CONFRONTING CHRONIC NEGLECT

The Education and Training of Health Professionals on Family Violence

Committee on the Training Needs of Health Professionals
to Respond to Family Violence

Felicia Cohn, Marla E. Salmon, and John D. Stobo, *Editors*

Board on Children, Youth, and Families

INSTITUTE OF MEDICINE

NATIONAL ACADEMY PRESS
Washington, DC

NATIONAL ACADEMY PRESS • 2101 Constitution Avenue, N.W. • Washington, DC 20418

NOTICE: The project that is the subject of this report was approved by the Governing Board of the National Research Council, whose members are drawn from the councils of the National Academy of Sciences, the National Academy of Engineering, and the Institute of Medicine. The members of the committee responsible for the report were chosen for their special competences and with regard for appropriate balance. The Board on Children, Youth, and Families is a joint effort of the Institute of Medicine and the Division of Behavioral and Social Sciences and Education.

Support for this project was provided by the Centers for Disease Control and Prevention, U.S. Department of Health and Human Services. The views presented in this report are those of the Institute of Medicine's Committee on the Training Needs of Health Professionals to Respond to Family Violence and are not necessarily those of the funding agencies.

Library of Congress Cataloging-in-Publication Data

Board on Children, Youth, and Families (U.S.). Committee on the Training
Needs of Health Professionals to Respond to Family Violence.
  Confronting chronic neglect : the education and training of health
professionals on family violence / Committee on the Training Needs of
Health Professionals to Respond to Family Violence, Board on Children,
Youth, and Families, Institute of Medicine ; Felicia Cohn, Marla E.
Salmon, and John D. Stobo, editors.
    p. ; cm.
Includes bibliographical references and index.
  ISBN 0-309-07431-2 (hardcover)
  1. Family violence. 2. Medical personnel—Training of—United States.

  [DNLM: 1. Domestic Violence—prevention & control—United States. 2.
Health Personnel—education—United States. HV 6626.2 B662 2002] I.
Cohn, Felicia. II. Salmon, Marla E. III. Stobo, John D. IV. Title.
  RC569.5.F3 B63 2002
  616.85'822—dc21
                              2002000875

Additional copies of this report are available for sale from the National Academy Press, 2101 Constitution Avenue, N.W., Box 285, Washington, D.C. 20055. Call (800) 624-6242 or (202) 334-3313 (in the Washington metropolitan area), or visit the NAP's home page at **www.nap.edu.** The full text of this report is available at **www.nap.edu.**

For more information about the Institute of Medicine, visit the IOM home page at: www.iom.edu.

The serpent has been a symbol of long life, healing, and knowledge among almost all cultures and religions since the beginning of recorded history. The serpent adopted as a logotype by the Institute of Medicine is a relief carving from ancient Greece, now held by the Staatliche Museen in Berlin.

"Knowing is not enough; we must apply.
Willing is not enough; we must do."
—Goethe

INSTITUTE OF MEDICINE

Shaping the Future for Health

THE NATIONAL ACADEMIES

National Academy of Sciences
National Academy of Engineering
Institute of Medicine
National Research Council

The **National Academy of Sciences** is a private, nonprofit, self-perpetuating society of distinguished scholars engaged in scientific and engineering research, dedicated to the furtherance of science and technology and to their use for the general welfare. Upon the authority of the charter granted to it by the Congress in 1863, the Academy has a mandate that requires it to advise the federal government on scientific and technical matters. Dr. Bruce M. Alberts is president of the National Academy of Sciences.

The **National Academy of Engineering** was established in 1964, under the charter of the National Academy of Sciences, as a parallel organization of outstanding engineers. It is autonomous in its administration and in the selection of its members, sharing with the National Academy of Sciences the responsibility for advising the federal government. The National Academy of Engineering also sponsors engineering programs aimed at meeting national needs, encourages education and research, and recognizes the superior achievements of engineers. Dr. Wm. A. Wulf is president of the National Academy of Engineering.

The **Institute of Medicine** was established in 1970 by the National Academy of Sciences to secure the services of eminent members of appropriate professions in the examination of policy matters pertaining to the health of the public. The Institute acts under the responsibility given to the National Academy of Sciences by its congressional charter to be an adviser to the federal government and, upon its own initiative, to identify issues of medical care, research, and education. Dr. Kenneth I. Shine is president of the Institute of Medicine.

The **National Research Council** was organized by the National Academy of Sciences in 1916 to associate the broad community of science and technology with the Academy's purposes of furthering knowledge and advising the federal government. Functioning in accordance with general policies determined by the Academy, the Council has become the principal operating agency of both the National Academy of Sciences and the National Academy of Engineering in providing services to the government, the public, and the scientific and engineering communities. The Council is administered jointly by both Academies and the Institute of Medicine. Dr. Bruce M. Alberts and Dr. Wm. A. Wulf are chairman and vice chairman, respectively, of the National Research Council.

REVIEWERS

This report has been reviewed in draft form by individuals chosen for their diverse perspectives and technical expertise, in accordance with procedures approved by the National Research Council's Report Review Committee. The purpose of this independent review is to provide candid and critical comments that will assist the institution in making its published report as sound as possible and to ensure that the report meets institutional standards for objectivity, evidence, and responsiveness to the study charge. The review comments and draft manuscript remain confidential to protect the integrity of the deliberative process. We wish to thank the following individuals for their review of this report:

Robert A. Burt, Yale University
Linda Chamberlain, Alaska Family Violence Prevention Project
Lynn Mouden, Arkansas Department of Health
Barbara Parker, University of Virginia
Desmond K. Runyan, University of North Carolina, Chapel Hill
Pat Salber, Kaiser Permanente
LuAnn Wilkerson, UCLA School of Medicine
Rosalie Wolf, The Medical Center of Central Massachusetts

Although the reviewers listed above have provided many constructive comments and suggestions, they were not asked to endorse the conclusions or recommendations nor did they see the final draft of the report before its release. The review of this report was overseen by Neal A. Vanselow, Tulane University, appointed by the Institute of Medicine and Luella Klein, Emory University School of Medicine, appointed by the National Research Council's Report Review Committee, both of whom were responsible for making certain that an independent examination of this report was carried out in accordance with institutional procedures and that all review comments were carefully considered. Responsibility for the final content of this report rests entirely with the authoring committee and the institution.

Preface

This report is not the first recent National Academies' report to focus on the issue of family violence. It is the third and, regrettably, it may not be the last. Family violence continues to plague society and we have not yet developed either the practical interventions or evidence base to address this important social issue.

When Congress passed the Health Professions and Education Partnerships Act of 1998, it issued an important challenge to government and the health professions. The bill's language suggested that education of health professionals is an important first step in mitigating the problem of family violence. The Board on Children, Youth, and Families of the Institute of Medicine and the Division of Behavioral and Social Sciences and Education of the National Research Council responded to this challenge by establishing the Committee on the Training Needs of Health Professionals to Respond to Family Violence.

The committee's point of departure for its work was to adopt three fundamental principles: (1) family violence is a health issue; (2) education of health professionals about the issue is therefore important; and (3) while education of health professionals about family violence is necessary to address the problem, it is not by itself sufficient. Other individuals and entities outside the health professions are involved in addressing issues related to family violence, and this larger societal context must not be forgotten.

As the committee began its deliberations, we quickly became aware that education of health professionals in family violence is not a consistent priority across or within health professions education curricula. The challenge of even identifying curricular content or strategies was compounded by the almost complete absence of either educational research or evaluation relating to family violence education and training for health professionals. In short, while family violence exacts a tremendous cost from its victims and society, it is not viewed as sufficiently important for society to invest the resources and expertise critical for developing the research and demonstrations necessary to improve the response of health professionals and others to this serious social and health problem. That must change.

The charge to our committee reflected a desire by Congress to encourage health professionals in education and practice to assume more responsibility for addressing this difficult, devastating issue. While the committee is sympathetic with this view, we also recognize that the complexity and breadth of this issue call for the involvement of professionals whose work lies outside the health arena. Responding to victims of family violence, and ultimately preventing its occurrence, is a societal responsibility. As such it must be shared.

The committee has chosen to limit the number of our recommendations in the hope that offering a few specific priorities will increase the likelihood of implementation. In our view, family violence should be treated like other public scourges such as heart disease, cancer, diabetes, and AIDS. Resources equivalent to those used to address these problems should be applied to address the problem of family violence. We recommend the creation of education and research centers that will not only generate significant new information with a beneficial impact on family violence but will also be useful in coordinating, integrating, and evaluating educational and intervention activities related to family violence. The work of such centers will benefit the development of sound, evidence-based curricula, contributing to the development of research and scholars around this issue. Such centers will provide focus to activities related to this very serious health problem.

Our recommendations reflect our consideration of the evidence and input that we worked diligently to uncover throughout the study process. It is important to note, however, that the committee members were both troubled and frustrated by the lack of scholarship in this area. We note here a finding that is not explicitly discussed elsewhere: the failure to make progress on education and practice in the area of family violence is in itself clear evidence that society has paid too little attention to what will remain a national shame and tragedy. For too long family violence has indeed been a case of chronic neglect.

> John D. Stobo, *Chair*
> Marla E. Salmon, *Vice Chair*
> Committee on the Training Needs of Health
> Professionals to Respond to Family Violence

Acknowledgments

No report is possible without the assistance of many people. The Committee on the Training Needs of Health Professionals to Respond to Family Violence would like to acknowledge the efforts of many who contributed to this report.

The study conducted by this committee was funded by the National Center for Injury Prevention and Control of the Centers for Disease Control and Prevention (CDC). CDC staff members Rodney Hammond, director for the Division of Violence Prevention, and Lynn Short, previously with the CDC and now executive director for Analytic Systems Associates, Inc., among others, provided useful background material and ongoing support. Joyce McCurdy, public health advisor in the Division of Violence Prevention, served as the project officer for this study and continuously provided invaluable assistance. This study, the result of federal legislation, also benefited from the support of Anne Marie Murphy, legislative assistant in the Office of the Honorable Richard J. Durbin, sponsor of the authorizing legislation.

Several consultants provided important background information, assisted in data collection, and contributed text for use in the report. Jane Koziol-Mclain of Johns Hopkins University prepared materials on issues related to funding and core competencies. Gina Espinosa Salcedo of Boston University assisted in the collection and organization of existing curricula for health professionals on family violence. Paul Mazmanian of the Medical College of Virginia provided background materials on clinician behavior change research. In addition to these formally appointed consultants, a number of other individuals offered background information and contributed text for this report. Kim Bullock of the Georgetown University Medical Center Department of Family Medicine prepared a comprehensive description and bibliography on cultural competencies for health professionals. William Rudman of the University of Mississippi provided extensive background materials on health care utilization data related to intimate partner violence. Deborah Horan of the American College of Obstetricians and Gynecologists (ACOG) developed the flowchart describing ACOG's work on family violence, and Donna Vivio of the American College of Nurse-Midwives (ACNM) developed the timeline of ACNM's family violence activities for inclusion in this report. Frank Putnam, director of the Mayerson Center for Safe and Healthy Children, provided helpful data and references. Bernice Parlak and Joan Weiss of the Health Resources and Services Administration and Diane Hanner of the Substance Abuse and Mental Health Services Administration provided essential information on the Geriatric Education Centers evaluation. Richard Hodis and Tony Phelps of the National Institute on Aging assisted with information on the Alzheimer's disease program. David Hemenway of the Harvard Injury Control Research Center provided useful information on the impact of that center. The committee is indebted to each of these individuals for their hard work and cooperation.

The committee's progress was possible, in part, due to the regular assistance of a number of speakers at committee meetings and other experts on family violence, health professional education, and related topics. Wanda Jones, deputy assistant secretary for health (women's health) of the U.S. Department of Health and Human Services; Denice Cora-Bramble, special advisor to the director of primary health care of the Health Resources and Services Administration; Lisa James, senior program specialist for the Family Violence Prevention Fund; Lori Stiegel, American Bar Association, Commission on the Problems of the Elderly; and David Cordray, professor of public policy and psychology and co-director, Center for Evaluation Research and Methodology, Institute for Public Policy Studies, Vanderbilt University, provided thoughtful presentations regarding current efforts to educate health professionals as well as frequent insights relevant to the committee's work. A number of others also served as resources for the committee, including Marcy Gross, Kate Rickard, and Carolina Reyes of the Agency for Healthcare Research and Quality; Angela Gonzalez-Willis of the Bureau of Health Professions; Debbie Lee of the Family Violence Prevention Fund; Hal Arkes and Ann Bostran of the National Science Foundation; Anita Rosen and Joan Zlotnick of the Council on Social Work Education; Rosalie Wolf of the Institute on Aging at the University of Massachusetts; Lynn Moudin of Prevent Abuse and Neglect Through Dental Awareness and the Arkansas Department of Health; Catherine Judd of the University of Texas Southwestern Medical Center at Dallas; Brian Rafferty of Talaria; and Calvin Hewitt of the University of Mississippi.

A number of other individuals provided helpful presentations and background materials on topics related to the committee's work. The committee appreciates the time and resources offered by the following individuals: Sidney

Stahl, chief, Health Care Organization and Older People in Society, National Institute on Aging; Mark Rosenberg, executive director, Task Force for Child Survival and Development; Brigid McCaw, director of the Family Violence Prevention Project, Kaiser Permanente Richmond and clinical lead for domestic violence prevention, Northern California Kaiser Permanente; Connie Mitchell, medical director for domestic violence, California Medical Training Center; Marilyn Peterson, director, California Medical Training Center, and director, University of California-Davis Child Protection Center; Ellen Taliaferro, medical director, Violence Intervention Prevention Center, Parkland Health and Hospital System, and co-founder, Physicians for a Violence Free Society; Bonnie Brandl, project coordinator, National Clearinghouse on Abuse in Later Life and Wisconsin Coalition Against Domestic Violence; Robert Spagnoletti, chief, Sex Offense and Domestic Violence Section, U.S. Attorney's Office; Billie Weiss, Injury and Violence Prevention Program, Los Angeles County Public Health and Program Service; Joanne Marlott Otto, program administrator, Adult Protection/ Elder Rights Services, Colorado State Department of Human Services; John Umhau, Laboratory of Clinical Studies, National Institutes for Alcohol Abuse and Alcoholism; Christopher Murphy, Department of Psychology, University of Maryland, Baltimore County; Larry Cohen, executive director, Prevention Institute; Suzanne Donovan, senior program officer, National Research Council; Deborah Danoff, assistant vice president for medical education, Association of American Medical Colleges; and Jeffrey Rachlinski, professor, Cornell Law School.

The committee conducted a public forum in Washington, DC, to inform its deliberations. The forum was designed to elicit the expertise of health professionals, policy makers, family violence advocates, and educators on the content and design of training programs for health professionals on family violence and information on existing guidelines and organizational positions. Representatives from over 20 organizations presented their policies, positions, educational initiatives, and research. The committee appreciates the insights these presentations provided into existing and potential educational approaches and is thankful to each participant and to all of those who submitted written materials.

Finally, the committee benefited tremendously from the support and assistance of several members of the Division on Behavioral and Social Sciences and Education and Institute of Medicine staff, as well as the administrative and research assistants of several committee members. A special thanks goes to Maura Shea, who provided administrative and research support to the committee, assisted in drafting pieces of the report, and helped prepare the report for publication. Drusilla Barnes, Amy Gawad, Rebekah Pinto, Michael Rosst, Mary Strigari, Kerry Williams, and Sonja Wolfe deserve much appreciation for their assistance with committee and meeting organization. The research needs of this report could not have been met without the able assistance of Adrienne Davis, Georgeann Higgins, James Igoe, and others in the National Research Council

Library. The substantive contributions and ongoing support of Nancy Crowell and Rosemary Chalk were inestimable. Bronwyn Schrecker was invaluable to the report review process. Christine McShane edited the report and Yvonne Wise was especially helpful in preparing the report for publication. The public release and dissemination of this report would not have been possible without the hard work of Mary Graham, Jennifer Otten, and Vanee Vines. Several assistants to specific committee members, including Eve Adams, Jandee Christensen, Sandy Froslan, Pat Knox, Latisha Lord, Drew Smith, JoEllen Stinchcomb, and Dianne Winsett, deserve thanks for facilitating the committee process, as do Samantha Coulombe, Caroline Han, Stacey Vaccaro Milonas, and Carla VandeWeerd. Finally, a heartfelt thanks to our study director, Felicia Cohn, who kept us organized and on time while guiding us through the entire process and who made significant contributions to the substance of the report.

Contents

CONFRONTING CHRONIC NEGLECT

Executive Summary

Family violence—child abuse and neglect, intimate partner violence, and elder abuse—is seen as a widespread and deeply troubling problem in American society. Studies consistently report that family violence affects as many as 25 percent of children and adults in America during their lifetimes—as victims, witnesses, or perpetrators. Combating such a major societal problem necessarily requires the involvement of multiple sectors, including the justice system, social services, and the health professions. For both practical and ethical reasons, health care professionals play a particularly important role in addressing family violence. They are often the first to encounter victims of family violence and consequently can play an important role in ensuring that victims, and also perpetrators, get the help they need.

Health professionals provide care for the physical and psychological problems associated with abuse and neglect, ranging from acute injuries to chronic medical conditions to psychiatric and psychological disorders. Because of their contact and relationship with actual and potential victims, health care professionals have a unique opportunity to screen for, diagnose, treat, and even prevent abuse and neglect. Despite this pivotal role, the training and education of health professionals about family violence are often inadequate to enable them to intervene effectively. Health professionals commonly report lack of support and feeling ill equipped and frustrated in dealing with family violence victims.

THE COMMITTEE CHARGE

At the request of Congress, and with support from the Centers for Disease Control and Prevention, the Institute of Medicine and the National Research

1

Council of the National Academies established a multidisciplinary committee to examine what is currently known about the training needs of health professionals to respond to family violence. The Committee on the Training Needs of Health Professionals to Respond to Family Violence was asked to examine existing curricula for health professionals on family violence and current efforts to foster their knowledge and skills in this area. The committee focused its review on the six professional groups it considered most likely to encounter family violence victims early in the evaluative process and thus to have significant educational needs related to screening, diagnosing, treating, and preventing family violence. The six groups are: physicians, physician assistants, nurses, psychologists, social workers, and dentists. This focus on these professions is not intended to suggest that other professions do not have important roles in responding to family violence.

A CASE OF CHRONIC NEGLECT

This committee is not the first to address the issue of family violence or to make recommendations for research, education, and practice to address it. Many of the difficulties identified in this report have been encountered before. Time and again in the past decade, groups of researchers, government officials, law enforcement professionals, social service providers, and health care professionals have convened to discuss the research and policy needed to address family violence. To date there has been little response to calls for improvements in the research base, increased funding, or collaboration among those concerned about family violence.

The problems identified by previous groups have not abated. In fact, the conclusions and recommendations in this report underscore problems that have been known to exist for decades. Building on the work of previous groups, we focus here specifically on the issues with the greatest impact on the training and education of health professionals to respond to family violence.

On the basis of its assessment and deliberations, the committee draws a number of conclusions regarding the current state of health professional training on family violence and makes recommendations to direct future efforts. These conclusions and recommendations address two major concerns: resources and coordination for education research and curricular development to expand the knowledge base and inform policy and practice, and curricular content and teaching strategies.

EDUCATION RESEARCH AND CURRICULAR DEVELOPMENT

Although the committee's review of available data suggests that family violence is widespread in the United States, its actual prevalence is unknown. Several critical examinations have eloquently described the paucity of data and research findings to reliably guide practice in the area of family violence. Previous reports have pointed specifically to the lack of a base of scientific findings sufficient to inform education and practice for health professionals, as well as inadequate funding for the teaching and evaluation of family violence curricula.

For example, in 1990, the U.S. Advisory Board on Child Abuse and Neglect reported that, although progress had been made, child maltreatment "may still be the most under-researched social problem." It identified as problems the unsystematic nature of the research on child maltreatment, a decline in public support for it from 1975 to 1990, a shortage of researchers in the field, and specific topics that have been especially understudied. The Advisory Board recommended establishment of state and regional resource centers for training, consultation, policy analysis, and research on child protection. Among its other recommendations were the development of a new data system, the creation of a U.S. Department of Health and Human Services-wide research advisory committee, a major role for the National Institute of Mental Health in research planning, implementation, and coordination, as well as in providing research training and career development awards.

In 1998, the National Research Council/Institute of Medicine's Committee on the Assessment of Family Violence Interventions noted a lack of rigorous evaluation, insufficient resources, and the failure of the research and practice communities to collaborate. The committee recommended that evaluation be integral to all family violence interventions and that policy incentives and leadership foster coordination among policy, program, and research agendas. The conclusions and recommendations in this report echo these calls for action to address a disturbing societal problem.

Conclusions

- **While family violence is understood to be widespread across the United States and to have significant health consequences, its full effects on society and the health care system have not been adequately studied or documented.**

The available data are inadequate to determine the full magnitude and severity of family violence in society or its impact on the health care professions. Furthermore, estimates of the scope of the problem vary according to the data source and research methods used. With respect to its impact on the health system, few studies have been conducted to trace the patterns of utilization or the costs of health care for conditions associated with family violence or its effects on the health status of the patient (or victim). A better understanding of baseline problems, health care needs, and costs associated with family violence could reinforce the need for more focused attention by health professionals, provide guidance on how best to respond, and inform and improve the education and practice of health care professionals.

- **Variation in the definitions, data sources, and methods used in research on family violence has resulted in inconsistent and unclear evidence about its magnitude and severity, as well as its effects on the health care system and society.**

As noted in previous reports published by the National Research Council and Institute of Medicine (*Understanding Child Abuse and Neglect, Understanding Violence Against Women, Violence in Families: Assessing Prevention and Treatment Programs*), clarity regarding definitions used to describe family violence is essential in order to compare studies and generalize from one setting to another. Similarly, clarity and consistency in data sources and research methods are needed to accurately describe the prevalence of family violence as encountered in health care settings and the health care needs of victims. Such an evidence base could shed new light on the roles of health professionals and their opportunities to intervene and respond more effectively to family violence and also provide a foundation for their more effective education.

- **Funding for research, education development and testing, and curricular evaluation on family violence is fragmented, and information about funding sources is not systematically available. No consistent federal sources of support for education research on family violence appear to exist.**

As the committee's review of existing programs and funding sources revealed, program development and funding for family violence programs are scattered among agencies of the U.S. Department of Health and Human Services and the U.S. Department of Justice. Among these agencies are the Centers for Disease Control and Prevention, the Agency for Healthcare Research and Quality, the Health Resources and Services Administration, the National Institutes of Health, the Administration on Children and Families, the National Institute of Justice, and the Office of Justice Programs. These federal agencies, departments, and offices share a mandate to address family violence, but the committee found that often one agency was unaware of either projects or funding opportunities for research and programs on family violence in other agencies. The fragmented information on funding is difficult to access for researchers and educators and others attempting to develop and conduct research, design training and practice interventions, and evaluate programs. The information must be collected piecemeal from numerous web sites and federal agency officials, making it difficult to determine if and when funds are available. Furthermore, while the committee was able to identify some sources of funding for intervention and training, we could find no consistent sources for federal support of education research on family violence to design and test innovative and responsive models for the education of health professionals or to evaluate existing models. Although their mandates differ in focus and scope, in the committee's judgment these agencies, as well as stakeholders in family violence, would benefit from sharing and coordinating information about their projects and funding opportunities.

Recommendation

Recommendation 1: The secretary of the U.S. Department of Health and Human Services should be responsible for establishing new multidisciplinary education and research centers with the goal of advancing scholarship and practice in family violence. These centers should be charged with conducting research on the magnitude and impact of family violence on society and the health care system, conducting research on training, and addressing concerns regarding the lack of comparability in current research. The ultimate goal of these centers will be to develop training programs based on sound scientific evidence that prepare health professionals to respond to family violence.

The committee suggests that a modest number of centers, three to five, be established in the next five years. That time period should be sufficient to establish and evaluate the early effects of the centers. The initial focus of the centers should be the evaluation of existing curricula on family violence and the expansion of scientific research on magnitude, health effects, and intervention effectiveness. Once the centers are established and the evidence base is developed, additional funding should be phased in to develop, test, evaluate, and disseminate education and training programs; to provide training at all levels of education; to develop policy advice; and to disseminate information and training programs.

In recommending the creation of education and research centers, the committee not only reiterates the recommendations of previous reports on family violence but also builds on the reported effectiveness of research and education centers in other fields. For example, centers dedicated to Alzheimer's disease, injury control research, and geriatric education have reported success in bringing multidisciplinary scholars together, expanding the research in their fields, producing scholars, providing training, and encouraging collaboration. In the committee's judgment, the reported successes of centers in other fields support this call for centers on family violence.

The committee therefore urges the secretary of the U.S. Department of Health and Human Services to instruct its agencies to determine how to allocate resources on a continuing basis to establish multidisciplinary centers on family violence. These centers could be connected to academic health centers, as recommended previously by others, or they could build on related efforts, such as the injury prevention and research centers of the Centers for Disease Control and Prevention. In addition, the centers should be linked to local and community resources and programs to facilitate and support the translation of research results into effective training efforts and real-world practices.

By providing a locus of activity, education and research centers can facilitate tracking and coordinating efforts to address family violence among federal agencies as well as those at the state and local levels and private organizations. Such coordination may result in: (1) the development of common research priorities; (2) the distribution of funding to studies and projects that continuously build the evidence base needed for the development of effective education and practice; (3) the broad dissemination of information about current research and programs; and (4) clear sources of information. Coordination would be aided by an analysis, perhaps undertaken by the U.S. General Accounting Office, about where investments are made, their level, and their adequacy.

CURRICULAR CONTENT AND TEACHING STRATEGIES

The committee's review indicates that existing curricula on family violence for health professionals are quite diverse. There are few scientific underpinnings to support the content, instructional methodologies, or extent of education now being provided in these training programs.

Conclusions

- **Curricula on family violence for health professionals do exist, but the content is incomplete, instruction time is generally minimal, the content and teaching methods vary, and the issue is not well integrated throughout their educational experiences. Moreover, studies indicate that health professionals and students in the health professions often perceive existing curricula on family violence to be inadequate or ineffective.**

Although a number of curricula exist, training is not consistently offered to those who have the responsibility to care for victims of family violence. When it is, it is typically of short duration, offered at only one point in the training program, and frequently limited to only one type of family violence (e.g., intimate partner violence). Elder maltreatment appears to be the most neglected area.

- **Evaluation of the effects of training has received insufficient attention. Few studies investigate whether curricula on family violence are having the desired impact on the delivery of health care to family violence victims. When evaluations are done, they often do not**

utilize the experimental designs necessary to provide an adequate understanding of effects.

At present, most studies appear to rely primarily on quasi-experimental research and short-term measurement of proximal effects and provider outcomes, such as increased knowledge and awareness of family violence. Evaluations required by law, funding agencies, or sponsoring organizations often assess only the process by which a program is implemented or participant satisfaction, without attention to program effectiveness—or they focus on program effects without considering implementation. Other experimental designs, particularly randomized experiments, would be useful in demonstrating the effects of training on the behavior of health professionals or on victims' health. Also helpful in improving understanding of the relationship between training and outcomes are high-quality quasi-experimental designs. Both could significantly improve the evidence base and its use to provide guidance as to what works best, for whom, and under what conditions.

- **Core competencies for health professional training on family violence can be developed and tested based on similarities in the content of current training programs. The important content areas include: (1) identification, assessment, and documentation of abuse and neglect; (2) interventions to ensure victim safety; (3) recognition of culture and values as factors affecting family violence; (4) understanding of applicable legal and forensic responsibilities; and (5) prevention. The level of competency necessary will vary with professional roles, functions, and interests.**

Core competencies are areas of knowledge, skills, and attitudes that health care professionals must possess in order to provide effective health care to patients. Currently, no definitive, evidence-based set of core competencies exists. An examination of existing programs, however, suggests some similarities in training objectives, content, and teaching methods. These reveal some common content areas across disciplines in which core competencies could be developed or tested for health professional education. These content areas regularly appeared in the existing curricula and the literature reviewed by the committee. In the committee's view, research to specify core competencies for health professionals on family violence should begin with the five content areas listed above. Their specification could facilitate the development of sound measures for assessing them.

- **Existing education theories about behavior change suggest useful teaching methods and approaches to planning educational interventions for health professionals tailored to the issue of family violence. These approaches include ways of changing behavior and practice in**

health care delivery systems, the use of techniques to address practitioners' biases or beliefs about victims, and the use of health care outcome measurement to inform evidence-based practice.

Studies demonstrate that traditional forms of didactic education designed to increase knowledge about a particular topic are ineffective to enhance skills and change clinical practice to improve patient outcomes. Research on behavior change and principles of adult learning instead support the use of teaching methods that employ multifaceted, skill-building, practice-enabling strategies as more effective at changing behavior in health care delivery. Such strategies involve interactive techniques, such as case discussion, role play, hands-on practice sessions, guided clinical experiences, and evaluative feedback to trainees about their behavior.

Strategies to change behavior are referred to as "systems change models." A number of such models exist, generally involving identifying areas in which change is needed, determining objectives, testing approaches, and assessing their impact. A few managed care organizations and hospitals are beginning to apply such approaches to the education and training of health professionals to identify and manage cases involving family violence. Early experiences with these techniques are demonstrating positive effects.

Techniques to reduce the assumptions that health professionals have about who family violence victims are and why they are maltreated may also be useful in developing effective education curricula. Research suggests that errors in victim identification and risk assessment could be reduced through exercises in which trainees compare their own judgments and assumptions about victims with data describing real victims.

Research on outcome measurement and evidence-based practice suggests potential for the creation of a standard set of expectations about effective practice to deal with family violence. Measurement using the Healthplan Education Data Information Set has demonstrated significant effects on the behavior of practitioners and health care delivery organizations in areas other than family violence. And evidence-based practice, which involves efforts to apply the best-available scientific evidence to day-to-day practice, is recognized as essential to ensure quality health care, yet even in areas in which best-practice standards are well established, incorporation into practice is extremely slow and uneven.

• **Challenges to developing, implementing, and sustaining training programs on family violence for health professionals include the nature of accreditation, licensure, and certification; characteristics of health professional organizations; the views of stakeholder groups; the attitudes of individual health professionals; and the existence of mandatory reporting laws and education requirements.**

Accreditation, licensure, and certification requirements do not consistently and explicitly address family violence and thus do not encourage training to address it. Without such requirements, health professionals may perceive family violence education as unnecessary, and educators may have little incentive to provide it. The influence of other stakeholder groups, including advocates, victims, and payers, has not been studied and so it is difficult to gauge what impact they may have. For individual health professionals, personal and professional factors may influence beliefs about the desirability of education about family violence and how such education is received and applied. Health care professionals have concerns regarding inadequate time or preparation, discomfort with dealing with family violence, and beliefs that it is a private issue in which they should not be involved. In addition, health care professionals may themselves have had personal experience with victimization or be affected by trauma experienced by their patients. Training programs therefore need to be sensitive to health professionals' specific needs and concerns.

The committee was particularly mindful of the use and effects of mandatory reporting and education legislation. Advantages of mandatory reporting include an increased likelihood that the health care provider will respond to family violence, refer victims for social and legal services, and assist with perpetrator prosecution. However, mandatory reporting is seen by some as a breach in confidentiality that undermines autonomy, trust, and privacy in the health care setting, particularly for intimate partner violence; interferes with efforts to ensure the safety of victims; serves to deter perpetrators from obtaining treatment; precipitates violent retaliation by perpetrators; decreases victims' use of health care services; and discourages inquiries by health care professionals who believe that if they do not ask, they have nothing to report.

Although the relationship between mandatory reporting requirements and education is unclear, the committee found that existing curricula, particularly for child abuse and neglect, often focus in part or in whole on legal reporting requirements. While reporting requirements may encourage education about screening and reporting family violence, given the time constraints on training, that may come at the cost of training about treating, referring, and preventing family violence.

A few states mandate family violence education for health professionals. The committee could find no formal evaluations of the impact of the education provided in accordance with those laws. However, studies demonstrate that health professionals who have obtained any continuing education about child maltreatment (not necessarily mandated) are no more likely—and in some study samples are less likely—to report child abuse and neglect than are those who have not attended such training.

• **In addition to effective training on family violence, a supportive environment appears to be critically important to producing desirable outcomes.**

Evaluation of curricula, while critical, is not sufficient to produce the desired outcomes. Having a proven curriculum will not ensure that health professionals receive the necessary training and adapt their practice behaviors. A commitment of time and resources is necessary to make attention to family violence a regular part of training and practice. Without such a supportive environment, the effects of training are likely to be short lived and may erode over time.

Recommendations

Recommendation 2: Health professional organizations—including but not limited to the Association of American Medical Colleges, the American Medical Association, the American College of Physicians, the American Association of Colleges of Nursing, the Council on Social Work Education, the American Psychological Association, and the American Dental Association—and health professional educators—including faculty in academic health centers—should develop and provide guidance to their members, constituents, institutions, and other stakeholders. This guidance should address (1) competency areas for health professional curricula on family violence, (2) effective strategies to teach about family violence, (3) approaches to overcoming barriers to training on family violence, and (4) approaches to promoting and sustaining behavior changes by health professionals.

In addition to federal efforts supporting research, scholarship, and curricular development, leadership and collaboration from the health sector are needed to develop effective training for health professionals on family violence. Health professional organizations are positioned to assist and influence their members who are likely to encounter victims of family violence. Efforts by the American Association of Colleges of Nursing, the American College of Obstetricians and Gynecologists, the American Academy of Pediatrics, and the American College of Nurse Midwives provide promising examples of how health professional organizations can actively work to encourage and implement education initiatives on family violence among their members.

Recommendation 3: Health care delivery systems and training settings, particularly academic health care centers and federally qualified health clinics and community health centers, should assume greater responsibility for developing, testing, and evaluating innovative training models or programs.

Health professional education often occurs in the health care delivery setting. Therefore, leadership from the health sector, including health care delivery systems and training settings, is needed to develop, test, and evaluate practical and effective training for health professionals on family violence. Training curricula should be linked to clinical evidence, including outcome measurement, should provide incentives, and should respond to factors that challenge the development, implementation, and sustainability of training programs. The literature on the principles of adult education, theories of behavior change, and performance measurement techniques offer informative models. Instruction should be based on clinical evidence and emphasize task-centered (problem-based) learning approaches. Mechanisms for the ongoing collection, analysis, and feedback of process and outcome data are needed for progressive improvements in education and practice.

Recommendation 4: Federal agencies and other funders of education programs should create expectations and provide support and incentives for evaluating curricula on family violence for health professionals. Curricula must be evaluated to determine their impact on the practices of health professionals and their effects on family violence victims. Evaluation must employ rigorous methods to ensure accurate, reliable, and useful results.

Evaluation of existing and future training programs is necessary to identify effective programs. However, for evaluation to be helpful, it must produce reliable and useful results so that any weaknesses that are discovered in the evaluated programs can be improved and effective programs replicated. Evaluation should include attention to: (a) the development of measurement tools and the assessment of quality, (b) the numbers of individuals being studied to ensure the numbers are sufficient for meaningful study, (c) accounting and controlling for the effect of previous training experiences, (d) the use of more rigorous methods, and (e) examination of trainee and practice characteristics and their interaction.

The committee's review of existing training programs for health professionals and the evaluation of those programs suggest evaluation is often not specifically funded. Funders should require that evaluations be conducted as a condition of funding and should provide funding at appropriate levels or the resources and support to ensure that evaluation is possible. In addition, funds should be allocated specifically for the evaluation of existing programs.

1

Introduction

Conservative estimates indicate that family violence affects as many as one in four children and adults in the United States during their lifetimes (Centers for Disease Control [CDC], 2000a, 2000b; Tjaden and Thoennes, 1998). Family violence results in a wide array of injuries, chronic medical conditions, and psychiatric and psychological disorders (National Research Council [NRC] and Institute of Medicine [IOM], 1998). The national data on health care service utilization by victims of child abuse and neglect, intimate partner violence, and elder maltreatment, though limited, indicate considerable contact between victims and health professionals. In 1994, 1.4 million persons were treated in emergency departments for injuries resulting from confirmed or suspected cases of interpersonal violence. Of these, 25 percent (350,000) were victims of family violence: 7 percent had been injured by a spouse or ex-spouse; 10 percent by a current or former boyfriend or girlfriend; and 8 percent by a parent, child, sibling, or other relative (Rand, 1997).[1]

While the numbers of victims of family violence seen in emergency departments are significant, the available data do not address the full extent of the problem. The emergency room data do not address the numbers of victims seen in other health care settings, such as primary care, pediatrics, obstetrics and gynecology, dentistry, and nursing homes. Research suggests that they are underreported (Ganley, 1996; Moore et al., 1998; Parsons et al., 1995; Rand, 1997; Rudman and Davey, 2000; Sabler, 1995, 1996). In addition, injuries and other health problems related to family violence often are not seen by health

---

[1]Data inclusive of all health care settings are not available, nor are more recent data.

professionals at all. For example, only about 1 in 10 women victimized by an intimate partner seeks professional medical treatment (Greenfeld et al., 1998). Therefore, the true size of the problem is larger than what available data suggest.

A comparison of incidence data suggests that family violence is equally or more prevalent than other serious health conditions (Putnam, 1998, 2001). For example, 1996 data reveal 3,195,000 reported cases of child abuse, of which 1,054,000 were substantiated. Based on substantiated cases, the incidence rate was 15 per 1,000 children/year, which represents a 47 percent increase over about a decade (Department of Health and Human Services [DHHS], 1998). Data on cancer from the same year reveal 1,339,156 cases with an incidence rate of 3.95 per 1,000 individuals/year, reflecting a 2.7 percent decrease over about 3 years (Ries et al., 1999).

In addition to the medical implications for individuals, family violence has been recognized as a public health problem that requires attention to its societal impact and opportunities for intervention (Mercy et al., 1993; White, 1994). Family violence is associated with numerous other problems that affect health, such as homelessness, alcohol and substance abuse, and delinquency (NRC and IOM, 1998).

The nature of their work suggests that health care professionals play a particularly important role in addressing health conditions associated with family violence. Beyond their role in direct treatment of health problems, the long-term and privileged nature of the provider-patient relationship creates unique opportunities to identify family violence victims and respond to their needs. Contact with actual and potential victims affords health professionals the occasion to screen, diagnose, treat, refer, and even prevent abuse and neglect. For example, health care professionals account for the reporting of up to about 23 percent of cases of child abuse and neglect (Administration for Children and Families [ACF], 1998). Work in the context of public health could move health professionals and others beyond the treatment of individual symptoms resulting from family violence to addressing the problems underlying the violence itself (Marks, 2000).

Yet studies consistently describe the lack of education for health professionals on family violence as a major barrier to the identification, treatment, and provision of assistance to family violence victims (e.g., Chiodo et al., 1994; Ferris, 1994; Hendricks-Matthews, 1991; King, 1988; Reid and Glasser, 1997; Sugg and Inui, 1992; Tilden et al., 1994). Some health professionals have expressed concern that they have never had the opportunity to learn how to ask patients about possible abuse; even with training, many report that they are ill equipped or are not encouraged in the practice setting to address family violence (Cohen et al., 1997; Schechter, 1996). Others express anxiety and frustration regarding their ability to respond appropriately if abuse is suspected or disclosed (e.g., Ferris, 1994; Sugg and Inui, 1992).

THE CHARGE TO THE COMMITTEE

In response to a congressional mandate under P.L. 105-392, the Health Professions Education Partnerships Act of 1998, the Board on Children, Youth, and Families of the Institute of Medicine (IOM) and the National Research Council (NRC) of the National Academies convened a committee to assess the training needs of health professionals with respect to the detection and referral of victims of family and acquaintance violence, including child physical abuse and sexual abuse and neglect, intimate partner violence, and elder abuse and neglect. The study was supported by the Centers for Disease Control and Prevention. The multidisciplinary committee included individuals with scientific, clinical, and policy expertise in the fields of pediatrics, obstetrics-gynecology and women's health, family medicine, emergency medicine, geriatrics, nursing, academic health education, mental health, social work, public health, family violence, evaluation, law, and ethics. The 15-member committee was asked to review and synthesize available research on:

1. the training needs of health care providers from the various disciplines that come into contact with family or acquaintance violence, including but not limited to physicians, nurses, and social workers, and the appropriateness with which providers are receiving training;

2. available curricula for screening, detecting, and referring family and intimate partner violence in health care delivery settings and the effectiveness of these curricula and training activities, as well as outcomes associated with these interventions; and

3. existing efforts, coalitions, and initiatives intended to foster the knowledge and skills base of health care providers.

When possible, the committee has looked for other opportunities and settings for training, including schools of medicine and nursing, graduate education programs for psychology and social work, clinical training, and continuing medical education. In addition, the committee has examined the strengths and limitations of indicators and outcome measures, as well as evaluation methodologies that are commonly used to assess curricula and training programs. Finally, the committee has worked to address issues regarding the implementation of these programs in light of competing patient-level needs and existing barriers and system-level disincentives for screening, detecting, and referring family violence.

THE COMMITTEE'S APPROACH

The committee began its work with an examination of the extent to which health professionals receive training about family violence. To do this, we identified and assessed existing curricula across health professions and educational levels. An exploration of the meaning of family violence and its impact on society and the health professions provided the background for this assessment. After reviewing the content and methods currently employed, the committee sought an understanding of how curricula have evolved, identifying and examining factors that potentially shape them. Then, an examination of available evaluation data provided insight into what is and is not working, as well as the limitations of the evaluation efforts to date. To determine the next steps in ascertaining and addressing health professional training needs, the committee considered the competencies necessary for training on family violence. Reflecting on principles of adult education and methods of behavior change, the committee also investigated effective training strategies.

To accomplish these tasks, the committee surveyed the published literature; unpublished health professional curricula on family violence; and existing requirements, policy statements, and guidelines for family violence education. We also consulted with numerous health professional organizations; policy makers; family violence advocacy groups; and researchers and scholars on family violence, education, law, and related issues.

Our review of the available literature, consultation with experts, and input from other interested parties reveal severe limits on the evidence base needed to develop the guidance requested by Congress. A number of training efforts exist, but little evidence supports their content, design, or methods and little is known about their effects. Nonetheless, the committee decided to adopt an approach used in previous reports that encountered a similar situation: we assess and build on the existing, though limited, evidence. For example, a previous study of interventions for victims of family violence[2] concluded that the research base was insufficient to yield any policy recommendations (NRC and IOM, 1998, pp. 289, 294). However the report recognized that the existing array of interventions offers a valuable body of experience and expertise from which lessons could be drawn to inform future interventions. Education cannot wait until definitive research is available, but must be improved by future research findings.

In the judgment of the current committee, existing efforts at training health professionals on family violence offer an important and instructive body of experience from which scientific determinations of efficacy can be made. Educators, education researchers, and curriculum architects will be challenged to develop rigorous evaluations and build on the results. We endeavored to make the most of the little evidence and substantial experience that are available. With this foundation, in our view, significant progress can be made to develop the field of family violence and training initiatives to address it. To emphasize the

---

[2]We refer the reader to the report, *Violence in Families: Assessing Prevention and Treatment Programs*, for a discussion about existing family violence interventions and their effects, as this material is not addressed in this report.

importance of research and evaluation for this development, the committee devotes an entire chapter to evaluation research and makes recommendations that target the development of the field and educational efforts.

DEFINITIONAL ISSUES

Addressing health professional training on family violence is complicated by several definitional issues. The use and meaning of the terms *family violence, health professionals, training,* and *response* are not consistent in the existing literature. The definitions of family violence and each of its subtypes also vary widely and are laden with controversy. The task of identifying and assessing all existing family violence curricula for every type of health professional across all education and practice settings proved to be enormous and was compounded by the lack of consensus about what constitutes a training program. To carry out its task, the committee established common descriptions and terms for its work, described below.

Family Violence

According to the committee's charge, family violence is defined to include "child physical and sexual abuse and neglect, intimate partner violence, and elder abuse and neglect." To inform this definition, the committee relied primarily on the description offered by the National Research Council/Institute of Medicine Committee on the Assessment of Family Violence Interventions. According to its report, the term *family violence* is applied to "a broad range of acts whose presence or absence results in harm to individuals who share parent-child or adult intimate relationships" (NRC and IOM, 1998, p. 18). The current committee understands violence to include physical, emotional, psychological, and sexual harms; the potential for harms; intentional and unintentional injury; and abuse and neglect. In addition, the committee reviewed some commonly referenced definitions, including those in both federal and state legislation, and drew on the descriptive overlap that emerges for our work. Among these are the types of abuse with which this report is concerned: child abuse and neglect, intimate partner violence, and elder maltreatment.

The committee considered whether to examine family violence as a single entity or to address the traditionally defined demographic groups separately. The charge suggests that family violence be considered as a single entity, and the need for health professional training on family violence generally suggests a unified approach. However, child abuse and neglect, intimate partner violence, and elder maltreatment are studied, described, and discussed separately in the majority of the literature. The committee opted to consider family violence both in the aggregate and by type. For example, in describing our review of the literature regarding the magnitude of family violence and existing curricula, generally we considered each type of family violence separately. The discussion reflects what we perceive to be an imbalance in attention to each of the types of family violence in research, current interventions, and educational initiatives. In drawing conclusions and making recommendations, the committee considers family violence in the aggregate, with the idea that evidence specific to training about one form of family violence may also be instructive for other forms.

Health Professionals

Victims of family violence seek help from a broad array of health professionals. Among these are physicians of many specialties; physician assistants; nurses and advanced-practice nurses of many specialties; certified nursing assistants; social workers; psychologists and other mental health professionals; dentists; emergency medical service providers; public health professionals; alternative and complementary medicine providers; allied health professionals, such as physical therapists, occupational therapists, and others; home health care personnel of various types; pharmacists; dieticians and nutritionists; medical assistants; veterinarians; hospital chaplains; patient advocates; case workers; clinical office and hospital receptionists; health educators; clinical administrators; and human resources personnel. This list is not intended to be comprehensive but illustrative of the diversity of health professionals involved in addressing family violence and the variety of roles they play, including prevention, recognition, treatment, education, and referral.

This report focuses on the following health professions: physicians, physician assistants, nurses (including advanced-practice nurses), social workers, psychologists, and dentists, because, in the committee's view, these health professional groups are among the most likely to encounter victims of family violence early in the evaluative process and to have a role in screening, diagnosing, treating, and preventing family violence. By limiting the focus, we do not mean to suggest that other health professional groups or disciplines are not important in the health care response to family violence. The commentary, conclusions, and recommendations in this report will be of value to a wide array of health professionals.

Training and Education

The terms *training* and *education* may be used synonymously or to express different meanings. Training is often described as practically useful skills development, while education refers to the promotion of conceptual understanding (e.g., Moran Campbell, 2000). The committee chose to use these terms interchangeably throughout the report to refer to formal efforts to provide information and experience about family violence to health professionals or students.

Based on the understanding of learning advanced by the National Research

Council (1999) and following the example of the Centers for Disease Control and Prevention (Osattin and Short, 1998), the committee elected to concentrate on formal curricula and agreed on the following working definition of *curriculum:* "a deliberate program of study, with explicit goals and objectives, that is designed for use as a regular component of professional education/training." This definition was used to collect information and examples of existing training programs. The committee limited its review of programs to those with formally developed curricula. Curricula were collected via a literature review, a web search, an extensive mailing to health professionals and organizations likely to be involved in family violence education, listserves, individual member knowledge, and word of mouth. The illustrative collection of existing curricula is available in Appendix E.

While relying on the previously described definition of curriculum for its review of programs, the committee did not limit its review of program evaluations to those that evaluated programs fitting the definition. Rather we reviewed all available literature on the evaluation of educational programs on family violence for health professionals, in order to garner as many lessons as possible.

Because in the committee's judgment successful training requires both appropriate content and effective educational methods, we also examined teaching practices: both traditional teaching approaches and newer approaches based on the emerging principles of the dissemination of knowledge and adult learning theory.

Responses of Health Professionals to Family Violence

The charge to the committee is very specific with regard to the meaning of the response of health professionals to family violence. According to the charge, response includes "detecting," "screening," and "referring" victims of family violence. Reflecting on the use of these terms in health care practice, the committee understands them to mean the following: *detection* refers to identification of the victims of various forms of abuse and neglect; *screening* refers to the clinical strategies used to detect and learn about a patient's specific situation of abuse; and *referral* means developing an action plan that involves locating, contacting, and providing appropriate and necessary services, such as community shelters, social services, safety planning, and law enforcement.

Although prevention is not explicitly included in the charge, the committee notes its importance and found that there is extensive and contentious debate about the roles of health professionals in preventing family violence. In limited instances, this report does address prevention, primarily in descriptions of existing and recommended curricular components.

ORGANIZATION OF THE REPORT

Report Content

Following this Introduction, Chapter 2 discusses definitions of the types of family violence addressed by health professional training, the magnitude of family violence in American society, and an estimate of the effects of family violence on health care professionals and the health care system. Chapter 3 describes current educational activities. In Chapter 4, the committee assesses forces that may affect health professional training. Evaluation data are the primary focus of Chapter 5, which identifies the methods used and what evaluation reveals. Chapter 6 moves from what is known about health professional education to what the evidence and expert opinion suggest it should be; the chapter includes a discussion of content issues, educational strategies, and techniques of behavior change. The concluding chapter provides the committee's recommendations on training health professionals about family violence.

Areas Not Addressed in the Report

The content of this report reflects the committee's fidelity to its explicit charge. Although we discussed a number of important and often controversial areas during our deliberations, those falling outside the scope of our charge do not appear in the report. Among these are the causes of family violence, the actual impact of training on the problem of family violence, the relationship between education and practice, the roles of health professionals in prevention, and the relationship of health professionals to their colleagues in law enforcement, social services, and broader community services systems. The committee also considered issues relating to the identification and treatment of batterers or perpetrators, distinctions between intentional and unintentional injuries as they relate to educational content, the impact of fragmented care on victims, and the overall meaning of health, but we did not explicitly address these issues in the report.

The breadth of these issues associated with family violence both underscores the committee's firm view that health professional training alone cannot fix the problem of family violence and reinforces our position on the importance of health professional training on this issue. This report addresses these issues, suggesting directions for a comprehensive and collaborative approach necessary to understand and move toward resolution of the problem of family violence.

2

Defining the Problem

This chapter provides important background for understanding the context of and the need for training health professionals about family violence. It presents the committee's operational definitions of the types of family violence, data describing the magnitude of the problem, a discussion of the roles of health professionals with regard to family violence, and evidence of the impact of family violence on health care utilization and costs.

DEFINITIONS AND MAGNITUDE

Family violence is widely regarded as a serious problem that affects large numbers of adults and children throughout the life span.[1] Although the exact figures are frequently disputed, conservative estimates suggest that the prevalence and incidence of child abuse and neglect, intimate partner violence, and elder maltreatment affect up to 25 percent of the population annually, involving millions of children, women, and men in the United States (CDC, 2000a, 2000b; Tjaden and Thoennes, 2000). The data describing the magnitude of family violence at the national level, however, are limited and do not appear to be collected systematically. The committee had difficulty discerning a complete picture of the problem due to variability in the definitions used, differences in the sources of data, and diversity in the study methodologies.

---

[1]For additional information on family violence, see previous reports of the National Research Council, including *Understanding Child Abuse and Neglect* (1993) and *Understanding Violence Against Women* (1996).

Determining when maltreatment has occurred continues to be challenging, as it can result from acts of commission (abuse) or omission (neglect) and can be acute or chronic, subtle or extreme (see Brassard and Hardy, 1997). Additional confusion has arisen in the field over defining abuse and neglect according to the perpetrator's behavior or injury to the victim or whether a single act or a pattern of repeated actions is required. For example, the original term "battered woman syndrome" implies that a pattern is required, but the more recent approach when collecting data is to obtain information on the type, severity, and frequency of the violence.

The confusion is exacerbated by the development of multiple definitions of maltreatment developed for different purposes (e.g., research, judicial action, clinical investigation; NRC, 1993). Some studies rely on reported cases and others estimate cases. The definition of a case varies from state to state, with some requiring that there be "reason to believe" abuse has occurred before "substantiating" abuse or neglect, others requiring that abuse "probably occurred," and still others requiring "clear and convincing" evidence. Interstate variability exists in the number of cases reported per population at risk. The heterogeneity of definitions and evidentiary requirements makes accuracy in incidence data extremely difficult to achieve.

Investigative methods and data sources also affect research results. For example, rates tend to be very low if only severe physical injury (e.g., fracture) is included, somewhat higher if milder injury (e.g., bruises) is included, and can increase even more if psychological violence and emotional violence are included (Wilt and Olson, 1996). Surveys of patients in health care settings tend to find higher rates than do surveys of the general population (Campbell et al., 2000; Wilt and Olson, 1996). Self-administered written questionnaires tend to result in higher rates than do personal interviews (Canterino et al., 1999; Thompson et al., 2000), although this is not always the case (Gazmararian et al., 1996). Higher rates tend to be obtained when victim and perpetrator are assessed separately (Bohannon et al., 1995). Rates also depend on how the survey is framed or introduced (Campbell et al., 2000).

All of this diversity can result in tremendous variation in research results and difficulty in comparing and interpreting data. Despite these constraints, the data do generally indicate the extent of the problem. In the following sections, the committee describes the definitions of types of family violence that informed its analysis in this report and what is known about the magnitude of each type. Table 2.1 presents the definitions of family violence terminology used in the report. Table 2.2 presents common elements of the three types of maltreatment.

Child Abuse and Neglect

The current understanding of child abuse and neglect has expanded greatly since Kempe and colleagues in 1962 first coined the term *battered child syn-*

TABLE 2.1 The Committee's Working Definitions of Family Violence Terminology

Term	Description
Physical abuse	The infliction of physical injury by punching, beating, kicking, biting, burning, shaking, or other actions that result in harm
Sexual abuse	Involves children or adults who are unable to fully comprehend and/or give informed consent in sexual activities that violate the taboos of society, including pedophilia (an adult's preference for or addiction to sexual contact with children), all forms of incest, rape, fondling genitals, intercourse, sodomy, exhibitionism, and commercial exploitation through prostitution or the production of pornographic materials
Psychological/emotional abuse	Involves psychological abuse, verbal abuse, or mental injury and includes acts or omissions by loved ones or caregivers that have caused or could cause serious behavioral, cognitive, emotional, or mental disorders
Neglect	Failure of a loved one or caregiver to provide for a person's basic physical, emotional, medical, educational, nutritional, or shelter needs
Financial exploitation	Taking advantage of a person for monetary gain or profit
Self-neglect[a]	The behavior of a person that threatens his or her own safety or health
Unwarranted control	Controlling a person's ability to make choices about living situations, household finances, and medical care
Victim	The person who is the target of violence or abuse, excessive controlling behavior, or neglect
Perpetrator	The person who inflicts the violence or abuse or causes the violence or abuse to be inflicted on the victim
Intimate partners	Current spouses (including common-law spouses); current nonmarital partners (including heterosexual, same-sex, dating, first date, boyfriend or girlfriend); former marital partners (divorced, separated, former common-law spouses); former nonmarital partners (dates, boyfriend or girlfriend, heterosexual, same-sex), cohabiting or not, involved in a sexual relationship or not

[a]Both technically and practically, self-neglect is not a form of family violence, but it is described here because adult protective services agencies typically have responsibility for self-neglecting elderly people alongside more "traditional" victims of elder abuse; in many states self-neglectors constitute the majority of the caseloads.

TABLE 2.2 Elements Commonly Found Among Published Definitions

Types of Violence	Common Definitional Elements
Child abuse and neglect	• a recognition that abuse and neglect present in many forms • a recognition that harm may be actual or potential • acknowledgment that the perpetrator of harm may be a parent or other caregiver within the family or extended family or outside the family in a community setting (e.g., day care, school) • the different forms of maltreatment may occur separately or in combination • maltreatment may occur once or throughout the life of the child
Intimate partner violence[a]	• recognition of events of abuse and patterns of abusive behavior • inclusion of psychological and sexual as well as physical abuse • inclusion of threats • demonstration of controlling behavior • perpetration by a current or former intimate partner, regardless of a marital relationship, cohabitation, sexual relationship, or the gender of the pair
Elder maltreatment	• emphasis on the victimization of elderly persons, defined by a particular age • recognition of financial or material abuse and abandonment in addition to physical, psychological, emotional, and sexual forms of abuse and neglect • recognition of self-neglect as an important entity

[a]The definition used in this report is broader than that used in the 1993 National Research Council report, in which the term was more narrowly defined to refer to physical violence.

drome to characterize "a clinical condition in young children who have received serious physical abuse, generally from a parent or foster parent" (p. 17). Recognizing that physical abuse is only one type of behavior that puts children at risk, four general categories are now generally recognized: physical abuse, sexual abuse, emotional abuse, and neglect (NRC, 1993; P.L. 104-235, Section 111; 42 U.S.C. 5106g).

Kempe estimated 749 battered children in the United States in 1960 (Kempe et al., 1962). In the 1979 annual incidence study required by the Child Abuse Prevention and Treatment Act, about 669,000 reports of suspected child abuse and neglect were filed. By 1990 the number of these reports had grown to more than 3 million. Other data sources suggest that the number of cases ranges from about 1 million (DHHS, 1998) to about 3 million annually (DHHS, 1996). More than half of all victims (54 percent) suffered neglect, almost one-quarter (23 percent) suffered physical abuse, almost 12 percent were sexually abused, less than 6 percent suffered psychological abuse, less than 6 percent were medically neglected, and one-quarter of victims suffered more than one type of abuse (DHHS, 1998). Other data sources vary with regard to the numbers of subtypes of abuse, but generally they indicate that neglect is more prevalent than abuse and that physical abuse and neglect are greater than emotional, sexual, and medical abuse and neglect (e.g., DHHS, 1996).

In addition to violence perpetrated against them, children are affected by witnessing other forms of family violence. Research suggests that between 3.3 million and 10 million children are exposed annually to intimate partner violence, usually committed against one of their parents, in the home (Carlson, 1984; Straus, 1992). Approximately half of the women who are victims of interpersonal violence have children in their home under age 12, and so the potential number of child witnesses is high (Greenfeld et al., 1998).

Intimate Partner Violence

Intimate partner violence is described by several names, including *domestic violence, gender violence, violence against women, and spousal abuse.*[2] Following the example of the Centers for Disease Control and Prevention, the committee elected to use the term *intimate partner violence* as the best choice to describe the situations of spousal, partner, and acquaintance violence addressed in this report. Violence is generally divided into four categories: (1) physical violence, (2) sexual violence, (3) the threat of physical or sexual violence, and (4) psychological or emotional abuse (Saltzman et al., 1999). Some descriptions also explicitly list stalking among the behaviors that constitute intimate partner violence.

Victims of intimate partner abuse include both women and men, in heterosexual and same-sex relationships, but women abused by current or former male partners are the most frequently abused and experience the highest rate of serious injury (Tjaden and Thoennes, 2000). Lifetime incidence rates vary widely, depending on the type of violence assessed, but they tend to be in the 15 to 30 percent range among women (Wilt and Olson, 1996). Intimate partner violence accounts for 22 percent of violent crimes against women, and the rate of female murder victims killed by intimate partners has remained at about 30 percent of all female murder victims since 1976 (Rennison and Welchans, 2000).

In contrast, intimate partner violence accounts for 3 percent of violence against men (Rennison and Welchans, 2000), and rates of violence by women against men are generally lower (Schafer et al., 1998). In 1996, for example, intimate partner violence victimization was reported by 150,000 men compared with 840,000 women (Greenfeld et al., 1998). In the National Violence Against

---

[2]Throughout this report, the original language has been retained in citations and in other instances ~~when a specific term is used. In addition to the controversy surrounding the label given to instances~~ of maltreatment between intimate partners, the term *domestic violence* has also been used synonymously with *family violence*, particularly in contexts of legal and social services.

Women Survey, almost 25 percent of the women surveyed and 7.5 percent of the men said they had experienced sexual or physical violence by a current or former intimate partner at some time in their life (Tjaden and Thoennes, 2000).

Special populations are often the focus of research: pregnant women, young adults, and persons in same-sex relationships. The risk for intimate partner violence for pregnant women appears to be similar to that for nonpregnant women (Gazmararian et al., 1996; Hedin et al., 1999). A large representative sample of teenage and young adult dating partners reveals 37 percent of women and 22 percent of men reported physical intimate partner violence (Magdol et al., 1997). Regarding same-sex partners, a review of 19 studies indicates that the rates and risk factors for violence in lesbian and gay male relationships are similar to those in heterosexual relationships and that the risk factors, other than gender, are similar (Burke and Follingstad, 1999). In a national probability sample, compared with heterosexual couples, the prevalence of intimate partner violence was higher between gay men and lower between lesbian partners (Tjaden et al., 1999).

Elder Maltreatment

Elder maltreatment is the most recently recognized form of family violence[3] and, like other categories of family violence, it can include a wide variety of acts beyond the willful infliction of physical harm on an older person (see, e.g., American Medical Association [AMA], 1992; Aravanis et al., 1993). Elder neglect has been more difficult to define than abuse, because norms are ambiguous about the duties that particular caregivers may have (Fulmer and O'Malley, 1987). Types of elder maltreatment, like other forms of family violence, include (1) *physical abuse,* (2) *emotional or psychological abuse,* (3) *neglect,* (4) *sexual abuse,* and (5) *abandonment.* In addition, (6) *financial exploitation,* (7) *self-neglect,* and (8) *unwarranted control* are categories unique to elder maltreatment.

Because of the recency of interest by health care researchers in elder maltreatment, there are substantially fewer data regarding the prevalence, incidence, and medical consequences of this problem compared with child abuse and neglect and intimate partner violence. Several prevalence studies conducted in the United States and abroad do allow tentative estimates of the prevalence of elder mistreatment. Approximately 3 percent of elderly persons experience maltreatment annually (Lachs et al., 1998; Pillemer and Finkelhor, 1988). Some studies have examined the relative frequency of the various subtypes of elder maltreatment. For example, according to one study, of 176 elderly persons in the protective services system as a result of allegations of maltreatment, 10 (6 percent) of

---

[3]The committee selected the term *elder maltreatment* instead of *elder abuse and neglect,* considering it to be broader and more inclusive.

these were for abuse, 30 (17 percent) for neglect, 8 (5 percent) for exploitation, and 128 (73 percent) for self-neglect (Lachs et al., 1998). The data also show that those who suffered from mistreatment by others had worse survival rates that those with self-neglect.

HEALTH PROFESSIONALS' ROLES

Professional Responsibility

With regard to family violence, a primary function of health care professionals is to treat resultant physical and psychological conditions and injuries. They may encounter family violence victims in the course of routine care (e.g., annual physicals) or specifically due to victimization.

In addition to this clinical role in the lives of victims, health professionals have a role defined by law. All states require that health professionals, among others, report situations of child abuse and neglect, and most require reporting for elder maltreatment (see Appendix C). A small minority requires reporting of intimate partner violence. The law enforcement and justice systems may also depend on health professionals' assessments as documented in medical records, in order to better provide protection to victims, prosecute abusers, and address custody issues.

Recognizing the clinical and legal responsibilities that health professionals may bear with regard to family violence, a number of health professional organizations have issued policy statements, recommendations, practice guidelines, and requirements for family violence education (see Appendix B) as well as practices related to family violence. Their positions variously emphasize recognition of types of family violence as significant public health threats and encourage their members to provide care, to identify and report (as appropriate per law or ethics) situations of family violence, and to assume positions of leadership in preventing and responding to family violence.

Numerous health professional organizations described and provided these positions and offered recommendations to the committee during a public forum held on June 22, 2000, at the National Academy of Sciences in Washington, DC. Among the participants were representatives from the American College of Nurse Midwives, the National Association of Orthopedic Nurses, the American Psychological Association, the World Psychiatric Association, the Council on Social Work Education, the American Medical Association, the American Academy of Pediatrics, and the American College of Obstetricians and Gynecologists. Many other health professional organizations submitted written materials to the committee. A review of their positions and recommendations indicates that all of these organizations recognize the impact of health professionals in detecting and responding to family violence and the need for comprehensive training on the signs of victimization and the medical needs of victims.

Health Effects of Family Violence

Drawing on a number of studies, the committee is able to describe some of the health care needs of victims of each type of family violence, but substantiating claims through current data systems that family violence results in an increased utilization of human, material, and financial resources is difficult. As with the data on magnitude, available research on the involvement of victims with the health care system is fragmented and limited. In the following section, we describe what is known about the health conditions associated with family violence, the workload related to treating those conditions, and the related costs to the health care system and society.

Child Abuse and Neglect

The effects of child abuse and neglect range from negligible to serious injury and even death (Feldman, 1997; Rosenberg and Krugman, 1991). Physical abuse may include single or multiple bruises, burns, fractures, abdominal injuries, and head injuries. The leading cause of death related to child abuse is shaken baby syndrome, which often involves a combination of subdural and subarachnoid hemorrhage and retinal hemorrhage. If the child survives, the effects of the syndrome can include developmental delays, blindness, and learning disabilities (Kirschner, 1997). The consequences of sexual abuse depend on the age of the child, the duration of the abuse, the relationship of the child to the abuser, and the amount of coercion used to sustain the relationship (Krugman and Jones, 1987). Effects may include medical conditions and behavioral disorders, but many victims have no symptoms. Among the more severe outcomes are sexual dysfunction, pregnancy, prostitution, and perpetration of sexual abuse to other children and adults. Emotional neglect can lead to significant later developmental, educational, and behavioral problems (Oates and Kempe, 1997). Early studies in the 1970s suggested that the mortality for children with severe nonorganic failure to thrive ranged from 4 to 15 percent (Oates and Kempe, 1997).

In addition to the immediate effects of maltreatment on children, there are well-documented long-term consequences that can occur in adulthood, especially increased risk for common somatic, psychosomatic, and psychiatric problems (Rosenberg and Krugman, 1991). One study indicates that child maltreatment is a risk factor for poor physical health, with multiple adverse childhood experiences with abuse and neglect increasing the risk (as expressed in odds ratios) for ischemic heart disease (2.2×), any cancer (1.9×), stroke (2.4×), chronic bronchitis/emphysema (3.9×), diabetes (1.6×), and hepatitus (2.4×) (Felitti et al., 1998). In addition, trauma can affect brain development and neurobiology in children (Putnam, 1998).

The effects of witnessing intimate partner violence in the home are not yet fully understood, but evidence suggests that there are both emotional and developmental effects (Grych et al., 2000). Literature reviews of studies on children exposed to intimate partner violence indicate that these children experience more behavioral problems than children from nonviolent homes. Among these are aggressive behaviors, depression, suicidal behaviors, anxiety, phobias, insomnia, bed-wetting, self-esteem problems, and impaired cognitive and academic functioning (Fantuzzo and Lindquist, 1989; Kolbo et al., 1996). Research suggests that there is some, but not a significant, relationship between exposure and social problems (Fantuzzo and Lindquist, 1989), but it indicates no causal relationship between exposure and physical health problems (Kolbo et al., 1996). The more severe the violence, the greater the consequences appear to be for the child (Attala and McSweeney, 1997). Children of a parent who commits intimate partner violence are also at increased risk for physical abuse themselves, and the risk is higher if the father is the perpetrator (Ross, 1996). Evidence also suggests that interventions to prevent child abuse are compromised when there is intimate partner violence in the home (Eckenrode et al., 2000).

For women who reported any abuse or neglect during childhood, median annual health care costs were $97 greater than those without histories of maltreatment, and the costs to those reporting histories of sexual abuse were $245 higher (Walker et al., 1999). Retrospective surveys of adolescents in detention facilities and psychiatric hospitals show significant rates of maltreatment in these populations. Abuse has been associated with increased rates of substance abuse, running away, and suicidal behavior in children, adolescents, and adults (Rosenberg and Krugman, 1991).

An analysis of data by Miller et al. (1996), based on data from 1986, indicates that direct costs (i.e., costs associated with the immediate needs of abused or neglected children, including medical care) due to child abuse were $7.3 billion and indirect costs (i.e., costs associated with the long-term or secondary effects of child abuse and neglect) were $48 billion. A 2001 study by Prevent Child Abuse America, based on data from the Department of Health and Human Services, the Department of Justice, the decennial census and other sources, indicates even higher costs (http.//www.preventchildabuse.org/research_ctr/ reports.html). In that study, direct costs total about $24.4 billion; this includes health care costs, which are those related to hospitalization, chronic health problems, and mental health care. Indirect costs totaled about $69.7 billion.

Another study, based on data collected between 1991 and 1994, reports the costs associated with pediatric intensive care for abused children. Cases of child abuse in this study represented 1.4 percent of admissions and 17 percent of deaths, and these patients had higher severity of illness (61 percent), hospitalization charges ($30,684), daily charges ($5,294), and mortality rates (53 percent) than any other group of patients admitted to the pediatric intensive care unit over almost four years (Irazuzta et al., 1997). The array of injuries and health conditions that result from child abuse and neglect suggests that health care utilization and costs are substantial.

Intimate Partner Violence

The impact of intimate partner violence on the health care system and on health professionals is addressed in a number of studies of discrete elements of the problem, such as injuries, particular medical conditions, and specific treatment costs. Virtually all the available data involve adult female victims.

As with other forms of family violence, the most severe medical consequence of intimate partner violence is death. A high proportion of women who are murdered, 30 to 40 percent, are victims of intimate partner violence. In fact, intimate partners constitute the largest single category of perpetrators in the homicide of women (CDC, 2000a, 2000b).

Nonfatal intimate partner violence is also associated with an increase in a wide range of psychological, psychosomatic, and physical effects, including headache, chronic pain, gastrointestinal and gynecological symptoms, sexually transmitted diseases, unintended pregnancies, urinary tract infections, depression and anxiety, suicide, substance abuse, and post-traumatic stress syndrome (Abbott et al., 1995; Bergman and Brismar, 1991; Campbell et al., 1996; Diaz-Olavarrieta et al., 1999; Domino and Haber, 1987; Drossman et al., 1995; el-Bayoumi et al., 1998; Felitti, 1991; Felitti et al., 1998; Gil-Rivas et al., 1996; Gin et al., 1991; Hegarty and Roberts, 1998; Jones et al., 1999; Leiman et al., 1998; Letourneau et al., 1999; Linares et al., 1999; Longstreth et al., 1998; Maman et al., 2000; McCauley et al., 1995, 1998; McFarlane et al., 1992; Schei and Bakketeig, 1989; Schei, 1990; Stark and Flitcraft, 1988; Talley et al., 1994; Walker et al., 1999). Head injury is common and can have a variety of long-term effects (Monahan and O'Leary, 1999; Muelleman et al., 1996). Even low-severity intimate partner violence (e.g., verbal threats, pushing, grabbing) has been linked to adverse health effects, although as violence escalates, so do the health consequences (McCauley et al., 1998). Abuse of pregnant women appears to increase the risk of first-trimester pregnancy loss, abruptio placentae (premature detachment of the placenta), premature labor, low-birthweight babies, and neonatal death (Campbell et al., 1999; Curry et al., 1998; Gazmararian et al., 1996; Shumway et al., 1999).

Of 4.8 million cases of intimate partner physical and sexual abuse of women estimated annually, approximately 2 million resulted in injury to the victim and, of these, 552,192 resulted in medical treatment (Tjaden and Thoennes, 2000). Of the 2.9 million cases of intimate partner physical abuse of men, 581,391 victims were injured and 124,999 received medical care (Tjaden and Thoennes, 2000). Approximately 7 percent of victims of nonfatal intimate partner violence sought care in emergency departments, which represents about 15 percent of those who experience an injury. Less than 1 percent of victims were hospitalized. For women seeking care for intentional injuries in an emergency department, about 30 percent of their injuries were found to be the result of intimate partner violence (Tjaden and Thoennes, 2000; Greenfeld et al., 1998; Wilt and Olson, 1996).

Intimate partner violence appears to be a significant predictor of hospitalizations, general clinic use, mental health services use, and out-of-plan referrals (Wisner et al., 1999). A study of sexual assault victims from all causes reported significantly higher severity of physical symptoms and medical utilization for victims of intimate partner violence compared with others from the same socioeconomic groups. A total of 72 percent of the identified victims sought medical treatment, and 19 percent sought psychiatric treatment (Kimerling and Calhoun, 1994). One study indicates that women experiencing victimization were more likely to seek physical than mental health treatment (Sansone et al., 1997).

Of the few longitudinal studies of intimate partner violence, several address utilization patterns (Bergman and Brismar, 1991; Kimerling and Calhoun, 1994; Koss et al., 1991; Sansone et al., 1997; Ulrich, in preparation). For example, Swedish investigators, in the longest follow-up study to date, examined automated hospital records for 10 years prior to and 8 years following identification in a group of 117 women with injuries from intimate partner violence. These women experienced a 3.5-fold higher hospital care and admissions rate than women in a comparison group (Bergman and Brismar, 1991; Bergman et al., 1992). A health maintenance organization study reported a 40 percent relative increase in health care utilization for victims (Koss et al., 1991). In this group of studies, the length of follow-up was commonly two years or less, with no retrospective or prospective studies systematically assessing the effects of intimate partner violence on patterns of utilization and costs at all levels of care. The longest-term study was hampered by small sample size and dealt only with hospital-level care (Bergman and Brismar, 1991; Bergman et al., 1992).

The full economic cost of intimate partner violence has not been determined, but what is known suggests that it is quite high. One study indicates that a hospitalized patient who has been identified as a victim of intimate partner violence will cost a median of $873 more than a patient with the same condition who has not been identified as a victim (Rudman et al., 2000). An examination of annual costs to a managed care plan for a group of women who had experienced intimate partner violence compared with randomly selected controls found that the overall cost to the plan was 1.9-fold higher in the abused group, with treatment of each victim resulting in net costs that were $1,775 more annually for each victim than for comparison patients. Differences in costs in emergency department utilization and hospitalizations between an abused group and a random sample were not significantly different, so extra costs for abused women are due to additional general ambulatory care and mental health care (Wisner et al., 1999). Direct medical costs of care for battered women are estimated at $1.8 billion per year (Miller et al., 1993, 1995). Physical and psychological effects contribute to increased costs and utilization of medical and other services

(Bergman et al., 1992; Drossman et al., 1995; Koss et al., 1991; Leiman et al., 1998; Sansone et al., 1997; Stark and Flitcraft, 1988, pp. 293-317, 1996; Ulrich, in preparation; Walker et al., 1999). When time lost from work, losses due directly to crimes, and other acute and long-term health care costs are added, the overall costs have been estimated to range between $5 billion and $67 billion (NRC and IOM, 1998).

Elder Abuse

The extent to which elder maltreatment affects the health care system is largely unknown. Common clinical findings associated with maltreatment include bruises, lacerations, abrasions, head injury, fractures, dehydration, and malnutrition (Bosker et al., 1990). These injuries commonly result in hospitalization. In one descriptive study that tracked the emergency department utilization of known elderly victims of physical abuse identified through adult protective services, 114 individuals had 628 emergency department visits during a 5-year window surrounding the referral; 30 percent of these visits resulted in hospital admission (Lachs et al., 1997).

Elder maltreatment differs from family violence experienced by younger individuals, in large part because of the higher prevalence of chronic disease in older people and issues of capacity or competence. This difference creates a higher prevalence of both false positives and false negatives in screening older adults for abuse (Lachs and Fulmer, 1995). For example, abuse may cause fractures, but so can osteoporosis. And osteoporosis may render an older person more vulnerable to fractures when abused. Common comorbidities in this population, such as Alzheimer's disease and related dementias, both increase the risk for abuse and make the diagnostic evaluation more difficult (Dyer et al., 2000). In case management, the lack of decision-making capacity because of dementia may greatly influence the choices available for intervention. In addition, older adults and health care providers may have to rely on the perpetrators of elder mistreatment to provide care (Quinn and Tomita, 1997).

Studies do indicate that the effects of elder mistreatment increase the medical needs of victims. One longitudinal study of elderly victims of maltreatment documented a threefold increased risk of death in the 3-year period following mistreatment, after adjusting for comorbidity and other factors that predict death in older cohorts (Lachs et al., 1998). In addition, maltreatment may exacerbate or interfere with the treatment of other medical and psychosocial conditions. For example, angina pectoris, emphysema, diabetes mellitus, and arthritis are much more challenging to treat in an abusive environment (Lachs et al., 1997). No studies of the costs associated with these increased medical needs have been published.

In view of the rapidly growing elderly population in the United States, health care providers are likely to see an increasing number of cases in the coming years. Supporting this view, most adult protective services agencies are reporting growing caseloads (Tatara, 1993).

CONCLUSIONS

- **Family violence is common and the health consequences are significant.**

The need for health professional training in family violence is a function of its magnitude coupled with the health care needs associated with it. The available data suggest that family violence results in significant health effects and that treatment requires substantial time and financial resources.

- **The effects of family violence on society and the health care system have not been adequately studied or documented.**

The available data are inadequate to determine the full magnitude and severity of family violence in society or its impact on the health care professions. Few studies describe the total and marginal patterns of utilization and the costs of health care or the cross-sectional and longitudinal effects on health status from the point of view of the patient (or victim). The results of such studies could indicate the full extent to which the health care system and professionals encounter family violence and the health care needs of victims. A better understanding of the baseline problems, health care needs, and costs associated with family violence could reinforce the need for health professionals' attention to the issue, provide guidance as to how to respond, and inform and improve health care professional education and practice.

- **The definitions, data sources, and methods used in research on family violence are variable and result in inconsistent research findings about its magnitude, severity, and effects on the health care system and society.**

The common use of explicit definitions, data sources, and methods could foster the capacity to make reliable comparisons between studies and allow research results to be generalized to other situations. The committee reiterates the conclusions of previous National Research Council and Institute of Medicine reports (NRC, 1993, 1996; NRC and IOM, 1998) regarding the importance of definitional clarity.

The committee recognizes that the determination of clear definitions and classification schemes and outcomes is a complex and time-consuming task, which is both affected by and affects empirical measurement, social concerns, legal and ethical issues, and politics. As such, the committee is encouraged by recent efforts to develop definitions and classification schemes for each type of family violence that will be tailored to the health care context and endorses the use of such definitions and data elements to assist in creating a more comprehensive and comprehensible picture of family violence. The Centers for Disease Control and Prevention have developed such uniform definitions and measurement terms for intimate partner violence (Saltzman et al., 1999). The definitions and data elements recommended in their report reflect attention to the potential health care uses of the terms, recognizing incidents of violence, threats of violence, and consequences of violence, including those relevant to medical settings.

Similar efforts are under way for child abuse and elder abuse. For example, in response to the recommendation for definitional work in the National Research Council report *Understanding Child Abuse and Neglect* (1993), the National Institute for Child Health and Human Development, with the Children's Bureau of the Department of Health and Human Services and other institutes of the National Institutes of Health, has convened a Child Abuse and Neglect Working Group, which among other activities has commissioned work on definitions and classifications of child abuse and neglect. Other efforts to standardize child abuse and neglect definitions have been made, most notably by the National Clearinghouse on Child Abuse and Neglect, although such efforts have not yet resulted in agreement or widespread usage. With regard to elder maltreatment, the National Institute on Aging has funded the Committee on National Statistics of the National Research Council to conduct a workshop to consider the development of a national survey on the prevalence of elder abuse; consideration of explicit definitions is part of the agenda.

3

Current Educational Activities in the Health Professions

This chapter reviews the current educational activities for health professionals on family violence, focusing on what, how, and when health professionals are taught to assess, evaluate, and treat patients experiencing family violence. The committee obtained information on educational programs that have been published in the professional literature and supplemented these published descriptions by soliciting input from educational institutions, health care provider settings, health professional organizations, family violence advocacy groups, researchers, public policy makers, and individual health care providers. The results of this search provide an illustrative sample that was useful in informing the committee's work (see Appendix E). The following descriptions are based on the committee's review of this illustrative sample.

PHYSICIAN EDUCATION

Medical School

A majority of medical schools report the existence of educational content on at least one form of family violence (Liaison Committee on Medical Education Annual Medical School Questionnaire, 1999-2000, questions 39a, 39b). Most often, education appears to focus on reporting requirements, patient/victim interviewing skills, screening tools, health conditions associated with violence, and services to which victims can be referred. The amount of training varies widely from very brief (e.g., a discussion of topics to cover during a patient interview) to more extensive (e.g., a series of lectures or case discussions during a clinical rotation).

About 95 percent of medical schools report curricular inclusion of material related to child abuse and neglect (Alpert et al., 1998). The curricula generally include content on the identification, reporting, and management of child abuse and neglect and are typically introduced during the pediatric rotation in medical school (Alexander, 1990; Bar-on, 1998). Teaching strategies are both didactic and interactive.

With regard to intimate partner violence, medical schools report an increase in education (AAMC, 2000). Content usually focuses on screening, history taking, and available community resources for victims. Sexual assault appears to receive more attention than other forms of maltreatment. Teaching appears to occur most often in the form of lectures, frequently involving presentations by victims, case discussions, and role-playing exercises. The content is usually integrated into courses on history taking and communication or is offered during emergency medicine and obstetrics-gynecology rotations. With the exception of the few schools that now offer problem-based intimate partner violence cases or clinical electives, most instruction on intimate partner violence and elder abuse still occurs in the preclinical years and is predominantly content focused, lecture based, isolated, and not integrated into the overall educational schema with clinical correlations and cross-disciplinary education (Alpert et al., 1998).

Elder maltreatment appears to be least often included in medical school curricula. When it is, content tends to focus on institutional abuse and abuse between older intimate partners rather than other forms of maltreatment in a family setting. The most common teaching method is case discussion, most likely to occur during patient interviewing courses or during emergency department rotations. Schools with a geriatrics rotation appear most likely to address elder abuse.

Residency Training

Family violence training during residency appears most common among programs whose residents are considered mostly likely to encounter victims: pediatrics, obstetrics-gynecology, emergency medicine, internal medicine (primary care), geriatrics, and psychiatry. The Residency Review Committees of the Accreditation Council for Graduate Medical Education require education on family violence in a number of residency and subspecialty residency programs. Programs in pediatrics, adolescent medicine, pediatric emergency medicine, and forensic psychiatry specifically are required to include training in child abuse or neglect. Obstetrics and gynecology residencies must include training on intimate partner violence. Family practice geriatric medicine and geriatric psychiatry residencies must include training on elder maltreatment. Family practice, internal medicine, and emergency medicine residencies must contain training on all forms of family violence. The time allocated for training about family violence appears to vary greatly from program to program, and content appears to focus on identification and treatment. The methods include primarily lectures and case discussions.

Pediatric residency programs report a mean of 8 hours of training on child maltreatment during the first and third years of training and a mean of seven hours during the second year (Dubowitz, 1988). The standardized experiences for pediatric emergency fellowship training include a curriculum developed by the American Board of Pediatrics, the American Academy of Pediatrics, and the American College of Emergency Physicians. Despite this program, fellowship directors in emergency medicine reported a need for an increase in training on child abuse (Biehler et al., 1996; Wright et al., 1999).

A number of residency and fellowship programs report intimate partner violence content. In a study of primary care internal medicine residency program directors on women's health issues, 40 percent stated they include structured teaching on intimate partner violence in their training programs, and 20 percent believed their residents had mastered the subject (Staropoli et al., 1997). In a similar study of family practice residencies, 80 percent reported that intimate partner violence was included in their curricula (Rovi and Mouton, 1999). Teaching methodology consisted predominantly of lectures and case vignettes. Compared with a previous study, the inclusion of intimate partner violence content in family medicine residency curricula has increased (Hendrick-Matthews, 1991; Rovi and Mouton, 1999). Among psychiatry residents, 28 percent reported receiving any training about intimate partner violence during any phase of their medical education (Currier et al., 1996). Emergency medicine programs report increased attention to intimate partner violence and a focus on identifying potential victims and preventing further abuse (Abbott et al., 1995; Dearwater et al., 1998; Goldberg, 1984; McLeer and Anwar, 1989).

Elder maltreatment training varies from program to program but is less frequently included in training programs. Information on residency program training about elder abuse is minimal. Emergency medicine and geriatrics programs appear most often to include content on elder maltreatment. However, in a survey of practicing emergency medicine physicians, only 25 percent could recall any education on elder abuse during residency (Jones et al., 1997).

Continuing Medical Education

Little information is available about the level and amount of continuing medical education on family violence, beyond what the legal requirements dictate (discussed in Chapter 4). A number of lectures appear to be offered around the country each year and web-based programs exist, for which credit is available. The effects of continuing medical education on physician practice are discussed in depth in Chapter 6.

PHYSICIAN ASSISTANTS

Physician assistants (PAs) are licensed health care providers who practice medicine under the supervision of physicians. Little information about the specific training for physician assistants is available. The American Academy of Physician Assistants and the Association of Physician Assistant Programs recognize family violence as a public health epidemic in the United States and encourage PA programs to include violence prevention, assessment, and intervention in program curricula. Physician asssistants sometimes participate with medical students in medical school coursework, some of which contains content on family violence. One example of curricula at Nova Southeastern University, Florida, includes three hours of lecture and case presentations on diagnosis, treatment, counseling, prevention, and legal requirements for all types of family violence.

DENTISTRY

Data are scarce about dental education on family violence, regardless of specialty. The available data show that dentists are becoming aware that they encounter victims of family violence but often do not recognize the signs of abuse and are uncertain about how to intervene (Chiodo et al., 1994). A study in Oregon showed that dentists who graduated from dental school after 1980 were more apt to have received family violence education than their colleagues who graduated earlier (Chiodo et al., 1994). In one study comparing the formal education available to physicians, nurses, psychologists, and dentists, the dentists reported the least amount of formal education on all areas of family violence— this was most notable in education on elder abuse (Tilden et al., 1994). A survey of the 64 accredited dental schools in North America, however, indicated that 96 percent of preprofessional dental students are taught to recognize and report child maltreatment. The majority of schools taught about child maltreatment through the pediatric dentistry rotation, with most providing one or two hours for teaching this subject (Jesse, 1995). In another survey, 43 of 55 predoctoral pediatric dental programs reported including the subject of child maltreatment in their curricula (Posnick and Donly, 1990).

Prevent Abuse and Neglect through Dental Awareness (PANDA), a pioneer program in Missouri, is a coalition of social service and health agencies, professional dental organizations, and dental schools that develops education and training programs for dental health practitioners. PANDA programs have been established in other states as well (Ramos-Gomez et al., 1998; Hazelrigg, 1995). A similar group, the Dental Coalition to Combat Child Abuse and Neglect, was formed in Massachusetts to educate dental professionals about how to detect and report cases of child maltreatment. The coalition conducted an intensive statewide program that included educational materials on child maltreatment, intensive media coverage, oral slide presentations at state society meetings, and publicity about their work in the local dental journal. Participation in the state-wide education program, however, was low (Needleman et al., 1995).

NURSING

Nursing education does include attention to family violence, particularly child abuse and neglect and intimate partner violence. In one major study, responses from 298 schools (48 percent of the total; 85 percent baccalaureate degree or higher) indicated that all of the responding schools of nursing had at least some family violence-related content in their curricula, but only 53 percent of the schools felt that content was adequately addressed (Woodtli and Breslin, 1996). In spite of reports of content in baccalaureate schools of nursing, a regional random sample survey of 1,571 practicing clinicians in six disciplines including nursing demonstrated that more than one-third of these practicing clinicians reported no educational content in family violence (Tilden et al., 1994).

Content on child abuse and neglect was systematically integrated into almost all nursing curricula and texts in the late 1960s and 1970s, primarily as a result of national legislation and publicity on the subject. The Woodtli and Breslin (1996) study indicates that child abuse and neglect were addressed by 90 percent of the schools and that child abuse had the greatest number of separate classroom hours devoted to it, with 56 percent of schools indicating 3 or more hours on the topic.

Attention to intimate partner violence in the literature on nursing research and practice appears to be increasing, accompanied by professional association and curriculum development. Curriculum content on intimate partner violence has increased with official nursing organization attention to the issue (e.g., American Nurses Association [ANA], 1995; American Association of Colleges of Nursing [AACN], 1999; American College of Nurse Midwives [ACNM], 1997; Association of Women's Health, Obstetric, and Neonatal Nurses [AWHONN], 2000; Emergency Nurses Association [ENA], 1998; Paluzzi and Quimby, 1998). A total of 91 percent of schools reported addressing intimate partner violence (Woodtli and Breslin, 1996). One-third of the programs reported specifically planned and professionally guided learning experiences in clinical settings (primarily domestic violence shelters) that particularly focused on aspects of family violence.[1]

The area of elder abuse has received the least attention and is represented

---

[1]Some preliminary or indirect descriptive-level evidence from attitude surveys and course evaluations suggests that guided clinical experience focusing on families experiencing violence and settings in which violence occurs is most effective in teaching clinical nursing skills on violence against women (Barnett et al., 1992; Campbell and Humphreys, 1993; King, 1988).

least well in nursing curricula. Currently, there are no curricular requirements for the topic. A total of 82 percent of responding schools reported having any elder abuse content, and 66 percent of responding schools spent only 1-2 classroom hours on the subject (Woodtli and Breslin, 1996). The AACN, in conjunction with the John A. Hartford Institute for Geriatric Nursing Practice, has done much in recent years to address the paucity of geriatric curricula. The Geriatric Education Center Program, funded by the Bureau of Health Professions, is one vehicle for continuing education programs for nurses who need classes on elder abuse and neglect.

Almost all major textbooks in undergraduate baccalaureate nursing programs do have content on at least one form of family violence. However, family violence content is noticeably lacking in the physical assessment textbooks commonly used at both baccalaureate and advanced-practice levels, except for child abuse and neglect. Nursing texts at both the associate degree and advanced-practice levels also have less content on family violence, except again for child abuse and neglect in pediatric nursing. The other advanced-practice exception is nurse midwifery, which has systematically addressed the issue of violence against women through programs and texts (Paluzzi and Quimby, 1998).

PSYCHOLOGY

Although the American Psychological Association's (APA) Presidential Task Force on Violence and the Family (1996) recommended that training occur on issues of family violence, implementation of such recommendations is not a simple matter. For example, a review of 24 recently published introductory psychology textbooks, used primarily in undergraduate education, revealed great disparities in covering child sexual abuse (Letourneau et al., 1999). Furthermore, unlike many health professionals-to-be, doctoral students in psychology do not participate in a standard curriculum (for the relevant accreditation guidelines, see www.apa.org/ed/gp2000.html). There are also no standard texts (even as a matter of conventional practice) for most graduate psychology courses and no standards for addressing family violence. Although licensing boards often require that candidates have completed course work in broad areas of psychology (e.g., biological bases of behavior), they do not prescribe the content of the courses (e.g., the biological bases requirement could be met through a survey course or a seminar on basic neuropsychology, physiological psychology, behavior genetics, or neuropsychological assessment). Indeed, the initial survey course in statistics is the only commonality that can be expected in the curricula experienced by doctoral students in clinical, counseling, and school psychology. Moreover, it is often possible to obtain a PhD in psychology without meeting the requirements (which vary substantially across states in any event) for admission to licensing exams for psychologists wishing to engage in clinical or counseling practice.

Most training about child maltreatment takes place in workshops and continuing education (Kalichman and Brosig, 1993). Fewer than 20 percent of psychologists in Colorado and Pennsylvania reported having had education about such issues in graduate school (Kalichman and Brosig, 1993). Most clinical psychologists in a national sample rated their graduate education about child maltreatment as poor, and ratings of internship training about the problem were not much better (Pope and Feldman-Summers, 1992). Approximately 90 percent of clinical, counseling, and school psychology programs reported that they do not have courses specifically on the topic (Howe et al., 1992). These findings, drawn from surveys conducted about a decade ago, may be somewhat outdated, given the increased interest in the problem of child maltreatment among psychologists and the attention that the problem has been given by the APA in recent years. At a minimum, however, the data indicate serious gaps in the education of psychologists graduating a decade or more ago and raise questions about the systematization of educational efforts now occurring.[2]

Recognizing these issues, the APA Working Group on Implications for Education and Training of Child Abuse and Neglect (Haugaard et al., 1995) developed several recommendations for training (including, for example, experiential training in all APA-accredited internships in clinical, counseling, and school psychology about services for abused and neglected children). The working group also generated materials to meet the needs for curricular resources that it had identified. Besides initiating some workshops for continuing education and other training activities, the working group prepared booklets for college and university teachers of graduate (Haugaard, 1996a) and undergraduate (Haugaard, 1996b) psychology students, relying on course syllabi and reading lists garnered from the field.

The booklet on graduate education presents suggestions of topics and reading lists for three situations: (a) integration of examples relating to child abuse and neglect into conventional courses (e.g., inclusion of discussion of the origins of abusive behavior in a course on personality); (b) focus of a lecture or two on child abuse and neglect in a conventional course (e.g., discussion of prevention of child maltreatment in a course on community psychology); and (c) entire courses on child maltreatment or a type of maltreatment (e.g., sexual abuse). The booklet is organized with reading lists and other materials (e.g., lists of commercially available videotapes) for (a) a graduate course on child abuse and neglect and (b) specialized training for clinical, counseling, and school psychologists.

---

[2]The degree to which psychologists have been involved in family violence appears to have varied dramatically across forms of family violence. For example, searches in August 2000 of the PsycINFO data base of behavioral science journals published since 1990 revealed the following results. Using the terms *child abuse* or *child maltreatment*, 5,228 hits occurred. For *intimate partner violence* or *domestic violence* or *spouse abuse*, 802 citations were identified. The term *elder abuse* elicited 133 articles. Adding *psychologists* as a qualifying term—for example, *child abuse* or *child maltreatment* and *psychologists*—reduced the number of hits to 186, 24, and 0, respectively.

The outline for the graduate course includes one section devoted to the "Recognition and Referral of Abused and Neglected Children and Adults." The three books that are suggested readings for that session all focus on mandated reporting (Besharov, 1990; Kalichman, 1993; Monteleone, 1994). The outline on specialized training for professional psychologists includes a section on "Identifying Abuse and Neglect Victims," and the suggested readings (i.e., Melton and Limber, 1989; Morgan and Edwards, 1995; Myers, 1992) all relate to the need for care in evidence gathering and opinion formation.

Approximately three-fifths of mental health practitioners report having had training about intimate partner violence, a substantially smaller proportion than now claim to have been trained about child sexual abuse (Campbell et al., 1999; Tilden et al., 1994). As with child maltreatment, such training, when it occurs, usually consists of continuing education workshops. A task force convened by the presidents of five APA divisions is, at this writing, near completion of curricula on intimate partner violence. The curricula are being designed for education of undergraduate and graduate students and mental health professionals. With special attention to experiences of gay and ethnic-minority couples, the curricula will present topics for study from the perspectives of victims, perpetrators, and others, including children who witness intimate partner violence, and will include lists of relevant readings, music, and videos.

No specialized guidelines or training programs for psychologists on responses to elder abuse appear to exist. The general lack of attention is illustrated by a booklet published in 1997 by an APA working group on *What Psychologists Should Know About Working with Older Adults*. The discussion of elder abuse is limited to two paragraphs in the chapter on "Psychological Problems of Aging." The only concrete advice given is to question the cause of physical injuries to an older client and to be aware of state reporting laws. The remainder of the passage focuses on the epidemiology of elder abuse and the circumstances under which it is most likely to occur.

However, the problem has not been ignored by organized psychology. In 1999, the APA Public Interest Directorate published a booklet informing both the general public and professionals serving older adults about *Elder Abuse and Neglect: In Search of Solutions* (available at www.apa.org/pi/aging/practitioners/homepage. html). This booklet provides an extensive overview of the nature of elder abuse, psychosocial and cultural factors in its occurrence, steps for laypersons to take when elder abuse is suspected, and resources for help and further information.

SOCIAL WORK

A preliminary review of the 407 Council on Social Work Education accredited bachelor of social work (BSW) programs and 136 accredited master's of social work (MSW) programs in the United States indicates that little systematic education is being offered on family violence in schools of social work.[3]

To date, of the 258 BSW programs with information obtainable from web sites, 15 have courses on child abuse, 3 have courses on intimate partner violence, none have a course on elder maltreatment, and 18 have a course covering all aspects of family violence. One school offers a course on elder mistreatment that is available to both BSW and MSW students. Of the 74 MSW programs with course information online, 8 schools offer course(s) on child abuse and neglect, 5 schools on intimate partner violence, 1 on elder mistreatment, and 17 on all aspects of family violence.

Of the deans and directors who responded to the inquiry about family violence education, several noted that information is included in their general courses on treatment methods or human behavior in the social environment, the course on problems in the human environment (the equivalent of a psychopathology course in many MSW programs), or in courses on welfare policies and programs. However, none of the responding deans and directors suggested that the amount of time spent on the issues of family violence in all its forms was anything more than minimal.

The initial information from deans and directors also clearly suggests that a number of schools are actively involved in continuing education efforts in the area of family violence. At least two schools indicated that they are affiliated with centers that study family violence or one of its component elements, i.e., child abuse and neglect, intimate partner violence, or elder abuse. These centers by report tend to be actively involved in continuing education, with at least three of the schools indicating that they have produced conferences and workshops in all areas of family violence.

CONCLUSIONS

This review of the current state of training suggests the following conclusions:

- **A number of curricula on family violence for health professionals do exist and the number appears to be increasing.**

---

[3]These initial data were developed from the committee's review of social work program web sites containing information about curricula. The committee sought information concerning any course listings that indicated the course was about family violence, violence in general, domestic violence, intimate partner violence, child abuse, child sexual abuse, or elder mistreatment. In addition, information was solicited directly from deans and program directors about educational content on family violence at either the BSW or MSW levels. Only 12 deans or program directors responded to the committee's written inquiry. Work remains to be done to gather information not available on the Internet and to check the accuracy of the web-based information.

- Studies indicate that health professionals and students often perceive curricula on family violence as inadequate (e.g., content is insufficient to address the issue) or ineffective (e.g., students cannot recall training).
- In formal curricula on family violence, content is incomplete, instruction time is generally minimal, content and teaching methods vary, and the issue is not well integrated throughout the educational experience.

4

Forces Influencing
Health Professionals' Education

Health professional curricula evolve in the larger societal context and may be influenced by a number of factors. The committee identified a number of forces with the potential to influence curriculum development, implementation, and sustainability and explored the impact of each. The factors considered include training environment issues; accreditation, licensure, and certification requirements; individual issues for health professionals; the influence of health professional organizations and other stakeholder groups; laws mandating reporting and education about family violence; and funding.

Throughout its discussion of challenges to training, the committee struggled with two issues. First, little research has been published regarding factors that challenge or become barriers to educational efforts or the relationship between such factors and education. Second, some research has been published to provide empirical support for the impact of various factors on health professional practice. The committee often had difficulty distinguishing among effects on practice and education, as the experiences of individual committee members suggest that factors that become barriers to practice are also barriers to education. Many teaching faculty are also clinically active practitioners in their fields, and much education received by health professional students takes place in clinical settings (either inside or outside the academic institution). Thus challenges to training are difficult to distinguish from issues related to the clinical care of patients at risk for family violence. Despite perceptions of a relationship or similarities between challenges to education and barriers to practice, without further research, only inferences can be made. The committee has attempted to distill those concerns pertinent to the education and training of health care professionals.[1]

INTRINSIC INFLUENCES ON THE TRAINING ENVIRONMENT

Forces intrinsic to settings of health professional training may shape curricula. Such factors include: (1) curricular time and educational priorities and (2) institutional culture and norms. Curricular time refers to the specific course(s), hours, or other time allotted to training on family violence. How the time is used is dictated in part by the recognition of educational needs and determinations of the extent to which those needs will be met, involving setting priorities for the limited time available. Institutional culture and norms refers to the professional values and beliefs within the training environment.

The following discussion relies on the data available, the experience of committee members, and reports of others in health professional education elicited during a public forum the committee held on this topic, as well as other communications. The majority of the available literature focuses on physician and nurse education.

Curricular Time and Educational Priorities

Recognition of the Need for Training on Family Violence

Family violence, although of ancient origins, is newly recognized as a substantial concern for the public health and health care systems. For many in health care, it is perceived more easily as a social or legal problem. In fact, historically, society in general and some health professions in particular have considered family violence to be primarily a social or legal problem and have been slow to recognize its significant health component. As recently as 15 years ago then-Surgeon General C. Everett Koop convened the first workshop linking violence and public health. In Dr. Koop's words:

> Identifying violence as a public health issue is a relatively new idea. Traditionally, when confronted by the circumstances of violence, the health professionals have deferred to the criminal justice system. . . . [Now] the professionals of medicine, nursing, and the health related social services must come forward and recognize violence as their issue. (1991:v)

---

[1]The committee refers the reader to a number of references that do discuss barriers to practice (e.g., Chamberlain and Perham-Hester, 2000; NRC and IOM, 1998; Parsons et al., 1995). The Parsons et al. study, for example, does indicate that a lack of education is commonly identified as a barrier to screening practices and suggests the importance of training. However, this study relied on a questionnaire in which a sample of obstetrician-gynecologists were asked to rank a series of potential barriers to screening. It suggests that training is an important factor in screening practices but does not establish a cause-and-effect relationship between education (or lack thereof) and practice.

Koop's 1985 Conference on Violence as a Public Health Problem (DHHS, 1986) provided leadership in recognizing violence in general, including all forms of family violence, as a health problem. Recommendations from that conference covered inclusion of information about all forms of family violence in basic and continuing education for all health professionals and in certification, licensing, credentialing, and board examinations. The conference also recommended that the professions develop standards of practice and care, to be incorporated into family violence education.

Progress appears to have been made on health professionals' recognition of family violence as a health issue. For example, in 1991, the American Nurses Association published guidelines for identifying and treating intimate partner violence (ANA, 1991); the American Medical Association did the same in 1992 (AMA, 1992).

Some evidence that the attitudes of individual health professionals have begun to shift also exists. For example, in a 1995 survey of obstetrics-gynecology physicians, 86 percent reported a belief that intimate partner violence is a medical problem (Parsons et al., 1995). This belief appears to be even stronger in the nursing profession. One survey shows that fewer than 4 percent of private office nurses, 5 percent of public health nurses, and 3 percent of hospital nurses agreed with the statement that intimate partner violence is not a medical problem (Moore et al., 1998). In a survey of 107 nursing educators representing associate degree (38 percent) as well as baccalaureate and higher programs, all respondents agreed that all nursing students need to be taught the signs of abuse across the age span (Woodtli and Breslin, 1997). More than 75 percent felt that content on family violence was inadequate, and only 15 percent felt that faculty had adequate knowledge and skills to teach the topic competently. The majority (86 percent) were of the opinion that the content should be integrated throughout the curriculum, but only 33 percent said that resources for faculty and students on the subject were accessible. Only a few programs have a specific course on family violence, and those are generally elective courses. Some clinicians assert that, while family violence is indeed an important health problem, it is not something they themselves encounter (Sugg and Inui, 1992; Reid and Glasser, 1997).

Currently, the sentiment among health care providers that family violence lies outside the purview of the health professions seems most persistent among dentists and dental hygienists. Studies demonstrate that dental professionals vary in their response to receiving education on child abuse in dental school (Ramos-Gomez et al., 1998; Von Burg and Hibbard, 1995). In a 1994 survey of dentists, dental hygienists, physicians, nurses, psychologists, and social workers, providers were asked to respond to the statement: "Professionals in my discipline have as much responsibility to deal with problems of family violence as they do to deal with other clinical problems." In this study, 98 percent of psychologists, 97 percent of social workers, 87 percent of nurses, and 85 percent of physicians agreed. However, 47 percent of dentists and 46 percent of dental hygienists disagreed (Tilden et al., 1994).

Educational Needs and Priorities

Health professional curriculum development occurs in an environment of competing needs in which diverse curricular objectives must be sorted and prioritized. With the continuing increase of knowledge and expertise in health care as more research is conducted and published, potential topics for education increase while the educational time available remains the same. The need to add any "new" topic, such as family violence, to an already-packed curriculum may mean reducing or eliminating some other topic. Despite the increasing belief that family violence is an important issue for health care, training efforts on family violence may be perceived as displacing other more established educational topics long considered necessary to prepare health care professionals for clinical practice (Alpert, 1995).

Historically, clinical practice and the education that informs it have focused on acute trauma, physical injury, and disease. The U.S. health care system currently reflects the medical needs of the mid-20th century, when most Americans sought care for acute illness, injury, or childbirth (IOM, 1997). The American health care system is well suited to handle physical illnesses and injuries that used to be the predominant causes of morbidity and mortality, but it is not so well prepared to handle complex health issues with social underpinnings that are in the legitimate purview of health care and of public health (Fox, 1993; Wilkinson and Forlini, 1999).

Family violence is a complex, multifactorial problem that extends beyond these traditional focuses of medicine to social and ethical issues. Treating an acute injury per se does not require that the provider investigate the cause of the injury or evaluate the predisposing factors (analysis of which may help to prevent a subsequent injury in the same patient or a similar injury in a different individual). Symptoms of family violence (e.g., injuries, suicide gestures) can be treated without identification of the underlying cause, leaving the patient at risk for subsequent episodes. Furthermore, some physicians feel that it is ill advised to commit time toward learning how to evaluate a frustrating and often incurable situation, especially when there are other, more pressing treatable issues that can be addressed (Mashta, 2000, http://www.bmj.com/cgi/content/full/320/7229/208/a). According to one physician (Sugg and Inui, 1992):

> I think we tend to look more on the technical side of medicine, things we can help, like appendicitis. Domestic violence is a big morass which we will never escape. I get a headache thinking about it. And that attitude translates into the type of care we give those patients. (p. 3159)

Existing clinical care and education around family violence issues attend disproportionately to physical injury, despite the broad spectrum of abuse presentations seen in pediatric, adult, and elder populations (Talley et al., 1994; McCauley et al., 1995; Domino and Haber, 1987; Drossman et al., 1990; Drossman et al., 1995; Walker et al., 1999; Post et al., 1980; Schei, 1990; Jacobson and Richardson, 1987; Longstreth and Wolde-Tsadik, 1993; McCauley et al., 1997; Eby et al., 1995; Eisenstat and Bancroft, 1999). Even when physical injury is documented, clinicians tend to record facts (injury location) without sufficient context (e.g., who inflicted the injury and the circumstances surrounding the event; Warshaw, 1989).

Determining educational needs and priorities becomes even more difficult when little is known about a particular condition, treatment, or outcome. Thus, existing research gaps may limit education on a subject or suggest that it is not a priority. The research base on family violence interventions is deficient (NRC and IOM, 1998). For example, little is currently known about effective methods to detect intimate partner violence, and no data are available to determine the impact of screening and treatment on the incidence, morbidity, and mortality of intimate partner abuse (Cole, 2000). Without such knowledge, providers may be ill equipped to detect intimate partner violence in the health care setting, and appropriate education is difficult to determine (Abbott et al., 1995).

As the perceptions about important topics for health professional education continue to grow, prioritization is likely to become even more difficult. The figures on the magnitude of family violence in society, the health care implications for patients, and the health care services provided by health professionals (discussed in Chapter 2) indicate that family violence is a significant issue for health care, and the available research provides content that can be taught. While the need for family violence education does not ameliorate the need for education on other important topics, neglecting health professional training on family violence will not make the need for it disappear.

Allocation of Training Time and Adequacy of Training

Despite the numbers of existing curricula and beliefs about the need for family violence education, the amount of time allocated to this subject matter has been minimal (MMWR, 1989; Alpert, 1995; Alpert et al., 1998; Kassebaum, 1995). A total of 33 percent of a sample of physicians, nurses, social workers, psychologists, dentists, and dental hygienists reported that they have received no education about child abuse, intimate partner violence, or elder abuse during graduate school, residency training, or continuing professional education (Tilden et al., 1994). Sugg and Inui (1992) found that 61 percent of their sample of primary care physicians reported having had no training on intimate partner violence in medical school, residency training, or continuing education. Although the percentage of subjects who reported having some family violence education increased as the year of graduation became more recent, the lack of training appears to remain prevalent, with social workers reporting the most overall education in each type of abuse and dentists and dental hygienists the least (Sugg and Inui, 1992). Another survey of 705 academic emergency physicians indicated that only 25 percent could recall receiving any training about elder abuse during their residencies, only 20 percent during continuing education, and only 31 percent had a written protocol for the reporting of elder abuse in their current environment (Jones et al., 1997). Since 1998, the Association of American Medical Colleges (AAMC) has surveyed graduating medical students to assess the treatment of the topic of domestic violence in their medical school curricula. Nationally, the student perception of inadequate treatment decreased from 33 percent in 1998, to 31 percent in 1999, and 28.4 percent in 2000 (AAMC, 2000). The survey addresses only student perceptions and does not evaluate the content or intensity of the curricula. In another study, 86 percent of 111 medical schools reported existing curricula in adult intimate partner violence, yet a comparison of deans' and students' perceptions about curricular coverage of intimate partner violence yielded significant differences about the adequacy of coverage (Alpert et al., 1998).

Even in professions expressing concern about inadequate training in family violence, training may not be inadequately addressed. The American Psychological Association's (APA) Presidential Task Force on Violence and the Family (1996) has addressed the issue, yet most clinical psychologists in a national sample rated their graduate training on child maltreatment as poor and their internship training about the issue as only slightly better (Pope and Feldman-Summers, 1992). In a 1992 study, approximately 90 percent of clinical, counseling, and school psychology programs reported that they had no courses specifically addressing child abuse and neglect (Howe et al., 1992). In addition, approximately two-fifths of mental health workers reported that they had not received any training on intimate partner violence (Campbell et al., 1999). Recognizing these issues, the APA Working Group on Implications for Education and Training of Child Abuse and Neglect (Haugaard et al., 1995) noted a number of impediments to curricular reform to reduce the gap between psychologists' modal and optimal levels of expertise in responding to child maltreatment. Among these was a "lack of appreciation of the importance of including information about child abuse and neglect in current curricula by administrators, teachers, and trainers" (p. 79).

Institutional Culture and Norms

Institutional culture can create subtle messages regarding the educational and practical value of particular topics to health professionals and the status of those who teach and work with those topics (see, e.g., Hafferty, 1998; Hundert et al., 1996; Marinker, 1997). Challenging cultural issues include inertia or resistance to change, the dynamics of power, the need for leadership, professional socialization, multidisciplinary collaboration, and marginalization. Curricular revision requires attention to the culture and norms within the institution.

Studies suggest that faculty resistance to change is a major barrier to curricular reform, as the drive to maintain the status quo often overrides the desire to make educational innovations (Bloom, 1989; Robins, 2000). Even when medical curricula do undergo major reform, the changes that are instituted tend to revert or "drift" back to previous educational patterns (Robins, 2000). The drift that is observed is quite consistently in the direction of a decrease in social science, humanities, and ethics instruction in the first-year curriculum, due at least in part to a feeling among basic scientists that this material is taught prematurely at the expense of essential basic science(s).

Moreover, establishing programs is more challenging if the topic is not embraced by academic leaders or widely recognized by the faculty (Hendricson et al., 1993; Kendall and Reader, 1988). Unless there is an internal mandate from an influential institutional leader (e.g., the dean or a department chair) or an external mandate from an accrediting body or legislative authority, curricular innovation may be difficult to achieve (Alpert et al., 1997a; Bussigel et al., 1988).

Health care professional students and trainees are socialized within this culture and power structure to emulate the beliefs and practice patterns of their teachers and role models in the clinical setting. Norms reinforced through practices that students observe in clinical training may reflect beliefs about professional roles and functions (Brandt, 1997). Issues such as family violence, often requiring multifaceted responses, frequent interdisciplinary cooperation, and attention to social or personal issues may challenge the norms underlying the professional socialization of many health care professionals, such as those related to independent practice, clinician-patient relationships, and awareness of social issues (Warshaw, 1997).

In addition, these professional norms can be understood against a backdrop of deeply embedded social norms and values regarding family violence in society. Like the general public, health professionals are raised and trained in a society in which public intervention in "private" family matters has been proscribed until recent years and in which victims of family violence, particularly women and children, historically have had relatively little public recourse.

American society has a long history of maintaining the privacy of family matters. For example, from the early colonial period onward, American courts affirmed a husband's right to physically "discipline" his wife (O'Faolain and Martines, 1974, p. 188). It was not until the late 19th century that states finally began to move away from actually condoning a husband's use of physical force against his wife (e.g., *Fulgham v. State,* 46 Ala. 143, 146-47 [1871]; *Commonwealth v. McAfee*, 108 Mass. 458, 461 [1971]; *Gorman v. State*, 42 Tex. 221, 223 [1875]).

No such laws exist on the books today, and over the past 30 years every state has enacted a protective order statute that allows judges to prohibit batterers from assaulting or threatening their intimate partners and to provide victims with a broad range of protective measures (Epstein, 1999). However, remnants of the reluctance to intervene on behalf of victims persisted into the 1990s. For example, a nationwide survey of intimate partner violence service providers documents that some judges hearing civil protection order cases apply artificially heightened standards of proof (e.g., requiring physical evidence or unbiased witnesses) that make it more difficult for victims to succeed (Kinports and Fischer, 1993).

Similarly, courts have long tolerated parental authority to discipline children in the name of family privacy (e.g., *State v. Jones*, 95 N.C. 588, 588 [1886]). However, in the 1960s, the United States began to take an active approach to decreasing violence against children. Since then, every state has designated a wide range of behaviors as illegal child abuse and neglect and has enacted mandatory reporting legislation, requiring certain professionals to report instances of child maltreatment. But the emphasis on the private domain of families persists; for example, most states still exempt parents from sanctions for forms of corporal punishment that otherwise would constitute criminal assaultive conduct (e.g., Johnson, 1998).

The beliefs about private family matters reflected in the legal system also appear to affect health professionals. Health professionals have expressed concern or discomfort with intervening in situations they view as private matters and may demonstrate these reservations when teaching or supervising students. Studies of the values and beliefs of emergency service staff, including physicians, physician assistants, and social workers at four hospitals, indicate that 90 percent of the study subjects believed that they should try to identify battered women, and 82 percent considered this to be "part of their job." But the same group failed to respond to intimate partner violence in any way in 40 percent of cases and responded only partially in 49 percent. The study's investigators hypothesized that medical staff want to help but feel uncomfortable doing so because they view inquiry and intervention about intimate partner violence as invading their patients' personal affairs (Kurz and Stark, 1988; Yllo and Bograd, 1998).

Open-ended interviews of primary care physicians regarding attitudes about intimate partner violence suggest that privacy concerns were among the most frequently identified barriers to identification and intervention (Sugg and Inui, 1992). Fear of offending the victim "often originated in the physician's discomfort with areas that are culturally defined as private. . . . The uncertainty of whether patients would consider domestic violence a legitimate area to probe was distressing. . . . Physicians felt that by even broaching the subject of violence, the patient would take offense." Reluctance to "overstep the bounds of what is private . . . leaves the physician wary of how to approach the issue" (Sugg and Inui, 1992, pp. 1358-1359). In a study of pediatric emergency medicine fellows, 40 percent labeled a reluctance to invade family privacy as either a major (7.7 percent) or a minor (32.8 percent) obstacle to identifying and reporting suspected battering of a child-patient's mother (Wright et al., 1997). And 58 percent of these physicians also reported some degree of personal discomfort with intimate partner violence cases.

The nursing and social work literature also identify concerns about intrusions into private or family matters when approaching issues of family violence.

For example, a survey of social workers, physicians, and nurses found that 63 percent of those surveyed cited personal discomfort and 57 percent cited concern about family privacy when asked about barriers to their own effective responses in intimate partner violence and sexual assault cases[2] (McGrath et al., 1997). Even if intervention on behalf of victims of family violence is accepted, contrary practices may suggest a different message. Instructional settings create learning environments in which what students learn may vary from what is taught (Hafferty, 1998). So, even if taught to intervene, students may not observe or be involved with practicing health professionals who do intervene. Thus, they may not learn to do what they were taught.

In addition to concerns about privacy, the need for multidisciplinary collaboration in responding to family violence may create challenges to training. For example, multidisciplinary and nonclinical teaching partners are considered important to health professional education on family violence, as intervening in abusive situations usually involves interaction among the health, social, and legal systems (e.g., American Academy of Family Physicians, 1994). However, the committee's review of existing health professional curricula indicates that collaborative practice may be discussed, but it is not usually demonstrated. The materials may suggest a health care team model for responding to family violence victims and may provide information on referral services but rarely involve members of other professions (e.g., social workers, district attorneys) in the educational efforts. What is taught is not reinforced in clinical experiences. For example, while nurses were more than twice as likely as physicians to consult with another professional when detecting situations of abuse, physicians were more likely to try to handle the situation alone with the patient (Tilden et al., 1994).

Social norms may also result in the marginalization of health professionals who do assume leadership roles in family violence. Students may make their career choices, in part, based on others' perceptions of particular fields (Hunt et al., 1996). A study of the response to family violence in five diverse communities indicates that health care professionals who chose to work consistently with family violence victims were marginalized by their colleagues and institutions. These professionals also reported economic, social, and psychological disincentives to providing care to this population (Cohen et al., 1997).

The presence and efforts of a singular charismatic faculty leader paradoxically can be an impediment to curricular innovation. That leader may singlehandedly take responsibility for family violence curricula or extracurricular activities. However, once the leader moves on to other pursuits, the programs generally wither due to insufficient institutional commitment (Cohen et al., 1997). Although charismatic

---

[2]The researchers did not break down the response rates among the different health professions represented in the sample.

leaders are an important impetus for curriculum development, alone they are insufficient for establishing permanence for education and training in family violence without concurrent institutional changes. Sole dependence on such individuals can create challenges for stability, given the fluidity of American society and the frequency with which individuals change their institutional affiliations.

An example of this phenomenon has been published in the intimate partner violence literature (McLeer et al., 1989). The initial success of a novel emergency department screening program for intimate partner violence reverted to its inadequate baseline screening rate following the departure of the individuals primarily involved with the intervention. To maintain such efforts, the reform must be institutionalized. The challenge is to establish systems and procedures that help create a foundation that is sufficiently flexible to sustain innovations and behavioral changes.

ACCREDITATION, LICENSURE, AND CERTIFICATION REQUIREMENTS

Health professions are subject to numerous legal and voluntary requirements or guidelines related to ensuring the competence of practicing professionals, practice standards, and professional and patient protections. These requirements can serve as leverage points for the inclusion of particular educational content in a profession's various modes of training. For example, students may be more likely to receive training on a particular topic if the requirements for professional accreditation demand it or subspecialty certification exams include it. Even without explicit requirements, a health professional organization can exert influence on training content by encouraging or supporting such efforts. The committee reviewed existing accreditation, licensure, and certification requirements to identify family violence components.

Accreditation

Accreditation of professional disciplines determines the course of study required to be part of the profession.[3] In some cases, this may be as explicit as indicating the number of didactic hours of a particular subject area or as broad as specifying the requisite focal areas of study for a profession. Thus, requirements for the accreditation of professional disciplines can influence, if not in part define, the educational content in health professional schools.

The committee reviewed the accreditation standards as of December 2000

---

[3]This process is different from the general accreditation of colleges and universities, in which the principal purpose is to ensure that the college or university is meeting the broader goals of postsecondary education.

for the professions included in this study to identify requirements related to family violence of any or all types (see Appendix A). The review indicates that, overall, few accreditation requirements related to family violence exist. The standards for medicine suggest that programs *should* (rather than *must*) assert the ramifications of family violence as a social problem. While social work requirements include no specific mention of family violence in its curriculum guidelines, it does allude to those who are at risk of victimization or are oppressed. Similarly, nursing, dentistry, psychology, and physician assistants do not specifically include family violence education as part of their accreditation process. Certain subspecialty areas do have education or training requirements in specific types of family violence. For example, the American Board of Obstetrics and Gynecology requires intimate partner violence training, and the American Board of Pediatrics requires training on child abuse and neglect.

Licensure

Licensure is the process by which a state, usually through an examination, regulates the practice of a specific profession. This examination can be administered on a national level, medicine being the principal example, but more often is administered by the state issuing the license. This state-directed exam may be a combination of both a nationally developed test and questions specific to certain state laws and regulations, or it may be state generated, with some questions drawn from a national data bank. The exam content can reflect required and desirable areas of study.

While a comprehensive review of state licensing laws for each health profession was beyond the scope of this report, the committee reviewed national exams for content on family violence, with the understanding that these exams play different roles with regard to licensure within the professions. This review revealed that licensure exams from the National Board of Medical Examiners and the National Council on Boards of Nursing provide the most explicit reference to family violence content. The National Board of Medical Examiners issues a three-step United States Medical Licensing Exam, the third step of which may include some questions related to child abuse, elder abuse, and sexual abuse.[4] The National Council on Boards of Nursing's Nursing Certification Licensure Exam contains a psychosocial adaptation section (5-11 percent of the questions). The content includes child abuse and neglect, elder abuse and neglect, and sexual abuse, as well as behavioral interventions, chemical dependency, crisis intervention, and psychopathology. Other organizations also indicate content on family violence on their exams but do not explicitly delineate the breakdown of components.

---

[4]For proprietary reasons, the National Board of Medical Examiners does not release the number or percentage of questions on family violence on the exam or a range of potential questions.

Certification

Certification of health professionals has two purposes. First, a state may protect a particular professional title, such as social worker or psychologist, by requiring that a person have a certain type and level of education in order to use it. These certification laws do not, however, regulate practice of the profession. Second, certification may recognize that an individual has successfully completed the national exam for a particular specialty and, in so doing, has demonstrated competence in that specialty. For example, certification by the American Board of Pediatrics suggests that a physician has the knowledge, skills, and attitudes to practice pediatrics in congruence with the national standard.[5] The Academy of Certified Social Workers certification indicates an individual's readiness for independent, unsupervised social work practice, including supervision of junior-level practitioners.

A review of current specialty certifications as of December 2000 suggests that several specialties require some training in the area of family violence. This requirement is usually closely linked to the target patient population for the specialty (e.g., pediatrics and child maltreatment). In such instances, a small number of questions on family violence appear on the certifying exam. Only a few specialties require training in all areas of family violence. Emergency medicine, for example, addresses all areas of family violence in section 18 on traumatic disorders (11 percent of the exam questions). The nurse midwife certification exam has specific questions on domestic violence and sexual assault, and the pediatric nurse practitioner exam contains questions on child abuse. However, specific content for exam questions can change from year to year and is dependent on the makeup of the committees assigned by the practice organizations.

INDIVIDUAL ISSUES:
PROFESSIONAL AND PERSONAL FACTORS

The development and impact of health professional education on family violence may be affected by professional or personal concerns, beliefs, or experiences. These may explain a lack of clinician initiative, one of the most common reasons cited for failing to detect abused women (Ferris and Tudiver, 1992). The following discussion is intended to demonstrate the extent to which individual factors can affect training about family violence, but it may apply differently to the health professions considered in this report.

---

[5]Recent petitions to the American Board of Pediatrics to establish a subboard on child abuse and neglect (to be called Child Abuse and Forensic Pediatrics) were deferred to allow time to document the scientific base of the field and to determine whether other medical organizations would have objections to the development of child abuse and neglect as a formal subspecialty.

Professional Issues

Professional issues at the individual level involve those related to health care professionals' roles and functions. Among the primary issues affecting individual response to family violence are time, inadequate training, uncertainty about how to respond, perceptions of patient noncompliance, and inadequate incentives for involvement.

Many health care providers feel they lack sufficient time to adequately assist victims of abuse. In one survey (Sugg and Inui, 1992), 71 percent of physicians interviewed stated that time constraints were a major reason they refrained from asking patients questions about family violence. Primary care practitioners frequently chose to refrain from involvement because they felt that the issue would consume their already limited time. One physician said (Sugg and Inui, 1992):

> I think that some physicians, and I do the same thing, if you are very busy and have lots of patients waiting, you just don't ask a question that you know is going to open a Pandora's box. Even if it crosses your mind, you don't ask. (p. 3158)

Many primary care physicians were frustrated with what they perceived as an "extra" societal responsibility, stating that they could quickly become overwhelmed in caring for "nonmedical" issues (Sugg and Inui, 1992). For example, in one survey, an estimated 37 percent of California primary care physicians cited lack of time as a major barrier to the identification and referral of patients experiencing intimate partner abuse (Rodriguez et al., 1999). Nevertheless, in a study of Alaskan physicians who provide prenatal care, time constraints were not associated with differences in screening rates (Chamberlain and Perham-Hester, 2000).

Even if time were not an issue, health care providers have expressed concerns regarding inadequate preparation, uncertainty about how to proceed if maltreatment is disclosed, and frustration with the inability to ensure positive outcomes for the victims. For example, one study indicates that many health professionals believe they have not had adequate medical education or training on intimate partner violence (Reid and Glasser, 1997; see also Chapter 3, this volume). In another study of emergency room physicians, an existing protocol recommended referral of victims of intimate partner violence to a social worker or mental health professional and also listed referrals for shelter, legal assistance, and counseling. Despite this, mental health consultation was documented in only 4 percent of 52 cases, social work referral was obtained in only 8 percent, and shelter information or other referrals were offered in only 2 percent, due in part to a lack of knowledge about referral resources and how to access them (Warshaw, 1989).

Receiving continuing education on intimate partner violence has been associated with increased screening for abuse (Carbonell et al., 1995; Chamberlain and Perham-Hester, 2000). However, other studies have shown this association to not be significant after adjustment for other factors (Rodriguez et al., 1999; Chamberlain and Perham-Hester, 2000). Evaluations of multifaceted domestic violence interventions that have included training have documented improvement in screening associated with the intervention (Thompson et al., 2000; Harwell et al., 1998). A review of the literature (Waalen et al., 2000) that examined interventions and barriers to screening for intimate partner violence reveals that interventions limited to the education of providers had no significant effect on screening or identification rates, but interventions that are multifaceted (e.g., education, protocols, posters) were associated with significant increases in screening and/or identification rates. A causal relationship between these interventions that include education and screening, however, has not been established.

Some health professionals indicate that they are frustrated even when they do offer treatment and provide referrals. According to one physician: "I get to the point where I feel discouraged because I feel like, with someone that's in . . . an abusive situation, until that person's ready to take care of it, I'm banging my head against the wall" (Sugg and Inui, 1992, p. 3159). Another believes he "is not sure he would have any effect anyway. I certainly find that most of my advice on smoking and alcohol and other self-destructive behaviors has no effect on people and it gets very frustrating" (p. 3159).

This sense of frustration is exacerbated by perceptions of patient noncompliance. Health care professionals work to develop plans of care to address the health complaints and concerns raised by their patients. The provider might want to see the patient get out of an abusive relationship and offer advice to this effect without fully considering the victim's beliefs, resources, and the context of her or his life at that time. Thus, for reasons that cannot be fully explored in the office setting, the patient may choose not to do "what the doctor says" (NRC and IOM, 1998). The provider inevitably feels frustrated and the patient feels blamed for not doing what she or he was told. The noncompliant patient thus becomes an obstacle for the provider, who then offers less and less attention and reinforcement, which in turn generates less of a reason for the patient to be compliant (Warshaw, 1993). In one study of family physicians, patient unresponsiveness was given as a common reason for failing to detect abused women (Ferris and Tudiver, 1992). The new movement toward shared decision making in health care holds promise of countering real and perceived issues of noncompliance (Angell, 1999). This dynamic is particularly important in family violence; a victim might feel particularly vulnerable in the health care setting and thus be reluctant to disclose abuse or act on the health professional's advice (Warshaw, 1993; Warshaw and Ganely, 1998).

In addition to a sense of inadequate capacity and frustration, the incentives for health professionals to participate in teaching appear inadequate. Academic faculty incentives, such as promotion, are based largely on publications generated by funded research and by service (patient care and service to the academic institution) and less so on education, particularly in medicine (Guze, 1995). Physicians, for example, who treat family violence victims believe that such work garners little respect from their peers and will not result in prestigious research grants and other support necessary for promotion and tenure (Cohen et al., 1997).

Personal Issues

Beyond professional issues, individual health professionals may also experience personal issues that create challenges for education related to family violence. Among these are personal values and biases, personal experience with family violence, and vicarious traumatization. Like anyone else, health care students and professionals bring personal values and biases to their educational and clinical experiences. For example, health care professionals and trainees may make assumptions about their patients based on socioeconomic status and lifestyle choices, which may or may not be borne out by the evidence. In some cases, for example, close identification by a health professional with a patient's lifestyle or socioeconomic class produces an assumption that no violence is occurring, whereas distinct differences in lifestyle and class produce an expectation of violence (Sugg and Inui, 1992; Newberger, 1977). This preconception also can foster a belief that "nothing will be done anyway" (Cohen et al., 1997), as the underlying socioeconomic differences will not change. These attitudes of disillusionment accompany a growing critique of victim "noncompliance" with the referrals and advice of the clinician (i.e., perceptions that victims will not change their situations). For example, an estimated 78 percent of California's primary care physicians felt patients' lack of disclosure was a major barrier to physician identification of intimate partner abuse and referral of patients (Rodriguez et al., 1999).

Some personal values regarding family violence and difficulty in addressing it may stem from personal experiences with victimization. Many health professionals report personal experiences with family abuse. For example, 57.5 percent of nurses in an urban trauma center reported such experiences (Ellis, 1999). Feelings of vulnerability related to personal experiences with abuse may pose a challenge to training health care professionals. However, surveys of nurses and physicians have found no significant association between having a personal history of violence and reported screening behavior for intimate partner violence (Rodriguez et al., 1999; Parsons et al., 1995; Moore et al., 1998). Having personally known a victim of abuse has been positively associated with an improved response to abuse (Saunders and Kindy, 1993).

While the evidence on the impact of personal experiences with family violence is inconclusive, some evidence suggests that vicarious or secondary traumatization occurs. A number of clinical reports reveal this phenomenon among professionals who work with victims of crime, abuse, or disasters (McCann and Pearlman, 1990; Neumann and Gamble, 1995; Talbot et al., 1992). Such reports indicate that clinicians, perhaps especially those who are inexperienced, sometimes themselves experience some of the symptoms of post-traumatic stress disorder after they hear accounts of victimization. Furthermore, clinicians' concepts of interpersonal situations (e.g., their perceptions of trustworthiness) may be affected adversely, although such an effect was not observed in the one large survey about therapists' experience with vicarious traumatization (Brady et al., 1999). Brady et al. did find that post-traumatic symptoms were positively related to therapists' level of work with survivors of child or adult sexual abuse. Whether this relationship reflected a selection factor or a causal linkage is unclear. The anecdotal reports of vicarious traumatization are sufficiently common to suggest a need for preparation of clinicians in training for the emotional reactions that they may have to victims' stories.

PROFESSIONAL ORGANIZATIONS AND STAKEHOLDER GROUPS

This section reviews the impact of health professional organizations and several stakeholder groups on professional education in family violence. Included in these stakeholder groups are advocacy groups, victims, and health care payers and providers.

Health Professional Organizations

Health professional organization statements, guidelines, positions, and policies that address health professional education or training on family violence explicitly are noted in Appendix B. Organizations such as the American Medical Association, the American Academy of Physician Assistants, the American Academy of Pediatrics, the American Nurses Association, the American Psychological Association, the American Dental Association, and the National Association of Social Workers have issued positions, policy statements, and guidelines designed to encourage or require training in family violence. For example, in 1992, the American Medical Association (AMA) issued a series of educational pamphlets about family violence to provide practicing physicians with background and clinical direction in caring for victims. Many state medical associations held statewide educational campaigns for their members following that AMA initiative. In 1972, the American Academy of Pediatrics published a slide series on child maltreatment, which was updated in 1996, and published guidelines on child maltreatment for the first time in 1991, updating them in 1999.

The American College of Obstetricians and Gynecologists (ACOG) was the first health care professional organization to address intimate partner violence systematically. In 1989, it sent all members a technical bulletin giving information on abuse during pregnancy, assessment, and referral. ACOG has continued its leadership in this area (see Figure 4.1), and its screening guidelines have been endorsed by other health professional organizations (Frye, 2001).

The American Nursing Association passed resolutions on violence against women in 1987 and 1991, calling for routine screening for domestic violence and "routine education" of nurses. The Emergency Nursing Association, the Association of Women's Health, Obstetric, and Neonatal Nurses, the American Association of Orthopedic Nursing, and the National Black Nurses' Association have also passed resolutions recognizing violence against women and intimate partner violence as areas of nursing concern, calling for increased nursing and other health care professional education. In 1997, the National Nursing Summit on Violence Against Women, under the auspices of the U.S. Public Health Service's Office on Women's Health of the Department of Health and Human Services, also called for preprofessional classroom and clinical content on violence against women. This was followed by the American Association of Colleges of Nursing position paper in 1999 calling for the same and detailing the objectives and the type of content to be included (see Chapter 6 for details). With a grant from the Health Research and Services Administration, the American College of Nurse Midwives included violence against women systematically in the education of its professionals. It developed a curriculum for basic education and continuing education materials and ensured ongoing attention to the issue through inclusion in certification exams and monitoring of programs for appropriate content (see Figure 4.2).

The Presidential Task Force on Violence and the Family of the American Psychological Association (1996) provided a general review of relevant research and considered psychology's potential contributions to responses to child abuse and neglect, intimate partner violence, and elder maltreatment. The task force appeared to start from an assumption that training about family violence for psychologists and other service providers has typically been inadequate, a perception echoed by most clinical psychologists themselves, especially those trained prior to 1985 (Pope and Feldman-Summers, 1992). The task force concluded (APA, 1996):

> Each year, large numbers of families who are victimized by violence seek help at a time of critical need, and they often are unable to locate professionals with specific training to help them take steps to stop violence at home and heal from their trauma. This situation is, in part, a consequence of the presently fragmented and irregular nature of professional education and training in family violence evidence interventions. Individual practitioners without institutional support conduct a great deal of family violence intervention training; university programs for training and research in these specialized interventions are rare. There is a pressing need for stable institutional resources with a critical mass of expertise to test promising new interventions, to train newcomers to the field, and to disseminate information about successful intervention models to practitioners in several professions. It is important to begin teaching about family violence in undergraduate psychology curricula and to integrate studies of trauma and violence throughout all levels of psychology education. (pp. 134-135)

The task force specifically recommended that "routine screening for a history

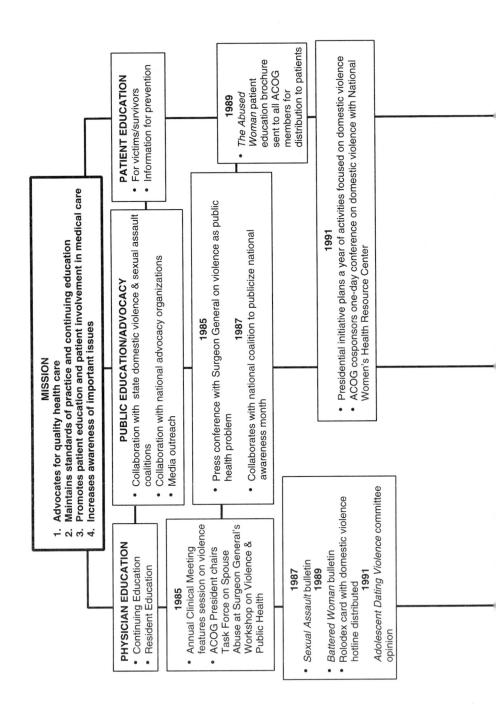

MISSION

1. Advocates for quality health care
2. Maintains standards of practice and continuing education
3. Promotes patient education and patient involvement in medical care
4. Increases awareness of important issues

PHYSICIAN EDUCATION
- Continuing Education
- Resident Education

1985
- Annual Clinical Meeting features session on violence
- ACOG President chairs Task Force on Spouse Abuse at Surgeon General's Workshop on Violence & Public Health

1987
- *Sexual Assault* bulletin

1989
- *Battered Woman* bulletin
- Rolodex card with domestic violence hotline distributed

1991
- *Adolescent Dating Violence* committee opinion

PUBLIC EDUCATION/ADVOCACY
- Collaboration with state domestic violence & sexual assault coalitions
- Collaboration with national advocacy organizations
- Media outreach

1985
- Press conference with Surgeon General on violence as public health problem

1987
- Collaborates with national coalition to publicize national awareness month

1991
- Presidential initiative plans a year of activities focused on domestic violence
- ACOG cosponsors one-day conference on domestic violence with National Women's Health Resource Center

PATIENT EDUCATION
- For victims/survivors
- Information for prevention

1989
- *The Abused Woman* patient education brochure sent to all ACOG members for distribution to patients

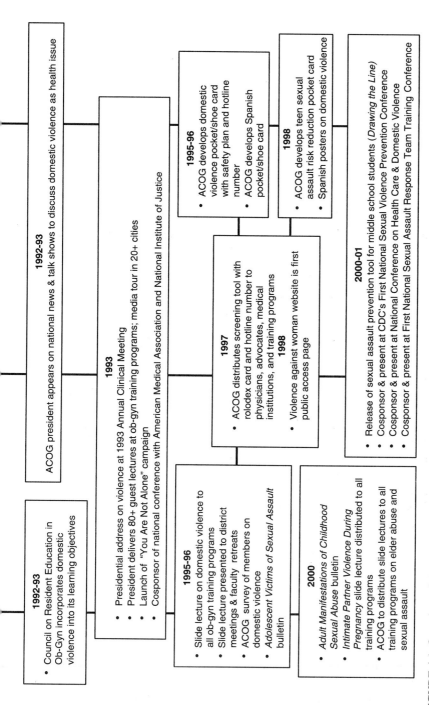

FIGURE 4.1 Overview of the American College of Obstetricians and Gynecologists response to violence against women. Source: American College of Obstetricians and Gynecologists. 2000. *Overview of the American College of Obstetricians and Gynecologists' Response to Violence Against Women.* Washington, DC.

of victimization be included in standard medical and psychological examinations and be considered in the development of individual treatment plans" (p. 134) and that the necessary training occur to enable such a change in psychologists' practice.

The National Association of Social Workers adopted a statement on family violence in 1987, reaffirmed it in 1993, and redrafted it in 2000. No other social work organizations, including the American Board of Examiners in Clinical Social Work and the Clinical Social Work Federation, appear to have specific expectations regarding family violence training for their members.

Advocacy Groups

A number of coalitions and initiatives have been developed to foster knowledge in the area of family violence. Generally, these groups and efforts target a particular type of family violence and appear to have been involved in increasing education on family violence issues. These groups include direct providers at shelters, other victims' services providers, members of grassroots movements that established those programs, and victims, as well as researchers and educators. However, their full impact is unknown. In addition, a number of advocates have expressed concerns about involvement with the health professions, believing health professionals may create obstacles to advocacy efforts and health professional education on family violence, if they do not understand or support the work the advocates are doing.

Systematic efforts were initiated in the 1960s and 1970s to integrate child maltreatment into the curricula of all of the health professions. The Child Abuse Prevention and Treatment Act of 1974 mandated the establishment of the National Center on Child Abuse and Neglect, which has since become the Office on Child Abuse and Neglect. The legislation resulted in part from efforts by advocacy groups to raise the awareness among helping professions about child maltreatment; it does not specifically address health professional training on child abuse and neglect.

Advocates were a primary force in bringing the issue of violence against women (including child sexual abuse and intimate partner violence) to the attention of health care providers. The first research by health professionals on the subject (outside psychiatry and psychology) was that of Carlson (1977) in social work, Parker and Schumacher (1977) from nursing and medicine, Stark and Flitcraft (1981) in medicine and sociology, Appleton (1980) in emergency medicine, and Campbell (1981) in nursing. Meanwhile, the 1970s were an era when the first battered-women's shelters were being established in the United States (Schechter, 1982) and when advocates of preventing sexual assault were beginning to address the issue of child sexual assault and rape.

Notable among advocacy efforts is the work of the Family Violence Prevention Fund. This organization has developed an extensive model educational program for health care providers (Ganley, 1998; Warshaw and Ganley, 1998). The

To be viewed as a continuum:

1994	1995	1996	1997	1998	1999	2000	And Beyond
* HHS Award to conduct Domestic Violence Education Project (Project MCJ#116084-01) * ACNM Board of Directors creates Ad Hoc Committee on Domestic Violence (later, Violence Against Women) * Committee recommends and BOD approves ACNM Position Statement on Violence Against Women	* ACNM Board of Directors recommends skills in Domestic Violence for all Midwives: Core Competency * DVEP activities and products in development: Video and manual on clinical skills; education materials for the public (video funded by Pharmacia & Upjohn Foundation)	* Continuing Education activities for ACNM members begin: Regional workshops using the tools; Training of Trainers workshops; workshops and education sessions at the ACNM Annual Meeting and Exhibit * Nurse-Midwifery Education Programs required to include domestic violence education in teaching and clinical skills development	* ACNM Certification Council (ACC) begins including item(s) about domestic violence in Certification Examination for CNMs/CMs * Journal of Nurse-Midwifery Home Study issue (Vol. 41, No.6) on domestic violence. ACNM members and others able to earn continuing education units * Continuing Education Workshops continue	* Proposal developed, together with the International Confederation of Midwives, for a project to work with midwifery associations in developing countries on the issue of domestic violence * Domestic Violence Education Project ends in October, with wide dissemination of materials to other groups and to the Maternal and Child Health Clearinghouse	* ACNM presents a paper on domestic violence and the role that midwives and midwifery associations can play at the Triennial Congress of the International Confederation of Midwives in Manila, the Phillipines * Ad Hoc Committee on Violence Against Women begins work on position statement on female genital mutilation (cutting)	* ACNM Board of Directors and membership approve position statement on female circumcision * ACNM presents at technical consultation on domestic violence sponsored by International Federation of Gynecology and Obstetrics (FIGO) in Naples, Italy * The ACNM's Domestic Violence Education Project: Evaluation and Results Journal of Midwifery and Women's Health, Vol. 45, No. 5	* ACNM's annual meeting and exhibit, 2001, with several sessions on violence against women

FIGURE 4.2 The American College of Nurse-Midwives activities and work in domestic violence: a timeline. Source: Vivio et al. (2000). Reprinted with permission.

program provides guidance to many educational and health care delivery institutions around the country that are in the process of developing or implementing training programs. The fund's training materials appear to have been distributed widely and serve as a reference for many health professionals. Plans to evaluate the program are under way. Other advocacy organizations, including provider advocacy organizations such as Physicians for a Violence-free Society and the Nursing Network on Violence Against Women International, have also been active in developing informational and educational materials and programs.

Advocates recognize the health care needs of victims of family violence, but they have also expressed reservations about the health care system's response, particularly with regard to victims of intimate partner violence. The concerns include: (1) the potential for the system to revictimize or blame female victims of violence (e.g., Faulk, 1974; Snell et al., 1964; Stark et al., 1981); (2) failure to identify victims (e.g., McLeer and Anwar, 1989); (3) the "medicalization" of a problem believed to be rooted in societal norms and systems; (4) interference with the development of strategies to escape from perpetrators; (5) emphasis on a medical solution to intimate partner violence that may enable society to continue to fail to hold perpetrators accountable; (6) insurance discrimination and loss of health care access (Fromson and Durborow, 1998); (7) overreliance on randomized clinical trials and quantitative measurement of outcomes that miss the complex nuances and intricate contexts of victims' lives (e.g., Campbell et al., 1999; NRC, 1996; Gondolf et al., 1997; NRC and IOM, 1998); and (8) loss of victim autonomy (NRC and IOM, 1998). Victims of both intimate partner violence and childhood sexual abuse have recounted how the health care system has failed them and how individual health care providers have made the situation worse (Herman, 1992; Sipes and Hall, 1996; Yllo and Bograd, 1998).

To address these concerns and to encourage health professional involvement with family violence issues and victims, advocates have been at the forefront in the training of health care professionals about family violence, particularly violence against women. Many training protocols (e.g., the Family Violence Prevention Fund, the Alaska Family Violence Prevention Project) prescribe the participation of advocates (as well as survivors) in training health care professionals. This joint partnership model of training remains to be evaluated for its efficacy.

In addition, advocates have promoted collaborative research involving partnerships with victims of family violence. Many researchers have undertaken this approach, and descriptions of these collaborations are beginning to be seen in the research literature (Campbell et al., 1999, 2001; NRC and IOM, 1998; Dutton et al., 1999; Gondolf et al., 1997).

Victims

Victims of family violence are being included in at least some of the research and policy decisions on the health care system's response to family violence. Many who work with domestic violence and sexual assault are themselves survivors of family violence. They speak, therefore, with the authentic voice of stakeholders as well as professionals in the field (e.g., Buel, 1994). Similarly, adult victims of child abuse have become active in advocacy. Victims of elder abuse, however, are often unable to advocate for themselves due to illness and incapacitation. At least in the area of intimate partner violence, victims have also begun to have a voice in research about needed directions in the health care system (e.g., Gielen, 2001; Rodriguez, 1998, 1999; Sipes and Hall, 1996). Current curricula appear often to include victims of intimate partner violence in educational efforts. These victims share their experiences with students and practicing professionals in an effort to personalize the problem.

The effect of these trends toward the inclusion of victims and victim advocates in professional education remains unclear. No available evaluation research addresses the impact of this trend. Research on educational strategies does suggest that case-based methods are effective (see Chapter 6), and victims and their advocates can provide real-life cases.

Health Care Payers and Providers

Payers have recently begun to express their views about health professional education. Groups such as the Pacific Business Group on Health and the Washington Business Group on Health are attempting to influence professional education in order to improve health care delivery. But neither of these groups to date has made any statements concerning training on family violence.

Blue Shield of California has been actively working in partnership with several large corporations to improve professional education on domestic violence. These programs tend to focus on a specific area of family violence. The extent of their impact has not been studied.

Similarly, several provider organizations (e.g., Kaiser-Permanente in California and Group Health Cooperative of Puget Sound) have included family violence in professional education. Although some of these programs have been publicized and evaluated (see Chapter 5), their impact appears to be limited largely to the areas served by these organizations.

Payers' reimbursement policies may also impact health professional training about family violence. The literature reflects a heated debate around third-party reimbursement generally, and limited research indicates that reimbursement issues can serve as a disincentive for health professional services for family violence (see, e.g., Krueger and Patterson, 1997; Socolara et al., 2001). One study notes, "[d]octors, nurses and other providers are urged to screen routinely for [intimate partner violence], yet progress is hindered because health systems lack the data, formalized procedures and the reimbursement schemes to fully implement and sustain published screening guidelines" (http://fvpf.org/programs/display.php3?DocID=54 8/8/01).

Without adequate reimbursement for screening and services provided to victims of family violence, little incentive would seem to exist to train health professionals to provide these services. The literature, however, does not appear to address the implications of reimbursement for training. Acknowledging the importance of this topic, the Agency for Healthcare Research and Quality and the Family Violence Prevention Fund sponsored a meeting in September 2001 of experts on various aspects of either intimate partner violence or coding and reimbursement issues to discuss existing systems, practices, and research. The group specifically addressed variation in reimbursement levels from system to system (e.g., Medicare, Medicaid, and private sector), financial incentives or disincentives associated with the current coding systems, and the implications of coding practices for patients and health care service delivery.[6] Further examination of the role third-party reimbursement plays in health professional training about family violence is needed and may result from this meeting.

LAWS MANDATING REPORTING AND EDUCATION

Mandatory reporting and mandated education laws have been conceived as possible means for ensuring that health professionals receive training in family violence. Legislatures may enact such laws, usually with the intention of improving the service system. The committee struggled with the relationship of these laws to the training of health professionals. Little evidence indicates the effect these laws have on health professional education, and the legislation has created much controversy among those who work in family violence. Numerous interpretations of what the laws actually require and how they differ around the country exist, but few comprehensive resources on these laws are available. In the committee's judgment, mandated reporting laws appear to drive the fields of child protection and elder protection and serve as a backdrop. And, in some states, they serve as a driver in intimate partner protection. Because they do appear to influence (and possibly distort) the content of education and ultimately of practice, the committee considered it important to examine these laws in detail to determine what is known about their actual impact. We sought to understand where such provisions are present, what they contain, and whether they achieve the intended effects. Having done the difficult work of collecting and examining all of the existing laws, the committee offers the details it has complied in the report appendixes and provides here the following descriptive analysis to assist others addressing the issue. The tables in Appendixes C and D describe state laws mandating reporting of and training about child abuse and

---

[6]The findings from this meeting were not available when this report went to press.

neglect, intimate partner violence, and elder maltreatment by health professionals as of August 2000.

In addition to the reporting mandates identified, several states encourage voluntary reporting or provide immunity for those who choose to report. Beyond the educational mandates identified, several states have enacted laws to encourage agencies to provide training to interested health professionals, to fund optional training programs, and to encourage licensing boards to consider educational mandates. Although such laws may serve an important policy objective, they were not included in the appendixes because they do not *require* individual health professionals to report or obtain training. Finally, a handful of states limit reporting mandates to institutionalized victims, and a few others mandate training solely for health professionals who serve as public employees. Although these are interesting alternatives to comprehensive mandates, these laws were not included because they apply to a relatively small subset of health professionals and victims.

Mandatory Reporting Laws

Requirements

Child Abuse and Neglect. All 50 states and the District of Columbia require health professionals to report child abuse and neglect. Virtually every state requires a report when a health professional either "knows" about abuse or has "reasonable grounds to suspect" or "reasonable grounds to believe" abuse has occurred. The states vary, however, on the question of whether health professionals must report behavior that they believe will result in a child's suffering abuse in the future, in addition to abuse that has already been perpetrated.

Health professionals are most often required to report directly to a local child protective services agency. Approximately one-half of the states give mandatory reporters the option of reporting to a law enforcement agency. The states vary as to whether reports must be oral, in writing, or both.

In every state, the reporting requirement applies to physicians, dentists, mental health professionals, nurses, social workers, and allied health professionals (except in Washington, where allied health professionals are exempt). Every state also requires reporting by some subset of allied health professionals, but this term is defined differently across jurisdictions and may include paramedics, emergency medical technicians, physical therapists, dental hygienists, chiropractors, "practitioners of the healing arts," or "persons having responsibility for care or treatment of children."

Intimate Partner Violence. Several states require health professionals to report injuries caused through the commission of a crime or the discharge of a firearm. Such injuries inevitably include instances of intimate partner violence.[7] In addition to these laws that address the issue indirectly, three states—California, Colorado, and Rhode Island—explicitly require the reporting of intimate partner abuse, and one—Kentucky—requires the reporting of abuse, neglect, or exploitation of any adult

California and Colorado require that reports be made to law enforcement agencies. Kentucky and Rhode Island, in contrast, require reporting solely for the purpose of documenting the incidence of family violence. As a result, it requires health professionals to report to monitoring agencies, rather than to law enforcement.

The typical legal standard that triggers these reporting requirements is "reasonable cause to suspect" or "reasonable cause to believe." Kentucky requires physicians, dentists, mental health professionals, nurses, social workers, and some allied health workers to report intimate partner violence. California and Rhode Island do not apply this requirement to mental health professionals or social workers. Colorado requires only physicians to report intimate partner violence.

Elder Maltreatment. In all, 43 states and the District of Columbia mandate the reporting of elder maltreatment by health professionals. (The exceptions are: Colorado, New Jersey, New York, North Dakota, Pennsylvania, South Dakota, and Wisconsin.) These states vary in terms of the types of injury that must be reported. Most states require reporting of "abuse, neglect, or exploitation." Others also require reporting of "mistreatment" (Minnesota); the "need [for] protective services" (Delaware, District of Columbia., Kansas, North Carolina, Missouri, and Pennsylvania); "isolation" (Nevada); "abandonment" (Alaska, California, Connecticut, Rhode Island, and Wyoming); or "financial exploitation" (California, Illinois, and Washington).

Some states have built in special exceptions to their elder maltreatment reporting requirements. For example, a California health professional need not report evidence of elder abuse if he or she "reasonably believes" that abuse did not occur in his or her "best clinical judgment."

The legal standard that triggers the reporting requirement also varies. In all, 39 states have adopted a "reasonable cause to believe" or "reasonable cause to suspect" standard. Other states dictate that a health professional "know," "observe," or "suspect" abuse before a report is required.

Just over half the states require reporting directly to the local department of health and human services or protective services agency. An additional 15 states also permit reporting to law enforcement officials. Two states—Alaska and

---

[7]New Hampshire has enacted such a law, but it includes a statutory exception that limits the mandatory reporting of intimate partner violence. Specifically, the law exempts reporting when a patient is the victim of sexual assault or domestic violence, is at least 18 years old, and objects to having the information reported to law enforcement. This exemption does not apply, however, if the victim is being treated for a gunshot wound or other "serious" injury.

Florida—limit reporting to data collection purposes, by mandating that reports be made only to local agencies responsible for maintaining elder abuse registries.

Most of the states require physicians, dentists, mental health professionals, nurses, social workers, and allied health workers to report, with a few exceptions. In Alaska, California, Nebraska, and Oregon, dentists are not required to report; in Idaho, mental health professionals are not required to report.

Impact

Research on health professionals' typical practice in cases of maltreatment and its divergence from optimal practice has focused in large part on clinicians' decisions about whether to report suspected maltreatment to authorities (Melton et al., 1995; Kalichman and Brosig, 1993; Kalichman, 1999). It is not uncommon for health professionals to refrain from reporting suspected child maltreatment that they do not regard as serious or clear-cut (Finlayson and Koocher, 1991; Kalichman and Brosig, 1993; Kalichman and Craig, 1991; Kalichman et al., 1988, 1989; Watson and Levine, 1989; Zellman, 1990a). Studies on elder abuse indicate that some health professionals do not report due to questions about the usefulness of reporting (i.e., repeated reports about the same patient do not appear to improve the situation; Clarke-Daniels et al., 1989, 1990) and beliefs that community resources are insufficient for appropriate responses (Jones et al., 1997). The tendency to ignore or bypass reporting mandates appears to be most prevalent among mental health professionals (Kalichman et al., 1988).

Although requirements for reporting suspected maltreatment are commonly recognized by health care professionals (Zellman, 1990a), many express concerns that reporting can be as harmful as helpful. Potential advantages of mandatory reporting, particularly for intimate partner violence, that have been cited include improvement of the health care response to family violence, aid in victim referral, and assistance with perpetrator prosecution (Rodriguez et al., 1999; Tilden et al., 1994). Concerns include beliefs that mandatory reporting may (1) breach confidentiality and so undermine autonomy, trust, and privacy in the health care setting (Kalichman and Craig, 1991; Kalichman et al., 1989; NRC and IOM, 1998; Rodriguez et al., 1998, 1999; Vulliamy and Sullivan, 2000; Warshaw and Ganley, 1998); (2) interfere with efforts to enhance patient safety (Levine and Doueck, 1995; NRC and IOM, 1998; Rodriguez et al., 1998, 1999; Tilden et al., 1994; Warshaw and Ganley, 1998; Zellman, 1990b); (3) serve as a deterrent to perpetrators obtaining treatment (Berlin et al., 1991; Kalichman et al., 1994); (4) precipitate violent retaliation by perpetrators against victims or health care professionals (Gerbert et al., 1999; Rodriguez et al., 1999); (5) decrease the utilization of health care services by abuse victims (Gerbert et al., 1999; Rodriguez et al., 1999); and (6) discourage inquiries by health care professionals who believe that if they do not ask, they have nothing to report (Gerbert et al., 1999).

Victims of family violence also express concerns about mandatory reporting. In studies of intimate partner violence (Gielen et al., 2001; Rodriguez et al., 2001a; Sachs et al., in press), a majority of participants supported reporting by health care professionals (73 to 91 percent) with the victim's consent. However, significantly more battered than nonbattered women favored nonmandatory options that would give decision-making authority to abused women (Gielen et al., 2001; Rodriguez et al., 2001a; Sachs et al., in press). Furthermore, one study found that women who had been abused within the past year were more likely to oppose mandatory reporting than women who had been abused more than one year ago (Rodriguez et al., 2001b). Battered women cited considerable concern about increased risk (44-54 percent) and resentment about loss of control (45-61 percent), and the majority (68-77 percent) believed that women would be less likely to tell their health care provider about abuse if disclosure would result in a mandatory report (Gielen et al., 2001; Sachs et al., in press).

Research on issues related to mandatory reporting requirements appears to focus on investigation and forensic assessment rather than the provision of therapeutic and preventive services[8] (Melton, 1994; Melton et al., 1995, 1997; NRC, 1993; U.S. Advisory Board on Child Abuse and Neglect, 1993).[9] Few studies indicate what happens over time once reports are made (Melton et al., 1995) or how effective health professional involvement is.

The relationship between mandatory reporting requirements and education is unclear, although it appears in some instances that training focuses on the legal reporting requirements, particularly in curricula on child abuse and neglect. Based on its review of existing health professional curricula, the committee concludes that mandatory reporting requirements may be both beneficial and detrimental to education. Reporting requirements appear to succeed in providing a place within health professional curricula for the issue of family violence and increasing attention to health professionals' responsibility for identifying and reporting it. However, existing curricula may focus on required reporting procedures to the exclusion of health professionals' roles in treating, referring, and preventing family violence. Research on the implications of mandatory reporting requirements for health professional education and practice is needed.

---

[8]The APA's Committee on Professional Practice and Standards (1995) published a question-and-answer-format article that addresses issues faced by clinicians and provides substantial background information, including suggested readings.

[9]See also U.S. General Accounting Office (1995) lamenting the general lack of attention to the health needs of children in state care.

Mandatory Education Laws

Requirements

Child Abuse and Neglect. Only three states—California, Iowa, and New York—mandate education on child abuse for health professionals. The training requirements appear to be driven at least in part by mandatory reporting laws; in all three states, training must focus on child abuse identification and the local statutory reporting requirements. The amount of required training varies. New York requires a one-time, 2-hour training session. California has a one-time training requirement of 7 hours over the course of a professional's career; Iowa goes further and requires at least 2 hours every 5 years.

Iowa requires physicians, dentists, mental health workers, nurses, and social workers to receive this form of education; New York does the same with the exception of social workers. California imposes this requirement only on its mental health professionals and social workers.

Intimate Partner Violence. Three states—Alaska, Florida, and Kentucky—mandate that health professionals receive education about intimate partner violence. The states require training on such topics as the nature and extent of such violence, safety planning, lethality and risk issues, and available community resources.

The amount of training required varies greatly: Florida mandates 1 hour every 2 years; Kentucky requires a one-time-only 3-hour training session; and Alaska does not specify. Florida and Kentucky require training for doctors, dentists, mental health workers, nurses, social workers, and allied health workers. Alaska does the same, except for allied health workers.

Elder Maltreatment. Iowa is the only state that requires its health professionals to receive training on elder maltreatment. Its law mandates education regarding identification and reporting dependent elder abuse, with a 2-hour initial session followed by two additional hours every 5 years. The education requirement applies to doctors, dentists, mental health professionals, nurses, social workers, and allied health workers.

Impact

The committee could find no formal evaluations of the impact of legally mandated family violence education. Studies demonstrate that health professionals who have obtained any continuing education (not necessarily mandated) about child maltreatment are no more likely—and in some samples are *less* likely—to report child abuse and neglect than are those who have not attended such workshops (Beck and Ogloff, 1995; Kalichman and Brosig, 1993; Reiniger et al., 1995). Accordingly, although one can hypothesize that such laws may have an array of positive as well as negative effects, until sound process and outcome evaluation data are acquired, in the committee's view these mandates are driven by assumptions and good intentions, rather than by a sound evidence base. What is known about continuing education for health professionals (summarized in Chapter 6) is that didactic instruction may result in increases in knowledge or changes in attitudes, but there is limited evidence that it influences practice behaviors. Therefore, there is no reason to believe that 1- to 3-hour instructional programs, the form that many of the mandates take, will result in lasting positive effects on screening or intervention in family violence. Critical evaluation questions for any educational program, particularly for those that are required by state statute or agency mandate, include: whether knowledge improvements can be demonstrated, whether any knowledge improvements are sustained over time, whether attitudes about family violence are affected, whether any attitudinal changes are sustained over time, whether and to what extent clinicians' practice behavior changes, and whether any such behavioral changes are sustained over time. Furthermore, questions are needed to assess the adequacy of the program, from the provider perspective, including measures of acceptance and satisfaction with the program and suggestions for improvement. Whether costs of care, severity of presentation, case mix, morbidity, and ultimately mortality are affected by mandatory training must be determined. Finally, it is necessary to question if any changes observed can be attributed to the education program itself.

RESOURCE ISSUES

Funding

Education development, implementation, maintenance, and evaluation require funding; however, federal funds for such activities appear to be meager, and state governments have actually decreased such funding (Reiser, 1995). Private investor funds appear be decreasing as well. Private investors tend to concentrate capital in areas that can demonstrate promising financial returns or, at the very least, clear savings to teaching institutions or society. Education and training programs often cannot produce such concrete results, especially in the short term, and therefore are at a serious and chronic disadvantage in terms of securing sufficient funding to develop and evaluate educational interventions (Mechanic, 1998; Blumenthal and Meyer, 1996).

Federal funding[10] may be provided through agencies such as the Health Resources and Services Administration of the Department of Health and Hu-

---

[10]A number of foundations (e.g., Commonwealth, Conrad-Hilton) have previously funded or currently fund family violence research and training initiatives. However, comprehensive search mechanisms for this type of support are not available. The committee chose to focus it discussion on federal funding sources.

TABLE 4.1 Selected Recent Federal Research Grant Opportunities

Agency	Title	Grant No. (Date)	Funding Allocation
Agency for Healthcare Research and Quality	Violence Against Women: Evaluating Health Care Interventions	RFA:HS-00-006 (FEB 2000)	$1 million FY2000
Centers for Disease Control and Prevention	Extramural Injury Research Grants for the Prevention of Intimate Partner Violence and Sexual Assault	PA: 00042	$1.2 million FY2000
Office of Community Services, Administration for Children and Families	Family Violence Prevention and Services Program	FA OCS-2000-06 (FEB 2000)	Varies (four priority areas)
Children's Bureau, Administration on Children, Youth, and Families	Administration for Children and Families: Child Abuse and Neglect (2000B)	CB-2001-01 (FEB 2000)	$3.5 million FY 2000

man Services when specific health professional training needs are identified.[11] Funds are provided for general health care professional training through the Public Health Services Act, but the act does not require training in family violence. In 1998, however, language was added that encourages grantees to "prepare practitioners" (physicians) or "provide care" (nurses) to "underserved populations and other high risk groups such as the elderly, individuals with HIV-AIDS, substance abusers, homeless, *and victims of domestic violence* [emphasis added]."

Federal agencies do occasionally fund family violence-related research in health care (see Table 4.1). However, for the most part these calls for proposals do not specify health professional training in family violence.

A review of individual federally funded projects indicates that few involve the training of health professionals in family violence research. The National Institute of Mental Health currently funds five pre- or postdoctoral research training grants related to family violence (see Table 4.2). General violence training grants (such as those from the National Consortium on Violence Research) may also include fellowships addressing family violence.

Family violence rarely emerges in a review of funding priorities among the

---

[11]Current goals for federally supported health professional training include (1) increasing underrepresented populations in the health professional workforce and (2) providing care to underserved communities. To meet these needs, the Bureau of Health Professions requested $103 million for fiscal year 2001.

TABLE 4.2 Family Violence Training Grants

Funding Source	Site	Principal Investigator	Title (grant number)	Funding Period	Doctoral Fellows	
					Pre	Post
NIMH	University of New Hampshire	Straus, Murray A.	Family Violence Research Training (T32MH15161)	SEP 77–JUN 02		X
NIMH	Johns Hopkins University	Campbell, Jacquelyn C.	Interdisciplinary Research Training on Violence (T32MH20014)	JUL 99–JUN 04	X	X
NIMH	Northern Illinois University	Milner, Joel S.	Family Violence and Sexual Assault Research Training (T32MH19952)	AUG 96–JUN 01	X	
NIMH	Boston University	Keane, Terence M.	Post-Doctoral Training on Post Traumatic Stress Disorder (T32MH19836)	AUG 96–JUN 01		X
NIMH	Medical University of South Carolina	Kilpatrick, Dean G.	Child and Adult Trauma Victims: A Training Program (T32MH18869)	JAN 98–JUN 03	X	X
NSF, HUD, NIJ	Carnegie Mellon University	Blumstein, Alfred	National Consortium on Violence Research (SBR-9513040)	MAY 95–APR 03	X	X

NIMH = National Institute of Mental Health; NSF = National Science Foundation; HUD = Department of Housing and Urban Development; NIJ = National Institute of Justice.

various institutes at the National Institutes of Health (NIH) (A.A. Perachio, personal communication, March 27, 2001). Among the seven research priorities of the National Institute of Nursing Research for 2001, for example, none specifically applies to developing new knowledge for nurses in the area of family violence (or to any other violence category). Although the National Institute on Aging included elder abuse and neglect as a Selected Future Research Direction, that topic is not named in the list of Areas of Special Emphasis (biology of brain disorders, new approaches to pathogenesis, new preventive strategies against disease, new avenues for the development of therapeutics, genetic medicine, and health disparities).

Other federal sources of training funds include projects set up in response to routine funding cycles (in which investigators submit proposals in their area of competency) and projects in direct response to requests for proposals (RFPs) or program announcements (PAs), the government's mechanism to encourage research in priority areas. A search of the *NIH Health Information Index* for family violence research by NIH or NIH-supported scientists revealed no entries for "family violence," "spouse abuse," "domestic violence," or "child abuse." The only family violence entry was for "elder abuse," accompanied by a link to the National Institute on Aging. The Computer Retrieval of Information on Scientific Projects (CRISP) database revealed 93 projects including the phrase "child abuse," 63 including "spouse abuse" (38 for "domestic violence"), and 4 for "elder abuse" currently (1999-2000) funded by several federal agencies (the National Institutes of Health, the Substance Abuse and Mental Health Administration, the Health Resources and Services Administration, the Food and Drug Administration, the Centers for Disease Control and Prevention, the Agency for Healthcare Research and Quality, and the Office of Assistant Secretary of Health). Some projects are listed twice (due to multiyear funding across the reporting year) and some projects only mention, rather than focus on, family violence. In other cases, currently funded projects are not included in the database. Funding amounts for these projects are not disclosed.

The allocation of federal funds for child abuse and neglect has been primarily in response to federal legislation, the Child Abuse Prevention and Treatment Act of 1974 (CAPTA—P.L. 93-247), which was reauthorized in 1996. As mentioned earlier, CAPTA established the National Center on Child Abuse and Neglect (NCCAN), defined child abuse and neglect, and supported other demonstration programs and projects to prevent, identify, and treat child abuse and neglect. In addition to allocating funds directly, CAPTA authorizes aid to states for child abuse and neglect programs. The program authorizes funds through 2001 and $99.3 million has been requested for 2001. These funds finance four broad programs, none of which explicitly include training: child abuse state grants, child abuse discretionary grants, community-based family resource and support grants, and an adoption opportunities program. The discretionary grants may include training. NCCAN did do a one-time funding of multidisciplinary training programs, a few of which remain (e.g., the Center on Child Abuse and Neglect, University of Oklahoma Health Sciences Center). NCCAN was reorganized as the Office of Child Abuse and Neglect (OCAN) in 1996 with 80 percent fewer staff. Among other activities, OCAN published the "Child Abuse and Neglect State Statutes Series" (NCCAN, 1997) to provide some information for health care providers about reporting mandates for child abuse and neglect. OCAN does not actively disseminate the information to health care providers or evaluate the impact of the information provided. State Victim Compensation and Assistance and Victim Assistance and Law Enforcement funds, allocated through the U.S. Department of Justice, have sometimes been used for the continued training of professionals in evaluating criminal forms of maltreatment, but the focus is not on health professionals.

Funding for health professional training for child abuse and neglect appears to be decreasing in proportion to the growth of the problem (Theodore and Runyan, 1999). For example, between 1980 and 1986, while the reported incidence of child abuse and neglect increased by 74 percent, the federal research budget for this topic increased only 2 percent (Kessler and New 1989), and between 1981 and 1995, while reported incidence increased by 150 percent, research funds decreased by 44 percent (Thompson and Wilcox 1995). Few efforts support training researchers and professionals (Jenny, 1997). For example, in 1996, the federal government spent $29.9 million or $28.47 per case on child abuse (Putnam, 1998, 2001) while spending $2.26 billion or $1,734.61 per case on cancer, despite the higher incidence of child abuse (NCI, 1996). In terms of research expenditure per lost life, violence accounted for $31, cancer for $794, heart and lung disease for $441, and AIDS for $697 (NRC, 1993).

Much of the funding for initiatives related to intimate partner violence is provided under the Violence Against Women Act (VAWA) of the Violent Crime Control and Law Enforcement Act (P.L. 102-322) of 1994. The goals of the legislation include preventing violence against women, increasing penalties for batterers, and supporting programs to prosecute offenders and assist women victims of violence. It is administered by the Department of Health and Human Services and the Department of Justice, and in fiscal year 2000, $223.6 million was appropriated to the Department of Health and Human Services for VAWA programs. The VAWA reauthorization bill, passed in October 2000, requested an increase to $660 million each year for the next 5 years. Services to victims account for the majority of the funds, and none is earmarked for health care professional training. The act does acknowledge (and dictate) funds for training for persons in the judicial and law enforcement domains.

The Older Americans Act (OAA) and the Social Security Act provide services for elders, including nutritional and caregiver services, and, to a limited extent, for abuse prevention. Pursuant to the OAA, the Department of Health and Human Services created the National Center on Elder Abuse in 1993 to help promote understanding among state and local networks of community workers, physicians, elderly volunteers, and others working to prevent elder abuse; it was reorganized in 1998. The center involves a consortium of six partners led by the National Association of State Units on Aging and was funded at $400,000 in 1998-1999, a similar amount for 1999-2000, and $800,000 for 2000-2001, under HHS grant no. 90-AP-2144. One purpose of the center is to facilitate training on elder abuse recognition and services through educational materials and technical assistance. Title IV-E of the Social Security Act also provides for training in the area of elder welfare. That training can include activities to educate health professionals collaborating with workers in social services. Table 4.3 summarizes the federal legislation authorizing funding for initiatives related to family violence.

Two National Research Council reports (1993, p. 318; 1996, pp. 152-155) have recommended that centers be funded to address family violence research needs, specifically that each of three centers be funded at $1 million. In actuality, a single center was funded by the Centers for Disease Control and Prevention,

TABLE 4.3 Family Violence Federal Funding Acts

Type of Violence	Legislation Authorizing Funding for Initiatives on Family Violence	Provision of Funding	Years	Funding
Intimate partner violence	Violence Against Women Act	DHHS DOJ-OJP	(1994-2000) 2000-	435.75 million
Child abuse and neglect	Child Abuse Prevention and Treatment Act; Social Security Act	Child Protective Services		
Elder maltreatment	Older Americans Act (Titles III and VII)	Social Services Block Grant	FY2000 (for all sx)^a	$1.5 bil
	Social Security Act (Title XX)	Adult Protective Services		
Family violence	Family Violence Prevention and Services Act		(1984) 1984	0
	Victims of Crime Act			

^{a}Through appropriation laws.

the National Violence Against Women Prevention Research Center. That center award, a consortium of the Medical University of South Carolina, the University of Missouri at St. Louis, and Wellesley College, was funded at approximately $500,000.

Federal funds for health professional training are closely linked to the priorities that are named by institutions such as HHS. However, earmarking of federal funds for health professional training in family violence is dependent on political considerations, not just on evidence that such training will make a difference. Moss recently stated, "It may be closer to the reality to say that politics is the basic science of public health," rather than epidemiology (Moss, 2000). Documents such as *Healthy People 2000* (and *Healthy People 2010*) and federal agency strategic plans set the health agenda for the nation in writing, reflecting, at least in part, the political priorities of the nation.[12] Even with such priorities,

---

[12]*The Healthy People 2000* objectives related to family violence are predominantly found in Priority Area 7: Violent and Abusive Behavior. They include for example: "[to] extend protocols for routinely identifying, treating, and properly referring suicide attempters, victims of sexual assault, and victims of spouse, elder and child abuse to at least 90% of hospital emergency departments" (National Center for Health Statistics, 2001).

the allocation of funds is another political process and is competitive within and across health care issues.

Overall, the information reviewed in this section suggests that funding for family violence is limited and inconsistent and that funds for health professional education research or training development on family violence specifically are even sparser. Until funds are proportionate to the known extent of the problem in society and in health care, progress in the area of health professional training on family violence is likely to be limited. Some potential for additional funding lies in the link between NIH's mission and the achievement of *Healthy People 2000* (and *Healthy People 2010*) objectives in which family violence has been identified as a national priority. The objectives related to family violence have yet to be achieved.

Human Resources

Although adequate and sustained financial resources are necessary to support curricular innovation, it is people who drive program development, staff classrooms and clinical practica, work to enhance training programs, and establish the systems needed to sustain education. Institutions are constrained financially by available funds, but they may have more control over the human resources involved. The nation is experiencing a shortage of faculty who are qualified and willing to teach in the health professions (Griner and Danoff, 1995). Furthermore, there are few researchers or educators nationwide who are recognized as scholars in family violence, and few programs appear to exist to prepare researchers or educators to achieve scholarship in this area. Health professional training programs, whether in undergraduate schools, graduate training programs, or continuing education, are in need of experienced, dedicated, sensitive, versatile, and experienced clinician-educators who can effectively teach this material (Alpert, 1995). Given the paucity of experts-educators in the field, it is also difficult to recruit and train educators, monitor their performance, and help them become more effective (Kassirer, 1995; Greenberg, 1995; Lesky and Hershman, 1995). Furthermore, developing the human resources necessary may not be achieved among health professionals at the teaching rates and hours currently evidenced in the literature (Alpert et al., 1998; Woodtli and Breslin, 1996). The problem becomes circular: research and training deficits yield few well-prepared educators, and an inadequate supply of educators and researchers results in inadequate training and research.

The committee could find little evidence of the educational infrastructure that is needed to teach about family violence. One study indicates that organized institutional response is not common (Cohen et al., 1997). Teaching about family violence could be enhanced by having an available cadre of survivors, standardized or simulated patients trained to portray actual patients accurately, library and computer resources, and community-based advocates and other direct service providers. Human, computational, and logistical infrastructure support for the evaluation of educational programs also appears to be unavailable in most institutions. The APA Working Group on Implications for Education and Training of Child Abuse and Neglect, for example, noted that "a lack of time and resources for teachers to develop curricula appropriate for the educational level of their students" and a "lack of readily available material to use in conjunction with child abuse and neglect curricula (e.g., textbooks and videotapes)" are impediments to curricular reform to reduce the gap between psychologists' modal and optimal levels of expertise in responding to child maltreatment (Haugaard et al., 1995, p. 79). An array of resource materials is available, including slide sets, handouts, videos, articles, book collections, and the like, but the extent to which these are distributed and in use is unknown. Attention to developing a research and training infrastructure in other health areas (e.g., muscular dystrophy, alcoholism) appears to have resulted in the growth of targeted funding and of a critical mass of faculty to ensure that the work will go on and the care for patients will improve (see, e.g., http://cysticfibrosis.com/centers.htm; http://www.mdausa.org/clinics/alsserv.html; http://www.niaaa.nih.gov/extramural/ResCtrs1198.htm).

CONCLUSIONS

The committee's assessment of the potential influences on health professional training on family violence suggests the following conclusions:

- **Institutional culture, norms, and priorities can influence the education offered, and they may also create challenges for developing, implementing, or sustaining family violence training for health.**

Common pathways for these challenges appear to include inadequate financial and human resources and institutional commitment to the problem at the national and local levels.

- **Accreditation, licensure, and certification requirements do not consistently and explicitly address family violence and thus do not appear to be a significant influence on family violence training for health professionals.**
- **Individual health professional concerns, beliefs, and experiences can create challenges to educating health professionals about family violence.**

Notable individual concerns include perceptions of inadequate time or preparation, personal values, and personal experience with victimization and traumatization.

- **A review of health professional organization statements, guidelines, positions, and policies reveals that the degree to which the various professions call for training differs greatly not only by profession but also by specialties within those professions.**
- **Health professional organizations can influence the existence and extent of family violence education within a profession.**

The American College of Obstetricians and Gynecologists, the American Academy of Pediatrics, and the American College of Nurse Midwives are excellent examples of health professional organizations actively working to encourage and implement education initiatives on family violence among members of their professions.

- **Stakeholder groups, including advocates, victims, and payers, have been or are becoming active in family violence issues, including education, but their impact on family violence education for health professionals is difficult to assess.**

No studies indicate the impact these efforts have had. However, curricula developed by organizations such as the Family Violence Prevention Fund appear to have been widely disseminated and in use by health professional educators.

- **The impact of mandatory reporting laws on family violence for health professionals is unclear, but the existence of such laws suggests a need for educational content about them.**

Based on the expressed concerns and research on rates of reporting, the committee sees a need for clear explanations of reporting laws for students and practitioners, as well as the provision of opportunities to discuss and resolve ethical issues that reporting raises for many health care providers. Additional studies are needed to determine whether reporting requirements are the appropriate mechanism for achieving the goals of increasing reporting rates and ensuring the necessary services for victims. Regardless of the existence of legal requirements, in the committee's view, students must learn to identify, report, and refer cases according to legal requirements, professional practice standards, and patient care goals. In addition, the training needs of health professionals extend beyond fulfilling legal requirements. The committee understands the intent underlying reporting requirements for health professionals generally to be the enhancement of their responses to family violence and ensuring that victims receive needed treatment and services. These goals suggest that health professionals need to know more than just how to report suspected and actual cases of family violence. Given the concerns about mandatory reporting cited by both health professionals and victims, it may be productive to orient training programs more toward planning and delivery of broad-based prevention and treatment services, rather than exclusively on case identification and forensic services.

- **The effect of mandated education requirements on health professional education is unknown.**
- **Funding for training programs in family violence education in the health professions does not appear to be a priority and does not appear to be consistently available. Information about funding is fragmented.**

The extensive effort required even to identify funding sources is noteworthy. The information must be collected piecemeal from numerous web sites for federal agencies and private foundations, rendering it difficult to determine if and when funds are available.

5

Evaluation of Training Efforts

As summarized in the earlier chapters, there has been some increased attention paid to training health care providers about child abuse and neglect, intimate partner violence, and, to a lesser extent, elder maltreatment. Descriptions of family violence curricula and training models for health professionals and experiences with their implementation have been published (e.g., Dienemann et al., 1999; Ireland and Powell, 1997; Spinola et al., 1998; Thompson et al., 1998; Wolf and Pillemer, 1994).

Attempts have been made to document the extent to which clinicians actually receive instruction in how to identify and respond to patients involved in these situations. Surveys of practicing clinicians have found that considerable segments of health professionals have had little or no training in this area. Some studies have found modest positive correlations between individuals' reported involvement in training and family violence assessment and management practices (Currier et al., 1996; Flaherty et al., 2000; Lawrence and Brannen, 2000; Tilden et al., 1994). Although this observed relationship cannot be mistaken for evidence that these practices are a direct product of training, it does suggest more careful examination of what is known about the effectiveness of family violence curricula and other training strategies on clinician behaviors and indicates the need for more explicit examination of causation.

At present, claims regarding what training is needed and how it should be carried out far outnumber the studies that provide empirical evidence to support them. Similar to many other areas of health provider training, several factors are most likely to contribute to this shortage of information. For example, accreditation criteria and other pressures on health professional schools place constraints on curricular content; limited funding interferes with evaluation; and legal, ethical, and patient barriers complicate evaluation efforts (e.g., Gagan, 1999; Sugg et al., 1999; Waalen et al., 2000).

Although this lack of evaluation is not unique to family violence training, increasing the number and quality of training opportunities in family violence has consistently been cited as central to narrowing the gap between recommended practices and professional behavior. To understand what improvements should be made, a strong evidential base for deciding how best to educate providers in this area is needed.

This chapter examines the available research base concerning the outcomes and effectiveness of family violence training. First, we summarize the search strategy used to locate and include evaluations of training interventions and then describe the characteristics of the training strategies and models that have been assessed, along with the basic features of the evaluation measures and designs. Finally, we discuss the inferences we can confidently draw from these studies so as to guide future training efforts. Due to the dearth of published studies on elder abuse training, the focus is on outcomes and effectiveness of child abuse and intimate partner violence training.

SEARCH STRATEGY

Four bibliographic databases were systematically searched for studies that evaluated training efforts in family violence and were published prior to November 2000. These included MEDLINE, PsycInfo, ERIC, and Sociological Abstracts. Search terms included *family violence, domestic violence, intimate partner violence, elder abuse/neglect,* and *child abuse/neglect* coupled with *training, assessment, evaluation, detection,* and *identification* as both subject terms and text words. These searches were augmented by published bibliographies (i.e., Glazer et al., 1997). The reference lists of all chosen articles also were screened for additional studies.[1]

This strategy identified 64 potential studies, the majority of which focused on intimate partner violence training ($n = 38$, or 59 percent). Another 31 percent ($n = 20$) addressed training efforts in child abuse and neglect, while only 9

---

[1]The unpublished literature was also examined for evaluation efforts, including formal committee requests to outside groups (e.g., relevant professional associations, government agencies, foundations, and advocacy groups). This uncovered the recent evaluation of the WomanKind program sponsored by the Centers for Disease Control and Prevention (Short et al., 2000), which was included in the set of studies reviewed. The evaluation of the Family Violence Prevention Fund training initiative has not yet been completed.

percent ($n = 6$) focused on elder maltreatment training.[2] Each was then reviewed to determine whether it met three inclusion criteria:

1. *Relevant training population.* Training participants had to include students pursuing degrees or practitioners in one or more of the six health professions chosen by the committee, i.e., physicians, nurses, dentists, psychologists, social workers, and physician assistants.

2. *Formal training effort.* The training evaluated had to be a *formal* educational intervention. This includes degree-related and continuing education courses, modules, clinical rotations, seminars, workshops, and staff training sessions but excludes training that was explicitly focused on clinical audits, feedback, or detailing. Also included were studies that assessed the use of a formal screening protocol, given that these efforts often involved highly organized training regarding information about family violence and was grounded in explicit models of instruction and behavior change (e.g., Harwell et al., 1998; Short et al., 2000; Thompson et al., 2000).

3. *Quantitative outcome measure(s).* A key requirement was that data were collected and reported on one or more quantitative measures of relevant *outcomes* related to responding to family violence. Outcome domains included: (a) knowledge, attitudes, beliefs, and perceived skills concerning family violence; (b) behaviors and performance associated with screening for abuse and case findings; and (c) practices and competencies needed to provide abuse victims with appropriate care (e.g., information, referrals, or case management).[3] Studies that focused on examining participant satisfaction were excluded, as were evaluations that employed only qualitative approaches.

Application of these criteria resulted in a pool of 44 articles.[4] Because three

---

[2]The study (Currier et al., 1996) evaluated trauma training, which included both intimate partner violence and child abuse, and the Thompson et al. (2000) evaluation of training for primary care providers assessed identification and management of violence for adults 18 or older, including elderly patients. Given that more attention was paid to intimate partner violence, both studies were assigned to this category.

[3] Measures of identification and intervention were limited to those that did not rely on provider self-report surveys. Studies using diaries completed by providers on a daily basis, however, were included.

[4]Two studies (Seamon et al., 1997; Weiss et al., 2000) dealt with the training of emergency medical technicians, a population that was not one of the professions targeted by the committee. Two studies of child abuse and neglect training programs were excluded, based on their training interventions. One involved a statewide educational program of mailings, workshops, and other activities for dentists, but the analysis did not distinguish between those who actually reported receiving materials and participating in the workshops (Needleman et al., 1995). Socolar et al.'s (1998) randomized trial evaluated the impact of feedback and audit strategies on physicians participating in a statewide child

reported additional follow-up data on interventions included in this group, a slightly smaller number of training efforts were actually evaluated ($n = 41$). Supporting the relative recency of interest in family violence training is the fact that only 7 percent ($n = 4$) appeared prior to 1990.

The final set of 41 evaluations resulted in a pool that was even more heavily populated by studies of intimate partner violence training. This area has received the most attention, with 30 (73 percent) of the studies assessing programs in this area.[5] With the exception of four studies that reported outcomes of an elder abuse training session, the remainder ($n = 7$, or 17 percent) examined child maltreatment training efforts.

The lack of evaluative information on elder abuse training may be partly a function of the relatively recent emphasis placed on the need for screening and the lack of available training opportunities. However, the reasons underlying the limited attention paid to evaluating child abuse training efforts are less clear. Descriptions of training strategies appeared in the literature more than 20 years ago (e.g., Hansen, 1977; Venters and ten Bensel, 1977), although published research on training did not surface until much later (1987). Despite the results of surveys conducted in the late 1990s that continued to report noticeable numbers of health care professionals who felt ill-equipped to fully address child abuse cases and labeled their training in this area as insufficient (e.g., Barnard-Thompson and Leichner, 1999; Biehler et al., 1996; Wright et al., 1999), efforts to assess training remain few in number. For example, in our search, we found 20 studies that described some type of training effort in child maltreatment for health professionals, but only 7 studies met the committee's criteria for selection.

---

abuse program, which fell outside the definition of formal training that was used. Another 14 studies either did not provide any evaluative data concerning the program, restricted their examination to qualitative observations, or collected information on such outcomes as participant satisfaction (Bullock, 1997; Delewski et al., 1986; Gallmeier and Bonner, 1992; Hansen, 1977; Ireland and Powell, 1997; Krell et al., 1983; Krenk, 1984; Nelms, 1999; Pagel and Pagel, 1993; Reiniger et al., 1995; Thurston and McLeod, 1997; Venters and ten Bensel, 1977; Wielichowski et al., 1999; Wolf and Pillemer, 1994). Finally, two studies had as their focus the development and assessment of new measures for assessing training rather than the observed outcomes of the training itself (Dorsey et al., 1996; Kost and Schwartz, 1989).

[5]Summaries of these studies in terms of training characteristics, outcomes assessed, evaluation designs, measurement strategies, and major results are provided in Appendix F for intimate partner violence training and Appendix G for child abuse training evaluations. For each type of outcome, studies are ordered by training target population (e.g., medical students, residents and fellows, emergency room staff, and providers in other health care settings).

TYPES OF TRAINING EFFORTS EVALUATED

Selected characteristics of the training efforts evaluated in the 37 studies of intimate partner violence and child abuse training are summarized in Table 5.1. Overall, training programs on intimate partner violence that were subjected to some formal evaluation targeted a more diverse group of training populations. For example, no study examined outcomes of child abuse training efforts for medical students; in contrast, 13 percent of the intimate partner violence evaluations examined formal medical school courses, modules, and other inten-

TABLE 5.1 Overview of Training Interventions Assessed in the Evaluations of Intimate Partner Violence and Child Abuse Training

	Area of Family Violence Addressed					
	Intimate Partner Violence (*n* = 7)		Child Abuse (*n* = 30)		Total (*n* = 37)	
Characteristic	*N*	*%*	*N*	*%*	*N*	*%*
Training population:						
Medical students	4	13.3	0	0.0	4	10.8
Residents or fellows	6	20.0	3	42.9	9	24.3
Emergency department staff (e.g., nurses, physicians, and social workers)	13	43.3	0	0.0	13	35.1
Staff in other health care settings (e.g., primary care and maternal health clinics)	7	23.3	0	0.0	7	18.9
Other (e.g., child protective services workers and participants from several disciplines)	0	0.0	4	57.1	4	10.8
Length of training:						
Less than 2 hours	9	30.0	0	0.0	9	24.3
2-4 hours	7	23.3	0	0.0	7	18.9
5-8 hours	2	6.7	4	55.1	6	16.2
More than 8 hours	5	16.7	3	42.9	8	21.6
Not specified	7	23.3	0	0.0	13	35.1
Training strategy:						
Didactic only	15	50.0	0	0.0	15	40.5
Didactic and interactive	11	36.7	7	100.0	18	48.6
Not specified	4	13.3	0	0.0	4	10.8
Training included screening form:	13	43.3	0	0.0	13	35.1
Training included other enabling devices (e.g., local resources list, checklists, and anatomically correct dolls)	12	40.0	1	12.5	13	35.1

Note: Percentages are column percentages and may not total 100.0 percent due to rounding.

sive instructional strategies (Ernst et al., 1998, 2000; Haase et al., 1999; Jonassen et al., 1999; Short et al., 2000).[6]

Providers in emergency departments and general health care settings are typically one of the first points of contact for abuse victims, and professional organizations have stressed the need to improve the identification and management of intimate partner violence (e.g., American College of Emergency Physicians, 1995; American College of Nurse Midwives, 1997; American Medical Association, 1992). Consequently, a substantial portion of intimate partner violence training evaluations have examined programs for emergency department staff (43 percent), and nearly one-quarter have involved providers in other organized health care settings (23 percent). Five (71 percent) of the seven training evaluations in child abuse were directed at professionals who are most likely to encounter child maltreatment cases— namely, pediatric residents and child protective services workers (Cheung et al., 1991; Dubowitz and Black, 1991; Leung and Cheung, 1998; Palusci and McHugh, 1995; Sugarman et al., 1997). No assessments of intimate partner violence or child maltreatment training efforts designed for the dental or physician assistant professions have been conducted.

Previous research on continuing medical education (e.g., Davis et al., 1999) has shown that if training is likely to have any impact on behavior, strategies that involve interaction among trainers and participants are important (see Chapter 6). These strategies have been a part of all child abuse training that has been subjected to any formal assessment (see Table 5.1). In contrast, only about 37 percent of the intimate partner violence training programs incorporated interactive instructional strategies, ranging from practice interviewing to group development of appropriate protocols and strategies for their implementation (e.g., Campbell et al., 2001).

Providing participants with materials that they can use in their clinical practice (e.g., assessment forms and diagnostic aids) also has been shown to facilitate the translation of what was learned from training into specific behaviors in the health care setting (see Chapter 6). A noticeable portion of the intimate partner violence evaluations was targeted at assessing outcomes associated with the introduction of a screening protocol that also involved training staff in its use. Approximately two-fifths of evaluated intimate partner violence training efforts provided additional "enabling" materials for use in clinical practice. Examples include posters or pocket-sized cue cards with screening questions or other checklists that were part of the materials provided to residents (Knight and Remington, 2000) and emergency department or health clinic staff (Fanslow et al., 1998; Roberts et al., 1997; Thompson et al., 2000). The dissemination of assessment

---

[6]A study by Palusci and McHugh (1995) did include medical students, but they accounted for a small proportion of the participants (2 individuals, or 13 percent of the 15 participants).

forms and other materials by child abuse training efforts was much less common. Of the seven training evaluation studies, one program provided participants with anatomically correct dolls for use in assessment (Hibbard et al., 1987).

ASSESSING THE AVAILABLE EVIDENCE

Understanding the effectiveness of family violence training programs necessitates estimating the unbiased effects of training (i.e., the impact of training above and beyond the influence of other variables that may have contributed to the observed outcomes). It is well known that this is best achieved by randomized field experiments in which individuals are randomly assigned to groups. This design, if successfully executed, controls nearly all common threats to internal validity (e.g., selection, history, and maturation).

However, randomization alone is not sufficient if these efforts are to be truly informative. Evaluation designs must also: (1) use outcome measures that are reliable, valid, and sensitive to change over time; (2) demonstrate that the training intervention was implemented as planned and that participants' experiences differed noticeably from those who did not receive such training; and (3) have sufficient sample sizes to allow statistical detection of group differences if they exist.[7]

Despite the strengths of randomized designs in determining program effectiveness, their execution in the field is not easy, and problems that are likely to introduce unexpected threats to internal validity can occur. For example, extended follow-up measurement waves—a desirable design component for examining how long training outcomes are sustained—also increases the chances that some study participants may not respond to later assessments. The resulting attrition may differ among study groups. Depending on its nature and magnitude, this differential attrition can either exaggerate or diminish the observed group differences.

Historical threats to internal validity can be introduced by unanticipated events, such as the introduction of new reporting requirements, the enactment of laws that mandate education, or increased attention by the media to family violence, all of which are beyond the control of the evaluator (see Campbell et al., 2001, for examples of these). Another problem occurs when settings permit interaction and contact among training group participants and their counterparts who did not receive such training (e.g., sharing of what was learned, or what is

---

[7]Statistical pooling of outcome results was not performed. Although such meta-analyses have provided valuable insight into the impact of problem-based learning and continuing education in medicine (e.g., Davis et al., 1999; Vernon and Blake, 1993), the small number of rigorous studies precluded this. In addition, data were not always reported for use in calculating effect sizes.

known as contamination). Members of the "no training" or "usual circumstances" comparison groups also may actually receive some relevant training through professional organizations or their own reading. Especially when the training is lengthy and involves multiple components, training participants themselves may not attend all sessions, complete homework assignments, and so forth (see Short et al., 2000). All of these circumstances narrow the difference that is likely to be found between groups and can lead to misleading conclusions when training is not monitored for both the intervention and comparison groups. Essentially, randomized designs then end up as quasi-experiments, and the ability to determine the net impact of training is reduced.

In some circumstances, randomization may not even be feasible, and quasi-experimental designs are the only alternative. These can involve the use of a comparison group that was not constructed by random assignment or the assessment of outcomes only for a training intervention group before training and at *multiple* points thereafter (time-series or cohort designs). Although these are unlikely to provide unbiased estimates of intervention effects, sophisticated statistical modeling procedures now exist for taking into account some pretreatment and post-treatment selection biases, given that the necessary information is collected as part of the study (e.g., Lipsey and Cordray, 2000; Murray, 1998). Along with other design features, such nonexperimental studies, if well done, can add to the knowledge base about training (e.g., evidence for a relationship between training and the observed outcomes). For this reason, these were included in our review of evaluation studies.

The most common training evaluation has involved the assessment of changes for the training participants only, typically before and immediately after training. Unfortunately, this is the weakest quasi-experimental design, as it yields little information on either the net effects of training or its relationship to outcomes. However, these studies can address the question "Did the expected improvements in knowledge, attitudes, and/or beliefs occur?" For example, did individuals who participated in the training show an increase in knowledge and self-confidence about treating family violence? This might be viewed as the first question of interest in any causal assessment. Results from such studies also may partly inform expectations about where improvements in performance may or may not be reasonable to expect and how long any observed gains might be sustained. Furthermore, if reliable change in outcomes is repeatedly not found, attention can be directed at understanding the reasons for these no-difference findings (e.g., poor engagement of participants, unreliable or insensitive measures, loss of organizational support for identification and management of family violence, poorly designed training curricula) so as to improve the development of training strategies and the choice and measurement of outcomes in the future. It also is possible that some of these studies were less subject to competing rival explanations for the observed changes due to other design features (e.g., very short pretest/posttest intervals and multiple pretest observations). Thus, the committee reviewed studies of this type to identify whether any general conclusions about the expected outcomes of training could be drawn.[8]

CHARACTERISTICS OF THE EVALUATION AND RESEARCH BASE

As previously noted, the outcomes of interest to the committee included those related to knowledge, attitudes, and beliefs; outcomes associated with screening and assessment of family violence (e.g., rates of asking about abuse, percentages of cases identified, and adequacy of documentation); and other patient outcome indicators (e.g., referrals made for individuals who were victims of violence). Table 5.2 summarizes the degree to which the 37 evaluations assessed each of these outcomes. There was a clear difference in the attention paid to the three outcome domains, depending on the type of training. About 57 percent of intimate partner violence training evaluations measured improvements in knowledge, attitudes, and beliefs. Given that a frequent goal of training was to implement a standard assessment protocol successfully, the evaluations paid considerable attention to determining changes in the frequency of screening and case finding (70 percent). A much smaller proportion of studies (27 percent) attempted to assess other changes in clinical practices. For example, the extent to which patient charts included a safety assessment and body map completed by emergency department staff was examined by Harwell et al. (1998), and changes in information and referral practices were assessed by Shepard et al. (1999) for public health nurses, Wiist and McFarlane (1999) for prenatal health clinic staff, and Short et al. (2000) for emergency department, critical care, and perinatal staff. Using an index for rating quality of care by medical record review, Thompson et al. (2000) tracked changes in both training intervention and comparison sites. The evaluation conducted by Campbell et al. (2001) was unique in attempting to assess quality of care in terms of both medical record review and patient satisfaction ratings. Moreover, this was one of the few studies to measure the extent of organizational support (e.g., commitment) for detecting and treating victims of intimate partner violence.

In contrast, evaluations of child abuse training focused primarily on investigating whether knowledge, attitudes, and beliefs improved. Assessment of other

---

[8]Admittedly, this group would be skewed toward those studies that observed the expected changes. Even with this limitation, however, it would have been useful to derive average effect sizes for these observed changes and compare their magnitude with that obtained in more rigorous studies. If similar magnitudes for these two groups had been found, this would have been informative. However, such an analysis was precluded once again due to the lack of necessary information (e.g., some reported means but no standard deviations, and others only reported overall statistical significance levels but no other statistics on group performance). Although not peculiar to this literature (e.g., Gotzsche, 2001, and Orwin and Cordray, 1985), a gap prevents this type of quantitative comparison.

TABLE 5.2 Outcomes Examined in Evaluations of Intimate Partner Violence and Child Abuse Training

| | Area of Family Violence Addressed | | | | | |
| | Intimate Partner Violence ($n = 30$) | | Child Abuse ($n = 7$) | | Total ($n = 37$) | |
Characteristic	N	%	N	%	N	%
Outcome domain:[a]						
Knowledge, attitudes, or beliefs (KAB)	17	56.7	6	75.0	23	62.2
Screening and identification of abuse	21	70.0	0	0.0	21	56.8
Other clinical skills (e.g., appropriate documentation and referrals)	8	26.7	2	25.0	10	27.0
Number of different outcome domains assessed:						
KAB only	9	30.0	5	71.4	14	37.8
Screening and detection of abuse only	9	30.0	0	0.0	9	24.3
Other clinical skills or outcomes only	0	0.0	1	14.3	1	2.7
KAB and screening/detection only	4	13.3	0	0.0	4	10.8
Screening/detection and other clinical only	5	16.7	0	0.0	5	13.5
KAB and other clinical only	0	0.0	1	14.3	1	2.7
KAB, screening, and other clinical	3	10.0	0	0.0	3	8.1

Note: Percentages are column percentages.

[a]Because a study can assess multiple outcomes, the percentages do not total 100.0 percent.

outcomes was not only infrequent but also more indirect. Cheung et al. (1991) used vignettes to rate the competency of trained protective services workers in case planning, goal formulation, and family contract development. These same researchers also assessed overall competency as indicated by supervisor job ratings (Leung and Cheung, 1998).

Evaluators of training efforts on intimate partner violence were more likely to measure multiple outcomes in the same study: 30 percent of the evaluations in this area reported findings on two outcomes, and another 10 percent assessed outcomes in all three domains. In contrast, only one (14 percent) of the seven child abuse studies gathered data on outcomes in more than one domain (Cheung et al., 1991).

Measurement of Outcomes

How outcomes are measured can influence what can be learned from evaluations. For example, unreliable measures can reduce the ability to detect intervention effects and therefore effectively decrease the power of a design (Lipsey, 1990). Even when gains among training participants and group differences are found, the measures used may have poor construct validity, serving as only pale surrogates of the relevant outcomes. These issues are especially relevant to research on family violence, given that study authors have frequently developed their own knowledge tests, attitude questionnaires, and chart review forms to assess practitioner attitudes and practices but either failed to assess their psychometric properties or reported marginal results, e.g., internal consistencies of less than 0.70 (e.g., Finn, 1986; Saunders et al., 1987).

Among the 16 evaluations that examined improvements in knowledge, attitudes, and beliefs about intimate partner violence, all but two developed their own measures. However, slightly less than half of these presented no data on the reliability (e.g., internal consistency) of these instruments, although total scores and subscale scores were derived. The remainder either referred readers to previously published data on the measures or provided their own assessments of internal consistency (the preferred strategy), which were generally at acceptable levels (Cronbach $\alpha = 0.70$ or higher).

The most concerted efforts at instrument development have been carried out by Short et al. (2000), Maiuro et al. (2000), and Thompson et al. (2000). In Short et al.'s (2000) evaluation of the domestic violence module for medical students at the University of California, Los Angeles, not only were both the internal consistency and test-retest reliability examined for the knowledge, attitudes, beliefs, and behaviors scale that she developed, but also attention was paid to assessing the construct validity of the intervention itself (i.e., expert ratings of whether it contained the appropriate content and utilized a problem-based approach and varied training methods). Maiuro and colleagues (2000) developed a 39-item instrument to assess practitioner knowledge, attitudes, and beliefs, and self-reported practices toward family violence identification and management. This instrument exhibited internal consistency ($\alpha = 0.88$), content validity, and sensitivity to change and was later used by Thompson et al. (2000) to assess training outcomes for primary health clinic staff.

When protocols for asking individuals about intimate partner violence were utilized, Campbell et al. (2001) and Covington and Dalton et al. (1997), Covington and Diehl et al. (1997) used items from the Abuse Assessment Screen, which has been investigated as to its validity (Soeken et al., 1998). Thompson et al. (2000) used items that had been validated by McFarlane and Parker. Clinical skills (e.g., asking about intimate partner violence or correctly diagnosing abuse) in medical students and residents were assessed with standardized patient visits and case vignettes, with two exceptions; Knight and Remington (2000) used a patient interview to determine whether trained residents had asked the woman about intimate partner violence, and Bolin and Elliott (1996) had residents report daily on the number of conversations they had about intimate partner violence with the patients seen.

With regard to measuring screening prevalence, identification rates, documentation, and referrals, evaluations of intimate partner violence training relied on reviewing patient charts. The typical practice was to use standardized forms developed by the researchers for collecting baseline and follow-up data. When multiple coders were used, the degree to which information was provided on the blinding of raters, how disagreements were resolved, and interrater reliability varied. For example, Tilden and Shepherd (1987) provided little information on intercoder reliability, whereas both Thompson et al. (2000) and Short et al. (2000) reported initial agreement levels (which ranged from 0.80 to 0.96) and a detailed description of the record review process.

In the area of child abuse training, all studies developed their own assessment instruments, but only three provided any data on the quality of their measures. Palusci and McHugh (1995) reported on the internal consistency of their 30-item knowledge test, which was only marginally acceptable ($\alpha = 0.69$). Leung and Cheung (1998) also reported coefficient alphas for their measures of the amount learned and supervisor ratings of job performance, and interrater reliability was provided for the grading of trainees' responses to case vignettes (Cheung et al., 1991).[9]

Timing of Measurement

An important question regarding training program outcomes involves the "half-life" of any observed improvements and whether changes are sustained or degrade over time. Studies that employ multiple and extended follow-up assessments are critical to informing this issue. The most common strategy has been to measure immediate improvement in knowledge, attitudes, and beliefs, typically within the first month after completion of training (see Figure 5.1). A handful of intimate partner violence training evaluations also assessed knowledge levels after a much longer time had elapsed (e.g., Campbell et al., 2001; Ernst et al., 2000; Short et al., 2000; Thompson et al., 2000). This is not true for child abuse training evaluations, for which there are no available data on the degree to which participants retained what they learned more than six months after training.

Outcomes associated with screening, case finding, and other clinical indicators have been assessed at much longer intervals for intimate partner violence training interventions. Nearly half (48 percent) of the evaluations measured screening and identification rates more than six months after the intervention, and four of these included data more than one year after training. For other clinical practices, approximately two-thirds attempted to measure outcomes 7 or more months after training, and 3 of these 6 studies collected data 12 or more

---

[9]Coefficient alpha or Cronbach's alpha is a statistic that measures the reliability of a test, scale, or measure in terms of its internal consistency. It is obtained from the correlations of each item with each other item. Like a correlation, it ranges from 0 to 1, with 0 meaning complete unreliability (the responses are essentially unrepeatable random responses) to 1 (all the items measure the same thing exactly).

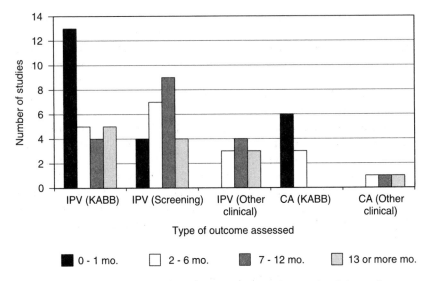

FIGURE 5.1 Timing of measurement in evaluations by type of training and outcome domain. IPV = intimate partner violence; CA = child abuse and neglect; KABB = knowledge, attitudes, beliefs, behaviors. Note: Percentages are column percentages. Because a study can have both a posttest and follow-ups, the numbers do not total to the number of studies in each training area.

months after training had been completed. Once again, the situation is much different for child abuse, for which the attention paid to measuring clinical outcomes has been infrequent, and follow-up data for extended periods was available in only one study.

Type of Design

The large majority of training program evaluations relied on some type of quasi-experimental design. The typical practice was to assess individual outcomes (e.g., knowledge levels of residents) with one-group, before-after designs and measure the health care outcomes of patients who were seen by the training recipients (e.g., percentage of patients who were screened by emergency department staff and identified as victims of family violence) before and one or more times after training. The most sophisticated design for determining causality—the individual or group randomized experiment—was employed in only six studies, and all of these were directed at training on intimate partner violence. Even here, however, some may be labeled more accurately as quasi-experiments due to problems encountered when sites varied in the degree to which they successfully implemented the training intervention or were possibly vulnerable to competing hypotheses related to self-selection caused by attrition from measurement and the occurrence of other events that affected the magnitude of group differences.

Because individual studies may examine different outcomes with different designs (e.g., incorporate a comparison group for selected outcomes only), Table 5.3 describes the evaluations in terms of the design used and the outcome of interest. As noted earlier, one-group, pretest-posttest designs were the most common when knowledge, attitudes, and beliefs were of interest. Approximately 63 percent of the studies assessing knowledge in both intimate partner violence and child abuse training relied on this design, and of this group, two-fifths limited their study to examining only changes that occurred immediately after the training session had concluded. The remaining studies were more ambitious, either incorporating a comparison group that received no training or a different type of training, but assignment to these comparison groups was nonrandom. In addition, the most rigorous studies randomly assigned individuals or training sites (e.g., clinics or hospitals) to receive or not to receive the training of interest.

For outcomes involving the identification of abused women, approximately one-third of the studies measured rates of screening, case finding, or both before and between 4 days and 12 months after staff training had occurred. Another 10 percent included lengthier follow-ups. Slightly more than two-fifths of the evaluations also collected similar screening and case-finding data from one or more comparison sites where staff did not receive such training; this group was nearly equally split between studies that managed to randomly assign sites to either a training or no-training group and those that did not randomize. A similar pattern pertained to evaluations that tracked other types of clinical outcomes.

TRAINING OUTCOMES AND EFFECTIVENESS

In general, the designs for most evaluations have effectively limited their contributions to enhancing the knowledge base with regard to the impact of training on health professionals' responsiveness to family violence. The variation in sophistication and rigor previously described must be taken into account when summarizing what is known about the effectiveness of family violence training. Because the large majority have used weak quasi-experimental designs (i.e., one-group, pretest and posttest), they can at best provide information for the much simpler question regarding whether the outcomes expected by training faculty actually occurred.

The remaining paragraphs attempt to summarize the evidence provided by the evaluations conducted to date. The majority of attention is paid to evaluations of intimate partner violence training, given the greater amount of available information. Outcomes for knowledge, belief, and attitudes; screening and identification; and other clinical outcomes are summarized separately. Because of the small number of child abuse evaluation studies and the even smaller

TABLE 5.3 Designs Used by Evaluations to Assess Training Outcomes by Type of Training and Outcome Domain

Type of Design	Intimate Partner Violence Training						Child Abuse Training			
	Knowledge, Attitudes, and Beliefs (n = 16)		Screening and Detection (n = 21)		Other Clinical Outcomes (n = 8)		Knowledge, Attitudes, and Beliefs (n = 6)		Other Clinical Outcomes (n=2)	
	N	%	N	%	N	%	N	%	N	%
Two-group, randomized (individual patients or practitioners or group randomization)										
Posttest only	0	0.0	3	14.3	1	12.5	0	0.0	0	0.0
Pretest and posttest	2	12.5	1	4.8	1	12.5	0	0.0	0	0.0
Pretest, posttest, and follow-up	1	6.3	1	4.8	1	12.5	0	0.0	0	0.0
Two- or three-group, nonequivalent comparison group										
Posttest only	1	6.3	2	9.5	0	0.0	0	0.0	0	0.0
Pretest and posttest	2	12.5	1	4.8	0	0.0	1	16.7	0	0.0
Pretest, posttest, and follow-up	1	6.3	1	4.8	2	25.0	1	16.7	1	50.0
Cohort										
Pretest and posttest (cohorts of patients)	0	0.0	7	33.3	1	12.5	0	0.0	0	0.0
Pretest, posttest, and follow-up (cohorts of patients)	0	0.0	2	9.5	1	12.5	0	0.0	0	0.0
One group										
Pretest and posttest	4	25.0	2	9.5	0	0.0	2	33.3	1	50.0
Pretest, posttest, and follow-up	6	37.5	1	4.8	0	0.0	2	33.3	0	0.0

Note: Percentages are column percentages. Because a few studies employed different designs for different outcomes (e.g., a one-group pretest and posttest to measure knowledge in training participants and a two-group nonequivalent comparison group design to assess clinical skills), the design used to assess each outcome domain rather than for the study itself was reported.

set of elder abuse training evaluations, brief summaries of what can be gleaned from published efforts in these two areas are presented below.

Child Abuse Training

Summarizing what is known about child abuse training efforts is difficult, given the small number of studies ($n = 7$) and their heterogeneity in terms of the professionals trained, the type of training delivered, and the designs themselves. The majority of evaluative data focuses on improvements in knowledge but restricts examination to training participants only (see Appendix G). In all cases, individuals who attended the training (whether they are residents in pediatrics, physicians, nurses, or caseworkers) exhibited increased knowledge levels, more appropriate attitudes, and perceived self-competency to manage child abuse cases. Such gains were typically measured immediately after training completion. For example, in two studies of child protective services workers, the trainees' perceptions about their ability to identify abuse and risk, along with attitudes about the value of family preservation and cultural differences, also improved after enrolling in a 3-month training program (Leung and Cheung, 1998), and greater ability in case planning, goal formulation, and family contract development was observed for individuals who had a 6-hour seminar in these skills (Cheung et al., 1991).

Relative to a comparison group, Dubowitz and Black (1991) found stronger improvement in knowledge, attitudes, and skills (including perceptions about their competency to manage child abuse cases) among pediatric residents who had attended several 90-minute sessions on child abuse immediately after training. However, with the exception of perceived self-competency, these differences were no longer evident at the 4-month follow-up. Palusci and McHugh (1995) also found that medical students, residents, fellows, and attending physicians who participated in a clinical rotation on child abuse had higher knowledge scores, on average, than their counterparts in other rotations. Once again, however, assessment was limited to immediately after the rotation had ended. In both these cases, the degree to which differences at the pretest between the training and intervention groups may have contributed to these group differences was not well examined.

For more direct indicators of clinical competency, Leung and Cheung (1998) found that child protective services workers who had received three months of focused training on child abuse improved between their six-month, nine-month, and first annual evaluation and between their first annual and second annual evaluation as measured by supervisor job performance ratings that covered such behaviors as case interviewing and documentation). At the same time, no significant differences between their performance and that of more seasoned workers without such formal training were found.

The above set of findings provides neither a broad nor strong evidence base on which to understand the outcomes and effects of child abuse training. Although training in this area appears to instill greater knowledge, appropriate attitudes, and perhaps self-efficacy for dealing with child abuse cases, these within-group changes have mainly been observed immediately after the conclusion of training. The extent to which they are sustained or can confidently be attributed to the training interventions themselves is unclear.

Training on Intimate Partner Violence

The degree to which health professionals involved in training on intimate partner violence actually change their knowledge, attitudes, and beliefs was addressed by 13 of the 15 training evaluations.[10] Typically, these evaluations did not go beyond examining changes before and after training, and posttests were usually administered immediately upon training completion or shortly thereafter (within one month).[11] In all but one evaluation (Knight and Remington, 2000),[12] statistically reliable differences between the pretest and posttest were found. Such gains were observed across a wide range of training interventions (ranging from a one-hour lecture to one or more days), questionnaires, and populations (medical students, residents, hospital staff, and community providers). Apparently, participants take something away from even a relatively brief exposure to material on family violence, but what the something is, how it changes with the content, nature, and length of training, how long it remains with them, and whether it was a direct result of training are not clear.

More informative are the seven evaluations that paid some attention to measurement issues (e.g., multi-item scales with acceptable levels of internal consistency) and had complete assessment data on the majority of training participants (70 percent or more). Many of these studies also had multiple or extended postbaseline assessments, and three collected outcome and other relevant data on comparison groups, two of which were designed as randomized field experiments. On the whole, pretest-posttest gains similar to those previously described were observed. In the Jonassen et al. (1999) study, medical students who completed an intensive interclerkship module (2 or 3.5 days) showed increases in knowledge, attitudes, and perceived skills at the time of completing the module, and these gains had not significantly eroded six months later. With the exception

---

[10]One study (Varvaro and Gesmond, 1997) involving emergency department house staff did not perform statistical analyses due to small sample sizes. Another study (Ernst et al., 1998) did report pre-post differences on 2 of 14 knowledge items but did not consider that this may be associated with the number of comparisons that were performed.

[11]Appendix F lists the evaluation studies and their characteristics regarding knowledge, attitudes, and belief outcomes for training on intimate partner violence.

[12]This "no-difference" finding in attitudes is most likely attributable to significant problems with respondent carelessness and a desire to complete the surveys quickly.

of perceived skills, similar results were found by Kripke et al. (1998) for a 4-hour workshop attended by internal medicine residents. Nearly 2 years after a focused, 2-day training workshop, emergency department staff evinced less blaming attitudes toward victims and were more knowledgeable about intimate partner violence and their role in addressing this problem than prior to training (Campbell et al., 2001). Furthermore, this group, which worked in hospitals that were randomly assigned to the training intervention, outperformed their counterparts at other hospitals who had not received the training.

Evaluations conducted by Short et al. (2000) and Thompson et al. (2000) provide a more differentiated picture of which attitudes and beliefs undergo the most modification. Medical students at the University of California, Los Angeles, who enrolled in a 4-week domestic violence module showed statistically reliable gains in knowledge, attitudes, and beliefs at the completion of the module and also improved more than medical students enrolled at a nearby school who did not have any organized opportunities for training on intimate partner violence. Further analyses highlighted that this improvement was primarily a function of increases in perceived self-efficacy—namely, the ability to identify a woman who had been abused and intentions to screen regularly upon becoming practicing clinicians. No such change was observed in other knowledge and attitude domains (e.g., how appropriate it is for physicians to intervene in these situations).

Similarly, primary care team members also experienced increased feelings of self-efficacy with regard to treating intimate partner violence victims both 9 and 21 months after an intensive training session (Thompson et al., 2000). This was in sharp contrast to staff in other clinics who had been randomly assigned not to receive the workshop and whose self-confidence in handling this problem decreased between the baseline and the nine-month follow-up period. Training participants also changed markedly and outperformed their comparison group counterparts in two other attitude domains—namely, fear of offending victims and provider or patient safety concerns in their interactions and stronger feelings that necessary organizational supports were in place.

Improvements in Screening and Identification Rates

Increased knowledge and more appropriate attitudes are important, but the ultimate goal is for professionals to translate these into their daily practice. Of the 18 evaluations that examined one or more of these behaviors, 7 collected data on variables related to asking or talking about intimate partner violence with their patients, and 11 monitored changes in case finding (e.g., the percentage of patients seen who were positively identified as victims of intimate partner violence).[13]

---

[13]Appendix F summarizes the studies on intimate partner violence screening and identification rates that included some type of training intervention.

In terms of explicitly inquiring about intimate partner violence, three of the five studies with data on this outcome found significantly higher percentages of patients asked about intimate partner violence after staff had participated in workshops or other staff training. For example, Knight and Remington (2000) observed that four days after hearing a lecture, internal medicine residents more frequently asked patients about intimate partner violence, based on reports of patients seen in their practice. Such changes do not seem limited to the short term but were also found 6 to 9 months later for community health center staff (Harwell et al., 1998) and primary care team members (Thompson et al., 2000). Moreover, this latter study demonstrated that such improvement did not occur among staff in teams that were randomly assigned not to receive such training. The training in all three studies provided either formal assessment protocols or a laminated cue card with screening questions. The other randomized field experiment (Campbell et al., 2000) found promising gains 24 months after a training intervention among emergency department staff and in contrast to their comparison group counterparts. The one study that showed no differences at a 6-month posttest involved a 4-hour training strategy aimed at internal medicine residents, but it involved no protocol or other enabling materials (Kripke et al., 1998).

The evidence on whether more frequent screening by practitioners is accompanied by increased case finding, however, is somewhat more mixed. A total of 13 evaluations monitored changes in relevant variables. Based on follow-ups conducted anywhere between 1 and 12 months after training, 7 (or 54 percent) of the evaluations found that the percentage of women who were positively identified as abused increased significantly in those emergency departments or clinics in which staff had received intimate partner violence training. In all these efforts, a protocol again was included as part of the training.

Four evaluations found no reliable change, and both programmatic and methodological factors most likely contributed to these results. In the evaluation of training for internal medicine residents, identification rates did not change, and no protocol or screening materials were provided as part of the training (Kripke et al., 1998). The other three evaluations did involve such forms. Among community health center staff, Harwell et al. (1998) found no change in the proportion of cases that were confirmed as intimate partner violence, but they did find that a greater percentage was suspected of it. Thompson et al. (2000) also found a 30 percent improvement in case finding, but this was not statistically reliable, most likely because of low statistical power and problems in medical record review. Finally, Campbell et al. (2001) found no statistically significant gains in the proportion of patients who self-reported intimate partner violence and had it documented in their charts; at the same time, this also may have been because of small sample size, events that may have increased relevant practices in the comparison sites (e.g., legislation on mandatory reporting and education), and the time required for modification of chart forms to facilitate reporting.

Furthermore, among the five studies that employed comparison hospitals or clinics, only two evaluations reported greater case finding in the intervention groups, but these increases may have been due to selection bias. No differences surfaced in those with randomized controls.

Overall, the above results suggest that if training is to result in increased screening for intimate partner violence, it must include instruction in and use of screening protocols and other types of standardized assessment materials. Clearly attesting to this are the findings from McLeer et al. (1989), who reported that the sizable increase in screening that followed training and protocol use essentially disappeared eight years later when administrative policy changed and the necessary infrastructure to support screening no longer existed. In addition, Larkin and his colleagues (2000) found dramatic improvements in screening rates by nursing staff, but only after disciplinary action for *not* screening was instituted as emergency department policy; neither training nor the availability of a protocol had previously enhanced screening in this site. Finally, Olson et al.'s (1996) work, while revealing a rise in domestic violence screening after a stamped query was placed on each patient's chart, also found that the addition of formal training following chart stamping produced no further improvement. Essentially, the net contribution made by training itself to screening and identification is less clear.

Improvements in Clinical Outcomes

Other clinical outcomes associated with identification include such behaviors as assistance in planning a course of action, providing referrals, and providing appropriate and quality care. Seven evaluations included measures relevant to these outcomes.[14] In general, there is some suggestion that training may be associated with staff's more frequently providing referrals for abused women. Harwell et al. (1998) found that trained community health center staff more often completed safety assessments (which had been provided as part of the training) and referred individuals to outside agencies. Wiist and McFarlane (1999) found similar results with regard to referrals for pregnant women who had been identified as intimate partner violence cases as did Fanslow et al. (1998, 1999) with emergency department staff. Although Shepard et al. (1999) did not find such gains with regard to trained public health nurses, the percentage of intimate partner violence cases that were provided information did significantly increase. In their randomized group trial, Campbell et al. (2001) found that patients were more satisfied with the care that they had received by trained emergency department staff compared with those in clinics in which staff had not received the training. This study also was unique in its measurement of institutional change: an index assessing departmental commitment to detecting inti-

---

[14]Appendix F describes the evaluations that examined these outcomes.

mate partner violence victims was stronger in the departments that participated in the training. Thompson et al. (2000), however, found no differences between intervention and comparison primary teams with regard to ratings of the quality of management as determined by record review. Saunders and Kindy (1993) also found no improvement among internal medicine and family practice residents in terms of history taking and planning.

In general, it may be that the materials provided do assist, particularly in terms of referrals. The reasons underlying the lack of differences in other variables may be several. These include site variation in implementing the necessary supports for system change, other events that may have contributed to increases in appropriate practices and weakened the difference between the training and comparison groups (Campbell et al., 2001), and problems resulting in accurately measuring certain outcomes such as quality of care (Thompson et al., 2000).

Training on Elder Abuse

As previously noted, the training of health professionals to identify elder abuse and neglect and intervene appropriately has received little attention in the literature. Descriptions of formal curricula and training models are few in number. Thus, it is not surprising that formal published evaluations of training efforts are also lacking.

The committee's literature search uncovered only four studies that explicitly provided any evaluative information on the outcomes of such training. These efforts were quite heterogeneous in terms of the recipients of training, the training provided, and the way in which outcomes were examined. Both Jogerst and Ely (1997) and Uva and Guttman (1996) reported data on the outcomes of resident training in elder abuse screening and management. Each study focused on a different specialty and training strategy. Whereas a home visit program to improve the skills of geriatric residents for carrying out elder abuse evaluations was the focus of Jogerst and Ely's work, Uva and Guttman provided data associated with a 50-minute didactic session for emergency medicine residents. Training for diverse groups of professionals was described and assessed by Vinton (1993) in her study of half-day training sessions of caseworkers, and Anetzberger et al. (2000) reported on the use of a 2.5-day training program that involved a formal curriculum—A Model Intervention for Elder Abuse and Dementia—that was delivered to adult protective services workers and Alzheimer's Association staff and volunteers.

Although all authors interpreted their findings as highlighting the benefits of training in terms of improved knowledge, level of comfort in handling elder abuse and neglect, and other outcomes (e.g., self-perceived competence), none of the four studies provided clear evidence regarding training effectiveness. For example, Vinton (1993) and Anetzberger et al. (2000) restricted their assessment to only pretest and posttest measurement of training participants immediately after training. Jogerst and Ely (1997) did employ a comparison group consisting of an earlier cohort who had not participated in the home visit program. With the exception of age, these groups were similar in terms of gender, type of practice, age of patients, and number of patients seen per week. Residents who had participated in the home visit rotation were more likely to rate their abilities to diagnose elder abuse and evaluate other important aspects (home environment) higher than the earlier cohort who did not have these training experiences. However, the latter group was *more* likely to have made home visits and to have provided statements regarding guardianships for their patients. Whether this was due to simply the added time in practice or to differences in patient mix or clinician skills cannot be determined from this design and its execution, and thus the effects of training (or lack thereof) remain ambiguous.

Uva and Guttman (1996) randomly assigned emergency residents to one of two groups, either: (a) to take a 10-item survey addressing their confidence in accurately recognizing elder abuse, level of comfort, and knowledge of how to report suspected cases and then attend a 50-minute educational session or (b) to participate in the session and then complete the survey. The two groups noticeably differed in terms of their confidence about detection and knowledge of reporting. While less than one-quarter of the residents who were administered the pretest trusted their skills in identification and knew to whom reports should be made, all residents who completed the questionnaire after training did so. Twelve months later, residents in both groups who responded to a follow-up survey all believed that they could identify and report elder abuse. Although a randomized design was used, this study is not very informative due to the lack of a comparison or control group and quite limited outcome measurement (i.e., assessment of knowledge and perceived self-confidence were each limited to one item).

Consequently, the knowledge base about the outcomes and effects of elder abuse training is sparse. Although these four studies conclude that training is beneficial, more comprehensive and rigorous assessments are needed in order to determine the types of training that are effective. Moreover, efforts to examine training for other populations, including medical students, nurses, and others, remain to be carried out.

QUALITY OF THE EVIDENCE BASE

A previous National Research Council and Institute of Medicine report (1998) concluded that the quality of the existing research base on family violence training interventions is "insufficient to provide confident inferences to guide policy and practice, except in a few areas. Nevertheless, this pool of studies and reviews represents a foundation of research knowledge that will guide the next generation of evaluation efforts and allows broad lessons to be derived" (p. 68). Unfortunately, the situation with regard to our evidence base on the associated outcomes and effectiveness of family violence training interventions is no different.

The research and evaluation base on family violence training interventions is mixed in terms of potentially contributing to understanding training effectiveness and the relationship between training and outcomes. This is especially true with regard to elder abuse training (for which there were too few studies to review systematically) and child abuse training. In terms of the latter, although descriptions of training strategies are available, there have been only a handful of attempts to provide corresponding evaluative information. When assessments have occurred, they have nearly all focused on gains in knowledge, and the majority have employed designs that cannot speak even to how training and outcomes may be related. Furthermore, no study was conducted in such a way that confident inferences could be made about the training intervention's effectiveness on patient outcomes.

The picture is somewhat more promising with regard to training on intimate partner violence. More than two dozen evaluation studies were located, although their methodological quality varied enormously. Again, assessing changes in knowledge, attitudes, and beliefs received the most attention, but concerted attempts have also been made to document changes in screening, identification, and other relevant clinical outcomes that are associated with training, particularly that which accompanies or includes the use of a screening protocol and other forms. Moreover, a small number of randomized field experiments have been conducted that can be used to address questions surrounding the effectiveness of training, and when such designs were not logistically possible (e.g., randomizing medical students to courses), there are notable instances of quasi-experimental designs that employ strong measurement strategies, measure differences in training participation, and attempt to address how well other rival explanations are ruled out.

As previously noted, several factors work against launching a concerted effort to improve the number of evaluations that can be conducted and to enhance how they are done. However, it is important to continue evaluating family violence training in ways that can contribute to the knowledge base about the outcomes of these efforts (even if in small increments). Clearly, these must include efforts to document outcomes and the effectiveness of training in child and elder maltreatment. The topic of child abuse and neglect offers an instructive example of evaluation needs. Training efforts for child abuse began to be described in the late 1970s, mandatory reporting requirements now exist, a handful of states require mandatory education in these reporting requirements and child abuse, and there is a national center devoted to addressing child abuse and neglect. However, only seven formal assessments, all of which suffered from methodological weaknesses, could be found.

Training efforts in intimate partner violence also can benefit from more serious scrutiny. The available evidence appears reasonably consistent in suggesting that training is positively associated with greater knowledge about family violence, stronger feelings of comfort and self-efficacy about interacting with battered women, and greater intentions to screen for intimate partner violence. When training is grounded in models of behavior change and how individuals learn, the data allow more confident determination of a link between training and increases in knowledge, attitudes, and behavioral intentions. Furthermore, for those training efforts aimed at practitioners, participants typically outperform their counterparts who did not receive such training in terms of increased rates of screening and identification—at least in the short term and up to two years after training. The same can be said for outcomes associated with safety planning, referrals for necessary services, and other clinical variables (e.g., patient satisfaction).

The available evidence also strongly indicates that training by itself, however, is not sufficient in terms of producing the desired outcomes. Unless the clinical settings display commitment to having their staff address the problem of family violence and provide the resources to do it, the effects of training will be short lasting and possibly erode over time. This suggests that training cannot be seen as a one-shot endeavor (e.g., a course in medical or social work school) and must include those who are responsible for creating the necessary infrastructure to support and reward practitioners for paying attention to identifying and intervening with family violence victims. Although the evidence for this conclusion derives mostly from evaluations of intimate partner violence training efforts, it is likely that the same could be said about child and elder maltreatment training activities.

CONCLUSIONS

- **Evaluation of the impact of training in family violence on health professional practice and effects on victims has received insufficient attention.**

- **Few evaluative studies indicate whether the existing curricula are having the desired impact.**

- **When evaluations are done, they often do not utilize experimental designs (randomized controlled trials and group randomized trials) necessary to determine training effectiveness. Also lacking are high-quality quasi-experimental designs necessary to provide a more complete understanding about the relationship of training to outcomes.**

- **In addition to effective training on family violence, a supportive environment appears to be critically important to producing desirable outcomes.**

6

Training Beyond the State of the Art

Moving beyond the current state of health professional training on family violence, the focus of this chapter is twofold: (1) to explore potential training content and (2) to examine behavior change in health professionals. With regard to training content, the committee describes and analyzes the concept of core competencies as an approach to establishing expectations for education and then proposes core competencies for health professionals in relation to family violence. These competencies refer to the basic knowledge, skills, and behaviors needed to respond effectively to family violence. In addition to specific core content areas for the health professions addressed in this report, the need for interdisciplinary core content is considered.

Following the discussion of what should be taught is a discussion of how teaching should proceed. The committee reflects on several key concepts that may affect behavior change and the ability of health professionals to learn about family violence: the diffusion of innovation, principles of adult learning, principles of continuing education, sustaining knowledge, building and maintaining what is effective, and independent forces with the potential to influence the education of health professionals, including evidence-based practice and routine outcome measurement.

Identifying appropriate content and teaching strategies is necessary for the development of effective training programs. In the committee's view, these tasks are at the very heart of its charge. However, progress is limited by the lack of research. A review of available literature reveals a great deal of expert opinion, and in some cases even consensus, about what is needed, but little scientific evidence about the necessary components or methods of family violence curricula. Key competencies may be normatively derived at least in part, but research is needed to support these norms. The literature on teaching methods and provider behavior change is growing, but little research is available on family violence training specifically. The committee's recommendations rely on the information available and underscore the need for extensive research.

TRAINING CONTENT: CORE COMPETENCIES

Competency is the ability to perform a complex task or function (Lane and Ross, 1998) and is closely linked to behaviors used as performance indicators for the accomplishment of competence. Knowledge, skills, and behaviors to be achieved on a particular topic typically define competencies. Competencies are not meant to be static; as new evidence is developed and systems change, competencies evolve. There is then a dynamic between research, practice, and educational competencies. The goal in articulating competencies is to set the current standards regarding expectations for training and practice in a field. Performance indicators provide the means to gather evidence as to whether training and practice objectives are achieved and whether stated objectives affect outcomes. Evaluation of competencies provides a method for measuring success in terms of process, outcome measures, and scope of training. The knowledge, skills, and behaviors necessary for effective health professional response to family violence are not yet established, and existing proposals for core competencies in family violence have not yet been evaluated.

Because of the substantial prevalence of family violence victims in health care settings, basic knowledge of all forms of family violence is necessary for all health care professionals who provide patient services. Those who ignore family violence, blame victims, or believe they can make decision about what is "right" without consulting the victim can potentially do additional harm (Brandt, 1995; Short et al., 1998). Basic standardized competencies can provide a powerful means to continue the process of educating and evaluating the ability of health care professionals to provide care to persons, families, and communities in the complex area of family violence.

Health care professionals, however, vary in their roles and responsibilities and have different degrees and types of interaction with family violence victims. Thus, beyond basic literacy, the committee considers competency levels appropriate to different health care professionals based on variations in perceived needs.

Levels of Competence

Differentiating competency levels is a means of acknowledging generalist and specialist foci (Adger et al., 1999; American Association of Colleges of Nursing, 1999; Auslisio et al., 2000; Brandt, 1995). For example, the National

Association for Children of Alcoholics recently published core competencies using a structure with levels (Adger et al., 1999). The first of three levels of competency is presented as the minimum for all health care providers and includes basic knowledge and skills in identifying cases, assessing needs and services, expressing concern, and offering support and referral. Health professionals who choose this role are "not expected to solve, manage, or treat the problem by themselves." However, they must "be able to collaborate with and refer to those who have the skill and expertise to provide these specialized services" (Adger et al., 1999, p. 1083). Competencies for persons at the next level include prevention, assessment, intervention, and coordination of care. At level three, long-term treatment is added to the list.

By not prescribing roles, this leveling schema has the advantage of allowing flexibility. Some health care professionals may need or be required to achieve competence at the advanced, specialized level based on the responsibilities of their roles and positions; others will choose to advance based on personal interest; and others may advance to fill local system gaps in services. The complexity of cases differentiates the need for varying levels of competence, defined in terms of amount of knowledge about the specified area (Auslisio et al., 2000).

The Oklahoma Principles, based on a multidisciplinary family violence conference of experts (Brandt, 1995, 1997), provide a detailed set of goals and objectives for three levels: Family Violence 101 includes core competencies to be mastered prior to graduating from a health professions school (e.g., medical school, nursing school, dental school). Family Violence 201 includes curricular principles for practicing primary care providers and for specialty-trained health professionals. Family Violence 301 includes curricular principles for scholars and leaders in family violence (expert clinicians, educators, researchers, curriculum architects, policy experts, and other experts in this field). The bulk of education for the 101 course or level is expected to take place during and within professional school, so that all graduating students can be assumed to have a stable foundation in the field. Education for the 201 level is expected to occur during postgraduate training (residency, advanced clinical work, or first-level graduate study) and is differentiated for primary care providers and specialty trainees, who would be expected to acquire more detailed expertise in more limited areas. Development of the 301 level expertise begins during fellowship or other advanced training and would continue as a dynamic, career-long process. These levels were formulated to guide curriculum development, program evaluation, career development, and policy formulation.

The American Association of Colleges of Nursing (1999) offers another scheme, classifying competencies for intimate partner violence according to educational program, baccalaureate versus master's. The master's education level moves beyond basic knowledge and skills to leadership competencies, such as developing, analyzing, and evaluating intimate partner violence programs.

Borrowing from the various approaches in use, the committee divides the development of competencies for addressing family violence into basic, advanced, and leadership competency levels (see Figure 6.1). Determining the specific content of each level for family violence requires further examination and explication.

Assigning Competency Roles

Who should bear responsibility for providing specialized, advanced care in family violence care is an issue for both national policy and local health care systems. Definition of competencies thus is entwined with the need to build a system of care delivery (Curran, 1995; Lane and Ross, 1998). Curran has identified core competencies in delivering care through integrated delivery networks, including "building a delivery system" (discussed below). Advanced competency (and the necessary education and training) may be distributed among health professionals in a community, as well as within community systems (such as criminal justice and victim advocates) to ensure that the complete spectrum of services is provided. For example, sexual assault nurse examiners provide advanced care for sexual assault victims in many communities, while in other communities other health professionals provide similar care. In any locality, what is vital is that roles are clarified and that health care professionals are adequately trained to provide competent care for victims of sexual assault (both familial and extrafamilial).

Advanced competencies may be profession specific or multidisciplinary. With regard to sexual assault, for example, knowledge of normal and abnormal genital anatomy is a basic competency for physicians and nurses but is not within the scope of social work, dentistry, or psychology. The ability to perform forensic examinations in cases of acute sexual assault (adult and pediatric) is a necessary basic competency for physicians, yet an advanced competency for nurses

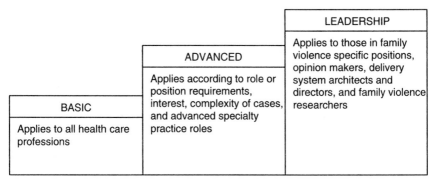

FIGURE 6.1 Levels of competency for addressing family violence.

(such as for sexual assault nurse examiners). Professional roles, duties, and ethics influence differences in specialized care. Both the number of providers in any single profession and the competencies themselves may vary by profession and type of family violence. For example, social workers may be likely to incorporate a host of social risks in their care planning (such as homelessness and substance abuse); physicians may focus their expertise on diagnosing and treating injuries and illnesses; nurses may focus on the complex interplay of physical, psychological, and social issues on health. Geriatricians may have advanced competence in elder abuse but only basic competence in child abuse. Health professionals working in primary and secondary prevention may focus on access and system-wide collaboration. However, there will still be a central nucleus of competencies that are the same for any health care professional at any level in any setting (see Figure 6.2).

Evidence Supporting Core Competencies

While core competencies have been suggested for health professional education on family violence, the committee could find no evidence to support specific content for them. Research is necessary to determine the effect of establishing core competencies, the degree to which health care providers achieve competencies (through training, education, and practice), and, more importantly,

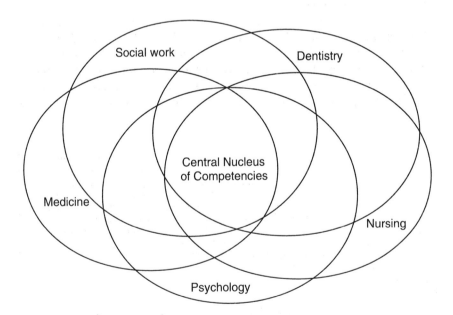

FIGURE 6.2 Overlapping professional core competencies for family violence.

whether client outcomes are improved when provided care by a "competent" provider. The specification of core competencies can provide a platform for learning, service delivery, and evaluation that proves quite useful in situations in which there is a limited scientific base. Evaluation should include both outcome and process measures to allow refinement of core competencies, including the addition of competencies as needs are identified.

However, in the committee's view, domains exist from which core competencies can be developed beginning with the basic level. A review of existing health professional curricula offers a starting point for identifying and detailing these domains. The committee's review indicates overlap in a number of content areas developed for health professionals (see Box 6.1).

BOX 6.1 Areas of Overlap Among Existing Family Violence Curricula

Common objectives include:
- To recognize family violence as a significant health problem.
- To develop a comprehensive understanding of the medical implications of family violence, including the signs and symptoms of abuse and neglect, associated health problems, and common treatments.
- To develop the skills necessary to detect, screen, treat, and protect victims of family violence.
- To understand and adhere to legal requirements for reporting situations of family violence.

To identify and learn to use medical, legal, social, and community services resources appropriately.

Common content:
- Dynamics of family violence
- Data on the magnitude and prevalence of the problem in various health care settings
- Family violence as a health care issue—physical and mental health symptoms and patterns of presentation
- Techniques for identifying victims of family violence
- Screening tools
- Documentation and encouragement to document all cases and suspected cases
- State mandatory reporting legal requirements
- Other legal issues (e.g., victims' rights, criminal sanctions, the role of the police and social services, the role of the courts, medical testimony for the courts in civil and criminal prosecutions, and child and adult protection)
- Referral services
- Collaborative health care team composition and roles
- Cultural issues, particularly with regard to variations in acts considered abusive

---

In a few cases, competency domains specific to family violence are addressed. For example, one review notes that competence in family violence "is now part of the expected standard of care for graduating and practicing physicians" (Alpert et al., 1998, p. 278). It describes the goal of curricula on family violence as competence in screening (how to ask the right questions), assessment (how to listen to the patient's responses and concerns), intervention (offering information, advice, and support), and referral for services. It also addresses some important interpersonal competencies, such as to "efficiently, yet compassionately, evaluate patients' concerns in the context of evolving life circumstances" (p. 277), appreciation for diversity, and awareness of one's own attitudes, beliefs, values, and history.

Another report identifies some traits for ethics consultations, including tolerance, patience, compassion, honesty, courage, prudence, humility, and integrity as being important and closely related to such skills as active listening and the communication of interest, respect, support, and empathy (Auslisio et al., 2000). These appear to be quite applicable to family violence as well. The complexity of addressing rights for individual autonomy while at the same time ensuring patient safety is a formidable task to be achieved in the family violence arena. However, competence here is necessary for all health care professionals encountering all forms of family violence (NRC and IOM, 1998). The American College of Nurse Midwives similarly supplemented knowledge, skill, and behavior competencies with the "hallmarks of midwifery" (1997), which include, for example, skillful communication, guidance, and counseling. In these and other cases, those proposing competencies acknowledge that practice involves not only science but also the artful application of knowledge in interpersonal relationships and ethical issues with clients. In family violence, this need to attend to interpersonal, ethical, and cultural competencies is considered crucial (American Nurses'Association, 1995; Ryan and King, 1998).

The foregoing review of the literature does not provide a scientific foundation for core competencies on family violence for health professionals. The committee struggled with the lack of a scientific evidence base from which to propose core competencies for health professionals and the need for such competencies. What and how much each type of health professional needs to know about family violence remains a matter of debate. However, the literature does suggest important elements and common themes. In the committee's judgment, the overlap it found in the literature, as well as the literature describing curricular development by consensus processes (e.g., Brandt, 1997), suggests some agreement in the field regarding the appropriate areas for educational intervention. The consensus opinions and products of the formal consensus panels that have developed core competencies provide a very valuable starting point from which to launch evaluative research.

Based primarily on the work of the American Association of Colleges of Nursing (1999), Alpert et al., (1998), Brandt (1995, 1997), Heise et al. (1999), and the multidisciplinary expertise of our committee members, the committee drafted proposed core competencies at the basic level within the domains identified in the literature (see Table 6.1). These core competencies reflect the committee's consensus on best practice, the ideal state of knowledge and skills, published expert opinion, and existing curricula. They were developed to address multidisciplinary care and to be inclusive of family violence across the life span.

Content was specified in accord with the areas of overlap found in the curricula the committee examined and proposals offered in the literature. As such, these proposed competencies build on the collective wisdom of those working in family violence. They are not intended as a definitive set of competencies but are offered as a springboard for research and evaluation. The committee emphasizes the need for research on these competencies, or any set that is chosen, to provide a scientific basis and to determine effectiveness. It is our judgment that current training initiatives and educational development should be suspended awaiting scientific evidence, but the need for such evidence must be addressed in the short term. The review of existing curricula and the literature indicate that much of the curricular development to date has largely been done within schools or particular professional groups or by organizations concerned specifically with one type of violence. Thus it appears that much "reinventing the wheel" occurs. In the committee's view, the various professions and organizations involved with victims of family violence could benefit greatly from collaboration in developing, testing, and evaluating core competencies on family violence.

Advanced competencies for responding to family violence have yet to be developed, with some notable exceptions. For example, the American Association of Colleges of Nursing (1999, http://www.aacn.nche.edu/publications/positions/violence.htm) recently published nursing education competencies for domestic violence (see Appendix H). To date, neither child abuse and neglect nor elder maltreatment have been addressed. The basic competencies set forth in Table 6.1 and the advance practice competencies of the American Association of Colleges of Nursing may provide all health professions with some helpful material to start to inform their own discussions leading to core competency descriptions and research. In addition, the list may provide a starting point from which collaborative work across professions can begin.

Advanced practice education does exist in other areas. For example, subspecialty residencies have been established for developmental pediatrics and adolescent health. Following increased research and a growing recognition of the need for cross-disciplinary training in these areas, the Maternal and Child Health Bureau of the Health Resources and Services Administration funded advanced-level training programs. The adolescent health program, for example, grew out of research on adolescence that began in the 1950s. In 1967, the Maternal and Child Health Bureau funded adolescent programs at 6 sites that included 14 physicians. In 1976, the bureau funded 9 new sites and extended training to

TABLE 6.1 Basic Level of Core Competencies Needed for Addressing Family Violence by Health Care Professionals

Competency	Performance Indicators
Identify, assess, and document abuse	1. Recognize risk factors for victimization and perpetration of violence. 2. Recognize physical and behavioral signs of abuse and neglect, including patterns of injury (including unusual forms of abuse such as Munchausen syndrome by proxy and poisoning), across the life span. 3. Screen for family violence experiences using valid and reliable instruments that are developmentally appropriate. 4. Assess clients via interview and appropriate health examination processes. 5. Document injuries and health effects, using forensic guidelines in obtaining and recording evidence (such as recording specific, concise, and objective information utilizing body maps and photographs). 6. Identify and address problems of emotional, physical, and sexual abuse and neglect.
Intervene to secure safety and reduce vulnerability	1. Assess for immediate danger. 2. Develop a safety plan with victims and families. 3. Consult with and refer to specialists and community resources for safety, education, caretaking, and support services (such as protective services, social work, shelter, child abuse hotlines, legal, mental health, substance abuse, and criminal justice) as appropriate. 4. Maintain appropriate clinical follow-up.
Recognize that cultural and value factors influence family violence	1. Communicate nonjudgmentally and compassionately. 2. Recognize the cultural factors important in influencing the occurrence and patterns of responses to family violence. 3. Provide culturally competent assessment and intervention to victims and perpetrators of family violence. 4. Explain culturally normative behaviors and relationship patterns that could be misconstrued as dysfunctional and/or violent. Recognize potential dilemmas in providing care and accessing resources that may arise from cultural differences.
Recognize legal and ethical issues in treating and reporting family violence	1. Know state reporting laws and mandates, local and state reporting agencies, and their procedures and regulations, including potential liability for failure to report. 2. Know ethical principles that apply to patient confidentiality for victims as well as the limits of that confidentiality. 3. Understand the need to balance respect for individual autonomy with concerns for safety of vulnerable persons when making reporting decisions. 4. Understand the health professional's role in court testimony (as either a regular or an expert witness).

TABLE 6.1 *(Continued)*

Competency	Performance Indicators
Engage in activities to prevent family violence	1. Promote activities to increase public awareness of family violence.
	2. Promote activities to address populations at risk.
	3. Participate in health policy activities to address family violence.
	4. Promote community action to establish and enhance programs to support victims and family members and for perpetrator interventions, especially at early stages.
	5. Understand the impact of services (such as home visitation nurses) on the prevention of physical abuse and neglect.
	6. Understand the principles of prevention of family violence (including sexual abuse of children).

professionals in nursing, social work, nutrition, and psychology. In 1994, adolescent medicine achieved the formal status of a subspecialty and became a 3-year program. In 1997, the Residency Review Committee for Pediatrics began requiring that pediatric residents complete a 1-month block rotation in adolescent medicine. Because of these requirements, 96 percent of programs report having an adolescent medicine block rotation, 90 percent of which are required (Emans et al., 1998). However, only 39 percent of programs felt that the number of adolescent faculty was adequate for teaching residents, and while many topics are believed to be adequately covered (e.g., sexually transmitted diseases, confidentiality, puberty, contraception, and menstrual problems), many others continue to be inadequately covered (e.g., psychological testing, violence in relationships, violence and weapon-carrying, and sports medicine) (Emans et al., 1998).

The development of such training programs demonstrates an approach to the advanced-level training necessary in family violence, but it also reveals the challenges. The programs became possible only with the increase in attention to and research on adolescent health needs and the subsequent availability of funds. Research indicated that adolescents have unique health care needs and a high rate of health problems (Athey et al., 2000). With funding from the Maternal and Child Health Bureau, support from the American Academy of Pediatrics, and the creation of the Society for Adolescent Medicine, appropriate training content was identified and training programs were implemented. Growth in the evidence base, increased support, and the availability of funding for research and training development appear to be critical factors for the evolution of such an advanced-level training program. Such a foundation does not yet appear to exist in family violence. For example, recent petitions to the American Board of Pediatrics to establish a subboard on child abuse and neglect (to be called Child Abuse and Forensic Pediatrics) have been deferred to allow time to document the scientific base of the field and to determine whether other medical organizations would have objections to the development of child abuse and neglect as a formal subspecialty. To date, no efforts have been made to develop an intimate partner violence, elder abuse, or family violence subspecialty.

Competency in Forensic Services

In addition to competencies related to working with victims of family violence and other health professionals, forensic assessment is an important competency domain due to the role of health professionals in screening and referring family violence victims. Although there are both ethical and practical reasons to try to separate forensic practice and other health services as much as possible (Melton et al., 1997, § 5.02), health professionals usually do not—and perhaps should not—have the luxury of avoiding involvement in legal processes related to cases of family violence.

Two reasons support the likelihood of such involvement and therefore the idea that health professionals in general should have some training in forensic practice, though the degree to which training is needed is likely to vary by profession, specialty, and practice setting. First, reporting laws mandate that all health professionals report suspected child maltreatment, most must report suspected elder abuse, and a few must report intimate partner violence itself or the abuse of any adult (see Chapter 3). In effect, such reports indicate suspicions that a crime has occurred, and they also trigger investigations that often may result in civil actions that involve coercive action for victim protection. Because such investigations are typically obligatory, health professionals are effectively in the position of legal decision makers at the initiation of the process.

Second, because health professionals may be among the first to see evidence that violence has occurred, they may be particularly credible fact witnesses, revealing exactly what they observed. Under some circumstances, health professionals may also be asked to testify as expert witnesses regarding their opinions about the meaning of particular observations—for example, at the adjudicatory phase, whether specific injuries could have resulted from particular abusive or neglectful actions by an intimate partner, a parent, or an adult child and, at dispositional phases, whether coercive action should be taken to prevent further harm to the victim. Furthermore, in many jurisdictions health professionals may be asked to testify about hearsay evidence (e.g., statements made by victims or colleagues). Because statements made to health professionals for the purpose of securing treatment are presumed to be especially reliable, clinicians often can provide hearsay testimony about what they were told by victims or other key informants. The relevant records, including opinions of other professionals on whom the clinician relied, may also be admissible.

Given the legal relevance of clinical evidence for various forms of family violence, the potential expansion of admissible evidence to include health professionals' opinions and their hearsay testimony and reports, and the frequency with which questions of family violence arise, health professionals often may become involved in legal proceedings related to family violence. Accordingly, all practicing health professionals should have some familiarity with forensic issues, and they should have access to consultation by forensic experts. Such expertise, whether held by or simply easily available to the health professional, is necessary to ensure that the quality of evidence gathered and the validity of opinions offered is maximized and that there is due sensitivity to the special ethical issues that arise in family forensic cases.

Such training and consultation appear to be needed especially because of the complexity and ambiguity of roles that health professionals often face in family violence cases. This complexity goes beyond usual role conflicts in forensic practice, because the nature of the role may change as a case goes through the various steps in the family and criminal courts (see Melton, 1994; Melton et al., 1997, § 15.04). In that regard, clinicians need to be especially sensitive to the fact that the nature of the opinions that may be offered ethically and admitted legally is likely to be different amid formal legal proceedings (in comparison with initial reporting, where required). According to generally prevailing evidentiary rules, experts make at least implicit representations that their opinions are based on specialized knowledge (Federal Rules of Evidence 702). Therefore, opinions, no matter how valid, should neither be sought by nor offered to legal authorities unless they are based on expert knowledge, not simply a common-sense inference that a layperson might make. Although an answer to the question about the nature of the foundation for an expert witness's opinion does not end the inquiry about its admissibility, that issue is central with regard to the witness's meeting his or her ethical obligation to avoid misleading the trier of fact (i.e., the judge or the jury) (see Melton et al., 1997, §§ 1.04 and 18.05).

Cultural Competencies

Increasingly visible diversity among patients has significant implications for health care delivery and for the education of health care professionals. Racial and ethnic minority populations now constitute fully 28 percent of the U.S. population (http://www.census.gov/population/estimates/nation/intfile3-1.txt). And 31 million U.S. residents are unable to speak the same language as their health care providers (Woloshin et al., 1995). Diversity can be described according to a number of characteristics, including age, gender, race, ethnic background, disability, religious affiliation, sexual orientation, socioeconomic status, and community setting (e.g., rural, urban, or international). Each of these characteristics contributes to the customary beliefs, social groupings, and material traits that account for cultural variations. In all health professional environments, the culture, background, and context of the patient, of clinicians, and of health care institutions converge and affect virtually every aspect of health care, including access to services, adherence to recommended treatment regimens, continuity of care, preventive care, screening practices, patient-clinician communication, immunization rates, and prescription practices (Flores, 2000).

Patient diversity occasions the need for cultural and linguistic competence. Such competence involves the knowledge and interpersonal skills that allow clinicians to understand and respond effectively to individuals from cultures and backgrounds other than their own (Campinha-Bacote, 1998, 1999). Culturally influenced definitions of abuse may influence patients' and also clinicians' expectations concerning interventions around family violence in the health care setting. When the health care professional does not speak the primary language of the patient, difficulty with identifying and intervening in family violence increases. For abused individuals with limited English proficiency, the use of family members as interpreters can present particular barriers to disclosure, confidentiality, assessment, reporting, safety, and referral. In addition, the health care professional's own cultural background and social class may influence the clinical care that is provided to patients experiencing family violence and their families. An understanding of the sociocultural backgrounds of individual patients and of their physical, cultural, social, and community environments is crucial to addressing family violence; therefore, clinicians who have limited cultural and linguistic competence also may have limited effectiveness in the assessment and management of family violence patients (Campbell and Campbell, 1996; Bell and Mattis, 2000).

Various ethnic groups comprise a large percentage of the American population. For example, in California, New Mexico, and Hawaii, "minority" groups make up more than 50 percent of the population (U.S. Census Bureau, 2000). These changing demographics pose a challenge to practitioners involved in offering services to abused immigrants. Victims of family violence who have immigrated illegally or who have recently relocated to the United States as refugees are in a particularly problematic situation, since their predominant fear of deportation may prevent them from contact with appropriate helping agencies, either governmental or private (Gelles, 1997; McGoldrick et al., 1996).

Of particular relevance to health care professionals, cultural practices can be mistaken for abuse, especially in the pediatric population (Bullock, 2000, 2001). For example, cupping or spooning (a method used to treat upper respiratory infections that leaves discrete markings on the skin) and certain treatments for empacho (a gastrointestinal illness) can be misunderstood by Western practitioners and labeled as abuse. A culturally sensitive physician familiar with some of these indigenous therapies may be able to address these issues, educating parents about negative effects on health, rather than reporting abuse.

Beyond these issues of ethnic cultures, community cultures may also create difficulties for health professionals. Family violence within rural, remote, or wilderness communities may present challenges distinct from those in urban settings. Although studies have shown that rates of abuse may be the same, unique features are associated with small communities in which family violence occurs, which may be due to socioeconomic differences, increasing isolation, dependence on geography, and more entrenched patriarchal sex-role stereotypes, among other factors. Providers may need an understanding of and appreciation for rural cultural and social life and other issues specific to the particular setting in order to be effective in nonurban environments (Websdale, 1998).

Despite the importance of providing culturally and linguistically competent health care to diverse patient populations, education about social and cultural factors that affect patients and influence the clinician-patient relationship is uncommon. One study documented that only 8 percent of U.S. medical schools offer separate instruction in cultural issues (Flores et al., 2000). While research is increasingly addressing issues of diversity in health care, more research is needed to identify effective components and methods for educational programs for health professionals (Loudon et al., 1999).

Cultural competency instruction that is either infrequent or insufficient poses a major challenge to optimal intervention in family violence, in which quality care depends on clinicians' sensitivity and understanding of patients' cultural backgrounds, complemented by self-reflection on personal cultural values and biases. Insufficient sensitivity and understanding of other cultures can lead to incorrect assessment and treatment, particularly when stereotypical and prejudicial notions about minority groups abound. Furthermore, culturally formed definitions of abuse can limit patients' ability to disclose information and can also affect patient expectations of treatment. A national survey of intimate partner violence treatment programs found that a deficiency in cultural understanding of minority populations was a major obstacle to better diagnosis and care (Williams and Becker, 1994). Thus, cultural "incompetence" can undermine the patient-provider relationship and jeopardize the delivery of quality health care, especially to ethnic minority populations.

Training and sensitizing health care professionals about cultural and linguistic issues is an important aspect of family violence education. The American Academy of Pediatrics and the Society of Teachers of Family Medicine each have published guidelines for the education and training of health care providers in cultural competency (AAP, 1999; Like et al., 1996). Recommendations to address the challenges of training health care professionals in the areas of family violence to include cultural and linguistic diversity have also been published (Pinn and Chunko, 1997). These recommendations include: (1) provision of training to help clinicians achieve and communicate a level of comfort with patients' cultures and environments and (2) inclusion of case study and standardized patient material that is representative of the racial, cultural, and linguistic groups in the community. In addition, the U.S. Department of Health and Human Services recently issued written policy guidance to assist health and social services providers in ensuring that persons with limited English skills can effectively access critical health and social services (Office of Minority Health,

2000). Although cultural competency can potentially improve outcomes of health care services, little research has been done to discern the need for cultural competency of health care providers in the delivery of care to patients who experience family violence (Brach and Fraser, 2000). However, cultural and linguistic competencies are important components of the education and training of health care professionals generally and appear relevant to family violence education.

ACHIEVING COMPETENCY THROUGH EDUCATION AND TRAINING

Training to achieve competency involves not only the relevant content and curricular space but also the timing, methods and strategies, and environment for conveying the content in ways that maximize comprehension, sustainability, and use. Thus, in addition to exploring the content of health professional training on family violence, the committee examined how such training might be accomplished. This section begins with a discussion of the diffusion of knowledge, goes on to address techniques for overcoming cognitive biases, moves to the literature on behavior change for health professionals, and then explores some strategies for enhancing education.

How Do People Get Knowledge?

People, including health care professionals, obtain knowledge in many ways, but some form of communication, generally defined as the provision of information (Tones, 1997, p. 794), is necessary. Theories about the provision of information may prove helpful in developing educational approaches for effecting behavioral changes in health professionals (NRC, 1999).

Several behavioral models populate the literature of change in health care. Among them are Rogers, *Diffusion of Innovations* (1995); Green and Kreuter, precede/proceed model (1991); Bandura, *The Social Foundations of Thought and Action: A Social Cognitive Theory* (1986); and Prochaska and Norcross, *Systems of Psychotherapy: A Transtheoretical Analysis* (1998).

Need is a concept central to each of the models, both behavioral and learning. Rogers reports that successful diffusion of innovations is dependent in part on compatibility, the degree to which an innovation is perceived as being consistent with the existing values, past experiences, and the needs of potential adopters. He notes that engaging the opinion leaders in a health care facility in order to convey the message about screening for family violence can boost prospects for the success of a training or intervention effort. These individuals have informal or formal influence in an institution, irrespective of their titles, and are recruited and trained to assist in making changes. Green and Kreuter suggest that attitudes that predispose systems to adopt innovations include appreciation of the importance of behavioral risk factors, the importance of intervening to modify risk factors, and the physician's diffidence in carrying out the intervention. Bandura explains that one needs to exercise control over events to accomplish desired goals. Prochaska and Norcross assert that increasing awareness of the causes, consequences, and cures for a particular problem behavior is required to enable successful change.

Some key innovation characteristics influence the acquisition of knowledge. Among these are simplicity, an accessible format with readily observable results, compatibility with existing norms, demonstration of a clear advantage compared with the status quo, and modest costs (Rogers, 1995; Tones, 1997).

In addition, the social system, including structure, norms, and the roles or potential roles of change agents, are important factors in determining how knowledge is received. For example, in institutions in which the importance of screening for family violence is not modeled by supervising health professional educators or written guidelines do not exist, students may perceive them as unnecessary.

Adult Education Principles

The principal message from research on the diffusion of knowledge is that most transfer of knowledge, including transfer to and among health professionals, occurs informally, based on perceived needs. And diffusion is maximized through informal communication by the early adopters or trailblazers. Such efforts are likely to be informed by attention to principles dominating the field of adult education, though general guidance for increasing participation in and the meaning of education is also derivable from learning principles generically (NRC, 1999). Among the most influential approaches in that regard is that of Knowles (1990), called *andragogy* (i.e., the methods of techniques used to teach adults).[1] For the most part, the andragogy principles reflect the roles and expectations of and for adults in our society, rather than developmentally specific learning principles per se. Six assumptions are basic to andragogy:

1. Adults must have a reason to learn something before they will undertake to do so.

2. Adults expect to be treated as self-directed beings.

3. Because of their life experience, adult learners themselves may possess the richest resources for learning. However, they may also have to overcome prejudices and experiences that they have incorporated into their own identity.

---

[1]There is some controversy about whether the principles are unique to adults and whether they have actually been widely used in practice (see Knowles, 1984, for examples of applications, including the University of Southern California's 1984 medical curriculum).

4. "Adults become ready to learn those things that they need to know and be able to do in order to cope effectively with their real-life situations" (p. 60).

5. Adults' learning is life (or task or problem) centered rather than subject based. Adults are motivated to learn when they perceive that the effort will enable them to perform tasks or solve problems in their daily lives. Accordingly, adults' education is most effective when information is presented in the context of application to real-life situations.

6. Adults respond best to intrinsic motivators, such as increased job satisfaction. There is an emerging consensus that the general principles of adult education, as embodied in continuing medical education, apply to health professionals as well.

The consensus is linked to the principles of adult learning (Abrahamson et al., 1999; Barrows, 1983; Green and Ellis, 1997; Knowles, 1984, 1990; Neame et al., 1981), emphasizing an adult's need to know why they should learn about a particular topic, how this knowledge or skill helps them cope with real-life situations; and that the learning is task centered (problem based) (Abrahamson et al., 1999; Boud and Felitti, 1991; Carlile et al., 1998; Dolmans and Schmidt, 1994; Schmidt, 1993; Slotnick et al., 1995).

Overcoming Cognitive Biases

Health professionals, like other individuals, possess belief systems that include prejudice, and these biases can affect their professional behavior, potentially resulting in errors in clinical judgment in family violence cases. Health professionals need to know about and improve the sensitivity, specificity, and positive predictive value of efforts to screen for or otherwise detect family violence.

Cognitive Heuristics

Errors result from ignorance about the relevant facts and how to pursue them efficiently and effectively, as well as from cognitive biases to which clinicians are subject. Although many health professionals may have substantially greater knowledge than laypersons about family violence, their process of judgment and decision making is likely to be similar to that of laypersons. The relevant body of research has grown from the recognition that *cognitive heuristics*—mental shortcuts that people learn to use to enable them to deal efficiently with information overload—sometimes lead to systematic biases in judgments and decision making (Kahneman and Tversky, 1982; Tversky and Kahneman, 1974).[2] Research on

---

[2] A thorough review of this literature is beyond the scope of this report.

cognitive heuristics does suggest several ways that biases are especially likely to affect clinicians' judgments in cases of actual or suspected family violence. These include overconfidence about assessments (Arkes, 1989; Lichtenstein and Fischhoff, 1980; Oskamp, 1965); the lack of objective feedback (Dawes, 1989); the vividness or emotional charge of personal experiences (Tversky and Kahneman, 1973); the tendency not to use statistical information (Plous, 1993; Melton et al., 1997); the format of the information (Slovic et al., 2000); and errors of attribution based on personal experiences (Heider, 1958).

Debiasing

Clinicians' biases in judgment and decision making thus can present major obstacles to accurate predictions of violent behavior and to resulting forensic decisions and safety planning. Educational programs for health professionals about family violence should take such obstacles into account. A body of research has begun to develop about effective techniques of debiasing to help prevent these errors of assessment (see, e.g., Arkes, 1981). For example, Plous (1993) has provided steps that research suggests should reduce tendencies to make errors as a result of cognitive heuristics.

Although some biases are difficult to correct even with training (see, e.g., Slovic et al., 2000), a theme of debiasing research is to increase accountability. Clinicians are less likely to reach erroneous conclusions when they are subject to divergent opinions, required to examine actuarial data, and given feedback about the validity of their judgments. These findings suggest that training programs on family violence should include exercises in comparing the participating clinicians' judgments with statistical information, including feedback about the accuracy of their own judgments. Research is also needed to increase the development and testing of actuarial measures available to make predictions specific to family violence (Campbell et al. 1995, 2000). These advances, coupled with better training for health care professionals, will lead to combinations of truly "expert" (debiased clinical experience and advanced knowledge base) judgment and valid actuarial predictions that are thought to be the optimal combination for accurate predictions of violence (Hess and Weiner, 1999; Campbell et al., 2000).

Training for Behavior Change: Continuing Education Principles That Work

At present for undergraduate and graduate education in the health professions, educational needs are determined largely by faculty members who develop and present the curriculum to persons interested in acquiring the knowledge, skills, and attitudes necessary to enter professional practice. In deliberating on the changing needs of society and the responsibility of preparing students for a future of lifelong professional learning, faculty select goals, content, and instructional methods, as they devise instructional objectives and compile the sequence of curricular activities (Ferren and Mussell, 2000).

When the effects of continuing medical education on physician practices and patient outcomes have been systematically examined, some insights emerge (see the systematic reviews of Haynes et al., 1984; Davis, Thomson et al., 1992, 1995; Davis, O'Brien et al., 1999). This group of researchers from McMaster University and the University of Toronto has noted that there is a wide range of rigorously tested interventions that substantially broaden the traditional definition of continuing medical education (Davis, Thomson et al., 1992). From this work, *formal* continuing medical education is defined as varying from "passive, didactic, large group presentations to highly interactive learning methods such as workshops, small groups and individual training sessions. Examples of such educational activities include rounds, educational meetings, conferences, refresher courses, programs, seminars, lectures, workshops and symposia" (Davis, O'Brien et al., 1999, p. 868). The broader view of continuing medical education also includes educational materials, outreach visits, local opinion leaders, patient-mediated interventions, audit and feedback, and reminders.

Formal Continuing Medical Education: Implications for Health Professional Training

In a recent systematic review of formal continuing medical education for the years 1970 to 1999, Davis, O'Brien et al. (1999) found 64 studies of which 14 met their selection criteria (only randomized controlled trials). The education approaches were divided into three categories: didactic only, interactive, and mixed. In their conclusions the authors state that "the use of traditional [continuing medical education] activities such as lectures has been widely criticized. This criticism appears justified because didactic interventions analyzed in this review failed to achieve success in changing professional performance or health care outcomes. In contrast studies that used interactive techniques such as case discussion [e.g., problem-based learning approaches] role-play, or hands on practice sessions were generally more effective in changing those outcomes documented in this review" (p. 870).

The research suggests that independent lecture-based courses are unlikely to be sufficient; rather if such courses or lectures occur, the knowledge provided must be reinforced at later points during the degree or certification program and throughout the learner's practical educational exposures to their profession. In the committee's view, such an approach is appropriate for family violence training as well. Family violence content may be integrated across courses and reinforced with clinical instruction. For example, students may learn to screen and identify family violence victims during coursework on patient interviewing or communication skills; to document suspected or actual cases of family violence for forensic purposes during diagnosis or history-taking coursework; to recognize the emotional and psychological manifestations of family violence during case-based or simulated patient instruction; and to understand culturally relevant issues during clinical rotations in diverse settings. Such an approach may build on knowledge and skills for addressing family violence and emphasize the importance of family violence as an important health care issue.

Health professional schools appear to be moving from offering specific courses on each topic to an integrated approach. With such an approach, content on a particular issue is woven throughout the curriculum both horizontally (in different courses that occur simultaneously) and vertically (reinforced throughout the length of the curriculum). Current time constraints and limits on financial and human resources may make the addition of another course difficult.

In addition to integrating components of family violence into health professional education, the literature also suggests incorporating multidisciplinary resources into training efforts. Given the complexity of family violence as a medical and social issue, no amount of training will allow health professionals alone to solve the problems of family violence. Education should include community-based professionals such as law enforcement, legal services, victim advocacy, batterer intervention, elder services, and child protection experts (Alpert et al., 1998). Brandt (1997) pointed out that a curriculum that involves a variety of professionals "models respect and collaboration, attributes that are essential to developing an effective team approach to caring for victims of violence" (p. S55), thus allowing students the opportunity to negotiate community-specific roles and competencies. This point was reiterated by the Committee on the Assessment of Family Violence Intervention Programs (NRC and IOM, 1998, pp. 261-262).

The Alaska Family Violence Prevention Project offers an important example of collaborative work (http://www.hss.state.ak.us/dph/mcfh/domestic violence/Backgnd.htm). Since 1993, the project has developed and provided community-based training to health care and other service professionals, including those in law, protective services, and education, and to advocates for victims of intimate partner violence throughout Alaska. In addition, the Alaska project is involved in the development of a statewide plan for a comprehensive health care system response to intimate partner violence. Other models of collaboration also exist. For example, the Pennsylvania Coalition Against Domestic Violence has developed a program to coordinate community and justice system responses to intimate partner violence (http://www.pcadv.org/coalition.html, June 4, 2001). Such collaborative programs have not yet been evaluated.

The Use of Systems Change Models

While research indicates that education that merely imparts knowledge is often insufficient to lead to improved skills, changed practices, and improved patient outcomes, a consensus is emerging that other strategies are more effective. These strategies are integral to the broader view of continuing medical education described by Davis and colleagues (Davis, Thomson et al., 1992; Davis, O'Brien et al., 1999). Multifaceted, skill-building, practice-enabling strategies that make the identification and receipt of services a routine part of care when combined with feedback mechanisms, including positive reinforcement (for health professionals or patients), have the highest success rates (Bero et al., 1998; Berwick and Nolan, 1998; Davis et al., 1995; Davis, O'Brien et al., 1999; Haynes et al., 1984; Oxman et al., 1995; Shekelle et al., 2000; Thompson, 1996; Thomson et al., 2001a, 2001b, 2001c).

Intervention planning models that are conceptually based provide a typology for categorizing intervention components, in addition to their more customary use in planning interventions (DHHS, 1994; Curry and Kim, 1999; Goodman, 1999; Green and Kreuter, 1991, 1999; Thompson, 1996; Walsh and McPhee, 1992). The exact planning model chosen is important but not paramount. The precede/proceed model (see Figure 6.3) offers one useful example of a planning model (Green and Kreuter, 1991, 1999). It specifies three categories of factors (predisposing, enabling, and reinforcing) supporting behavior change.[3]

Predisposing factors influence a person's willingness to change (i.e., barrier identification and other factors); the possession of and the confidence in (sense of self-efficacy) his or her skills to perform a task; the providers' knowledge, attitudes, and beliefs; and personal health behaviors or experiences. Enabling factors, such as supporting policies or computer systems, are environmental factors at the practice, organization, or community level that make change possible. Reinforcing measures, such as the right incentives or measurement and feedback, can amplify the intervention. The McMaster-Toronto group used this model to categorize the interventions that they considered to be part of the broader view of continuing medical education (Davis, Thomson et al., 1992).

Recognizing that passive conveyance of information in writing or by course is generally an ineffective educational strategy (Bero et al., 1998; Davis, Thomson et al., 1995; Shekelle et al., 2000), the committee sought evidence on effective strategies. Employing the precede/proceed model (Green and Kreuter, 1991, 1999), the committee categorized interventions to change practitioner behavior, both of the formal continuing medical education variety and those encompassed in a broader view of continuing education. Table 6.2 provides a list of potential "tools for change" for the precede/proceed planning model chosen, but they can also be applied to other models. The tools listed are those for which there is some evidence of effectiveness. For interventions directed to predisposing factors of health professionals, there is solid support in the literature for measuring and addressing barriers, academic detailing (i.e., a maneuver derived from the practices of drug salespersons, consisting of a series of brief informa-

---

[3]See the web site for Lawrence Green (http://www.lgreen.net/precede.htm) for over 850 applications of the precede/proceed model to a wide range of health conditions.

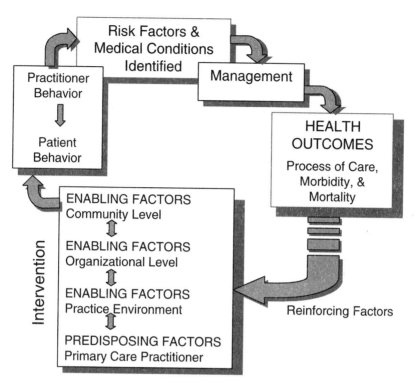

FIGURE 6.3 Conceptual basis for the intervention: precede/proceed model. SOURCE: Thompson (1996). Reprinted with permission.

tional encounters that are built into the practitioner's daily appointment schedule), and the use of interactive educational meetings. The evidence for the use of opinion leaders and cooperation/collaboration among health professionals is less substantial. There is firm evidence to support the use of financial incentives and reminders as enablers of change in patient outcomes. The use of posters is less solidly grounded. The evidence for decision support for providers, including computerized support and reminders, is solid. The evidence for the use of checklists, flow sheets, health questionnaires, and chart stickers is less well established. The evidence for process redesign is beginning to emerge.

At the organizational level, interventions that make the identification of the need for and the delivery of services routine, the use of rules and policies, and the engagement of top management are supported by research (see Shekelle et al., 2000). The use of clinical computing systems to drive the care process is developing rapidly and holds much promise for the future. There is moderately solid evidence for the use of measurement and feedback, financial incentives for

TABLE 6.2 Continuing Education to Change Behavior: What Works?

Interventions directed to predisposing factors: changing health professionals' knowledge, attitudes, and beliefs

■ Measuring and addressing barriers at the outset	Basch, 1987; Ward et al., 1991; Davis, Thomson et al., 1992, 1995; Grol, 1997; Haines and Donald, 1998; Haynes and Haines, 1998; Shekelle et al., 2000
■ Interactive educational meetings: small-group training with role playing; start-and-stop action videos; interactive role modeling	Wenrich et al., 1971; Eisenberg, 1982; Stross et al., 1983; Rich et al., 1985; Maiman et al., 1988; Davis, Thomson et al., 1992; Katon et al., 1995; Davis, O'Brien et al., 1999
■ Academic detailing	Davis, Thomson et al., 1995; Bero et al., 1998; Thomson et al., 2001a
■ Use of opinion leaders	Becker, 1970; Haynes et al., 1984; Davis, Thomson et al., 1995; Bero et al., 1998; Berwick and Nolan, 1998; Thomson et al., 2001a; Larson, 1999
■ Cooperation/collaboration between the different professionals involved	Berwick and Nolan, 1998; Shekelle et al., 2000

Interventions directed to environmental enabling factors

For patients:

■ Financial incentives	Shekelle et al., 2000
■ Reminders	Larson et al., 1979, 1982; Thompson, 1986; McDowell et al., 1986; Mullooly, 1987; Leininger et al., 1996; Brimberry, 1988; Shekelle et al., 2000
■ Posters in clinical areas	Lane et al., 1991; Savage, 1991

For health professionals:

■ Practice environment—clinical decision support	
■ Computerized decision support	Bero et al., 1998; Haynes and Haines, 1998
■ Checklists, flow sheets	Cohen et al., 1982; Prislin et al., 1986; Madlon-Kay, 1987; Cheney and Ramsdell, 1987; Shank et al., 1989; Dietrich et al., 1992; Johns et al., 1992
■ Health questionnaires	Thompson et al., 2000
■ Reminders	Barnett et al., 1983; McDonald et al., 1984; Tierney et al., 1986; McPhee et al., 1991; Rind et al., 1994; Davis, Thomson et al., 1995; Oxman et al., 1995; Overhage et al., 1996; Shekelle et al., 2000
■ Chart stickers	Cohen et al., 1987, 1989; Solberg et al., 1990

TABLE 6.2 Continued

■ Practice environment—process redesign	Pommerenke and Dietrich, 1992a, 1992b; Berwick, 1996, 1998; Berwick and Nolan, 1998; Nelson et al., 1998
■ The Plan, Do, Study Act (PDSA) cycle and others	
■ Clear roles	
■ Patient flow	
■ Organized follow-up	
■ Organizational environment—to make identification of the need for and delivery of the services a routine part of care	Shekelle et al., 2000
■ Rules or policies	McGowan and Finland, 1974; Durbin et al., 1981; Vayda and Mindell, 1982; Ruchlin et al., 1982; Martin et al., 1982; Gryskiewicz and Detmer, 1983; Wong et al., 1983
■ Top management support, such as enlisting the aid of the CEO	Shekelle et al., 2000
■ Clinical computing systems	Thompson, 1996; Nelson et al., 1998
Interventions designed to reinforce the program	
■ Measurement and feedback	Schroeder et al., 1973; Griner, 1979; Hillman et al., 1979; Young, 1980; Check, 1980; Eisenberg and Williams, 1981; Myers and Schroeder, 1981; Eisenberg, 1982; Rosser, 1983; Thompson et al., 1983; Wong et al., 1983; Fineberg et al., 1983; Haynes et al., 1984; Winickoff et al., 1984; Gehlbach et al., 1984; Marton et al., 1985; McPhee et al., 1989; Nattinger et al., 1989; Oxman et al., 1995
■ Financial incentives for professionals	Larson, 1999
■ Requirement for accreditation measurement: Healthplan Employer Data and Information Set (HEDIS) and other accrediting organizational requirements	Dalzell, 1998, 1999; Eddy, 1998

health professionals, and accreditation-driven measurement of care, such as the Healthplan Employer Data and Information Set (HEDIS).

Creating and Sustaining Behavior Change Through Systems Approaches: Case Studies from the Field

As reviews of continuing medical education illustrate, conventional continuing education workshops using lectures alone have shown little effectiveness in improving practice or even increasing knowledge that is retained over the long term. However, when a systematic approach is used for the application of information, positive effects on health outcomes can be achieved. Three examples of the process and tools used in systems successes are described below.

Example 1. The University of Virginia Institute of Law, Psychiatry & Public Policy had been involved for some time in training community mental health professionals about forensic issues (Melton et al., 1985). However, information was acquired, retained, and applied only after a system was put into place that included a joint memorandum from the state authorities about payment for evaluations, drafting of model orders, and meetings with key court constituencies to allay concerns about the quality of community-based evaluations. After those steps were taken, in just a few days of didactic workshops, the community clinicians acquired a level of forensic expertise commensurate with professionals in the field, and their reports were evaluated by legal authorities as substantially superior to those produced by hospital-based forensic clinicians. Furthermore, the clinicians expanded their expertise on their own, and they began to be used as experts on issues that were not included in the original training.

Example 2. The domestic violence prevention project at Kaiser Permanente, Northern California, utilizes the precede/proceed planning model and involves an assortment of tools for change in their program to improve the identification and management of family violence.

•   **Predisposing factors** are addressed through a training program for the team of health care providers, including small group training with role modeling and role playing, reinforced by video presentation.

•   **Enabling factors** in the clinic practice environment include posters, brochures, member wallet cards, provider toolkits with checklists and assessment forms, referral information, and linkages to community advocacy groups. Safe telephone numbers for subsequent contact with victims are elicited at the time of identification.

•   **Reinforcing factors** include departmental meetings with feedback and process measurement data and pay incentives for performance.

This program addresses personal and environmental factors in patient care and encompasses some of the multifaceted strategies that have higher success rates for behavior change.

Example 3. At Group Health Cooperative, the approach, funded by grants, includes use of the precede/proceed planning model and, to the maximum extent possible, the application of evidence-based intervention components.

• **Predisposing factors** were addressed by provider team training for the entire team for two half days. The training used role modeling and role playing. Start-and-stop action videos were used. Opinion leaders were recruited and received additional training.

• **Enabling factors** included placing and replacing posters in the reception areas, cue cards for providers, two questions about intimate partner violence incorporated on physical exam questionnaires and information pamphlets for patients placed in the bathrooms. The care guideline for intimate partner violence was placed on the cooperative's internal web site.

• **Booster sessions** included four additional training sessions conducted at each of the clinics. The opinion leaders helped in the conduct of these additional sessions. A newsletter containing clinic-level results and new information from the literature was circulated on a regular basis. The results of this work have been published (Maiuro et al., 2000; Sugg et al., 1999; Thompson et al., 1998, 2000) and are now being adapted for system-wide application.

The Melton et al. (1985) study and the Kaiser Permanente and Group Health Cooperative initiatives provide examples of systematic efforts to communicate a specific body of knowledge and to integrate it into ongoing processes of care.

Another strategy is to develop an organizational culture that rewards ongoing searches for, and syntheses of, knowledge germane to practice. Learning organizations are typified by "hallway learning" (Merriam and Caffarella, 1999):

> The heart of the learning organization is the willingness of organizations to allow their employees and other stakeholders related to the organization to suspend and question the assumptions within which they operate, then create and examine new ways of solving organizational problems and means of operating. . . . Creating learning organizations could allow educators of adults, whether they are associated with formal or nonformal settings, to develop learning communities in which change is accepted as the norm and innovative practices are embraced. (p. 44)

A climate of reflective practice is highly consistent with the general movement toward evidence-based health practice (see discussion below). Such an approach may be particularly important in relation to family violence for two reasons. First, family violence and the resulting response by the community are unusually complex phenomena. Not only is there a multitude of causes and correlates to be considered in interaction, but numerous community institutions (e.g., law enforcement, social services, health and mental health services, victim assistance programs, housing agencies, grassroots organizations) have roles in responding to the problem. Second, family violence is a politically charged topic (Melton, 1987; Nelson, 1984) in which advocates (often including health professionals themselves) have strongly held beliefs about what "everybody knows" (or should know).

INFLUENCING FAMILY VIOLENCE EDUCATION IN THE FUTURE

Based on the committee's understanding of the adult learning, continuing education, and systems change literature, it suggests and explores two emerging forces in health care, which have the potential to influence the training of health professionals about family violence. These forces are evidence-based practice and routine outcome measurement and reporting, as exemplified by the Healthplan Employer Data Information Set (HEDIS). The committee considers the following questions: What are the effects of these movements, when encompassed in a broader view of continuing education as described above, on teaching for the health professions in general? Does their adoption change health professionals' behavior or lead to improved patient outcomes? What do we know about their specific application to family violence? What might their effects be in the future?

Evidence-Based Practice

Evidence-based practice, also known as evidence-based medicine, can be broadly defined as the attempt to take the best-available scientific evidence and apply it to day-to-day practice.[4] It involves converting information needs into focused questions, identifying and critically appraising the evidence available to answer each question, applying the results in clinical practice, and evaluating the clinical application. Evidence-based practice can be understood as "a shift in thinking from an authoritarian model to an authoritative model" (Liberati et al., 1999, p. 363).

The formal evidence-based practice movement is relatively new, but the roots can be traced back to the late 1960s (see McKeown, 1968). Major advances in the approach have been made in Canada (Evidence-Based Medicine Working Group, 1992), the United Kingdom (Guyatt et al., 1997; Sackett et al., 1996), and the United States (e.g., Eddy, 1996). The intense interest in the subject is demonstrated by a web site devoted to definitions of evidence-based medicine (http://www.shef.ac.uk/scharr/ir/defe.html). In addition, a sizeable number of electronic databases devoted to evidence-based practice have emerged; three examples

---

[4]The committee uses evidence-based practice synonymously with evidence-based medicine, judging these concepts to be applicable to all health care professionals.

include the Cochrane Collaboration (http://hiru.mcmaster.ca/COCHRANE); the Centre for Evidence-Based Medicine (http://cebm.jr2.ox.ac.uk); and the Agency for Healthcare Research and Quality Clinical Practice Guidelines (http://www.ahrq.gov/query/query.htm).

As evidence of the recent interest and rapid growth in evidence-based practice, a search of the National Library of Medicine, using the term *evidence-based medicine* either as a medical subject heading (MeSH) or as a text word, revealed no citations from 1966 through 1991, 33 from 1992 through 1996, and 3,328 from 1997 through the first quarter of 2000. The increased interest in evidence-based practice has been worldwide (Dickson et al., 1998; Garner et al., 1998). In the United States, the Agency for Healthcare Research and Quality has created evidence-based practice centers across the country, sponsored guideline development, and established a guideline clearinghouse (Geyman, 1998). The Centers for Disease Control and Prevention has established a task force to develop evidence-based recommendations for the practice of public health (Pappaioanou and Evans, 1998; Task Force on Community Preventive Services, 2000).

Evidence-Based Practice in Health Professional Education

With the major new focus in the literature on rules of evidence, experts agree that evidence-based practice is an increasingly important concept in continuing medical education and medical school curricula (Michaud et al., 1996; Geyman, 1998; Estabrooks, 1998). It is a focused approach to interpretation and clinical translation of research findings that provides a valuable tool for managing the knowledge base of medicine by synthesizing and compressing the explosion in available information—over 1 million journal publications a year (Berg et al., 1997; Culpepper and Gilbert, 1999). Straus and Sackett (1998) suggest that using evidence-based practice and other summary sources could cut the clinical literature reading burden by 98 percent.

Furthermore, research demonstrates that textbooks are sometimes systematically biased, often inaccurate, and always outdated (Antman et al., 1992). These findings provide additional impetus for incorporating evidence-based practice into teaching curricula.

Evidence-based practice is beginning to influence medical school curricula and graduate student medical education in a wide range of teaching hospitals, practice settings, and geographic areas of the United States and Canada (Barnett et al., 1999; Chessare, 1998; Green and Ellis, 1997; Grimes, 1995; Grimes, et al., 1998; Hudak et al., 1997; McCarthy and Zubialde, 1997; Neal et al., 1999; Norman and Shannon, 1998; Poses, 1999; Reilly and Lemon, 1997; Sackett and Straus, 1998; Wadland et al., 1999). Effects on the curricula for other health professionals include reports of its development and use for public health (Brownson et al., 1999), nursing (French, 1999), behavioral scientists (medical social workers, psychologists, and counselors; Gambril, 1999), and dentistry (Newman, 1998).

However, general surveys on the degree of curricular institutionalization of evidence-based practice suggest that there is still a long way to go. A survey of 417 internal medicine programs showed that 37 percent of respondents had a freestanding evidence-based practice curriculum, while only 33 percent provided best evidence or the Cochrane Collaboration in their programs, 51-54 percent provided on-site electronic information, and 31-45 percent provided site-specific faculty development in evidence-based practice (Green, 2000). There were only two data-based studies found on evidence-based practice from nursing, (Estabrooks, 1998; Morin et al., 1999), both suggesting that quality evidence is little recognized or used for decision making in nursing, in spite of many calls in their literature to increase evidence-based practice.

Effects on Provision of Care and Patient Outcomes

The impact of evidence-based practice on health care decisions, provision of services, and patient outcomes remains unclear (Jadad and Haynes, 1998). Norman and Shannon (1998) performed a systematic review of seven studies with a comparison group and reporting measures of performance from 1966 through 1995 and found that evidence-based practice implemented in undergraduate programs resulted in significant gains in knowledge, as assessed by written tests of epidemiology, a mean gain of 17 percent, and a standard deviation of 4 percent. Studies based at the residency level showed minuscule mean gains in knowledge (1.3 percent), leading to the conclusion that the knowledge gain from evidence-based practice was not demonstrably applied in clinical practice. A subsequent search (1996-2000) identified eight studies that addressed the link between teaching the general principles of evidence-based practice (not disease-specific) and health professionals' knowledge, behavior, process of care, and patient outcomes (Bazarian et al., 1999; Green and Ellis, 1997; Humphris, 1999; Ibbotson et al., 1998; Michaud et al., 1996; Slawson and Shaughnessy, 1999; Wadland et al., 1999; Wainwright et al., 1999). Two studies indicate effects of the use of evidence-based practice.[5] The results of one study were moderately suggestive of a positive effect on the use of literature for patient care decisions and perceived competence, using a quasi-experimental group design (Green and Ellis, 1997). In another study (Bazarian et al., 1999) using a quasi-experimental design with before and after measurements, the results were negative. However, the intervention was not strong (a 1-hour journal club that met

---

[5]Using an adaptation of the study design quality rating criteria developed by the Centers for Disease Control and Prevention (Briss et al., 2000; Zaza et al., 2000), these two studies were deemed to be at least moderately appropriate in design and execution for assessing effect.

monthly for 1 year), the numbers were small ($N = 32$), and the outcome assessment measured test-taking skills, not application of evidence-based practice skills.

Potential Influences

The effects of the evidence-based practice movement on teaching about family violence are presently unclear. The drive to evidence-based practice appears likely to lead to increased interest in proving the effectiveness of various family violence interventions, since present knowledge is limited as to what works beyond the short term. Information on the effects of intervention as measured from the patient perspective is needed, especially in the longer term. The drive for evidence-based practice could serve as a stimulus for effectiveness research on family violence interventions. Conversely, it is also possible that it may have a negative effect on family violence teaching in some locales, due to the current lack of evidence regarding the ideal content of health professional education on family violence. Research shows, however, that even in areas in which best practice standards are well established, incorporating them into practice is extremely slow and uneven (IOM, 2001).

The Healthplan Employer Data and Information Set

The Healthplan Employer Data and Information Set (HEDIS) is a standard set of performance measures designed to provide purchasers and consumers with information on effectiveness of care. It is used by the National Committee for Quality Assurance (NCQA) to compare the performance of managed health care plans and to provide health care plans and professionals with data needed to improve quality of care (Dalzell, 1998; Hill and Spoeri, 1997; National Committee for Quality Control, 1999; Rulon and Sica, 1997). Since the early 1990s, the use of HEDIS measures as a quality index has grown rapidly. By 1999, 247 health care organizations encompassing 410 health plans and 52 million people were reported to be using the HEDIS performance measures (National Committee for Quality Control, 1999). According to Eddy (1998):

> Once performance measurement is launched, its importance can be profound. When the [National Committee for Quality Assurance] publishes a HEDIS measure, the effect is as if every health plan in the country went on a retreat to set their clinical goals for the coming year, and all came back with the same answer. I cannot think of a more powerful single instrument for shifting healthcare resources than a national set of performance measurements would be. . . . Science has no effect until it is properly implemented, and measuring performance is one of the most powerful tools for implementation. (p. 8)

These views are corroborated by others (Bader et al., 1999; Epstein, 1998; Harris et al., 1998; Hill and Spoeri, 1997; Kelly, 1997).

Health plans make major improvements in care after new HEDIS measures are devised (National Committee for Quality Control, 1999). For example, at the Group Health Cooperative, after HEDIS measurement was instituted, complete immunization in 2-year-olds improved from 63 percent in early 1993 to 91 percent by 1995 (Thompson, 1996). These changes were driven by the measurement, feedback, and education and training activities for health care professionals of all stripes engendered by the institution of HEDIS measures for immunizations. There are other published examples on immunization (Hughes, 1997; Family Violence Education, 1996), management of hypertension (Elliott et al., 1999), and diabetes care (Peters et al., 1996). Some health professionals claim that "in ten years, we are going to look back at these measures and we will say that their introduction had as much public health significance as almost anything we have been involved in in our careers" (Dalzell, 1999, p. 57).

HEDIS measurement and evidence-based practice appear to be directly linked in that most HEDIS measures are based on health conditions posing a significant disease burden and for which intervention can be expected to make a positive difference. The future of HEDIS will increasingly entail its use as a measurement system for the implementation status of evidence-based guidelines and programs. HEDIS measurement and evidence-based practice will become increasingly synergistic. The synergism may well express itself as a new HEDIS process of care measure for family violence. Such a move would provide a major stimulus for training efforts.

CONCLUSIONS

Although core competencies and teaching methods in family violence education are developing, both their foundation and their effect on professional behavior and patient outcomes are largely unexamined in the research literature. The committee is not able to identify a single educational model but recognizes key areas of overlap in curriculum content that have emerged among existing family violence curricula. These suggest starting points for core competencies that can then be evaluated for effectiveness. In addition, research on teaching techniques now employed for other content areas suggests possibilities for family violence. A few promising training initiatives for health professionals in family violence merit additional attention.

The committee makes the following observations based primarily on reports of expert and consensus opinion and experience:

- **Content areas exist in which core competencies for health professional training on family violence can be developed. These areas include: (1) the identification, assessment, and documentation of abuse and neglect, (2) interventions to ensure victim safety, (3) rec-**

ognition of cultural and value factors affecting family violence, (4) understanding the applicable legal and forensic responsibilities of health care professionals, and (5) action to prevent family violence.

Research is needed to verify that this educational content, perceived to be necessary, is in fact necessary, as well as to identify other educational needs to enable health professionals to respond to family violence. In addition, agreement as to the content of specific core competencies and who should develop them is needed.

• **The competency necessary will vary with professional roles, functions, and interests.**

The appropriate level of competency for a given health care provider is a function of an individual clinician's roles and responsibilities in the clinical and educational setting. Some basic competencies regarding family violence may serve as a foundation of best practice for further specified, advanced, and leadership competencies.

Based on reviews of the scientific evidence base, the committee makes the following observations:

• **Studies demonstrate that traditional didactic education that merely imparts knowledge is often insufficient to lead to improved skills, changed practices, and improved patient outcomes. Research on behavior change and adult learning principles indicates that teaching methods that employ multifaceted, skill-building, practice-enabling strategies are more effective.**

• **Research on debiasing may provide helpful methods for overcoming cognitive biases that result in systematic errors in judgment and may affect clinical decision making related to family violence.**

Cognitive biases may have particular effects on the identification of victims and attributions of risk in cases of actual or suspected family violence. Research on debiasing suggests that such errors could be reduced if training programs on family violence included exercises in which trainees compared their own judgments with statistical information and the integration of feedback into systems of reflective practice, as in learning organizations and evidence-based health care.

• **Systems change models that are based on the science of behavior change may be useful in planning educational interventions for health professionals tailored to the issue of family violence.**

Systems change models build on research about effective behavior change and adult learning. A number of systems change models exist, generally involving the identification of areas in which change is needed, determining objectives for change, trying out approaches for achieving those changes, and testing the impact of those approaches. Such approaches are being applied to the issue of education and training for health professionals in the identification and management of family violence (Campbell et al., 2000; Thompson et al., 2000). The use of these initiatives may result in changes in health professionals' knowledge and practices and the health outcomes of their patients.

•   **Healthplan Employer Data Information Set (HEDIS) measures for health care outcomes and the use of evidence-based practice may have potential for improving health professionals' identification and care processes for family violence.**

HEDIS measurement, in its short existence, has had profound effects on the behavior of health care delivery organizations and on practitioners. For example, managed care organizations have made major changes to meet new requirements and training health care personnel is part of this process. Currently, there are no HEDIS measures for family violence. The committee's review of what is known about the health professional's response to family violence at this time indicates insufficient evidence on which to base the development and adoption of HEDIS measures for family violence. Given the impact of HEDIS measures, however, the development of a standard set of measures for effective practice for family violence appears to have the potential to drive education, practice, and measurement changes for this issue. Evidence-based practice currently appears to be another strong and emerging force in health care professional education. The linkage between HEDIS measurement and evidence-based practice may increasingly drive the use of HEDIS or HEDIS-like measurement into the education of health care professionals.

7

Priorities for Health Professional Training on Family Violence

The committee's review of the current state of health professional training on family violence reveals that some efforts are being made to train health professionals to respond to family violence; however, the evidence base provided by the available information overall is too thin to indicate clear directions for training. Existing curricula are quite diverse; in general, they tend to focus on only one type of violence, target only specific health professionals or students, and usually lack evaluation. As a result, little evidence exists to indicate what, when, or how to teach health professionals about responding to family violence, the success of current educational programs, or the impact of the training on victims of family violence.

BUILDING A FIELD

Several reports (U.S. Advisory Board on Child Abuse and Neglect, 1990, 1991, 1993; NRC and IOM, 1998) over the last decade have eloquently described the paucity of research findings to inform practice in the area of family violence. This report is not the first to note difficulties in addressing the issue. For example, the U.S. Advisory Board on Child Abuse and Neglect in its 1991 (p. 109) report summarized the state of research in the field:

• Although progress has been made, child maltreatment may still be the most underresearched social problem.
• Research on child maltreatment has grown unsystematically. When major findings have occurred, there have been few efforts to pursue them.

- Public support for research on child abuse and neglect may actually have fallen over the last 15 years.
- There is a serious shortage of researchers in the field and some important researchers have left the field.
- Some particular research topics important to the development of effective prevention and treatment programs have been especially understudied.

Another study, by the Education Development Center and Children's Hospital and funded by the Robert Wood Johnson Foundation, examined the health care system's response to family violence in five communities. It found that, despite recognition in the health care community that family violence is an important problem, health care systems are not playing a central role in responding to it. Health care professionals pay little attention to the identification, treatment, follow-up, or prevention of family violence, and those who do are often marginalized (De Vos et al., 1992).

These previous reports and studies raise the question of how to build the field of family violence in order to create the capacity to address the problem effectively. A number of approaches are possible. Efforts may focus on producing scholars, supporting research, developing training capacity, encouraging collaborative efforts, or some combination of these goals. To facilitate the growth of scholars in particular research areas, for example, the National Institutes of Health offer awards called K Awards for individual career development in new areas of research. Health professional organizations and federal agencies have developed subspecialty training to develop clinical scholars in particular fields (see Chapter 6 for a discussion of the developmental pediatrics and adolescent medicine subspecialties). Private foundations sponsor fellowships to develop clinical scholars in specific areas. Examples of these include the Robert Wood Johnson Clinical Scholars program and the W.K. Kellogg Foundation Fellowships in Health Policy Research. To encourage research, a number of federal agencies and private foundations have offered grant programs in family violence, calling for research proposals and funding a select few. This research support has been offered through grant programs that specify topics or allow investigators to propose topics within general categories. Other efforts have the primary goal of developing training programs and providing training. For example, geriatric education centers were created to develop, support, and provide health professionals with training in geriatrics.

Each of these approaches offers advantages and disadvantages. The benefits of a focus on developing scholars include the creation of a core of individuals who are competent to handle working with family violence victims and possess the knowledge and experience to provide training to other health care professionals. However, this approach is limited in the number of scholars that can be produced; other health care professionals and interested parties in need of training may not have access to these experts. Developing research opportunities can generate information that all health professionals need in order to address family violence. But the applicability of the research is limited without dissemination and training, especially given the overwhelming amount of health care research being published. Usually, research centers not only conduct and fund research but also disseminate their findings. They do not usually provide training, however. Education centers can fill this gap, but they may be dependent on other mechanisms for the research on which the training programs are to be based.

No definitive evidence indicates the best approach to building a field. The committee's examination of existing mechanisms suggests that each appears to have arisen from the needs perceived by those working in the field or other interested parties. Individual or organizational champions work to engender financial and political support from government and private funders. In recommending an approach for the field of family violence, the committee explored suggestions from previous reports and studies on family violence as well as reports of successful approaches in other fields.

A brief review of efforts to develop the field of family violence reveals some consensus on the needs of the field and how they might be addressed. For example, the U.S. Advisory Board on Child Abuse and Neglect called for the development of a new data system; creation of a U.S. Department of Health and Human Services-wide research advisory committee; and a primary or lead role for the National Institute of Mental Health in research planning, implementation, and coordination, as well as in providing research training and career development awards. The advisory board also recommended establishment of state and regional resource centers for training, consultation, policy analysis, and research on child protection.

A few months after the advisory board's report was issued, the commissioner for children, youth, and families (who had received the 1990 and 1991 reports of the advisory board) asked the National Academies "to convene an expert panel to develop a research agenda for future studies of child maltreatment." The report, *Understanding Child Abuse and Neglect,* made a series of wide-ranging recommendations, many of which expanded on the advisory board's recommendations. Importantly, the panel stated as a research priority (NRC, 1993):

> When a sufficient research budget is available to support an expanded corps of research investigators from multiple disciplines, multidisciplinary research centers should be established to foster collaboration in research on child maltreatment. The purpose of these centers should be to assemble a corps of researchers and practitioners focused on selected aspects of child abuse and neglect, including medical, psychological, social, legal, and cultural aspects of child abuse and neglect. The proposed centers could provide a critical mass in developing long-term research studies and evaluating major demonstration projects to build on and expand the existing base of empirical knowledge. The proposed centers should have a regional distribution, be associated with major academic centers, have the capacity to educate professionals of various disciplines, and launch

major research efforts. Examples of the cancer and diabetes centers funded by the National Institutes of Health could serve as models, as could the Prevention Intervention Research Centers of the National Institute of Mental Health. (pp. 358-359)

In 1993, another group of researchers, government officials, law enforcement professionals, social service providers, and health care professionals convened at the Wingspread Conference Center in Racine, Wisconsin, to discuss the research and policy needed to address family violence. This group recognized the need to identify and analyze existing evaluations of relevant programs to inform future practice. The National Research Council and the Institute of Medicine established the Committee on the Assessment of Family Violence Interventions to do just that. That committee's report noted a lack of rigorous evaluation, insufficient resources, and failure of the research and practice communities to collaborate (NRC and IOM, 1998). It recommended that evaluation be integral to all family violence interventions and that policy incentives and leadership foster coordination among policy, program, and research agendas.

A study of the response of health professionals to family violence in five communities resulted in similar recommendations (De Vos et al., 1992). That report recommended improving victim access to care, increasing health professionals' knowledge and improving attitudes, implementing institutional policies that provide incentives for improving detection and care, improving coordination among health care institutions and community services, developing the knowledge base on family violence, and stimulating health professionals organizations to address the issue.

In the years since these reports were published, their dozens of recommendations have largely been ignored, although the problems identified have not abated. One analysis suggests that a lack of champions in the legislative and executive branches of the federal government and an inability to create for the public an ongoing sense of crisis have contributed to the inattention these recommendations have received (Krugman, 1997). According to this analysis, a coherent collaborative policy, leadership at the national level, and a continuing program of research and evaluation are necessary to develop the field.

There is significant correspondence between the needs of the field and all these proposals for addressing them. Commonly noted needs include the need to build the knowledge base, to evaluate programs, to develop scholars, to provide training, to increase health professionals' response, to facilitate collaborative efforts, and to develop ongoing support for the field.

In the committee's judgment, confronting the long history of ignored recommendations and the broad array of needs requires a multipronged approach. Resources should be focused in a way that provides a locus of attention to the problem; facilitates interdisciplinary collaboration; bridges science, practice, and policy in the various disciplines, professions, and agencies that address family violence; and establishes systems for preprofessional and continuing education.

Taking such a comprehensive approach, family violence can become an integral part of education, the relevant service systems, and communities of research. Individual research grant and training programs can help, but they cannot individually meet the broad goals that have been repeatedly described in this and previous reports. The committee recommends a more comprehensive approach involving the development of education and research centers, greater responsibility for the health care sector in health professional training, increased attention to evaluation, and improved collaboration.

This chapter summarizes the conclusions the committee drew from our review of available information. Detailed recommendations based on these conclusions suggest ways to improve the training of health professionals to respond to family violence. These conclusions and recommendations are congruent with those offered in previous reports but are focused intensively on health professional training.

CONCLUSIONS

Responding to its charge, the committee's conclusions address what is known about health professionals' training needs to respond to family violence, available training programs and program evaluation, and particular challenges to and opportunities for training development and implementation. Each of the previous chapters includes specific conclusions relevant to its content. What follows is a summary of these conclusions.

• **While family violence is understood to be widespread across the United States and to have significant health consequences, its full effects on society and the health care system have not been adequately studied or documented.**

The available data are inadequate to determine the full magnitude and severity of family violence in society or its impact on the health care professions. Furthermore, few studies describe the total and marginal patterns of utilization or the costs of health care, or the cross-sectional and longitudinal effects on health status from the point of view of the patient (or victim). The results of such studies could indicate the full extent to which the health care system and professionals encounter family violence and the health care needs of victims. A better understanding of the baseline problems, health care needs, and costs associated with family violence could reinforce the need for health professionals' attention to the issue, provide guidance as to how to respond, and inform and improve the education and practice of health care professionals.

• **Variation in the definitions, data sources, and methods used in research on family violence has resulted in inconsistent and unclear**

evidence about its magnitude and severity, as well as its effects on the health care system and society.

The definitions, data sources, and research methods used for research on family violence vary from study to study. As noted in previous National Research Council and Institute of Medicine reports (NRC, 1993, 1996; NRC and IOM 1998), definitional clarity for family violence terminology is necessary to understand the extent to which data can be reliably compared between studies or reliably generalized to other situations. The same holds true for clarity and consistency in data sources and research methods. Clear and consistent definitions, data sources, and methods are important for developing the evidence base to detail the prevalence of the problem as encountered in health care settings and the health care needs of victims, as well as to indicate the opportunities and roles of health professionals to address family violence. Such an evidence base is necessary to provide a foundation for effective health professional education.

- **Curricula on family violence for health professionals do exist, but the content is incomplete, instruction time is generally minimal, the content and teaching methods vary, and the issue is not well integrated throughout their educational experience. Moreover, studies indicate that health professionals and students in the health professions often perceive curricula on family violence to be inadequate or ineffective.**

Although a number of curricula exist, training does not appear to be consistently offered and is usually of short duration at only one point in the training program, is usually targeted to one professional group, and is frequently limited to one type of family violence. Elder maltreatment appears to be the most neglected type of family violence in existing curricula. Health care professionals who have received training on family violence frequently describe it as insufficient (e.g., Biehler et al., 1996; Wright et al., 1999) or report that they cannot recall having had such training (e.g., Jones et al., 1997).

- **Evaluation of the effects of training has received insufficient attention. Few studies investigate whether curricula on family violence are having the desired impact on the delivery of health care to family violence victims. When evaluations are done, they often do not utilize the experimental designs necessary to provide an adequate understanding of effects.**

At present, a majority of studies appear to rely primarily on quasi-experimental research and short-term measurement of proximal effects and provider outcomes, such as increased knowledge and awareness of family violence. Evaluations, required by law, funding agencies, or sponsoring organizations often assess only the process by which a program is implemented or participant satisfaction, without attention to program effectiveness—or they focus on effects without considering implementation. Other experimental designs, particularly randomized experiments, would be useful in demonstrating the effects of training on health professionals' behavior or victims' health. Also helpful in improving understanding of the relationship between training and outcomes are high-quality quasi-experimental designs. Both could significantly improve the evidence base and its use to provide guidance as to what works best, for whom, and under what conditions.

- **In addition to effective training on family violence, a supportive environment appears to be critically important to producing desirable outcomes.**

The available evidence from evaluation studies indicates that an evaluated curriculum, while critical, is not sufficient to produce the desired outcomes. That is, having a proven curriculum will not ensure that health professionals receive the necessary training and adapt their practice behaviors. A commitment of time and resources is necessary to make attention to family violence a regular part of training and practice. Without such a supportive environment, the effects of training are likely to be short lived and may erode over time.

- **Core competencies for health professional training on family violence can be developed and tested based on similarities in the content of current training programs. The important content areas include: (1) identification, assessment, and documentation of abuse and neglect; (2) interventions to ensure victim safety; (3) recognition of culture and values as factors affecting family violence; (4) understanding of applicable legal and forensic responsibilities; and (5) prevention. The level of competency necessary will vary with professional roles, functions, and interests.**

Core competencies are areas of knowledge, skills, and attitudes that health care professionals must possess in order to provide effective health care to patients. Currently, no definitive, evidence-based set of core competencies exists. An examination of existing programs indicates some similarities in objectives, content, and teaching methods, suggesting some coherence in domains across disciplines in which core competencies could be developed or tested for health professional education. While the committee could find little research to determine specific core competencies and content, these content areas regularly appeared in existing curricula and in the literature on health professional training on family violence. In our view, these areas offer useful starting points for research to specify core competencies for health professional training and educational content that reflects stages of learning, educational setting, profession, specialty, intensity of educational need, and patient populations likely to be encountered. In addition, the specification of core competencies could facilitate the development of sound measures for assessing them. This, in turn, would lead to better measures for assessing outcomes and competencies in training evaluation studies.

- **Existing education theories about behavior change suggest useful teaching methods and approaches to planning educational interventions for health professionals tailored to the issue of family violence. These approaches include ways of changing behavior and practice in health care delivery systems, the use of techniques to address practitioners' biases or beliefs about victims, and the use of health care outcome measurement (e.g., Health Employer Data Information Set measures) to inform evidence-based practice.**

Studies demonstrate that traditional forms of didactic education intended to increase knowledge about a particular topic are insufficient to enhance skills and change clinical practice to improve patient outcomes. The research literature on behavior change and strategies and principles of adult learning indicate that teaching methods that employ multifaceted, skill-building, practice-enabling strategies are more effective at changing behavior in health care delivery. Such strategies involve interactive techniques, such as case discussion, role play, hands-on practice sessions, and guided clinical experiences and provide evaluative feedback to trainees about their behavior in these situations.

Evidence from research on continuing medical education further reveals that these teaching methods are effective at changing professionals' behavior and health care outcomes, particularly when they are supported and reinforced in both training and practice settings, when the outcomes associated with the trainee's behaviors are measured, and when the trainees are given positive feedback when positive outcomes are achieved (Bero et al., 1998; Berwick and Nolan 1998; Davis et al., 1995; Haynes et al., 1984; Oxman et al., 1995; Shekelle et al., 2000; Thompson, 1996; Thomson et al., 2001a, 2001b, 2001c).

Strategies—referred to as systems change models—for changing practices within institutions are based on findings about effective ways to change behavior. A number of such models exist, generally involving identifying areas in which change is needed, determining objectives for change, testing approaches for achieving those changes, assessing the impact of those approaches, and making further adjustments. Kaiser Permanente of Northern California, the Group Health Cooperative, and the University of Virginia have demonstrated success with the use of systems change models in health care institutions (Melton et al., 1985; Maiuro et al., 2000; Sugg et al., 1999; Thompson et al., 1998, 2000). A few managed care organizations and hospitals are beginning to apply such approaches to the education and training of health professionals to identify and manage cases involving family violence (Thompson et al., 2000; Campbell et al., 2000). Early experiences with these techniques are demonstrating positive effects.

In addition to efforts to change systems, techniques to reduce health professionals' biases—the assumptions health professionals have about who family violence victims are and why they are maltreated—may be useful in developing effective education on family violence. As with other professions that deal with family violence, cognitive biases held by health practitioners may have particular effects on the identification of victims and attributions of risk in cases of actual or suspected family violence. Research on techniques to address these assumptions or biases, known as "debiasing," suggests that errors in identifying victims and assessing risk could be reduced if training programs on family violence included exercises in which trainees compared their own judgments and assumptions about victims with data describing real victims.

Research on outcome measurement, such as measures included in the Healthplan Employer Data Information Set (HEDIS), and evidence-based practice suggest potential for the creation of a standard set of measures for effective practice for family violence. HEDIS measurement, in its short existence, has demonstrated profound effects on the behavior of health care delivery organizations and on practitioners (Bader et al., 1999; Eddy, 1998; Epstein, 1998; Harris et al., 1998; Hill and Spoeri, 1997; Kelly, 1997). For example, managed care organizations have made major changes to meet new requirements, and training of health care personnel is widely conducted as part of this process (National Committee for Quality Control, 1999). Examples of the success of HEDIS measures include changing health care delivery for immunizations (Hughes, 1997; Family Violence Education, 1996; Thompson, 1996), the management of hypertension (Elliott et al., 1999), and diabetes care (Peters et al., 1996). Currently, no HEDIS measures exist for diagnosing and treating family violence.

Evidence-based practice currently appears to be another strong and emerging force in health care professional education. Evidence-based practice is recognized as essential to ensure quality health care (e.g., Green and Ellis, 1997; Norman and Shannon, 1998). As it involves efforts to apply the best-available scientific evidence to day-to-day practice, the drive for it could serve as a stimulus for effectiveness research on family violence interventions. Yet research shows that even in areas in which best-practice standards are well established, incorporation into practice is extremely slow and uneven (IOM, 2001).

- **Challenges to developing, implementing, and sustaining training programs for health professionals on family violence include the nature of accreditation, licensure, and certification; characteristics of health professional organizations; views of stakeholder groups; attitudes of individual health professionals; and the existence of mandatory reporting laws and education requirements.**

A number of factors may influence whether or not as well as the extent to which family violence is included in health professional training. Accreditation, licensure, and certification requirements do not consistently and explicitly address family violence and thus do not appear to be significant influences encouraging such training for health professionals. Without such requirements, health professionals may perceive family violence education as unnecessary, and educators may have little incentive to provide it. The influence of other stakeholder groups, including advocates, victims, and payers, has not been studied and so it is difficult to gauge what impact they may have. For individual health professionals, as for other individuals, personal and professional factors may influence beliefs about the desirability of education about family violence and how such education is received and applied. Health care professionals have concerns regarding inadequate time or preparation, discomfort with dealing with family violence, and beliefs that it is a private issue in which they should not be involved (e.g., Sugg and Inui, 1992; Newberger, 1977; Cohen et al., 1997). Overcoming these concerns is another challenge to be addressed. In addition, health care professionals may themselves have had personal experience with victimization (e.g., Ellis, 1999) or be affected by trauma experienced by their patients ("vicarious traumatization"; McCann and Pearlman, 1990; Neumann and Gamble, 1995; Talbot et al., 1992). Training programs therefore need to be sensitive to health professionals' specific needs and concerns.

The committee was particularly mindful of the use and effects of mandatory reporting and education legislation. Reporting suspected abuse and neglect has become common in health practice (Zellman, 1990a), but some health care professionals express concerns that reporting can be more harmful than helpful to the victim. The advantages of mandatory reporting include the increased likelihood that the health care provider will respond to family violence, refer victims for social and legal services, and assist with perpetrator prosecution. However, with regard to intimate partner violence in particular (Rodriguez et al., 1999; Tilden et al., 1994), some health professionals and others voice concern that mandatory reporting is a breach in confidentiality that undermines autonomy, trust, and privacy in the health care setting (Kalichman and Craig, 1991; Kalichman et al., 1989; NRC and IOM, 1998; Rodriguez et al., 1998, 1999; Vulliamy and Sullivan, 2000; Warshaw and Ganley, 1998); interferes with efforts to ensure the safety of victims (Levine and Doueck, 1995; NRC and IOM, 1998; Rodriguez et al., 1998, 1999; Tilden et al., 1994; Warshaw and Ganley, 1998; Zellman, 1990b); serves to deter perpetrators from obtaining treatment (Berlin et al., 1991; Kalichman et al., 1994); precipitates violent retaliation by perpetrators (Gerbert et al., 1999; Gielen et al., 2001; Rodriguez et al., 1999); decreases victims' use of health care services (Gerbert et al., 1999; Rodriguez et al., 1999); and discourages inquiries by health care professionals who believe that if they do not ask, they have nothing to report (Gebert et al.,1999).

Although the relationship between mandatory reporting requirements and education is unclear, the committee found that existing curricula, particularly on child abuse and neglect, often focus in part or in whole on legal reporting requirements. While reporting requirements may be useful in promoting health professional education about screening and reporting family violence, it appears that existing curricula may focus on required reporting procedures to the detriment of health professionals' roles in treating, referring, and preventing family violence. A previous report of the National Research Council and Institute of Medicine, *Violence in Families,* recommended that "states initiate evaluations of their current reporting laws" and that they "refrain from enacting mandatory reporting laws for domestic violence until such systems have been tested and evaluated by research" (NRC and IOM, 1998, pp. 295-296). Such research continues to be necessary and should include the impact of reporting laws on health professional training.

A few states mandate family violence education for health professionals, but the committee could find no formal evaluations of the impact of the education provided in accordance with those laws. However, studies demonstrate that health professionals who have obtained any continuing education about child maltreatment (not necessarily mandated) are no more likely—and in some study samples are less likely—to report child abuse and neglect than are those who have not attended such training (Beck and Ogloff, 1995; Kalichman and Brosig, 1993; Reininger et al., 1995). In addition, the legal requirements tend to take the form of lecture-based programs that education research suggests have little effect on influencing practice behaviors (e.g., Davis et al., 1999). Mandated education requirements provide an opportunity for evaluation to determine whether changes and improvements in knowledge, attitudes, and skills related to family violence result from such requirements and whether they can be sustained over time; whether costs of care, severity of presenting health problems, case mix, morbidity, and mortality are affected; and whether any changes observed can be attributed to the education program itself.

- **Funding for research, education development and testing, and curricular evaluation on family violence is fragmented, and information about funding sources is not systematically available. No consistent federal sources of support for education research on family violence appear to exist.**

The fragmented information on funding is particularly difficult to access for researchers and educators and others attempting to develop and conduct research, design training and practice interventions, and evaluate programs. The information must be collected piecemeal from numerous web sites and federal agency officials, making it difficult to determine if and when funds are available. Furthermore, while the committee was able to identify some sources of funding for intervention and training, we could find no consistent sources for education research on family violence to design and test innovative and responsive models for health professional education or to evaluate existing models.

RECOMMENDATIONS

Recommendation 1: The secretary of the U.S. Department of Health and Human Services should be responsible for establishing new multidisciplinary education and research centers with the goal of advancing scholarship and practice in family violence. These centers should be charged with conducting research on the magnitude and impact of family violence on society and the health care system, conducting research on training, and addressing concerns regarding the lack of comparability in current research. The ultimate goal of these centers will be to develop training programs based on sound scientific evidence that prepare health professionals to respond to family violence.

In recommending the creation of education and research centers, the committee reiterates and builds on recommendations from previous reports on family violence (U.S. ABCAN, 1990, 1991; NRC, 1993; NRC and IOM, 1998). In addition, there are some indications that the use of centers is effective in building a field. For example, Tony Phelps, director of the Alzheimer's disease centers program of the National Institute on Aging, reports:

> While there has been no comprehensive formal evaluation of the Alzheimer's Disease Centers Program, there is substantive agreement that the ADCs have played and will continue to play a major role in Alzheimer's disease research by providing an infrastructure and core resources around which institutions can build innovative research programs. Centers not only conduct research projects and provide resources locally, but also join together with other ADCs to perform collaborative studies on important research topics and serve as regional or national resources for special purpose research.

Among the accomplishments of the centers Phelps describes are multidisciplinary undertakings in research that have significantly advanced understanding of Alzheimer's disease; the development of new lines of research; the dissemination of research findings to the professional and lay communities; and support for professional education through training programs, conferences, presentations, collaboration with state and local agencies and other Alzheimer's professional groups, and technology-based information dissemination. Of note, he writes, "By pooling resources and working cooperatively, the Centers have produced research findings that could not have been accomplished by individual investigators working alone" (Phelps, personal communication to the committee, July 7, 2001).

Similarly, David Hemenway, director of the Harvard Youth Violence Prevention Center, reports that centers offer the advantages of coordination and continuity. In addition, they allow a group of people to build a field by collaborating on several projects instead of working project by project. The center focuses on the interdisciplinary study of the causes and etiology of injury and its application for the development and evaluation of prevention and intervention strategies and policy. In its first two years of existence, the Harvard Youth Violence Prevention Center was able to win major grant funding; assemble a multidisciplinary team of faculty; have 78 peer-reviewed articles on injury prevention published or accepted by journals in the field; initiate five major research projects as well as several others; provide graduate student and professional training and research opportunities; offer information and training to community leaders and members; and collaborate with state and local governments and community groups (Harvard Injury Control Research Center, 2001).

The Geriatric Education Centers, which are funded by the Health Resources and Services Administration to develop and disseminate curricula and to support training on geriatrics for health professionals, were the subject of a formal national impact evaluation four years after their inception in 1983 (Engle and Jackson, 1991). The number of centers grew from 4 in 1983 to 38 in 1989. The evaluation found that enrollees in the training programs came from a number of disciplines, primarily nursing, social work, and medicine. The majority reported the intensive training experience as excellent to good in providing direct experience with the range of clinical problems related to geriatrics (91.9 percent), in helping develop professional skills in geriatrics (89.3 percent), and in contributing to their decision to begin or continue working in geriatrics (70.9 percent). The enrollee respondents also reported that their impression of geriatric health care had changed positively since their training experience. They indicated that they had made changes to increase their work or activities relating to older adults and that they considered the training to be change producing, although the evaluation does not prove a cause-and-effect relationship.

The trainees' supervisors reported that their institutions did provide some support, with 32 percent reporting financial support and 50 percent reporting the provision of paid leave for the trainees. The responding supervisors also reported that, following training, staff involvement in geriatric-related activities increased and the institution offered more geriatric-related training. Administrators in the trainees' institutions also reported increased interest in geriatric activities, including increased enrollment in geriatric programs, the development of policies on geriatric-related issues, more courses on geriatrics, and an increase in the number of funded grants related to geriatrics or gerontology.

In the committee's judgment, the reported successes of centers in other fields support the call for centers on family violence. The committee therefore urges the secretary of the U.S. Department of Health and Human Services to instruct its agencies to determine how to allocate resources on a continuing basis to establish multidisciplinary centers on family violence. These centers could be connected to academic health centers, as recommended previously by others, or they could build on related efforts in other existing centers. For example, the National Center for Injury Prevention and Control of the Centers for Disease Control and Prevention already conducts and funds activities related to health professional training on family violence, among other activities (http://www.cdc. gov/ncipc/about/about.htm). These resource centers should be linked to local and community resources and programs (e.g., domestic violence shelters, community clinics, and local assistance hotlines) as well as the health care delivery system. Such linkage is necessary to facilitate and support translating research results into real-world practices.

The committee suggests that a modest number of centers, three to five, be established in the next 5 years. That time period should be sufficient to establish and evaluate the early effects of the centers. The initial focus of the centers should be the evaluation of existing curricula on family violence and the expansion of the scientific research on magnitude, health effects, and interventions. Once the centers are established and the evidence base is developed, additional funding should be phased in to develop, test, evaluate, and disseminate education and training programs; to provide training at all levels of education; to develop policy advice; and to disseminate information and training programs.

Research conducted or funded by these centers should include attention to:

- an examination of the variability in definitions, data sources, and methods used in research on family violence to determine how to address and overcome the concerns and limitations this variability produces;
- the epidemiology of family violence, particularly its magnitude, severity, and health consequences in society;
- the underlying causes and psychodynamics of family violence;
- ongoing assessment and surveillance mechanisms related to the utilization and costs of health care services associated with family violence; and
- assessment of current family violence interventions and the development, testing, and evaluation of new intervention programs to determine effective practices.

The development of training programs for health professionals should involve educational research on:

- identification of the range and extent of training needs within and across professions;
- assessment of current education efforts, including both content and teaching strategies;
- the development, testing, and evaluation of model educational strategies (including content and methods) for education and training;

- the identification and evaluation of factors that influence education, research, and practice (e.g., mandatory reporting requirements, mandated education laws, accreditation, advocacy groups) and strategies for overcoming barriers;
- the determination of training needs for health professionals at all educational levels, including the needs of trainers; and
- systems or setting changes and educational strategies that promote the institutionalization of appropriate new or changed behaviors by those caring for victims of family violence.

The centers should offer training to:

- translate research findings into educational and clinical practice;
- expand the number of scholars and educators from multiple disciplines working in the area of family violence who can provide training in health professional schools and other training settings; and
- provide settings in which multidisciplinary training efforts are modeled.

Based on research findings and collaborative experience, advice on policy should be developed regarding a number of issues, including:

- education funding, including the role of third-party reimbursement in training and
- infrastructure (human and financial resources and other needs within the training setting) development to support education on family violence.

Dissemination should be undertaken to:

- inform educators, researchers, policy makers, grant funders, and the public about research findings and funding opportunities related to family violence research and education;
- foster multidisciplinary collaboration on family violence research, education, and practice;
- encourage public and professional understanding of family violence and its significance in society; and
- offer leadership in policy development related to family violence research and education.

By providing a locus of activity, education and research centers can facilitate the tracking and coordination of efforts to address family violence among federal agencies as well as those at the state and local levels and private organizations. As the committee's review of existing programs and funding sources revealed, program development and funding for family violence programs are currently scattered among agencies of the U.S. Department of Health and Human Services and the U.S. Department of Justice. Among these are the Centers for Disease Control and Prevention, the Agency for Healthcare Research and Quality, the Health Resources and Services Administration, the National Institutes of Health, the Administration on Children and Families, the National Institute of Justice, and the Office of Justice Programs. These federal agencies, departments, and offices share a mandate to address family violence, but the committee found that often one agency was unaware of either projects or funding opportunities for research and programs on family violence in other agencies. Although their mandates differ in focus and scope, in the committee's judgment these agencies, as well as stakeholders in family violence, would benefit from sharing and coordinating information about their projects and funding opportunities.

Such coordination may result in: (1) the development of common research priorities; (2) the distribution of funding to studies and projects that continuously build the evidence base needed for the development of effective education and practice; (3) the broad dissemination of information about current research and programs; and (4) clear sources of information. Coordination would be aided by an analysis, perhaps undertaken by the U.S. General Accounting Office, about where investments are made, their level, and their adequacy.

In addition to the development of centers, the committee endorses continued funding of individual research and program initiatives that focus on family violence. These efforts can enhance the effectiveness of the proposed centers.

Recommendation 2: Health professional organizations—including but not limited to the Association of American Medical Colleges, the American Medical Association, the American College of Physicians, the American Association of Colleges of Nursing, the Council on Social Work Education, the American Psychological Association, and the American Dental Association—and health professional educators—including faculty in academic health centers—should develop and provide guidance to their members, constituents, institutions, and other stakeholders. This guidance should address: (1) competency areas for health professional curricula on family violence, (2) effective strategies to teach about family violence, (3) approaches to overcoming barriers to training on family violence, and (4) approaches to promoting and sustaining behavior changes by health professionals.

In addition to federal efforts supporting research, scholarship, and curricular development, leadership and collaboration from the health sector are needed to develop effective training for health professionals on family violence. Health professional organizations are positioned to assist and influence their members who are likely to encounter victims of family violence.

Efforts by the American Association of Colleges of Nursing, the American College of Obstetricians and Gynecologists, the American Academy of Pediatrics, and the American College of Nurse Midwives provide promising examples of how health professional organizations can actively work to encourage and implement education initiatives on family violence among their members. The organizations provide insight into strategies to overcome barriers to developing, implementing, and sustaining curricula and to promote changes in behavior. In addition, their experiences suggest promising directions for other organizations. The committee encourages other organizations to undertake similar initiatives and evaluate the impact of their efforts. The models developed could help to inform educational efforts. The education and research centers recommended above can undertake further research into these issues as well.

Recommendation 3: Health care delivery systems and training settings, particularly academic health care centers and federally qualified health clinics and community health centers, should assume greater responsibility for developing, testing, and evaluating innovative training models or programs.

In addition to federal efforts supporting research, scholarship, and curriculum development, leadership from the health sector, including health care delivery systems and training settings, is needed to develop, test, and evaluate practical and effective health professional training on family violence. Much health professional training occurs in the health care delivery setting, so these settings provide an opportunity to develop practices that enhance the care of victims of family violence. Efforts to develop training curricula should be linked to clinical evidence, include outcome measurement, provide incentives, and respond to factors that challenge development, implementation, and sustainability of training programs.

The literature on the principles of adult education, theories of behavior change, and performance measurement techniques offer informative models. Instruction should be based on clinical evidence and emphasize task-centered (problem-based) learning approaches. Mechanisms for the ongoing collection, analysis, and feedback of process and outcome data are needed for progressive improvements in education and practice; in this way, evaluation becomes integral to training. Evaluation is important to identifying effective curricula and determining areas in which change is needed. The goal of evaluation is not simply to assess a particular program but to determine how to change behaviors and create systems of practice that improve the health outcomes of victims of family violence. Working with evaluated materials is an important step in developing effective and sustainable education efforts.

Kaiser Permanente of Northern California, the GroupHealth Cooperative, and the University of Virginia offer examples of health care delivery systems making innovations in education techniques and overcoming barriers to behavior change. These organizations are or have been actively involved in developing, testing, and improving training programs.

Other health care delivery system and training leaders can likewise take advantage of the influence they may have with health professions and professionals as part of the broader societal efforts to address the general need for health professional education, determine appropriate content and effective teaching strategies, and provide support for health professional training development and evaluation. Sound development, evaluation, and funding are necessary to ensure that these systems are sustainable, as sustainability in health professional training programs is as important as the development of effective curricula.

Recommendation 4: Federal agencies and other funders of education programs should create expectations and provide support for the evaluation of curricula on family violence for health professionals. Curricula must be evaluated to determine their impact on the practices of health professionals and their effects on family violence victims. Evaluation must employ rigorous methods to ensure accurate, reliable, and useful results.

To ensure that evaluation is useful, a number of methodological issues are in need of attention:

• **Measurement development and assessment of quality.** In order to add to the evidence base regarding the effectiveness of family violence interventions, future studies should pay greater attention to. Priority should be given to the development of measures with demonstrated reliability, validity, and sensitivity to change, which evaluators could then adopt for more widespread use. Refining alternative measures of knowledge and attitudes (e.g., the use of vignettes and standardized patients) and strategies for assessing clinical outcomes are also important.

• **The number of individuals studied: strategies to improve statistical power include increasing sample sizes.** Evaluations of training interventions have often been based on small samples of trainees (and comparison group members) that lack sufficient statistical power to detect meaningful effects. This is particularly a problem with regard to outcomes involving knowledge and attitude change, for which metaanalyses have found that effects of behavioral interventions are reasonably small. The expectation of small effects, therefore, needs to be considered in the design of evaluations.

Conventional statistical estimates point to the fact that large sample sizes of 300 or more are necessary to detect whether desired effects exist (Cohen, 1988). It is unlikely that such sample sizes are possible in most training evaluation studies. Other strategies for improving the power of the design are possible. More reliable measurement can help in terms of reducing the variability within groups caused by measurement error (Lipsey, 1990); examining a training intervention implemented in multiple sites can increase the statistical strength of studies as long as each site adequately implements the key training components.

• **Better information on variation in training received for both the**

training intervention and comparison groups. In any type of training, particularly those involving multiple sessions and activities, individuals vary in their levels of engagement or participation. Differences in student training experiences and tutor preparation affect changes observed in knowledge, attitudes, and skills. Differences in baseline knowledge and preparation may also influence the magnitude of change in training participants (Short et al., 2000). Measuring training also is important for the nonintervention groups, who may in fact have received different amounts of previous education or have acquired somewhat similar information as those who participated in the training.

  • **Rigorous evaluation studies.** Well-designed evaluations are urgently needed to expand knowledge of what and how much training should be delivered to whom, when, how often, and at what cost. Properly conducted, they can also highlight the level of other resources necessary for successful implementation (e.g., administrative support). Priority for evaluation funding should be assigned to training interventions designed around strategies shown to be effective in fostering learning and changing provider behaviors (e.g., Davis, O'Brien et al., 1999; NRC, 1999).

Randomized field experiments of individuals are difficult. Single-site evaluations that rely on quasi-experimental designs can improve the degree to which they address the relationships between training and outcomes and even rule out certain plausible rival hypotheses. Examples include paying more attention to the timing of follow-ups and, when possible, having multiple pre- and posttest observations of the outcomes of interest. Employing strategies to reduce attrition from measurement is important (e.g., incentives for participants to complete the measures). Finally, both experimental and quasi-experimental designs must attend to assessing the environment in which individuals function and the degree to which it facilitates or impedes translation of the knowledge learned from training to actual practice. This may also be useful in exploring whether training actually results in any system changes.

  • **Programmatic research on training.** Research is needed that more closely examines how trainee characteristics, their perceptions of training and its quality, and the characteristics of the practice context in which they work (e.g., integrated delivery systems versus small-group practices) interact in effectively translating the knowledge and skills into daily practice (see Huba et al., 2000; Ottoson and Patterson, 2000; and Panter et al., 2000, for examples in HIV/AIDS education and continuing education). With such research, evaluated programs can contribute to enhancing practice by health professionals to improve the health outcomes of victims of family violence.

Evaluation is critical to the development of effective training programs on family violence. The committee's review of existing training programs for health professionals and the evaluation of those programs suggests that even when program development is funded, evaluation is usually not funded. Funders should require that evaluations be conducted as a condition of funding and should provide funding at appropriate levels or the technical support to ensure that evaluation is possible. In addition, funds should be allocated specifically for the evaluation of existing programs.

FINAL THOUGHTS

A limited evidence base and the emotional responses that family violence inspires combined to make the committee's task in responding to its charge complex and difficult. Guided by the judgment that health professional training on family violence is necessary, the committee drew on the existing science to discern important starting points for research and development on training content and teaching methods. These represent opportunities for educators, researchers, and policy makers to address and help reduce, if not resolve, problems related to the responses of health professionals to family violence and to develop the responsive health care system that family violence victims need. With sufficient human and financial investment and collaboration among diverse stakeholders, the committee is confident that significant progress can be made in meeting the training needs of health professionals and the health care needs of family violence victims.

References

Abbott, J., Johnson, R., Koziol-McLain, J., & Lowenstein, S. R. (1995). Domestic violence against women: Incidence and prevalence in an emergency department population. *Journal of the American Medical Association, 273* (22), 1763–1767.

Abrahamson, S., Baron, J., Elstein, A. S., Hammond, W. P., Holzman, G. B., Marlow, B., Taggart, M. S., & Schulkin, J. (1999). Continuing medical education for life: Eight principles. *Academic Medicine, 74,* 1288–1294.

Adger, H. Jr., Macdonald, D. I., & Wenger, S. (1999). Core competencies for involvement of health care providers in the care of children and adolescents in families affected by substance abuse. *Pediatrics, 103* (5, Pt 2), 1083–1084.

Administration for Children and Families. (1998). *Reports by Source 1998 Figure 3-1.* Available: http://www.acf.dhhs.gov/programs/cb/publications/cm98/c3f1.gif [March 2, 2001].

Alexander, R. C. (1990). Education of the physician in child abuse. *Pediatric Clinics of North America, 37* (4), 971–988.

Alpert, E. J. (1995). Making a place for teaching about family violence in medical school. *Academic Medicine, 70* (11), 974–978.

Alpert, E. J., Cohen, S., & Sege, R. D. (1997a). Family violence: An overview. *Academic Medicine, 72* (1 Suppl), S3–S6.

Alpert, E. J., Sege, R. D., & Bradshaw, Y. S. (1997b). Interpersonal violence and the education of physicians. *Academic Medicine, 72* (1 Suppl), S41–S50.

Alpert, E. J., Tonkin, A. E., Seeherman, A. M., & Holtz, H. A. (1998). Family violence curricula in U.S. medical schools. *American Journal of Preventive Medicine, 14* (4), 273–282.

American Academy of Family Physicians. (1994). Kansas City, MO: American Academy of Family Physicians.

American Academy of Pediatrics. (1999). Guidelines for the evaluation of sexual abuse of children: Subject review. American Academy of Pediatrics, Committee on Child Abuse and Neglect. *Pediatrics, 103* (1), 186–191.

American Association of Colleges of Nursing. (1999). *Violence as a public health problem.* Washington, DC: AACN.

American Cancer Society. (1996). *(Cancer facts and figures 1996.* Available: http://www.cancer.org/statistics/96cff/costs.html [March 9, 2001].

American College of Emergency Physicians. (1995). Emergency medicine and domestic violence. American College of Emergency Physicians. *Annals of Emergency Medicine, 25* (3), 442–443.

American College of Nurse Midwives. (1997). The core competencies for basic midwifery practice. Adopted by the American College of Nurse-Midwives. May 1997. *Journal of Nurse Midwifery, 42* (5), 373–376.

American Medical Association. (1992). American Medical Association Diagnostic and Treatment Guidelines on Child Physical Abuse and Neglect. *Archives of Family Medicine, 1* (2), 187–197.

American Nurses Association. (1995). *Managed care curriculum for baccalaureate nurses foundation.* Washington, DC: American Nurses Publishing.

American Psychological Association. (1996). *Violence and the family.* Washington, DC: American Psychological Association.

Anetzberger, G. J., Palmisano, B. R., Sanders, M., Bass, D., Dayton, C., Eckert, S., & Schimer, M. R. (2000). A model intervention for elder abuse and dementia. *Gerontologist, 40* (4), 492–497.

Angell, M. (1999). The American health care system revisited—A new series. *New England Journal of Medicine, 340* (1), 48.

Antman, E., Lau, J., Kupelnick, B., Mosteller, F., & Chalmers, T. (1992). A comparison of results of meta-analyses of randomized control trials and recommendations of clinical experts. Treatments for myocardial infarction. *Journal of the American Medical Association, 268* (2), 240–248.

Appleton, W. (1980). The battered woman syndrome. *Annals of Emergency Medicine, 9* (1), 84-91.

Aravanis, S. C., Adelman, R. D., Breckman, R., Fulmer, T. T., Holder, E., Lachs, M., O'Brien, J. G., & Sanders, A. B. (1993). Diagnostic and treatment guidelines on elder abuse and neglect. *Archives of Family Medicine, 2* (4), 371–388.

Arkes, H. R. (1981). Impediments to accurate clinical judgement and possible ways to minimize their impact. *Journal of Consulting and Clinical Psychology, 49,* 323–330.

Arkes, H. R. (1989). Principles in judgement/decision making research pertinent to legal proceedings. *Behavioral Sciences and the Law, 7,* 429–456.

Association of American Medical Colleges. *Graduation Questionnaire 1998, 1999, 2000.* Available: http://www.aamc.org/meded/gq/ [March 7, 2001].

Association of Women's Health, Obstetric, and Neonatal Nurses. (2000). *Education for entry.* Washington, DC: AWHONN.

Athey, J., Kavanagh, L., Bagley, K., & Hutchins, V. (2000). *Building the future: The maternal and child health training program.* Washington, DC: Georgetown University Press.

Attala, J., & McSweeney, M. (1997). Preschool children of battered women identified in a community setting. *Issues in Comprehensive Pediatric Nursing, 20* (4), 217–225.

Auslisio, M. P., Robert, A., & Youngner, S. J. (2000). Health care ethics consultation: Nature, goals and competencies. A position paper from the Society for Health and Human Values-Society for Bioethics Consultation Task Force on Standards for Bioethics Consultation. *Annals of Internal Medicine, 113* (1), 56–69.

Bader, J., Shugars, D., White, B., & Rindal, D. B. (1999). Development of effectiveness of care and use of services measures for dental care plans. *Journal of Public Health Dentistry, 59* (3), 142–149.

Bandura, A. (1986). *The social foundations of thought and action: A social cognitive theory.* Englewood Cliffs, NJ: Prentice Hall.

Bar-on, M. E. (1998). Teaching residents about child abuse and neglect. *Academic Medicine, 73* (5), 573–574.

Barnard-Thompson, K., & Leichner, P. (1999). Psychiatric residents' views on their training and experience regarding issues related to child abuse. *Canadian Journal of Psychiatry, 44* (8), 769–774.

Barnett, G. O., Winickoff, R. N., Morgan, M. M., & Zielstorff, R. D. (1983). A computer-based monitoring system for follow-up of elevated blood pressure. *Medical Care, 21* (4), 40040–40049.

Barnett, R., Marshall, N., & Singer, J. (1992). Job experiences over time, multiple roles, and women's mental health: A longitudinal study. *Journal of Personality and Social Psychology, 62* (4), 634–644.

Barnett, S., Smith, L., & Swartz, M. (1999). Teaching evidence-based medicine skills to medical students and residents. *International Journal of Dermatology, 38* (12), 893–894.

Barrows, H. S. (1983). Problem based, self-directed learning. *Journal of the American Medical Association, 250,* 3077–3080.

Basch, C. E. (1987). Focus group interview: An underutilized research technique for improving theory and practice in health education. *Health Education Quarterly, 14* (4), 411–448.

Bazarian, J., Davis, C., Spillane, L., Blumstein, H., & Schneider, S. (1999). Teaching emergency medicine residents evidence-based critical appraisal skills: A controlled trial. *Annals of Emergency Medicine, 34* (2), 148–154.

Beck, K. A., & Ogloff, J. R. P. (1995). Child abuse reporting in British Columbia: Psychologists' knowledge of and compliance with the reporting laws. *Professional Psychology: Research and Practice, 26,* 245–251.

Becker, M. H. (1970). Factors affecting diffusion of innovations among health professionals. *American Journal of Public Health and the Nation's Health, 60* (2), 294–304.

Bell, C., & Mattis, J. (2000). The importance of cultural competence in ministering to African American victims of domestic violence. *Violence Against Women, 6* (5), 515–532.

Berg, A., Atkins, D., & Tierney, W. (1997). Clinical practice guidelines in practice and education. *Journal of General Internal Medicine, 12* (Suppl 2), S25–S33.

Bergman, B., & Brismar, B. (1991). A 5-year follow-up study of 117 battered women. *American Journal of Public Health, 81* (11), 1486–1489.

Bergman, B., Brismar, B., & Nordin, C. (1992). Utilisation of medical care by abused women. *British Medical Journal, 305* (6844), 27–28.

Berlin, F., Malin, H., & Dean, S. (1991). Effects of statutes requiring psychiatrists to report suspected sexual abuse of children. *American Journal of Psychiatry, 148,* 449–453.

Bero, L. A., Grilli, R., Grimshaw, J. M., Harvey, E., Oxman, A. D., & Thomson, M. A. (1998). Closing the gap between research and practice: An overview of systematic reviews of interventions to promote the implementation of research findings. The Cochrane Effective Practice and Organization of Care Review Group. *British Medical Journal, 317* (7156), 465–468.

Berwick, D. M. (1996). A primer on leading the improvement of systems. *British Medical Journal, 312* (7031), 619–622.

Berwick, D. M. (1998). Developing and testing changes in delivery of care. *Annals of Internal Medicine, 128* (8), 651–656.

Berwick, D. M., & Nolan, T. W. (1998). Physicians as leaders in improving health care: A new series in Annals of Internal Medicine. *Annals of Internal Medicine, 128* (4), 289–292.

Besharov, D. J. (1990). *Recognizing child abuse: A guide for the concerned.* New York: Free Press.

Biehler, J. L., Apolo, J., & Burton, L. (1996). Views of pediatric emergency fellows and fellowship directors concerning training experiences in child abuse and neglect. *Pediatric Emergency Care, 12* (5), 365–369.

Bloom, S. W. (1989). The medical school as a social organization: The sources of resistance to change. *Medical Education, 23* (3), 228–241.

Blumenthal, D., & Meyer, G. S. (1996). Academic health centers in a changing environment. *Health Affairs, 15,* 201–215.

Bohannon, J. R., Dosser, D. A. Jr., & Lindley, S. E. (1995). Using couple data to determine domestic violence rates: An attempt to replicate previous work. *Violence and Victims, 10* (2), 133–141.

Bolin, L., & Elliott, B. (1996). Physician detection of family violence. Do buttons worn by doctors generate conversations about domestic abuse? *Minnesota Medicine, 79* (6), 42–55.

Bosker, G., Schwartz, G., Jones, J., & Sequeira, M. (1990). *Geriatric emergency medicine.* St. Louis: C.V. Mosby.

Boud, D., & Feletti, G. (1991). *The challenge of problem-based learning.* London: Kogan Page.

Brach, C., & Fraser, I. (2000). Can cultural competency reduce racial and ethnic health disparities? A review and conceptual model. *Medical Care Research and Review, 57* (Suppl 1), 181–217.

Bradley, S., & Moran, R. (1998). Better continence. *Nursing Times, 94,* 52–53.

Brady, J., Guy, J., Poelstra, P., & Brokaw, B. (1999). Vicarious traumatization, spirituality, and the treatment of sexual abuse survivors: A national survey of women psychotherapists. *Professional Psychology: Research and Practice, 30,* 386–393.

Brandt, E. N. Jr. (1995). Education and research in adult family violence: A perspective. *Academic Medicine, 70* (11), 968–970.

Brandt, E. N. Jr. (1997). Curricular principles for health professions education about family violence. *Academic Medicine, 72* (1 Suppl), S51–S58.

Brassard, M., & Hardy, D. (1997). Psychological maltreatment. In M. Helfer, R. Kempe, & R.D. Krugman (Eds.), *The battered child* (5th ed., ch. 17). Chicago: University of Chicago Press.

Brimberry, R. (1988). Vaccination of high-risk patients for influenza: A comparison of telephone and mail reminder methods. *Journal of Family Practice, 26* (4), 397–400.

Briss, P., Zaza, S., Pappaioanou, M., et al. (2000). Developing an evidence-based guide to community preventive services methods. The Task Force on Community Preventive Services. *American Journal of Preventive Medicine, 18* (1 Suppl), 35–43.

Brownson, R. C., Gurney, J. G., and Land, G. H. (1999). Evidence-based decision making in public health. *Journal of Public Health Management Practices, 5* (5), 86–97.

Buel, S. (1994). *Combating domestic violence intervention and opportunities for partnerships.* Pinellas Park, FL: Juvenille Welfare Board.

Bullock, K. (1997). Domestic violence training at an inner-city hospital found helpful. *Journal of Emergency Nursing, 23* (4), 299–300.

Bullock, K. (2000). Child abuse: The physician's role in alleviating a growing problem. *American Family Physicians, 61,* 2977–2980.

Bullock, K. (2001). Cultural controversies on child abuse. Letter to the Editor. *American Family Physicians, 64* (7), 1142–1143.

Burke, L. K., & Follingstad, D. R. (1999). Violence in lesbian and gay relationships: Theory, prevalence, and correlational factors. *Clinical Psychology Review, 19* (5), 487–512.

Bussigel, M. N., Barzansky, B. M., & Grenholm, G. G. (1988). *Innovation processes in medical education.* New York: Praeger.

Campbell, C., Parboosingh, J., Gondocz, T., Babitskaya, G., & Pham, B. (1999a). A study of the factors that influence physicians' commitments to change their practices using learning diaries. *Academic Medicine, 74* (10 Suppl), S34–S36.

Campbell, J. (1981). Misogyny and homocide of women. *Advanced Nursing Sciences, 3* (2), 67–85.

Campbell, J., Kub, J. E., & Rose, L. (1996). Depression in battered women. *Journal of American Medical Women's Association, 51* (3), 106–110.

Campbell, J. C., & Campbell, D. W. (1996). Cultural competence in the care of abused women. *Journal of Nurse Midwifery, 41* (6), 457–462.

Campbell, J. C., & Humphreys, J. (1993). *Nursing care of survivors of family violence.* St. Louis: Mosby.

Campbell, J. C., Harris, M. J., & Lee, R. K. (1995). Violence research: An overview. *Scholarly Inquiry for Nursing Practice, 9* (2), 105–126.

Campbell, J. C., Dienemann, J., Kub, J., Wurmser, T., & Loy, E. (1999b). Collaboration as a partnership. *Violence Against Women, 5* (10), 140–156.

Campbell, J. C., Sharps, P. W., & Glass, N. E. (2000). Risk assessment for intimate partner violence. In G. F. Pinard & L. Pagani (Eds.), *Clinical assessment of dangerousness: Empirical contributions* (pp. 136–157). New York: Cambridge University Press.

Campbell, J. C., Coben, J. H., McLoughlin, E., Dearwater, S., Nah, G., Glass, N., Lee, D., & Durborow, N. (2001). An evaluation of a system-change training model to improve emergency department response to battered women. *Academic Emergency Medicine, 8* (2), 131–138.

Campinha-Bacote, J. (1998). Cultural diversity in nursing education: Issues and concerns. *Journal of Nursing Education, 37* (1), 3–4.

Campinha-Bacote, J. (1999). A model and instrument for addressing cultural competence in health care. *Journal of Nursing Education, 38* (5), 20320–20327.

Canterino, J. C., VanHorn, L. G., Harrigan, J. T., Ananth, C. V., & Vintzileos, A. M. (1999). Domestic abuse in pregnancy: A comparison of a self-completed domestic abuse questionnaire with a directed interview. *American Journal of Obstetric Gynecology, 181* (5, Pt 1), 1049–1051.

Carbonell, J., Chez, R., & Hassler, R. (1995). Florida physician and nurse education and practice related to domestic violence. *Women's Health Issues, 5,* 203–207.

Carlile, S., Barnet, S., Sefton, A., & Uther, J. (1998). Medical problem based learning supported by intranet technology: A natural student centered approach. *International Journal of Medical Informatics, 50,* 225–233.

Carlson, B. E. (1984). Children's observations of interpersonal violence. In A. R. Roberts (Ed.), *Battered women and their families.* New York: Springer.

Carlson, L. D. (1977). *Pre-merger: guidelines for conducting an internal feasibility study.* St. Louis.

Centers for Disease Control. About NCIPC. Available: http://www.cdc.gov/ncipc/about/about.htm [July 9, 2001].

Centers for Disease Control. (1989). Education about adult domestic violence in U.S. and Canadian medical schools, 1987–88. *Morbidity and Mortality Weekly Report, 38* (2), 17–19.

Centers for Disease Control. (1996). Physical violence and injuries in intimate relationships—New York, Behavioral Risk Factor Surveillance System, 1994. *Morbidity and Mortality Weekly Report, 45* (35), 765–767.

Centers for Disease Control. (2000a). Prevalence of intimate partner violence and injuries—Washington, 1998. *Morbidity and Mortality Weekly Report, 49* (26), 589–592.

Centers for Disease Control. (2000b). Use of medical care, police assistance, and restraining orders by women reporting intimate partner violence—Massachusetts, 1996–1997. *Morbidity and Mortality Weekly Report, 49* (22), 485–488.

Chamberlain, L., & Perham-Hester, K. (2000). Physicians' screening practices for female partner abuse during prenatal visits. *Maternal and Child Health Journal, 4,* 141–148.

Chapman, L. J., & Chapman, J. P. (1967). Genesis of popular but erroneous psychodiagnostic observations. *Journal of Abnormal Psychology, 72,* 193–204.

Chapman, L. J., & Chapman, J. P. (1969). Illusory correlation as an obstacle to the use of valid psychodiagnostic signs. *Journal of Abnormal Psychology, 74,* 271–280.

Check, W. A. (1980). How to affect antibiotic prescribing practices. *Journal of the American Medical Association, 244* (23), 2594–2595.

Cheney, C., & Ramsdell, J. W. (1987). Effect of medical records' checklists on implementation of periodic health measures. *American Journal of Medicine, 83* (1), 129–136.

Chessare, J. B. (1998). Teaching clinical decision-making to pediatric residents in an era of managed care. *Pediatrics, 101* (4, Pt 2), 762–766.

Cheung, K. F., Stevenson, K. M., & Leung, P. (1991). Competency-based evaluation of case-management skills in child sexual abuse intervention. *Child Welfare, 70* (4), 425–435.

Chiodo, G. T., Tilden, V. P., Limandri, B. J., & Schmidt, T. A. (1994). Addressing family violence among dental patients: Assessment and intervention. *Journal of the American Dental Association, 125* (1), 69–75.

Clarke-Daniels, C., Daniels, R., & Baumhover, L. (1989). Physicians mandatory reporting of elder abuse. *Gerontologist, 29* (3), 321–327.

Clarke-Daniels, C., Daniels, R., & Baumhover, L. (1990). Abuse and neglect of the elderly: Are emergency department personnel aware of mandatory reporting laws? *Annals of Emergency Medicine, 19*, 970–977.

Cohen, B. J., Levin, R. F., Bashoff, M. L., Ellis, E., Condie, V., & Gelfand, G. (1997). Educators' responses to changes in the health care system. *Journal of the New York State Nurses' Association, 28* (2), 4–7.

Cohen, D. I., Littenberg, B., Wetzel, C., & Neuhauser, D. (1982). Improving physician compliance with preventive medicine guidelines. *Medical Care, 20* (10), 1040–1045.

Cohen, J. (1988). *Statistical power analysis for the behavioral sciences* (2nd ed.). Hillsdale, NJ: Lawrence Erlbaum.

Cohen, S. J., Christen, A. G., Katz, B. P., Drook, C. A., Davis, B. J., Smith, D. M., & Stookey, G. K. (1987). Counseling medical and dental patients about cigarette smoking: The impact of nicotine gum and chart reminders. *American Journal of Public Health, 77* (3), 313–316.

Cohen, S. J., Stookey, G. K., Katz, B. P., Drook, C. A., & Smith, D. M. (1989). Encouraging primary care physicians to help smokers quit: A randomized, controlled trial. *Annals of Internal Medicine, 110* (8), 648–652.

Cole, T. (2000). Is domestic violence screening helpful? *Journal of the American Medical Association, 284* (5), 551–553.

Covington, D. L., Dalton, V. K., Diehl, S. J., Wright, B. D., & Piner, M. H. (1997a). Improving detection of violence among pregnant adolescents. *Journal of Adolescent Health, 21* (1), 18–24.

Covington, D. L., Diehl, S. J., Wright, B. D., & Piner, M. (1997b). Assessing for violence during pregnancy using a systematic approach. *Maternal and Child Health Journal, 1* (2), 129–133.

Culpepper, L., & Gilbert, T. (1999). Evidence and ethics. *Lancet, 353* (9155), 829–831.

Curran, C. R. (1995). IDN core competencies: Nursing's role. *Nursing Economics, 13* (4), 192, 249.

Currier, G. W., Barthauer, L. M., Begier, E., & Bruce, M. L. (1996). Training and experience of psychiatric residents in identifying domestic violence. *Psychiatric Services, 47* (5), 529–530.

Curry, M. A., Doyle, B. A., & Gilhooley, J. (1998). Abuse among pregnant adolescents: Differences by developmental age. *MCN The American Journal of Maternal Child Nursing, 23* (3), 144–150.

Curry, S. J., & Kim, E. L. (1999). A public health perspective on addictive behavior change interventions: Conceptual frameworks and guiding principles. In J. A. Tucker, D. M. Donovan, & G. A. Donovan (Eds.), *Changing addictive behavior: Moving beyond thearpy assisted change.* New York: Guilford.

Dalzell, M. D. (1998). Helping hands for HEDIS. *Managed Care, 7* (6), 34A-H.

Dalzell, M. D. (1999). Physician, HEDIS (Health Employer Data and Information Set) thyself. *Managed Care, 8* (3), 54, 57.

Davis, D. (1998). Does CME work? An analysis of the effect of educational activities on physician performance or health care outcomes. *International Journal of Psychiatry in Medicine, 28* (1), 21–39.

Davis, D., O'Brien, M. A., Freemantle, N., Wolf, F. M., Mazmanian, P., & Taylor-Vaisey, A. (1999). Impact of formal continuing medical education: Do conferences, workshops, rounds, and other traditional continuing education activities change physician behavior or health care outcomes? *Journal of the American Medical Association, 282* (9), 867–874.

Davis, D. A., Thomson, M. A., Oxman, A. D., & Haynes, R. B. (1992). Evidence for the effectiveness of CME: A review of 50 randomized controlled trials. *Journal of the American Medical Association, 268* (9), 1111–1117.

Davis, D. A., Thomson, M. A., Oxman, A. D., & Haynes, R. B. (1995). Changing physician performance. A systematic review of the effect of continuing medical education strategies. *Journal of the American Medical Association, 274* (9), 700–705.

Dawes, R. M. (1989). Experience and the validity of clinical judgement: The illusory correlation. *Behavioral Sciences and the Law, 7,* 457–467.

Dawes, R. M., Faust, D., & Meehl, P. E. (1989). Clinical versus actuarial judgement. *Science, 243,* 1668–1674.

De Vos, E., Barkan, S., Cohen, S., Flint, S., Singer, A., Whitcomb, D., Ames, N., Ley, J., Peeler, N., & Stober, M. (1992). *Family violence and the health care system: Lessons from five communities.* Report No. PC234. Robert Wood Johnson Foundation.

Dearwater, S. R., Coben, J. H., Campbell, J. C., Nah, G., Glass, N., McLoughlin, E., & Bekemeier, B. (1998). Prevalence of intimate partner abuse in women treated at community hospital emergency departments. *Journal of the American Medical Association, 280* (5), 433–438.

Delewski, C. H., Pecora, P. J., Smith, G., & Smith, V. (1986). Evaluating child protective services training: The participant action plan approach. *Child Welfare, 65* (6), 579–591.

Department of Health and Human Services. (1986). *Surgeon General's Workshop on Violence and Public Health.* Washington, DC: Health Resources and Services Administration.

Department of Health and Human Services. (1994). *Clinical Practice Guideline Development: Methodology Perspectives.* Report No. AHCPR Pub. No. 95-0009. Washington, DC: DHHS, Agency for Health Care Policy and Research.

Department of Health and Human Services. (1996). *Third National Incidence Study of Child Abuse and Neglect: Final Report (NIS-3).* Washington, DC: U.S. Government Printing Office.

Department of Health and Human Services. (1998). *Child Maltreatment 1996: Reports from the States to the National Child Abuse and Neglect Data Systems.* Washington, DC: U.S. Government Printing Office.

Dewey, J. (1938). *Experience and education.* New York: Collier.

Diaz-Olavarrieta, C., Campbell, J., Garcia de la Cadena, C., Paz, F., & Villa, A. R. (1999). Domestic violence against patients with chronic neurologic disorders. *Archives of Neurology, 56* (6), 681–685.

Diaz-Olavarrietta, C., Paz, F., Garcia de la Cadena, C., & Campbell, J. (2001). Prevalence of intimate partner abuse among nurses and nurses' aides in Mexico. *Archives of Medical Research, 32,* 79–87.

Dickson, R., Abdullahi, D., Flores W, et al. (1998). Putting evidence into practice. *World Health Forum, 19* (3), 311–314.

Dienemann, J., Trautman, D., Shahan, J. B., Pinnella, K., Krishnan, P., Whyne, D., Bekemeier, B., & Campbell, J. (1999). Developing a domestic violence program in an inner-city academic health center emergency department: The first 3 years. *Journal of Emergency Nursing, 25* (2), 110–115.

Dietrich, A. J., O'Connor, G. T., Keller, A., Carney, P. A., Levy, D., & Whaley, F. S. (1992). Cancer: Improving early detection and prevention. A community practice randomised trial. *British Medical Journal, 304* (6828), 687–691.

Dolmans, D. H., & Schmidt, H. G. (1994). What drives the student in problem-based learning? *Medical Education, 28,* 372–380.

Domino, J. V., & Haber, J. D. (1987). Prior physical and sexual abuse in women with chronic headache: Clinical correlates. *Headache, 27* (6), 310–314.

Dorsey, J. K., Gocey, J., Murrell, K., Rinderer-Rand, H., Hall, C., & Myers, J. H. (1996). Medical student response to an interactive patient simulation program used to supplement child abuse education. *Child Abuse and Neglect, 20* (10), 973–977.

Drossman, D. A., Leserman, J., Nachman, G., Li, Z. M., Gluck, H., Toomey, T. C., & Mitchell, C. M. (1990). Sexual and physical abuse in women with functional or organic gastrointestinal disorders. *Annals of Internal Medicine, 113* (11), 828–833.

Drossman, D. A., Talley, N. J., Leserman, J., Olden, K. W., & Barreiro, M. A. (1995). Sexual and physical abuse and gastrointestinal illness. Review and recommendations. *Annals of Internal Medicine, 123* (10), 782–794.

Drossman, D. A., Li, Z., Leserman, J., Toomey, T. C., & Hu, Y. J. (1996). Health status by gastrointestinal diagnosis and abuse history. *Gastroenterology, 110,* 999–1007.

Dubowitz, H. (1988). Child abuse programs and pediatric residency training. *Pediatrics, 82* (3, Pt 2), 477–480.

Dubowitz, H., & Black, M. (1991). Teaching pediatric residents about child maltreatment. *Journal of Developmental Behavioral Pediatrics, 12* (5), 305–307.

Durbin, W. A. Jr, Lapidas, B., & Goldmann, D. A. (1981). Improved antibiotic usage following introduction of a novel prescription system. *Journal of the American Medical Association, 246* (16), 1796–1800.

Dutton, M. A., Goodman, L. A., & Bennett, L. (1999). Court-involved battered women's responses to violence: The role of psychological, physical, and sexual abuse. *Violence Victims, 14* (1), 89–104.

Dyer, C. B., Pavlik, V. N., Murphy, K. P., & Hyman, D. J. (2000). The high prevalence of depression and dementia in elder abuse or neglect. *Journal of the American Geriatric Society, 48* (2), 205–208.

Eby, K. K., Campbell, J. C., Sullivan, C. M., & Davidson, W. S. (1995). Health effects of experiences of sexual violence for women with abusive partners. *Health Care for Women International, 16* (6), 563–576.

Eckenrode, J., Ganzel, B., Henderson, C. R. Jr., Smith, E., Olds, D. L., Powers, J., Cole, R., Kitzman, H., & Sidora, K. (2000). Preventing child abuse and neglect with a program of nurse home visitation: The limiting effects of domestic violence. *Journal of the American Medical Association, 284* (11), 1385–1391.

Eddy, D. (1996). *Clinical decision making from theory to practice: A collection of essays from the American Medical Association.* Sudbury, MA: Jones and Bartlett.

Eddy, D. M. (1998). Performance measurement: Problems and solutions. *Health Aff (Millwood), 17* (4), 7–25.

Eisenberg, J. M. (1982). The use of ancillary services: A role for utilization review? *Medical Care, 20* (8), 849–861.

Eisenberg, J. M., & Williams, S. V. (1981). Cost containment and changing physicians' practice behavior. Can the fox learn to guard the chicken coop? *Journal of the American Medical Association, 246* (19), 2195–2201.

Eisenstat, S. A., & Bancroft, L. (1999). Domestic violence. *The New England Journal of Medicine, 341* (12), 886–892.

el-Bayoumi, G., Borum, M. L., & Haywood, Y. (1998). Domestic violence in women. *The Medical Clinics of North America, 82* (2), 391–401.

Elliott, W., Toth, S., Stemer, A., & Cadwalader, J. (1999). Detection, treatment, and control of adult hypertension in northwest Indiana. *American Journal of Hypertension, 12* (8, Pt 1), 830–834.

Ellis, J. M. (1999). Barriers to effective screening for domestic violence by registered nurses in the emergency department. *Critical Care Nursing Quarterly, 22* (1), 27–41.

Emans, S. J., Bravender, T., Knight, J., Frazer, C., Luoni, M., Berkowitz, C., Armstrong, E., & Goodman, E. (1998). Adolescent medicine training in pediatric residency programs: Are we doing a good job? *Pediatrics, 102* (3), 588–595.

Emergency Nurses Association. (1998). *Role of the registered nurse in the prehospital environment.* [Position Statements, 7th ed.] Available: http://www.ena.org/services/posistate/data/rolreg.htm.

Engle, M., & Jackson, J. R. (1991). *Final report: Analysis of geriatric education center national impact evaluation data.* Birmingham: University of Alabama School of Medicine.

Epstein, A. M. (1998). Rolling down the runway: The challenges ahead for quality report cards. *Journal of the American Medical Association, 279* (21), 1691–1696.

Epstein, D. (1999). Effective intervention in domestic violence cases: Rethinking the roles of prosecutors, judges and the court system. *Yale Journal Law and Feminism, 11.*

Ernst, A. A., Houry, D., Nick, T. G., & Weiss, S. J. (1998). Domestic violence awareness and prevalence in a first-year medical school class. *Academic Emergency Medicine, 5* (1), 64–68.

Ernst, A. A., Houry, D., Weiss, S. J., & Szerlip, H. (2000). Domestic violence awareness in a medical school class: 2-year follow-up. *Southern Medical Journal, 93* (8), 772–776.

Estabrooks, C.A. (1998). Will evidence-based nursing practice make practice perfect? *The Canadian Journal of Nursing Research, 30* (1), 15–36.

Evidence-Based Medicine Working Group. (1992). Evidence-based medicine: A new approach to teaching the practice of medicine. *Journal of the American Medical Association, 268* (17), 2420–2425.

Family Violence Education. (1996). Family violence education in medical school-based residency programs—Virginia, 1995. *Morbidity and Mortality Weekly Report, 45* (31), 669–671.

Fanslow, J. L., Norton, R. N., Robinson, E. M., & Spinola, C. G. (1998). Outcome evaluation of an emergency department protocol of care on partner abuse. *Australian and New Zealand Journal of Public Health, 22* (5), 598–603.

Fanslow, J. L., Norton, R. N., & Robinson, E. M. (1999). One year follow-up of an emergency department protocol for abused women. *The Australian and New Zealand Journal of Public Health, 23* (4), 418–420.

Fantuzzo, J., & Lindquist, C. (1989). The effects of observing conjugal violence on children: A review of empirical literature. *Journal of Family Violence, 4,* 77–94.

Faulk, M. (1974). Men who assault their wives. *Medicine, Science, and the Law,* 180–183.

Feldman, K. (1997). The evaluation of physical abuse. In M. Helfer, R. Kempe, & R.D. Krugman (Eds.), *The battered child* (5th ed., pp. 175–220). Chicago: University of Chicago Press.

Felitti, V. J. (1991). Long-term medical consequences of incest, rape, and molestation. *Southern Medical Journal, 84* (3), 328–331.

Felitti, V. J., Anda, R. F., Nordenberg, D., Williamson, D. F., Spitz, A. M., Edwards, V., Koss, M. P., & Marks, J. S. (1998). Relationship of childhood abuse and household dysfunction to many of the leading causes of death in adults. The Adverse Childhood Experiences (ACE) Study. *American Journal of Preventive Medicine, 14* (4), 245–258.

Ferren, A., & Mussell K. (2000). Leading Curriculum Renewal. In A. Lucas (Ed.), *Leading academic change* (pp. 246–274). San Francisco: Jossey-Bass.

Ferris, L. E. (1994). Canadian family physicians' and general practitioners' perceptions of their effectiveness in identifying and treating wife abuse. *Medical Care, 32* (12), 1163–1172.

Ferris, L. E., & Tudiver, F. (1992). Family physicians' approach to wife abuse: A study of Ontario, Canada, practices. *Family Medicine, 24* (4), 276–282.

Fineberg, H. V., Funkhouser, A. R., & Marks, H. (1983). Variation in medical practice: A review of the literature. *Conference on Cost-Effective Medical Care: Implication of Variation in Medical Practice.* Institute of Medicine, National Academy of Sciences, Washington, DC.

Fineberg, H. V., Funkhouser, A. R., & Marks, H. (1985). Variation in medical practice. A review of the literature. *Industry and Health Care, 2,* 143–168.

Finlayson, L., & Koocher, G. P. (1991). Professional judgement in child abuse reporting in sexual abuse cases. *Professional Psychology: Research and Practice, 22,* 464–472.

Finn, J. (1986). The relationship between sex role attitudes and attitudes supporting marital violence. *Sex Roles, 14,* 235–244.

Flaherty, E. G., Sege, R., Binns, H. J., Mattson, C. L., & Christoffel, K. K. (2000). Health care providers' experience reporting child abuse in the primary care setting. Pediatric Practice Research Group. *Archives of Pediatric and Adolescent Medicine, 154* (5), 489–493.

Flores, G. (2000). Culture and the patient-physician relationship: Achieving cultural competency in health care. *The Journal of Pediatrics, 136* (1), 14–23.

Fox, D. M. (1993). *Power and illness: The failure and future of American health policy.* Berkeley: University of California Press.

Fox, R., Mazmanian, P., & Putnam, R. (1989). Change and learning in the lives of physicians. Westport, CT: Praeger.

Fox, R., & Miner, C. (1999). Motivation and the facilitation of change, learning, and participation in educational programs for health professionals. *Journal of Continuing Education in the Health Professions, 19,* 132–141.

French, P. (1999). The development of evidence-based nursing. *Journal of Advanced Nursing, 29* (1), 72–78.

Fromson, T., & Durborow, N. (1998). *Insurance Discrimination Against Victims of Domestic Violence.* Pennsylvania: PCADV publications.

Frye, V. (2001). Examining homicide's contribution to pregnancy-associated deaths. *Journal of the American Medical Association, 285* (11), 1510–1511.

Fulmer, T. T. (1989). Mistreatment of elders: Assessment, diagnosis, and intervention. *The Nursing Clinics of North America, 24* (3), 707–716.

Fulmer, T. T., & O'Malley, T. A. (1987). *Inadequate care of the elderly: A health care perspective on abuse and neglect.* New York: Springer.

Gagan, M. J. (1999). Clinical implications of a study of nurse practitioner performance with suspected domestic violence victims. *Journal of the American Academy of Nurse Practitioners, 11* (11), 467–470.

Gallmeier, T. M., & Bonner, B. L. (1992). University-based interdisciplinary training in child abuse and neglect. *Child Abuse and Neglect, 16* (4), 513–521.

Gambrill, E. (1999). Evidence-based clinical practice. *Journal of Behavior Therapy and Experimental Psychiatry, 30* (1), 1–14.

Ganley, A. L. (1996). Understanding domestic violence. In C. Warshaw & A. L. Ganely (Eds.), *Improving the healthcare response to domestic violence: A resource manual for health care providers* (pp. 1–14). San Francisco, CA: The Family Violence Prevention Fund.

Ganley, A. L. (1998). Improving the health care response to domestic violence: A trainer's manual for health care providers. San Francisco, CA: Family Violence Prevention Fund.

Garner, P., Kale, R., Dickson, R., Dans, T., & Salinas, R. (1998). Getting research findings into practice: Implementing research findings in developing countries. *British Medical Journal, 317* (7157), 531–535.

Gazmararian, J. A., Lazorick, S., Spitz, A. M., Ballard, T. J., Saltzman, L. E., & Marks, J. S. (1996). Prevalence of violence against pregnant women. *Journal of the American Medical Association, 275* (24), 1915–1920.

Gehlbach, S. H., Wilkinson, W. E., Hammond, W. E., Clapp, N. E., Finn, A. L., Taylor, W. J., & Rodell, M. S. (1984). Improving drug prescribing in a primary care practice. *Medical Care, 22* (3), 193–201.

Gelles, R. J. (1997). *Intimate violence in families* (3rd ed.). Thousand Oaks, CA: Sage Publications.

Gerbert, B., Caspers, N., Bronstone, A., Moe, J., & Abercrombie, P. (1999). A qualitative analysis of how physicians with expertise in domestic violence approach the identification of victims. *Annals of Internal Medicine, 131* (8), 578–584.

Geyman, J. P. (1998). Evidence-based medicine in primary care: An overview. *Journal of the American Board of Family Practice, 11* (1), 46–56.

Gielen, A. C., O'Campo, P. J., Campbell, J. C., Schollenberger, J., Woods, A. B., Jones, A. S., Dienemann, J. A., Kub, J., & Wynne, E. C. (2000). Women's opinions about domestic violence screening and mandatory reporting. *American Journal of Preventive Medicine, 19* (4), 279–285.

Gielen, A. C., Wilson, M. E., McDonald, E. M., Serwint, J. R., Andrews, J. S., Hwang, W. T., & Wang, M. C. (2001). Randomized trial of enhanced anticipatory guidance for injury prevention. *Archives of Pediatrics and Adolescent Medicine, 155* (1), 42–49.

Gil-Rivas, V., Fiorentine, R., & Anglin, M. D. (1996). Sexual abuse, physical abuse, and posttraumatic stress disorder among women participating in outpatient drug abuse treatment. *Journal of Psychoactive Drugs, 28* (1), 95–102.

Gin, N. E., Rucker, L., Frayne, S., Cygan, R., & Hubbell, F. A. (1991). Prevalence of domestic violence among patients in three ambulatory care internal medicine clinics. *Journal of General Internal Medicine, 6* (4), 317–322.

Glazer, A., Glock, M. H., & Page, F. E. (1997). Current bibligraphies in medicine; no. 97–3. Bethesda, MD: National Library of Medicine.

Goldberg, M. F. (1984). Training family practice residents in university obstetrics-gynecology departments: A national survey. *Journal of Family Practice, 19* (2), 162, 167.

Gondolf, E. W., Yllo, K., & Campbell, J. C. (1997). Collaboration between researchers and advocates. G. K. Kantor & J. L. Jasinski (Eds.), *Out of the darkness: Contemporary perspectives on family violence* (pp. 255–267). Thousand Oaks, CA: Sage.

Goodman, N. W. (1999). Who will challenge evidence-based medicine? *The Journal of the Royal College of Physicians of London, 33* (3), 249–251.

Gotzsche, P. C. (2001). Reporting of outcomes in arthritis trials measured on ordinal and interval scales is inadequate in relation to meta-analysis. *Annals of the Rheumatic Diseases, 60,* 349–352.

Green, L., & Kreuter, M. (1991). *Application of PRECEDE/PROCEED in community settings. Health promotion planning: An educational and environmental approach.* Mountain View, CA: Mayfield.

Green, L. W., & Kreuter, M. (1999). *Health Promotion Planning: An Educational and Ecological Approach REV* (3rd ed.). Mountainview, CA: Mayfield.

Green, M. L. (2000). Evidence-based medicine training in internal medicine residency programs: A national survey. *Journal of General Internal Medicine, 15* (2), 129–133.

Green, M. L., & Ellis, P. J. (1997). Impact of evidence-based medicine curriculum based on adult learning theory. *Journal of General Internal Medicine, 12* (12), 129–133.

Greenberg, L. W. (1995). Managed care, re-engineering and downsizing: Will medical education survive change? *Pediatrics, 96,* 1146–1147.

Greenfeld, L. A., Rand, M. R., Craven, D., Klaus, P. A., Perkins, C. A., Ringel, C., Warchol, G., Maston, C., & Fox, J. A. (1998). Report No. NCJ–167237. U.S. Department of Justice, Office of Justice Programs, Bureau of Justice Statistics.

Grimes, D. A. (1995). Introducing evidence-based medicine into a department of obstetrics and gynecology. *Obstetrics and Gynecology, 86* (3), 451–457.

Grimes, D. A., Bachicha, J. A., & Learman, L. A. (1998). Teaching critical appraisal to medical students in obstetrics and gynecology. *Obstetrics and Gynecology, 92* (5), 877–882.

Griner, P., & Danoff, D. (1995). Sustaining change in medical education. *Journal of the American Medical Association, 18,* 2429.

Griner, P. F. (1979). Use of laboratory tests in a teaching hospital: Long-term trends: Reductions in use and relative cost. *Annals of Internal Medicine, 90* (2), 243–248.

Grol, R. (1997). Beliefs and evidence in changing clinical practice. *British Medical Journal, 315* (7105), 418–421.

Grych, J. H., Jouriles, E. N., Swank, P. R., McDonald, R., & Norwood, W. D. (2000). Patterns of adjustment among children of battered women. *Journal of Consulting and Clinical Psychology, 68* (1), 84–94.

Gryskiewicz, J. M., & Detmer, D. E. (1983). Waste not, want not: Use of blood in elective operations—improved utilization of blood by use of blood-ordering protocols and the type and screen. *Current Surgery, 40* (5), 371–377.

Guyatt, G. H., Haynes, R. B., McKibbon, K. A., & Cook, D. J. (1997). Evidence-based health care. *Molecular Diagnosis, 2* (3), 209–215.

Guze, P. A. (1995). Cultivating curricular reform. *Academic Medicine, 70* (11), 971–973.

Haase, C. E., Short, P. D., Chapman, D. M., & Dersch, S. A. (1999). Domestic violence education in medical school: Does it make a difference? *Academic Emergency Medicine, 6* (8), 855–857.

Hafferty, F. W. (1998). Beyond curriculum reform: Confronting medicine's hidden curriculum. *Academic Medicine, 73* (4), 403–407.

Haines, A., & Donald, A. (1998). Making better use of research findings. *British Medical Journal, 317* (7150), 72–75.

Hansen, C. M. (1977). A program to introduce medical students to the problem of child abuse and neglect. *Journal of Medical Education, 52* (6), 522–524.

Harris, J.R., Caldwell, B., Cahill, K. (1998). Measuring the public's health in an era of accountability: Lessons from HEDIS, Health Plan Employer and Information Set. *American Journal of Preventive Medicine, 14* (3 Suppl), 9–13.

Harvard Injury Control Research Center. (2001). Protecting vulnerable populations. Advisory Board Meeting Harvard School of Public Health: HICRC.

Harwell, T. S., Casten, R. J., Armstrong, K. A., Dempsey, S., Coons, H. L., & Davis, M. (1998). Results of a domestic violence training program offered to the staff of urban community health centers. Evaluation Committee of the Philadelphia Family Violence Working Group. *American Journal of Preventive Medicine, 15* (3), 235–242.

Haugaard, J. J. (1996a). A guide for including information on child abuse and neglect in graduate and professional education and training. Washington, DC: American Psychological Association, Child Abuse and Neglect Working Group and Section on Child Maltreatment of the Division of Child, Youth and Family Services.

Haugaard, J. J. (1996b). A guide for including information on child abuse and neglect in the undergraduate curriculum. Washington, DC: American Psychological Association, Child Abuse and Neglect Working Group and Section on Child Maltreatment of the Division of Child, Youth and Family Services.

Haugaard, J. J., Bonner, B. L., Linares, O., Tharinger, D., Weisz, V., & Wolfe, D. A. (1995). Recommendations for education and training in child abuse and neglect: Issues from high school through postdoctoral levels. *Journal of Clinical Child Psychology, 24* (Suppl.), 78–83.

Haynes, B., & Haines, A. (1998). Barriers and bridges to evidence based clinical practice. *British Medical Journal, 317* (7153), 273–276.

Haynes, R. B., Davis, D. A., McKibbon, A., & Tugwell, P. (1984). A critical appraisal of the efficacy of continuing medical education. *Journal of the American Medical Association, 251* (1), 61–64.

Hazelrigg, C. O. (1995). A report on Indiana PANDA. Prevention of abuse and neglect through dental awareness. *Journal of the Indiana Dental Association, 74* (4), 40–43.

Hedin, L. W., Grimstad, H., Moller, A., Schei, B., & Janson, P. O. (1999). Prevalence of physical and sexual abuse before and during pregnancy among Swedish couples. *Acta Obstetricia Gynecologica Scandinavica, 78* (4), 310–315.

Hegarty, K., & Roberts, G. (1998). How common is domestic violence against women? The definition of partner abuse in prevalence studies. *Australian and New Zealand Journal of Public Health, 22* (1), 49–54.

Heider, F. (1958). *The psychology of interpersonal relations.* New York: Wiley.

Heise, L., Ellsberg, M., & Gottemoeller, M. (1999). *Ending violence against women.* Baltimore, MD: Johns Hopkins University School of Public Health, Population Information Program.

Hendricks-Matthews, M. K. (1991). A survey on violence education: A report of the STFM Violence Education Task Force. *Family Medicine, 23* (3), 194–197.

Hendricson, W. D., Payer, A. F., Rogers, L. P., & Markus, J. F. (1993). The medical school curriculum committee revisited. *Academic Medicine, 68* (3), 183–189.

Herman, J. (1992). *Trauma and recovery.* New York: Basic Books.

Hess, A. K., & Weiner, I. B. (1999). *The handbook of forensic psychology* (2nd ed.). New York: John Wiley.

Hibbard, R. A., Serwint, J., & Connolly, M. (1987). Educational program on evaluation of alleged sexual abuse victims. *Child Abuse and Neglect, 11* (4), 513–519.

Hill, J., & Spoeri, R. (1997). How does HEDIS affect quality improvement strategies in an HMO? *Managed Care Interface, 10* (11), 60–65.

Hillman, R. S., Helbig, S., Howes, S., Hayes, J., Meyer, D. M., & McArthur, J. R. (1979). The effect of an educational program on transfusion practices in a regional blood program. *Transfusion, 19* (2), 153–157.

Howe, A. C., Bonner, B., Parker, M., & Sausen, K. (1992). Graduate training in child maltreatment in APA-approved psychology programs. Meeting of the American Psychological Association. Washington, DC.

Huba, G. J., Panter, A. T., Melchior, L. A., Anderson, D., Colgrove, J., Driscoll, M., German, V. F., Henderson, H., Henderson, R., Lalonde, B., Rahimian, A., Rohweder, C., Uldall, K. K., Wolfe, L., & Zalumas, J. (2000). Effects of HIV/AIDS education and training on patient care and provider practices: A crosscutting evaluation. *AIDS Education and Prevention, 12* (2), 93–112.

Hudak, R. P., Jacoby, I., Meyer, G. S., Potter, A. L., Hooper, T. I., & Krakauer, H. (1997). Competency in health care management: A training model in epidemiological methods for assessing and improving the quality of clinical practice through evidence-based decision making. *Quality Management in Health Care, 6* (1), 23–33.

Hughes D. (1997). Innovation + incentives + HEDIS = high immunization rates. *Managed Care, 6* (9), 99–106.

Humphris, D. (1999). A framework to evaluate the role of nurse specialists. *Professional Nurse, 14* (6), 377–379.

Hundert, E. M., Hafferty, F., & Christakis, D. (1996). Characteristics of the informal curriculum and trainees' ethical choices. *Academic Medicine, 71* (6), 624–642.

Hunt, D. D., Scott, C., Zhong, S., & Goldstein, E. (1996). Frequency and effect of negative comments ("badmouthing") on medical students' career choices. *Academic Medicine, 71* (6), 665–669.

Ibbotson, T., Grimshaw, J., & Grant, A. (1998). Evaluation of a programme of workshops for promoting the teaching of critical appraisal skills. *Medical Education, 32* (5), 486–491.

Institute of Medicine. (1997). *Approaching death: Improving care at the end of life.* Committee on Care at the End of Life, M. Field, & C. Kassel (Eds.), Institute of Medicine. Washington, DC: National Academy Press.

Institute of Medicine. (2001). *Crossing the quality chasm: A new health system for the 21st century.* Committee on Quality of Health Care in America, Institute of Medicine. Washington, DC: National Academy Press.

Irazuzta, J. E., McJunkin, J. E., Danadian, K., Arnold, F., & Zhang, J. (1997). Outcome and cost of child abuse. *Child Abuse and Neglect, 21* (8), 751–757.

Ireland, L. M., & Powell, C. (1997). Development of an introductory course in child protection. *British Journal of Nursing, 6* (12), 686–690.

Jacobson, A., & Richardson, B. (1987). Assault experiences of 100 psychiatric inpatients: Evidence of the need for routine inquiry. *American Journal of Psychiatry, 144* (7), 908–913.

Jadad, A. R., & Haynes, R. B. (1998). The Cochrane Collaboration—advances and challenges in improving evidence-based decision making. *Medical Decision Making, 18* (1), 2–9; discussion, 16–18.

Jenny, C. (1997). Pediatrics and child sexual abuse: Where we've been and where we're going. *Pediatric Annals, 26* (5), 284–286.

Jesse, S. A. (1995). Child abuse and neglect curricula in North American dental schools. *Journal of Dental Education, 59* (8), 841–843.

Jogerst, G. J., & Ely, J. W. (1997). Home visit program for teaching elder abuse evaluations. *Family Medicine, 29* (9), 634–639.

Johns, M. B., Hovell, M. F., Drastal, C. A., Lamke, C., & Patrick, K. (1992). Promoting prevention services in primary care: A controlled trial. *American Journal of Preventive Medicine, 8* (3), 135–140.

Johnson, K. (1998). Crime or punishment: The parental corporal punishment defense—reasonable and necessary or excused abuse? *University of Illinois Law Review, 413,* 416.

Joint Commission on Accreditation of Healthcare Organizations (JCAHO). (1995). *1996 Comprehensive Accreditation Manual for Hospitals.* Oakbrook, IL: JCAHO.

Jonassen, J. A., Pugnaire, M. P., Mazor, K., Regan, M. B., Jacobson, E. W., Gammon, W., Doepel, D. G., & Cohen, A. J. (1999). The effect of a domestic violence interclerkship on the knowledge, attitudes, and skills of third-year medical students. *Academic Medicine, 74* (7), 821–828.

Jones, A. S., Gielen, A. C., Campbell, J. C., Schollenberger, J., Dienemann, J. A., Kub, J., O'Campo, P. J., & Wynne, E. C. (1999). Annual and lifetime prevalence of partner abuse in a sample of female HMO enrollees. *Women's Health Issues, 9* (6), 295–305.

Jones, J. S., Veenstra, T. R., Seamon, J. P., & Krohmer, J. (1997). Elder mistreatment: National survey of emergency physicians. *Annals of Emergency Medicine, 30* (4), 473–479.

Kahneman, D., & Tversky, A. (1982). *Judgment under uncertainty: Heuristics biases.* Cambridge: Cambridge University Press.

Kalichman, S. C. (1993). *Mandated reporting of suspected child abuse: Ethics, law and policy.* Washington, DC: American Psychological Association.

Kalichman, S. C. (1999). *Mandated reporting of suspected child abuse: Ethics, law, and policy* (2nd ed.). Washington, DC: American Psychological Association.

Kalichman, S. C., & Brosig, C. L. (1993). The effects of child abuse reporting laws on psychologists' reporting behavior: A comparison of two state statutes. *Law and Human Behavior, 17,* 83–93.

Kalichman, S. C., Brosig, C. L., & Kalichman, M. O. (1994). Mandatory child abuse reporting laws: Issues and implications for the treatment of offenders. *Journal of Offender Rehabilitation, 21,* 27–43.

Kalichman, S. C., & Craig, M. E. (1991). Professional psychologists' decisions to report suspected abuse: Clinician and situation influences. *Professional Psychology: Research and Practice, 22,* 84–89.

Kalichman, S. C., Craig, M. E., & Follingstad, D. R. (1988). Mental health professionals and suspected cases of child abuse: An investigation of factors influencing reporting. *Community Mental Health Journal, 24* (1), 43–51.

Kalichman, S. C., Szymanowski, D., McKee, G., Taylor, J., & Craig, M. E. (1989). Cluster analytically derived MMPI profile subgroups of incarcerated adult rapists. *Journal of Clinical Psychology, 45* (1), 149–155.

Kassebaum, D. (1995). Introduction: Why another conference on family violence? *Academic Medicine, 70* (11), 614–1446.

Kassirer, J. P. (1995). Teaching problem solving—how are we doing? *New England Journal of Medicine, 332* (22), 1507–1509.

Katon, W., Von Korff, M., Lin, E., Walker, E., Simon, G. E., Bush, T., Robinson, P., & Russo, J. (1995). Collaborative management to achieve treatment guidelines: Impact on depression in primary care. *Journal of the American Medical Association, 273* (13), 1026–1031.

Kelly, J. T. (1997). The need for improved access to information about clinical performance measurement. *Journal of Clinical Outcome Management, 4* (3), 22–24.

Kempe, C., Silverman, F. N., Steele, B., Droegemueller, W., & Silver, H. (1962). The battered-child syndrome. *Journal of the American Medical Association, 181,* 17–24.

Kendall, P. L., & Reader, G. G. (1988). Innovations in medical education of the 1950s contrasted with those of the 1970s and 1980s. *Journal of Health and Social Behavior, 29* (4), 279–293.

Kessler, D. B., & New, M. I. (1989). Emerging trends in child abuse and neglect. *Pediatric Annals, 18* (8), 471–472, 474–475.

Kimerling, R., & Calhoun, K. S. (1994). Somatic symptoms, social support, and treatment seeking among sexual assault victims. *Journal of Consulting and Clinical Psychology, 62* (2), 333–340.

King, M. C. (1988). *Helping battered women: A study of the relationship between nurses' education and experience and their preferred models of helping.* Notes Available at Dissertation Abstracts International   493105

Kinports, K., & Fischer, K. (1993). Orders of protection in domestic violence cases: An empirical assessment of the impact of the reform of statutes. *Texas Journal of Women and Law, 2* (163), 200–205.

Kirschner, R. (1997). The pathology of child abuse. M. Helfer, R. Kempe, & R. Krugman (Eds.), *The battered child* (5th ed., pp. 248–295). Chicago: Chicago University Press.

Knight, R. A., & Remington, P. L. (2000). Training internal medicine residents to screen for domestic violence. *Journal of Women's Health and Gender Based Medicine, 9* (2), 167–174.

Knowles, M. S. (1984). *The adult learner: A neglected species.* Houston, TX: Gulf Publishing Co.

Knowles, M. S. (1990). *The adult learner: A neglected species* (4th ed.). Houston, TX: Gulf Publishing Co.

Knox, A. (1990). Influences on participation in continuing education. *Journal of Continuing Education in the Health Professions, 10,* 261–274.

Kolbo, J. R., Blakely, E. H., & Engelman, D. (1996). Children who witness domestic violence: A review of empirical literature. *Journal of Interpersonal Violence, 11,* 281–293.

Koop, C. E. (1991). Foreword. M. L. Rosenberg & M. A. Fenley (Eds.), *Violence in America: A public health approach* (pp. v-vi). New York: Oxford University Press.

Koss, M. P., Koss, P. G., & Woodruff, W. J. (1991). Deleterious effects of criminal victimization on women's health and medical utilization. *Archives of Internal Medicine, 151* (2), 342–347.

Kost, S., & Schwartz, W. (1989). Use of a computer simulation to evaluate a seminar on child abuse. *Pediatric Emergency Care, 5* (3), 202–203.

Krell, H. L., Richardson, C. M., LaManna, T. N., & Kairys, S. W. (1983). Child abuse and worker training. *Journal of Contemporary Social Work,* 532–538.

Krenk, C. J. (1984). Training residence staff for child abuse treatment. *Child Welfare, 63* (2), 167–173.

Kripke, E. N., Steele, G., O'Brien, M. K., & Novack, D. H. (1998). Domestic violence training program for residents. *Journal of General Internal Medicine, 13* (12), 839–841.

Krueger, P., & Patterson, C. (1997). Detecting and managing elder abuse: Challenges in primary care. *Canadian Medical Association Journal, 157* (8), 1095–1100.

Krugman, R., & Jones, D. (1987). Incest and other forms of sexual abuse. R. Helfer, & R. Kempe (Eds.), *The battered child* (4th ed.,). Chicago: Chicago University Press.

Krugman, R. (1997). Child protection policy. M. E. Helfer, R. Kempe, & R. Krugman (Eds.), *The battered child* (5th ed., pp. 627–641). Chicago: University of Chicago Press.

Kurz, D., & Stark, E. (1988). Not-so-benign neglect. K. Yllo & M. Bograd (Eds.), *Feminist perspectives on wife abuse* (pp. 249–265). Newbury Park, CA: Sage Publications.

Lachs, M., & Fulmer, T. (1995). Recognizing elder abuse and neglect: Clinics in geriatric medicine. *Geriatric Emergency Care, 9* (3), 665–675.

Lachs, M. S., & Pillemer, K. (1995). Abuse and neglect of elderly persons. *New England Journal of Medicine, 332* (7), 437–443.

Lachs, M. S., Williams, C., O'Brien, S., Hurst, L., & Horwitz, R. (1997). Risk factors for reported elder abuse and neglect: A nine-year observational cohort study. *Gerontologist, 37* (4), 469–474.

Lachs, M. S., Williams, C. S., O'Brien, S., Hurst, L., Kossack, A., Siegal, A., & Tinetti, M. E. (1997). ED use by older victims of family violence. *Annals of Emergency Medicine, 30* (4), 448–454.

Lachs, M. S., Williams, C. S., O'Brien, S., Pillemer, K. A., & Charlson, M. E. (1998). The mortality of elder mistreatment. *Journal of the American Medical Association, 280* (5), 428–432.

Lane, D. S., Polednak, A. P., & Burg, M. A. (1991). Effect of continuing medical education and cost reduction on physician compliance with mammography screening guidelines. *The Journal of Family Practice, 33* (4), 359–368.

Lane, D. S., & Ross, V. (1998). Defining competencies and performance indicators for physicians in medical management. *American Journal of Preventive Medicine, 14* (3), 229–236.

Larkin, G. L., Rolniak, S., Hyman, K. B., MacLeod, B. A., & Savage, R. (2000). Effect of an administrative intervention on rates of screening for domestic violence in an urban emergency department. *American Journal of Public Health, 90* (9), 1444–1448.

Larson, E. B. (1999). Evidence-based medicine: Is translating evidence into practice a solution to the cost-quality challenges facing medicine? *The Joint Commission Journal of Quality Improvement, 25* (9), 480–485.

Larson, E. B., Bergman, J., Heidrich, F., Alvin, B. L., & Schneeweiss, R. (1982). Do postcard reminders improve influenza compliance? A prospective trial of different postcard "cues." *Medical Care, 20* (6), 639–648.

Larson, E. B., Olsen, E., Cole, W., & Shortell, S. (1979). The relationship of health beliefs and a postcard reminder to influenza vaccination. *Journal of Family Practice, 8* (6), 1207–1211.

Lawrence, L. L., & Brannen, S. J. (2000). The impact of physician training on child maltreatment reporting: A multi-specialty study. *Military Medicine, 165* (8), 607–611.

Leiman, J. M., Rothschild, N., Meyer, J. E., & Kott, A. (1998). *Addressing domestic violence and its consequences.* Policy Report of the Commonwealth Fund Commission on Women's Health. The Commonwealth Fund.

Leininger, L. S., Finn, L., Dickey, L., Dietrich, A. J., Foxhall, L., Garr, D., Stewart, B., & Wender, R. (1996). An office system for organizing preventive services: A report by the American Cancer Society Advisory Group on Preventive Health Care Reminder Systems. *Archives of Family Medicine, 5* (2), 108–115.

Lesky, L. G., & Hershman, W. Y. (1995). Practical approaches to a major educational challenge: Training students in an ambulatory setting. *Archives of Internal Medicine, 155,* 897–904.

Letourneau, E. J., Holmes, M., & Chasedunn-Roark, J. (1999). Gynecologic health consequences to victims of interpersonal violence. *Women's Health Issues, 9* (2), 115–120.

Leung, P., & Cheung, K. M. (1998). The impact of child protective service training: A longitudinal study of workers' job performance, knowledge and attitudes. *Research on Social Work Practice, 8* (6), 668–684.

Levine, M., & Doueck, H. J. (1995). *The impact of mandated reporting on the therapeutic process.* Newbury Park, CA: Sage.

Liberati, A., Pistotti, V., & Telaro, E. (1999). Evidence-based medicine and practice: What's new for the physicians? *Forum (Genova), 9* (4), 361–371.

Lichtenstein, S., & Fischoff, B. (1980). Training for calibration. *Organizational Behavior and Human Performance, 20,* 159–183.

Like, R. C., Steiner, P. R., & Rubel, A. J. (1996). Recommended core curriculum guidelines on culturally sensitive and competent health care. *Family Medicine, 28,* 291–297.

Linares, L. O., Groves, B. M., Greenberg, J., Bronfman, E., Augustyn, M., & Zuckerman, B. (1999). Restraining orders: A frequent marker of adverse maternal health. *Pediatrics, 104* (2, Pt 1), 249–257.

Lipsey, M. W. (1990). *Design sensitivity.* Thousand Oaks, CA: Sage.

Lipsey, M. W., & Cordray, D. S. (2000). Evaluation methods for social intervention. *Annual Review of Psychology, 51,* 345–375.

Longstreth, G. F., Mason, C., Schreiber, I. G., & Tsao-Wei, D. (1998). Group psychotherapy for women molested in childhood: Psychological and somatic symptoms and medical visits. *International Journal of Group Psychotherapy, 48* (4), 533–541.

Longstreth, G. F., & Wolde-Tsadik, G. (1993). Irritable bowel-type symptoms in HMO examinees: Prevalence, demographics, and clinical correlates. *Digestive Diseases and Sciences, 38* (9), 1581–1589.

Loudon, R. F., Anderson, P. M., Gill, P. S., & Greenfield, S. M. (1999). Educating medical students for work in culturally diverse societies. *Journal of the American Medical Association, 282* (9), 875–880.

Madlon-Kay, D. J. (1987). Improving the periodic health examination: Use of a screening flow chart for patients and physicians. *Journal of Family Practice, 25* (5), 470–473.

Magdol, L., Moffitt, T. E., Caspi, A., Newman, D. L., Fagan, J., & Silva, P. A. (1997). Gender differences in partner violence in a birth cohort of 21-year-olds: Bridging the gap between clinical and epidemiological approaches. *Journal of Consulting and Clinical Psychology, 65* (1), 68–78.

Maiman, L. A., Becker, M. H., Liptak, G. S., Nazarian, L. F., & Rounds, K. A. (1988). Improving pediatricians' compliance-enhancing practices. A randomized trial. *American Journal of Diseases of Children, 142* (7), 773–779.

Maiuro, R. D., Vitaliano, P. P., Sugg, N. K., Thompson, D. C., Rivara, F. P., & Thompson, R. S. (2000). Development of a health care provider survey for domestic violence: Psychometric properties. *American Journal of Preventive Medicine, 19* (4), 245–252.

Maman, S., Campbell, J., Sweat, M. D., & Gielen, A. C. (2000). The intersections of HIV and violence: Directions for future research and interventions. *Social Science and Medicine, 50* (4), 459–478.

Marinker, M. (1997). Myth, paradox and the hidden curriculum. *Medical Education, 31* (4), 293–298.

Marks, J. (2000). Challenges and strategies for enhancing health care's response to domestic violence. *Family Violence Prevention Fund National Conference on Health Care and Domestic Violence.* San Francisco, CA.

Martin, S. G., Shwartz, M., Whalen, B. J., D'Arpa, D., Ljung, G. M., Thorne, J. H., & McKusick, A. E. (1982). Impact of a mandatory second-opinion program on Medicaid surgery rates. *Medical Care, 20* (1), 21–45.

Marton, K. I., Tul, V., & Sox, H. C. Jr. (1985). Modifying test-ordering behavior in the outpatient medical clinic: A controlled trial of two educational interventions. *Archives of Internal Medicine, 145* (5), 816–821.

Mashta, O. (2000). *Mental health experts should offer training to GPs.* BMJ Publishing Group.

McCann, I., & Pearlman, L. (1990). Vicarious traumatization: A framework for understanding the psychological effects of working with victims. *Journal of Traumatic Stress, 3,* 131–149.

McCarthy, L. H., & Zubialde, J. P. (1997). An integrated, evidence-based medicine program for FP residents. *Family Medicine, 29* (10), 687–688.

McCauley, J., Kern, D. E., Kolodner, K., Dill, L., Schroeder, A. F., DeChant, H. K., Ryden, J., Bass, E. B., & Derogatis, L. R. (1995). The "battering syndrome": Prevalence and clinical characteristics of domestic violence in primary care internal medicine practices. *Annals of Internal Medicine, 123* (10), 737–746.

McCauley, J., Kern, D. E., Kolodner, K., Dill, L., Schroeder, A. F., DeChant, H. K., Ryden, J., Derogatis, L. R., & Bass, E. B. (1997). Clinical characteristics of women with a history of childhood abuse: Unhealed wounds. *Journal of the American Medical Association, 277* (17), 1362–1368.

McCauley, J., Kern, D. E., Kolodner, K., Derogatis, L. R., & Bass, E. B. (1998). Relation of low-severity violence to women's health. *Journal of General Internal Medicine, 13* (10), 687–691.

McCauley, J., Yurk, R. A., Jenckes, M. W., & Ford, D. E. (1998). Inside "Pandora's box": Abused women's experiences with clinicians and health services. *Journal of General Internal Medicine, 13* (8), 549–555.

McDonald, C. J., Hui, S. L., Smith, D. M., Tierney, W. M., Cohen, S. J., Weinberger, M., & McCabe, G. P. (1984). Reminders to physicians from an introspective computer medical record. A two-year randomized trial. *Annals of Internal Medicine, 100* (1), 130–138.

McDowell, I., Newell, C., & Rosser, W. (1986). Comparison of three methods of recalling patients for influenza vaccination. *Canadian Medical Association Journal, 135* (9), 991–997.

McFarlane, J., Parker, B., Soeken, K., & Bullock, L. (1992). Assessing for abuse during pregnancy: Severity and frequency of injuries and associated entry into prenatal care. *Journal of the American Medical Association, 267* (23), 3176–3178.

McFarlane, J., & Parker B. (1994). Preventing abuse during pregnancy: An assessment and intervention protocol. *American Journal of Maternal and Child Nursing, 19* (6), 321–324.

McGoldrick, M., Giordano, J., Pearce, J. K., & Giordano, J. (1996). *Ethnicity and family therapy* (2nd ed.). New York: Guilford Press.

McGowan, J. E. Jr., & Finland, M. (1974). Usage of antibiotics in a general hospital: Effect of requiring justification. *Journal of Infectious Diseases, 130* (2), 165–168.

McGrath, M. E., Bettacchi, A., Duffy, S. J., Peipert, J. F., Becker, B. M., & St. Angelo, L. (1997). Violence against women: Provider barriers to intervention in emergency departments. *Academic Emergency Medicine, 4* (4), 297–300.

McKeown, T. (1968). *Screening in medical care, reviewing the evidence—A collection of essays.* London: Oxford University Press.

McLeer, S. V., & Anwar, R. (1989). A study of battered women presenting in an emergency department. *American Journal of Public Health, 79* (1), 65–66.

McLeer, S. V., Anwar, R. A., Herman, S., & Maquiling, K. (1989). Education is not enough: A systems failure in protecting battered women. *Annals of Emergency Medicine, 18* (6), 651–653.

McPhee, S. J., Bird, J. A., Fordham, D., Rodnick, J. E., & Osborn, E. H. (1991). Promoting cancer prevention activities by primary care physicians. Results of a randomized controlled trial. *Journal of the American Medical Association, 266* (4), 538–544.

McPhee, S. J., Bird, J. A., Jenkins, C. N., & Fordham, D. (1989). Promoting cancer screening: A randomized, controlled trial of three interventions. *Archives of Internal Medicine, 149* (8), 1866–1872.

Mechanic, D. (1998). *Managed behavioral health care: Current realities and future potential.* San Francisco, CA: Jossey-Bass Publishers.

Mechanic, R. E., & Dobson, A. (1996). The impact of managed care on clinical research: A preliminary investigation. *Health Affairs, 15,* 72–89.

Melton, G. B. (1987). The clashing of symbols: Prelude to child and family policy. *American Psychologist, 42,* 345–354.

Melton, G. B. (1994). Doing justice and doing good: Conflicts for mental health professionals. *Future of Children, 4* (2), 102–118.

Melton, G. B., Goodman, G. S., Kalichman, S. C., Levine, M., Saywitz, K. J., & Koocher, G. P. (1995). Empirical research on child maltreatment and the law. *Journal of Clinical Child Psychology, 24* (Suppl), 47–77.

Melton, G. B., & Limber, S. (1989). Psychologists' involvement in cases of child maltreatment: Limits of role and expertise. *American Psychologist, 44* (9), 1225–1233.

Melton, G. B., Petrila, J., Poythress, N. G., & Slobogin, C. (1997). *Psychological evaluations for the courts: A handbook for mental health professionals and lawyers* (2nd ed.). New York: Guilford.

Melton, G. B., Weithorn, L. A., & Slobogin, C. (1985). *Community mental health centers and the courts: An evaluation of community-based forensic services.* Lincoln: University of Nebraska Press.

Mercy, J. A., Rosenberg, M. L., Powell, K. E., Broome, C. V., & Roper, W. L. (1993). Public health policy for preventing violence. *Health Affairs, 12* (4), 7–29.

Merriam, S. B., & Caffarella, R. S. (1999). *Learning in adulthood: A comprehensive guide* (2nd ed.). San Francisco: Jossey-Bass.

Michaud, G. C., McGowan, J. L., van der Jagt, R. H., Dugan, A. K., & Tugwell, P. (1996). The introduction of evidence-based medicine as a component of daily practice. *Bulletin of the Medical Library Association, 84* (4), 478–481.

Miller, T., Cohen, M., & Rossman, S. (1993). Victim costs of violent crime and resulting injuries. *Health Affairs,* 293–317.

Miller, T., Cohen, M., & Wierseman, B. (1995). *Crime in the US: Victim costs and consequences.* Washington, DC: Urban Institute and the National Public Services Research Institute.

Miller, T., Cohen, M., & Wiersema, B. (1996). Washington, DC: U.S. Department of Justice.

Monahan, K., & O'Leary, K. D. (1999). Head injury and battered women: An initial inquiry. *Health and Social Work, 24* (4), 269–278.

Monteleone, J. A. (1994). *Recognition of child abuse for the mandated reporter.* St. Louis: G.W. Medical Publishing.

Moore, D. Jr. (1998). Needs assessment in the new health care environment: Combining discrepancy analysis and outcomes to create more effective CME. *Journal of Continuing Education in the Health Professions, 18,* 133–141.

Moore, M. L., Zaccaro, D., & Parsons, L. H. (1998). Attitudes and practices of registered nurses toward women who have experienced abuse/domestic violence. *Journal of Obstetric, Gynecologic and Neonatal Nursing, 27* (2), 175–182.

Moran Campbell, E. (2000). On education and training. *The Lancet, 356,* 1116.

Morgan, M., & Edwards, V. (1995). *How to interview sexual abuse victims: Including the use of anatomical dolls.* Thousand Oaks, CA: Sage.

Morin, K. H., Bucher, L., Plowfield, L., Hayes, E., Mahoney, P., & Armiger, L. (1999). Using research to establish protocols for practice: A statewide study of acute care agencies. *Clinical Nurse Specialist, 13* (2), 77–84.

Moss, A. (2000). Epidemiology and the politics of needle exchange. *American Journal of Public Health, 90* (9), 1385–1387.

Muelleman, R. L., Lenaghan, P. A., & Pakieser, R. A. (1996). Battered women: Injury locations and types. *Annals of Emergency Medicine, 28* (5), 486–492.

Muelleman, R. L., Reuwer, J., Sanson, T. G., Gerson, L., Woolard, B., Yancy, A. H., & Bernstein, E. (1996). An emergency medicine approach to violence throughout the life cycle. SAEM Public Health and Education Committee. *Academic Emergency Medicine, 3* (7), 708–715.

Mullooly, J. P. (1987). Increasing influenza vaccination among high-risk elderly: A randomized controlled trial of a mail cue in an HMO setting. *American Journal of Public Health, 77* (5), 626–627.

Murray, D. M. (1998). *Design and analysis of group randomized trials.* Oxford, England: Nye.

Muscular Dystrophy Association. *MDA ALS Research and Clinical Centers.* Available: http://www.mdausa.org/clinics/alsserv.html [May 2001].

Myers, J. (1992). *Legal issues in child abuse and neglect.* Newbury Park, CA: Sage.

Myers, L. P., & Schroeder, S. A. (1981). Physician use of services for the hospitalized patient: A review, with implications for cost containment. *The Milbank Memorial Fund Quarterly. Health and Society, 59* (4), 481–507.

National Association for Injury Control Research Centers. *NAICRC member research project databank.* Available: http://www.quickbase.com/db/6tejwf5t [June 7, 2001].

National Association of Social Workers Delegate Assembly. (1999). Policy Statement on Domestic Violence 3rd Ed. Washington, DC: NASW.

National Cancer Institute. (1996). NCI Factbook. Bethesda, MD: National Cancer Institute.

National Center for Health Statistics. (2001). Healthy People 2000 Final Review. Report No. DHHS 01-0256. Hyattsville, MD: Public Health Service.

National Center for Injury Prevention and Control. *NCIPC Extramural Research Grants Program, Injury Control Research Centers.* Available: http://www.cdc.gov/ncipc/res-opps/icrcs.htm [June 7, 2001].

National Clearinghouse on Child Abuse and Neglect. (1997). Washington, DC: Department of Health and Human Services.

National Committee for Quality Control. *NCQA's State of Managed Care Quality Report, Quality Compasso '99 Show Simple Formula for Health Care Quality: Accountability.* Available: http://www.ncqa.org/pages/communications/news/somcqrel.html [April 27, 2000].

National Institute for Occupational Safety and Health (NIOSH). (1999). Report No. 99–142. Cincinnati, OH: DHHS.

National Institute on Alcohol Abuse and Alcoholism. *National Alcohol Research Centers.* Available: http://www.niaaa.nih.gov/extramural/ResCtrs1198.htm [May 2001].

National Research Council. (1993). *Understanding child abuse and neglect.* Panel on the Understanding and Control of Violent Behavior, A. Reiss, Jr. & J. Roth (Eds.), Commission on the Behavioral and Social Sciences and Education. Washington, DC: National Academy Press.

National Research Council. (1996). *Understanding violence against women.* Panel on Research on Violence Against Women, N. Crowell & A. Burgess, (Eds.), Commission on the Behavioral and Social Sciences and Education. Washington, DC: National Academy Press.

National Research Council. (1999). *How people learn: Brain, mind, experience, and school.* Committee on Developments in the Science of Learning, Commissions on the Behavioral and Social Sciences and Education. Washington, DC: National Academy Press.

National Research Council & Institute of Medicine. (1998). *Violence in families: Assessing prevention and treatment programs.* Committee on the Assessment of Family Violence Interventions, R. Chalk & P. King (Eds.), Commission on the Behavioral and Social Sciences and Education. Washington, DC: National Academy Press.

Nattinger, A. B., Panzer, R. J., & Janus, J. (1989). Improving the utilization of screening mammography in primary care practices. *Archives of Internal Medicine, 149* (9), 2087–2092.

Neal, J., Brown, T., & Rojjanasrirat, W. (1999). Implementation of a case coordinator role: A focused ethnographic study. *Journal of Professional Nurses, 15* (6), 349–355.

Neame, R., Panzer, R., & Janus, J. (1981). Toward independent learning: Curricular design for assisting students to learn how to learn. *Journal of Medical Education, 56,* 886–893.

Needleman, H. L., MacGregor, S. S., & Lynch, L. M. (1995). Effectiveness of a statewide child abuse and neglect educational program for dental professionals. *Pediatric Dentistry, 17* (1), 41–45.

Nelms, T. P. (1999). An educational program to examine emergency nurses' attitudes and enhance caring intervention with battered women. *Journal of Emergency Nurses, 25* (4), 290–293.

Nelson, B. (1984). *Making an issue of child abuse: Political agenda setting for social problems.* Chicago: University of Chicago Press.

Nelson, E. C., Splaine, M. E., Batalden, P. B., & Plume, S. K. (1998). Building measurement and data collection into medical practice. *Annals of Internal Medicine, 128* (6), 460–466.

Neumann, D., & Gamble, S. (1995). Issues in the professional development of psychotherapists: Counter transference and vicarious traumatization in the new trauma therapist. *Psychotherapy, 32,* 341–347.

Newberger, E. H. (1977). Child abuse and neglect: Toward a firmer foundation for practice and policy. *American Journal of Orthopsychiatry, 47* (3), 374–376.

Newman, M. G. (1998). Improved clinical decision-making using the evidence-based approach. *Journal of the American Dental Association, 129* (Suppl), 4S–8S.

Norman, G. R., & Shannon, S. I. (1998). Effectiveness of instruction in critical appraisal (evidence-based medicine) skills: A critical appraisal. *Canadian Medical Association Journal, 158* (2), 177–181.

O'Faolain, J., & Martines, L. (1974). *Not in God's image: Women in history.* Glasgow: Fontana/Collins.

Oates, R. K., & Kempe, R. E. (1997). Growth failure in infants. M. Helfer, R. Kempe, & R. Krugman (Eds.), *The battered child* (5th ed.). Chicago: University of Chicago Press.

Office of Minority Health. (2000). Assuring cultural competence in health care: Recommendations for national standards and an outcomes-focused research agenda. Washington, DC: Federal Register.

Olson, L., Anctil, C., Fullerton, L., Brillman, J., Arbuckle, J., & Sklar, D. (1996). Increasing emergency physician recognition of domestic violence. *Annals of Emergency Medicine, 27* (6), 741–746.

Orwin, R. G., & Cordray, D. S. (1985). Effects of deficient reporting on meta-analysis: A conceptual framework and reanalysis. *Psychological Bulletin, 97* (1), 134–147.

Osattin, A., & Short, L. (1998). Intimate partner violence and sexual assault: A guide to training materials and programs for health care providers. Atlanta, GA: Centers for Disease Control and Prevention, National Center for Injury Prevention and Control.

Oskamp, S. (1965). Overconfidence in case study judgments. *Journal of Consulting Psychology, 29,* 261–265.

Ottoson, J. M., & Patterson, I. (2000). Contextual influences on learning application in practice: An extended role for process evaluation. *Evaluation and the Health Professions, 23* (2), 194–211.

Overhage, J. M., Tierney, W. M., & McDonald, C. J. (1996). Computer reminders to implement preventive care guidelines for hospitalized patients. *Archives of Internal Medicine, 156,* 1551–1556.

Oxman, A. D., Thomson, M. A., Davis, D. A., & Haynes, R. B. (1995). No magic bullets: A systematic review of 102 trials of interventions to improve professional practice. *Canadian Medical Association Journal, 153* (10), 1423–1431.

Pagel, J. R., & Pagel, P. R. (1993). Participants' perceptions of a mandated training course in the identification and reporting of child abuse. *Pediatric Nursing, 19* (6), 554–558.

Palusci, V. J., & McHugh, M. T. (1995). Interdisciplinary training in the evaluation of child sexual abuse. *Child Abuse and Neglect, 19* (9), 1031–1038.

Paluzzi, P.A., & Quimby, C.H. (1998). *Domestic violence education.* Washington, DC: American College of Nurse Midwives.

Panter, A. T., Huba, G. J., Melchior, L. A., Anderson, D., Driscoll, M., German, V. F., Henderson, H., Henderson, R., Lalonde, B., Uldall, K. K., & Zalumas, J. (2000). Trainee characteristics and perceptions of HIV/AIDS training quality. *Evaluation and the Health Professions, 23* (2), 149–171.

Pappaioanou, M., & Evans, C. Jr. (1998). Development of the Guide to Community Preventive Services: A U.S. Public Health Service initiative. *Journal of Public Health Management and Practice, 4* (2), 48–54.

Parker, B., & Schumacher, D. (1977). The battered wife syndrome and violence in the nuclear family of origin: A controlled pilot study. *American Journal of Public Health, 67* (8), 760–761.

Parsons, L. H., Zaccaro, D., Wells, B., & Stovall, T. G. (1995). Methods of and attitudes toward screening obstetrics and gynecology patients for domestic violence. *American Journal of Obstetrics and Gynecology, 173* (2), 381–386; discussion 386–387.

Peters, A. L., Legorreta, A. P., Ossorio, R. C., Davidson, M. B. (1996). Quality of outpatient care provided to diabetic patients: A health maintenance organization experience. *Diabetes Care, 15* (1), 73–85.

Pillemer, K., & Finkelhor, D. (1988). The prevalence of elder abuse: A random sample survey. *Gerontologist, 28* (1), 51–57.

Pinn, V. W., & Chunko, M. T. (1997). The diverse faces of violence: Minority women and domestic abuse. *Academic Medicine, 72* (Suppl 1), S65–S71.

Plous, S. (1993). *The psychology of judgment and decision making.* Philadelphia: Temple University Press.

Pommerenke, F. A., & Dietrich, A. (1992a). Improving and maintaining preventive services. Part 1: Applying the patient path model. *Journal of Family Practice, 34* (1), 86–91.

Pommerenke, F. A., & Dietrich, A. (1992b). Improving and maintaining preventive services, Part 2: Practical principles for primary care. *Journal of Family Practice, 34* (1), 92–97.

Pope, K. S., & Feldman-Summers, S. (1992). National survey of psychologists' sexual and physical abuse history and their evaluation of training and competence in these areas. *Professional Psychology: Research and Practice, 23,* 353–362.

Poses, R. M. (1999). Money and mission? Addressing the barriers to evidence-based medicine. *Journal of General Internal Medicine, 14* (4), 262–264.

Posnick, W. R., & Donly, K. J. (1990). Instruction in child abuse and neglect in the predoctoral curriculum. *Journal of Dental Education, 54* (2), 158–159.

Post, R. D., Willett, A. B., Franks, R. D., House, R. M., Back, S. M., & Weissberg, M. P. (1980). A preliminary report on the prevalence of domestic violence among psychiatric inpatients. *American Journal of Psychiatry, 137* (8), 974–975.

Prevent Child Abuse America. (2001). *Total estimated cost of child abuse and neglect in the United States.* Available: http://www.preventchildabuse.org/research.ctr/reports.html [June 1, 2001].

Prislin, M. D., Vandenbark, M. S., & Clarkson, Q. D. (1986). The impact of a health screening flow sheet on the performance and documentation of health screening procedures. *Family Medicine, 18* (5), 290–292.

Prochaska, J. O., & Norcross, J. C. (1998). *Systems of psychotherapy: A transtheoretical analysis* (4th ed.). Brooks/Cole.

Putnam, F. (2001). Why is it so difficult for the epidemic of child abuse to be taken seriously? K. Franey, R. Geffner, & R. Falconer (Eds.), *The cost of child maltreatment: Who pays? We all do* (pp. 185–198). San Diego, CA: Family Violence and Sexual Assault Institute.

Putnam, F. W. (1998). We all pay: The costs of child abuse and neglect. Mayerson Center for Safe and Healthy Children, Children's Hospital Medical Center Cincinnati, OH.

Quinn, M. J., & Tomita, S. K. (1997). *Elder abuse and neglect: Causes, diagnosis, and intervention strategies* (2nd Ed.). New York: Springer.

Ramos-Gomez, F., Rothman, D., & Blain, S. (1998). Knowledge and attitudes among California dental care providers regarding child abuse and neglect. *Journal of the American Dental Association, 129* (3), 340–348.

Rand, M. (1997). Measuring violence related injuries treated in hospital emergency departments: Results from the 1994 study of injured victims of violence. *4th World Conference on Injury Prevention and Control.*

Reid, S. A., & Glasser, M. (1997). Primary care physicians' recognition of and attitudes toward domestic violence. *Academic Medicine, 72* (1), 51–53.

Reilly, B., & Lemon, M. (1997). Evidence-based morning report: A popular new format in a large teaching hospital. *American Journal of Medicine, 103* (5), 419–426.

Reiniger, A., Robison, E., & McHugh, M. (1995). Mandated training of professionals: A means for improving reporting of suspected child abuse. *Child Abuse and Neglect, 19* (1), 63–69.

Reiser, S. (1995). Teaching excellence and departments' budgets. *Academic Medicine, 70,* 273.

Rennison, C. M., & Sarah Welchans. (2000). Intimate partner violence. Report No. NCJ–178247. U.S. Department of Justice, Office of Justice Programs, Bureau of Justice Statistics.

Rich, E. C., Crowson, T. W., & Connelly, D. P. (1985). Evidence for an informal clinical policy resulting in high use of a very-low-yield test. *American Journal of Medicine, 79* (5), 577–582.

Ries, L., Kosary, C., Hankey, B., Miller, B., Clegg, L., & Edwards, B. (1999). Bethesda, MD: National Cancer Institute.

Rind, D. M., Safran, C., Phillips, R. S., Wang, Q., Calkins, D. R., Delbanco, T. L., Bleich, H. L., & Slack, W. V. (1994). Effect of computer-based alerts on the treatment and outcomes of hospitalized patients. *Archives of Internal Medicine, 154* (13), 1511–1517.

Roberts, G. L., Lawrence, J. M., O'Toole, B. I., & Raphael, B. (1997). Domestic violence in the emergency department: 2. Detection by doctors and nurses. *General Hospital Psychiatry, 19* (1), 12–15.

Roberts, G. L., Raphael, B., Lawrence, J. M., O'Toole, B., & O'Brien, D. (1997). Impact of an education program about domestic violence on nurses and doctors in an Australian emergency department. *Journal of Emergency Nursing, 23* (3), 220–227.

Robins, L. S. (2000). The difficulty of sustaining curricular reforms: A study of "drift" at one school. *Academic Medicine, 75* (8), 801–805.

Rodriguez, M. A., Craig, A. M., Mooney, D. R., & Bauer, H. M. (1998). Patient attitudes about mandatory reporting of domestic violence: Implications for health care professionals. *The Western Journal of Medicine, 169* (6), 337–341.

Rodriguez, M. A., Bauer, H. M., McLoughlin, E., & Grumbach, K. (1999). Screening and intervention for intimate partner abuse: Practices and attitudes of primary care physicians. *Journal of the American Medical Journal, 282* (5), 468–474.

Rodriguez, M. A., Nah, G., Mcloughlin, E., & Campbell, J. (2001a). Mandatory reporting of domestic violence injuries to the police: What do emergency department patients think? *Journal of American Medical Association, 286,* 580–583.

Rodriguez, M. A., Sheldon, W. R., Bauer, H. M., & Perez-Stable, E. J. (2001b). The factors associated with disclosure of intimate partner abuse to clinicians. *Journal of Family Practice, 50* (4), 338–344.

Rodriguez, M. A., Sheldon, W. R., & Rao, N. (2001c). Factors that influence abused women's preferences for the mandatory reporting of intimate partner violence by medical clinicians to police. *Women and Health.*

Rogers, E. (1995). *Diffusion of innovations* (4th ed.). New York: The Free Press.

Rosenberg, D. A., & Krugman, R. D. (1991). Epidemiology and outcome of child abuse. *Annual Review of Medicine, 42,* 217–224.

Ross, S. M. (1996). Risk of physical abuse to children of spouse abusing parents. *Child Abuse and Neglect, 20* (7), 589–598.

Rosser, W. W. (1983). Using the perception-reality gap to alter prescribing patterns. *Journal of Medical Education, 58* (9), 728–732.

Rovi, S., & Mouton, C. P. (1999). Domestic violence education in family practice residencies. *Family Medicine, 31* (6), 398–403.

Ruchlin, H. S., Finkel, M. L., & McCarthy, E. G. (1982). The efficacy of second-opinion consultation programs: A cost-benefit perspective. *Medical Care, 20* (1), 3–20.

Rudman, W. (2000). *Coding and documentation of domestic violence.* Available: http://fvpf.org/programs/display.php3?DocID=54 [August 1, 2001].

Rudman, W. J., & Davey, D. (2000). Identifying domestic violence within inpatient hospital admissions using medical records. *Women Health, 30* (4), 1–13.

Rudman, W. J., Reyes, C., & Hewitt, C. (2000). Use of medical records in identifying intimate partner violence. *Family Violence Prevention Fund Conference.* San Francisco, CA.

Rulon, V., & Sica, J. (1997). The evolution of HEDIS: 3.0 and beyond. *Journal of the American Health Information Management Association, 68* (6), 32, 34–38; quiz 39–40.

Ryan, J., & King, M. C. (1998). Scanning for violence. *AWHONN Lifelines, 2* (3), 36–41.

Sabler, P. R. (1995). What do we know about domestic violence? Z. Brown (Ed.), *The physicians guide to domestic violence.* Volcano City, CA: Volcano Press.

Sabler, P. R. (1996). Improving the healthcare response. C. Warshaw & A. L. Ganely (Eds.), *Improving the healthcare response to domestic violence: A resource manual for health care providers* (pp. 1–14). San Francisco, CA: The Family Violence Prevention Fund.

Sachs, C., Koziol-McLain, J., Glass, N., Webster, D., & Campbell, J. A. (in press). Population-based survey assessing support for mandatory domestic violence reporting by healthcare personnel.

Sackett, D. L., & Straus, S. E. (1998). Finding and applying evidence during clinical rounds: The "evidence cart." *Journal of the American Medical Association, 280* (15), 1336–1338.

Sackett, D. L., Rosenberg, W. M., Gray, J. A., Haynes, R. B., & Richardson, W. S. (1996). Evidence based medicine: What it is and what it isn't. *British Medical Journal, 312* (7023), 71–72.

Saltzman, L. E., Fanslow, J. L., McMahon, P. M., & Shelley, G. A. (1999). Intimate partner violence surveillance: Uniform definitions and recommended data elements. Atlanta, GA: National Center for Injury Prevention and Control, Centers for Disease Control and Prevention.

Sansone, R. A., Wiederman, M. W., & Sansone, L. A. (1997). Health care utilization and history of trauma among women in a primary care setting. *Violence Victim, 12* (2), 165–172.

Saunders, D., & Kindy, J. (1993). Predictors of physicians' responses to woman abuse: The role of gender, background and brief training. *Journal of General Internal Medicine, 8,* 606–609.

Saunders, D., & Kindy, P. (2000). Predictors of physicians' responses to woman abuse: The role of gender, background, and brief training. *Journal of General Internal Medicine, 19* (4), 253–263.

Saunders, D. G., Lynch, A. B., Grayson, M., & Linz, D. (1987). The inventory of beliefs about wife beating: The construction and initial validation of a measure of beliefs and attitudes. *Violence Victim, 2* (1), 39–57.

Savage, B. (1991). Utility of clinical preventive services age-specific tables in the medical exam room. *26th Annual USPHS Professional Association Conference.* Atlanta, GA

Schafer, J., Caetano, R., & Clark, C. L. (1998). Rates of intimate partner violence in the United States. *American Journal of Public Health, 88* (11), 1702–1704.

Schechter, C. B. (1996). Costs and benefits of alternative rescreening strategies. *Acta Cytologica, 40* (5), 1111–1114.

Schechter, S. (1982) *Women and male violence: The visions and struggles of the battered women's movement.* Cambridge, MA: South End Press.

Schei, B. (1990). Psychosocial factors in pelvic pain: A controlled study of women living in physically abusive relationships. *Acta Obstetrica Et Gynecologica Scandinavica, 69* (1), 67–71.

Schei, B., & Bakketeig, L. S. (1989). Gynaecological impact of sexual and physical abuse by spouse: A study of a random sample of Norwegian women. *British Journal of Obstetrics and Gynaecology, 96* (12), 1379–1383.

Schmidt, H. G. (1993). Foundations of problem-based learning: Some explanatory notes. *Medical Education, 27,* 422–432.

Schroeder, S. A., Kenders, K., Cooper, J. K., & Piemme, T. E. (1973). Use of laboratory tests and pharmaceuticals: Variation among physicians and effect of cost audit on subsequent use. *Journal of the American Medical Association, 225* (8), 969–973.

Seaman, D. F., & Fellenz, R. A. (1989). *Effective strategies for teaching adults.* Columbus, OH: Bell and Howell.

Seamon, J. P., Jones, J. S., Chun, E., & Krohmer, J. R. (1997). Identifying victims of elder abuse and neglect: A training video for prehospital personnel. *Prehospital Disaster Medicine, 12* (4), 269–273.

Shank, J. C., Powell, T., & Llewelyn, J. (1989). A five-year demonstration project associated with improvement in physician health maintenance behavior. *Family Medicine, 21* (4), 273–278.

Shekelle, P. G., Kravitz, R. L., Beart, J., Marger, M., Wang, M., & Lee, M. (2000). Are nonspecific practice guidelines potentially harmful? A randomized comparison of the effect of nonspecific versus specific guidelines on physician decision-making. *Health Services Research, 34* (7), 1429–1448.

Shepard, M. F., Elliott, B. A., Falk, D. R., & Regal, R. R. (1999). Public health nurses' responses to domestic violence: A report from the Enhanced Domestic Abuse Intervention Project. *Public Health Nursing, 16* (5), 359–366.

Short, L. M., Johnson, D., & Osattin, A. (1998). Recommended components of health care provider training programs on intimate partner violence. *American Journal of Preventive Medicine, 14* (4), 283–288.

Short, L. M., Hadley, S. M., & Bates, B. (2000). CDC's evaluation of the WomanKind Program: An integrated model of the 24-hour health care response to domestic violence. *Women's Health Issues.*

Shumway, J., O'Campo, P., Gielen, A., Witter, F. R., Khouzami, A. N., & Blakemore, K. J. (1999). Preterm labor, placental abruption, and premature rupture of membranes in relation to maternal violence or verbal abuse. *Journal of Maternal-Fetal Medicine, 8* (3), 76–80.

Sipes, B., & Hall, E. J. (1996). *I am not your victim.* Thousand Oaks, CA: Sage.

Slawson, D. C., & Shaughnessy, A. F. (1999). Teaching information mastery: Creating informed consumers of medical information. *Journal of the American Board of Family Practice, 12* (6), 444–449.

Slotnick, H. B., Raszkowski, P. R., & Lichtenauer, D. F. (1995). Rethinking continuing medical education. *Journal of Continuing Education for Health Professionals, 15,* 8–22.

Slovic, P., Monahan, J., & MacGregor, D. G. (2000). Violence risk assessment and risk communication: The effects of using actual cases, providing instruction, and employing probability versus frequency formats. *Law and Human Behavior,* (24).

Snell, J., Rosenwald, R., & Robey, A. (1964). The wifebeater's wife. *Archives of General Psychiatry, 11,* 107–112.

Socolar, R. R., Raines, B., Chen-Mok, M., Runyan, D. K., Green, C., & Paterno, S. (1998). Intervention to improve physician documentation and knowledge of child sexual abuse: A randomized, controlled trial. *Pediatrics, 101* (5), 817–824.

Socolara, R., Fredrickson, D., Block, R., Moore, J., Tropez-Sims, S., & Whitworth, J. (2001). State programs for medical diagnosis of child abuse and neglect: Case studies of five established or fledging programs. *Child Abuse and Neglect, 25* (4), 441–455.

Soeken, K., Parker B., McFarlane J., & Lominak M. C. (1998). The abuse assessment screen: A clinical instrument to measure frequency, severity, and perpetrator of abuse against women. *Beyond diagnosis: Changing the health care response to battered women and their children* (pp. 195–203). Newbury Park, London: Sage.

Solberg, L. I., Maxwell, P. L., Kottke, T. E., Gepner, G. J., & Brekke, M. L. (1990). A systematic primary care office-based smoking cessation program. *Journal of Family Practice, 30* (6), 647–654.

Spinola, C., Stewart, L., Fanslow, J., & Norton, R. (1998). Developing and implementing an intervention: Evaluation of an emergency department pilot on partner abuse. *Evaluation and the Health Professions, 21* (1), 91–119.

Stark, E., & Flitcraft, A. (1988). *Violence among intimates—An epidemiological review.* V. Van Hasselt, R. Morrison, A. Bellack, & M. Hersen (Eds.), pp. 293–317. New York: Plenum Press.

Stark, E., & Flitcraft, A. (1996). *Women at risk: Domestic violence and women's health.* London: Sage Publications.

Stark, E., Flitcraft, A., Zuckermanh, D., Grey, A., Robinson, J., & Frazier, W. (1981). *Wife abuse in the medical setting.* Rockville, MD: National Clearinghouse on Domestic Violence.

Staropoli, C. A., Moulton, A. W., & Cyr, M. G. (1997). Primary care internal medicine training and women's health. *Journal of General Internal Medicine, 12* (2), 129–131.

Straus, M. A. (1992). *Children as witnesses to marital violence: A risk factor for lifelong problems among a nationally representative sample of American men and women.* Columbus, OH: Ross Laboratories.

Straus, S. E., & Sackett, D. L. (1998). Using research findings in clinical practice. *British Medical Journal, 317* (7154), 339–342.

Stross, J. K., Hiss, R. G., Watts, C. M., Davis, W. K., & Macdonald, R. (1983). Continuing education in pulmonary disease for primary-care physicians. *American Review of Respiratory Disease, 127* (6), 739–746.

Sugarman, J. M., Hertweck, S. P., & Giardino, A. P. (1997). An approach to teaching pediatric residents about the evaluation of children suspected of having been sexually abused. *Pediatric Emergency Care, 13* (1), 84–85.

Sugg, N. K., & Inui, T. (1992). Primary care physicians' response to domestic violence: Opening Pandora's box. *Journal of the American Medical Association, 267* (23), 3157–3160.

Sugg, N. K., Thompson, R. S., Thompson, D. C., Maiuro, R., & Rivara, F. P. (1999). Domestic violence and primary care: Attitudes, practices, and beliefs. *Archives of Family Medicine, 8* (4), 301–306.

Talbot, A., Manton, M., & Dunn, P. (1992). Debriefing the debriefers: An intervention strategy to assist psychologists after a crisis. *Journal of Traumatic Stress, 5,* 45–62.

Talley, N. J., Fett, S. L., Zinsmeister, A. R., & Melton, L. J. (1994). Gastrointestinal tract symptoms and self-reported abuse: A population-based study. *Gastroenterology, 107* (4), 1040–1049.

Task Force on Community Preventive Services. (2000). Introducing the guide to community preventive services: Methods, first recommendations and expert commentary. *American Journal of Preventive Medicine, 18* (1S), 1–142.

Tatara, T. (1993). Understanding the nature and scope of domestic elder abuse with the state aggregate data; Summaries of key findings of a national survey of state APS and aging agencies. *Journal of Elder Abuse and Neglect, 5,* 35–57.

Theodore, A. D., & Runyan, D. K. (1999). A medical research agenda for child maltreatment: Negotiating the next steps. *Pediatrics, 104* (1, Pt 2), 168–177.

Thompson, R. A., & Wilcox, B. L. (1995). Child maltreatment research: Federal support and policy issues. *American Psychology, 50* (9), 789–793.

Thompson, R. S. (1996). What have HMOs learned about clinical prevention services? An examination of the experience at Group Health Cooperative of Puget Sound. *Milbank Quarterly, 74* (4), 469–509.

Thompson, R. S., Kirz, H. L., & Gold, R. A. (1983). Changes in physician behavior and cost savings associated with organizational recommendations on the use of "routine" chest X rays and multichannel blood tests. *Preventive Medicine, 12* (3), 385–396.

Thompson, R. S., Meyer, B. A., Smith-DiJulio, K., Caplow, M. P., Maiuro, R. D., Thompson, D. C., Sugg, N. K., & Rivara, F. P. (1998). A training program to improve domestic violence identification and management in primary care: Preliminary results. *Violence Victim, 13* (4), 395–410.

Thompson, R. S., Michnich, M. E., Gray, J., Friedlander, L., & Gilson, B. (1986). Maximizing compliance with hemoccult screening for colon cancer in clinical practice. *Medical Care, 24* (10), 904–914.

Thompson, R. S., Rivara, F. P., Thompson, D. C., Barlow, W. E., Sugg, N. K., Maiuro, R. D., & Rubanowice, D. M. (2000). Identification and management of domestic violence: A randomized trial (1). *American Journal of Preventive Medicine, 19* (4), 253–263.

Thompson, R. S., Rivara, F. P., Thompson, D. C., Barlow, W. E., Sugg, N. K., & Maiuro, R. D. (2001). A randomized trial to improve identification and management of domestic violence in primary care practice. *American Journal of Preventive Medicine, 19,* 253–263.

Thomson, O., Oxman, A., Davis, D., Haynes, R., Freemantle, N., & Harvey, E. (2001a). Audit and feedback: Effects on professional practice and health care outcomes. *Cochrane Review, The Cochrane Library* (2).

Thomson, O., Oxman, A., Davis, D., Haynes, R., Freemantle, N., & Harvey, E. (2001b). Audit and feedback versus alternative strategies: Effects on professional practice and health care outcomes. *Cochrane Review, The Cochrane Library* (2).

Thomson, O., Oxman, A., Davis, D., Haynes, R., Freemantle, N., & Harvey, E. (2001c). Local opinion leaders: Effects on professional practice and health care outcomes. *Cochrane Review, The Cochrane Library* (2).

Thurston, W. E., & McLeod, L. (1997). Teaching second-year medical students about wife battering. *Women's Health Issues, 7* (2), 92–98.

Tierney, W. M., Hui, S. L., & McDonald, C. J. (1986). Delayed feedback of physician performance versus immediate reminders to perform preventive care: Effects on physician compliance. *Medical Care, 24* (8), 659–666.

Tilden, V. P., Schmidt, T. A., Limandri, B. J., Chiodo, G. T., Garland, M. J., & Loveless, P. A. (1994). Factors that influence clinicians' assessment and management of family violence. *American Journal of Public Health, 84* (4), 628–633.

Tilden, V. P., & Shepherd, P. (1987). Increasing the rate of identification of battered women in an emergency department: Use of a nursing protocol. *Research in Nursing and Health, 10* (4), 209–215.

Tjaden, P., & Thoennes, N. (1998). Prevalence, incidence, and consequences of violence against women: Findings from the national violence against women survey. Atlanta, GA: National Institute of Justice Centers for Disease Control and Prevention.

Tjaden, P., & Thoennes, N. (2000). *Extent, Nature, and Consequences of Intimate Partner Violence Findings from the National Violence Against Women Survey.* Report No. NCJ 181867. Atlanta, GA: National Institute of Justice, Centers for Disease Control and Prevention.

Tjaden, P., Thoennes, N., & Allison, C. J. (1999). Comparing violence over the life span in samples of same-sex and opposite-sex cohabitants. *Violence Victim, 14* (4), 413–425.

Tones, K. (1997). Health education, behaviour change, and the public health. R. Detels, W. W. Holland, J. McEwen, & G. Omenn (Eds.), *Oxford textbook of public health, the methods of public health* (3rd ed., vol. 2, pp. 783–814). New York: Oxford University Press.

Travis, J. (2000). Remarks at the Workshop on Children and Domestic Abuse. National Research Council and Institute of Medicine Workshop on Children and Domestic Abuse. National Academy of Sciences, Washington, DC. April 10, 2000.

Tversky, A., & Kahneman, D. (1973). Availability: A heuristic for judging frequency and probability. *Cognitive Psychology, 4,* 207–232.

Tversky, A., & Kahneman, D. (1974). Judgment under uncertainty: Heuristics and biases. *Science, 185,* 1124–1131.

U.S. Advisory Board of Child Abuse and Neglect 1. (1990). *Child abuse and neglect: Critical first steps in responding to a national emergency.* Washington, DC: U.S. Government Printing Office.

U.S. Advisory Board on Child Abuse and Neglect 2. (1991). *Creating caring communities: Blueprint for an effective federal policy on child abuse and neglect.* Washington, DC: U.S. Government Office of Printing.

U.S. Advisory Board on Child Abuse and Neglect 3. (1993). *Neighbors helping neighbors: A new national strategy for the protection of children.* Washington, DC: U.S. Government Printing Office.

U.S. Department of Justice. (2001). *Criminal victimization in the United States, 1999 statistical tables.* Report No. NCJ 184938. Washington, DC: U.S. Department of Justice, Office of Justice Programs, Bureau of Justice Statistics.

Ulrich, Y. C., Cain, K. C., Sugg, N. K., Rivara, F., & Thompson, R. S. (in preparation). Burden of disease: Medical care utilization patterns in women with diagnosed domestic violence. *American Journal of Preventive Medicine.*

U.S. Census Bureau. (2000). *U.S. Census 2000 fact finder.* Available: http://factfinder.census.gov/servlet/BasicFactsServlet.

Uva, J. L., & Guttman, T. (1996). Elder abuse education in an emergency medicine residency program. *Academic Emergency Medicine, 3* (8), 817–819.

Varvaro, F. F., & Gesmond, S. (1997). ED physician house staff response to training on domestic violence. *Journal of Emergency Nursing, 23* (1), 17–22.

Vayda, E., & Mindell, W. R. (1982). Variations in operative rates: What do they mean? *The Surgical Clinics of North America, 62* (4), 627–639.

Venters, M., & ten Bensel, R. (1977). Interdisciplinary education in child abuse and neglect. *Journal of Medical Education, 52* (4), 334–337.

Vernon, D. T., & Blake, R. L. (1993). Does problem-based learning work? A meta-analysis of evaluative research. *Academic Medicine, 68* (7), 550–563.

Vinton, L. (1993). Educating case managers about elder abuse and neglect. *Journal of Case Management, 2* (3), 101–105.

Von Burg, M. M., & Hibbard, R. A. (1995). Child abuse education: Do not overlook dental professionals. *ASDC Journal of Dentistry for Children, 62* (1), 57–63.

Vulliamy, A. P., & Sullivan, R. (2000). Reporting child abuse: Pediatricians' experiences with the child protection system. *Child Abuse and Neglect, 24* (11), 1461–1470.

Waalen, J., Goodwin, M. M., Spitz, A. M., Petersen, R., & Saltzman, L. E. (2000). Screening for intimate partner violence by health care providers: Barriers and interventions. *American Journal of Preventive Medicine, 19* (4), 230–237.

Wadland, W. C., Barry, H. C., Farquhar, L., Holzman, C., & White, A. (1999). Training medical students in evidence-based medicine: A community campus approach. *Family Medicine, 31* (10), 703–708.

Wainwright, J. R., Sullivan, F. M., Morrison, J. M., MacNaughton, R. J., & McConnachie, A. (1999). Audit encourages an evidence-based approach to medical practice. *Medical Education, 33* (12), 907–914.

Walker, E. A., Unutzer, J., Rutter, C., Gelfand, A., Saunders, K., VonKorff, M., Koss, M. P., & Katon, W. (1999). Costs of health care use by women HMO members with a history of childhood abuse and neglect. *Archives of General Psychiatry, 56* (7), 609–613.

Walsh, J. M., & McPhee, S. J. (1992). A systems model of clinical preventive care: An analysis of factors influencing patient and physician. *Health Education Quarterly, 19* (2), 157–175.

Ward, V. M., Bertrand, J. T., & Brown, L. F. (1991). The comparability of focus group and survey results. *Evaluation Review, 15* (226–283).

Warshaw, C. (1989). Limitations of the medical model in the care of battered women. *Gender and Society, 3* (4), 506–517.

Warshaw, C. (1993). Domestic violence: Challenges to medical practice. *Journal of Women's Health, 1,* 28.

Warshaw, C. (1997). Intimate partner abuse: Developing a framework for change in medical education. *Academic Medicine, 72* (Suppl 1), S26–S37.

Warshaw, C., & Ganley, A. (1998). *Improving the health care response to domestic violence: A resource manual for health care providers.* San Francisco, CA: Family Violence Prevention Fund.

Watson, H., & Levine, M. (1989). Psychotherapy and mandated reporting of child abuse. *American Journal of Orthopsychiatry, 59* (2), 246–256.

Websdale, N. (1998). *Rural women battering and the justice system: An ethnography.* Thousand Oaks, CA: Sage Publications.

Weiss, S. J., Ernst, A. A., Blanton, D., Sewell, D., & Nick, T. G. (2000). EMT domestic violence knowledge and the results of an educational intervention. *American Journal of Emergency Medicine, 18* (2), 168–171.

Wenrich, J. W., Mann, F. C., Morris, W. C., & Reilly, A. J. (1971). Informal educators for practicing physicians. *Journal of Medical Education, 46* (4), 299–305.

White, J. (1994). Violence: a public health epidemic. *Health Progress, 75* (1), 18–21.

Wielichowski, L., Knuteson, C., Ambuel, B., & Lahti, J. (1999). A model for collaborative nursing and medical education within the context of family violence. *Journal of Nursing Education, 38* (1), 13–16.

Wiist, W. H., & McFarlane, J. (1999). The effectiveness of an abuse assessment protocol in public health prenatal clinics. *American Journal of Public Health, 89* (8), 1217–1221.

Wilkinson, A., & Forlini, J. (1999). Medicaring: Quality end-of life Care. *Journal of Health Care Law and Policy, 2,* 501–530.

Williams, O. J., & Becker, R. L. (1994). Domestic partner abuse treatment programs and cultural competence: The results of a national survey. *Violence and Victims, 9* (3), 287–296.

Wilt, S., & Olson, S. (1996). Prevalence of domestic violence in the United States. *Journal of the American Medical Women's Association, 51* (3), 77–82.

Winickoff, R. N., Coltin, K. L., Morgan, M. M., Buxbaum, R. C., & Barnett, G. O. (1984). Improving physician performance through peer comparison feedback. *Medical Care, 22* (6), 527–534.

Wisner, C. L., Gilmer, T. P., Saltzman, L. E., & Zink, T. M. (1999). Intimate partner violence against women: Do victims cost health plans more? *Journal of Family Practice, 48* (6), 439–443.

Wolf, R. S., & Pillemer, K. (1994). What's new in elder abuse programming? Four bright ideas. *Gerontologist, 34* (1), 126–129.

Woloshin, S., Bickell, N. A., Schwartz, L. M., Gany, F., & Welch, H. G. (1995). Language barriers in medicine in the United States. *Journal of the American Medical Association, 273* (9), 724–728.

Wong, E. T., McCarron, M. M., & Shaw, S. T. Jr. (1983). Ordering of laboratory tests in a teaching hospital. Can it be improved? *Journal of the American Medical Association, 249* (22), 3076–3080.

Wood, R., & Bandura, A. (1996). Social cognitive theory of organizational management. R. Steers, L. Porter, & G. Bigley (Eds.), *Motivation and leadership at work* (pp. 84–94). New York: McGraw-Hill.

Woodtli, M. A., & Breslin, E. (1996). Violence-related content in the nursing curriculum: A national study. *The Journal of Nursing Education, 35* (8), 367–374.

Woodtli, M. A., & Breslin, E. T. (1997). Violence and the nursing curriculum: Nurse educators speak out. *Nursing and Health Care Perspectives, 18* (5), 252–259.

Wright, R. J., Wright, R. O., Farnan, L., & Isaac, N. E. (1999). Response to child abuse in the pediatric emergency department: Need for continued education. *Pediatric Emergency Care, 15* (6), 376–382.

Wright, R. J., Wright, R. O., & Isaac, N. E. (1997). Response to battered mothers in the pediatric emergency department: A call for an interdisciplinary approach to family violence. *Pediatrics, 99* (2), 186–192.

Yllo, K., & Bograd, M. (1998). *Feminist perspectives on wife abuse.* Newbury Park, CA: Sage.

Young, D. W. (1980). An aid to reducing unnecessary investigations. *British Medical Journal, 281* (6255), 1610–1611.

Zaza, S., Wright-De Aguero, L. K., Briss, P. A., Truman, B. I., Hopkins, D. P., Hennessy, M. H., Sosin, D. M., Anderson, L., Carande-Kulis, V. G., Teutsch, S. M., & Pappaioanou, M. (2000). Data collection instrument and procedure for systematic reviews in the Guide to Community Preventive Services. Task Force on Community Preventive Services. *American Journal of Preventive Medicine, 18* (Suppl 1), 44–74.

Zellman, G. (1990a). Child abuse reporting and failure to report among mandated reporters: Prevalence, incidence, and reasons. *Journal of Interpersonal Violence, 14,* 325–336.

Zellman, G. L. (1990b). Report decision-making patterns among mandated child abuse reporters. *Child Abuse and Neglect, 14* (3), 325–336.

Appendixes

Appendix A
Accreditation Requirements

Health Care Discipline	Accreditation Institutions	Requirements Related to Family Violence	Description
Medical Schools	Liaison Commission on Medical Education (LCME)	S	"The curriculum should prepare students for their role in addressing the medical consequences of common societal problems, for example, providing instructions in the diagnosis, prevention, appropriate reporting and treatment of violence and abuse." Standards can be found on the LCME web site at www.lcme.org.
	Accreditation Council for Graduate Medical Education (ACGME)	X	The institutional requirements of the ACGME are very practical in nature and do not outline any single curriculum requirements including any dealing with family violence.
	American Osteopathic Healthcare Association (AOHA)	NS	Institutions are required to include within the spectrum of "Emergency Procedures" some instruction regarding "abuse and neglect" of children. While these standards are not a requirement onto themselves, they do seem to be somewhat quantifiable.
Physician Residencies	Residency Review Committees (RRC) of the ACGME	S	The residency review committees of the ACGME, which accredit programs rather than institutions, do have provisions for family violence in certain fields. Though the genetics area does not mention family violence, the areas of family practice and obstetrics indicate how to identify signs of family violence and the steps to take.
Dental Schools	American Dental Association, Commission on Dental Accreditation (ADA)	NS	There is no specific mention of family violence in the accreditation commission's standards. Such training is believed to fall under the purview of a provision for "ethical reasoning" and "professional responsibility."

Nursing Schools	Commission on Collegiate Nursing Education Accreditation (CCNE)	X	CCNE guidelines are very generic and do not provide for any particular curriculum requirements. The guidelines allow schools to choose their own direction and philosophy and subsequently measures them against the standard they have chosen.
Nurse Practitioners	National League for Nursing Accrediting Commission (NLNAC)	NS	"NLNAC does not include specific curriculum content areas within its standards and criteria. When specific curriculum content is designated it is usually from the State Boards of Nursing since NLNAC is voluntary." Standards can be accessed on the website at www.nlnac.org.
	National Association of Pediatric Nurse Associates & Practitioners, Inc. (NAPNAP)	NS	NAPNAP recognizes that there is "substantial scientific evidence that children who are abused physically, sexually, emotionally or who are neglected, are prevented from optimal development." NAPNAP has in place a thorough position statement on child abuse/neglect.
Psychology Programs AND Internship Sites	Committee on Accreditation of the American Psychological Association: accredits both schools and internship sites (APA)	X	There is no mention of family violence in the APA accreditation guidelines. They take a broad stance on evaluating the goals that institutions set for themselves.

continued on next page

Health Care Discipline	Accreditation Institutions	Requirements Related to Family Violence	Description
Social Work Programs	Council on Social Work Education (CSWE)	NS	CSWE has no specific requirements mandating that the issue of family violence be discussed on any level. There is an expectation that a program dealing with social work must at some point address the problem. Should an institution not do this, it would probably be cited.
Physician Assistant	Commission on Accreditation of Allied Health Education (CAAHEP) Programs Effective January 1, 2001, CAAHEP no longer will be the accreditor of physician assistant education programs. All current accreditations are being transferred from CAAHEP to the Accreditation Review Commission on Education of the Physician Assistant (ARC-PA). http://www.CAAHEP.org/caahep_pa.htm	X	There is no reference to family violence made in the CAAHEP standards or guidelines. Curriculum is the responsibility of the sponsoring institution with the exception of a few general study education requirements.

Note:
S = specific existing requirements;
NS = nonspecific requirements;
X = no identifiable requirements.

Appendix B
Policy Statements of Health Professional Organizations

Organization Name	Policy Name, Source, and Date Established	Key Points Related to Education and Training
American Academy of Family Physicians (AAFP)	AAFP Paper on Family Violence From "AAFP Paper on Family Violence" Developed by the 1994 Commission on Special Issues and Clinical Interests	Among projects for the AAFP to consider are the following: *An ongoing education program for members on the recognition and treatment of violence, including distribution of the American Medical Association's (AMA) guidelines for history taking around issues of violence and abuse. *Offering a series of continuing medical education courses for members to increase their skills in discussing this issue with patients.
American Academy of Pediatrics (AAP)	The Role of the Pediatrician in Recognizing and Intervening on Behalf of Abused Women (RE9748) From web site June 1998	The AAP recognizes that family and intimate partner violence is harmful to children. The AAP recommends that: *Residency training programs and continuing medical education (CME) program leaders incorporate education on family and intimate partner violence and its implications for child health into the curricula of pediatricians and pediatric emergency department physicians.
	Oral and Dental Aspects of Child Abuse and Neglect (RE9920) Pulled from web site (www.aap.org/policy/) August 1999	Pediatric dentists and oral and maxillofacial surgeons, whose advanced education programs include a mandated child abuse curriculum, can provide valuable information and assistance to physicians about oral and dental aspects of child abuse and neglect.
American Academy of Physician Assistants (AAPA)	AAPA Policies	The AAPA shall support the development of educational programs concerning early prevention, recognition, reporting, and treatment of child abuse.

PA programs are encouraged to include in their curricula techniques of violence prevention, assessment, and intervention that promote safety and protection for battered individuals.

Physician assistants are encouraged to be familiar with multi-disciplinary educational resources and public health and safety efforts directed at pediatric and adolescent violence prevention. The AAPA believes that access and availability of reliable information in these areas can enhance the efforts of PAs to address the problem of violence as it relates to the pediatric and adolescent population.

AACN recommends that:

*Faculty in schools of nursing should acknowledge their own assumptions about domestic violence and stay current in their knowledge on the concomitant health problems.

*Content relative to domestic violence across the lifespan and across settings should be included in all baccalaureate and higher degree programs in nursing.

*If content is integrated or threaded throughout the curriculum, it is recommended that the faculty adopt a curriculum plan that specifies the location of violence-related content along with a plan for periodically tracking the implementation of this plan.

*Students should have opportunities to practice in clinical settings where they have experiences related to screening, assessing, and/or caring for victims of violence.

*High-quality materials related to domestic violence should be available for professional continuing education in formats compatible with nontraditional learners at times and places convenient to the practicing professional.

American Association of Colleges of Nursing (AACN)

Position Statement: Violence as a Public Health Problem

From AACN Position Statement "Violence as a Public Health Problem"

March 1999

Available at www.aacn.nche.edu/ publications/positions/position.htm

continued on next page

Organization Name	Policy Name, Source, and Date Established	Key Points Related to Education and Training
American College of Emergency Physicians (ACEP)	Domestic Violence: The Role of EMS Personnel From ACEP online (www.acep.org/policy/) Approved by the ACEP Board of Directors April 1995 Policy number 400279 Approved by the ACEP Board of Directors January 2000	*ACEP believes that training in the evaluation and management of victims of domestic violence should be incorporated into the initial and continuing education of emergency medical services personnel. This training should include the recognition of victims and their injuries, an understanding of the patterns of abuse and how this affects care, scene safety, preservation of evidence, and documentation requirements. ACEP recommends that: Emergency medical services, medical school, and emergency medicine residency curricula include training in recognition, assessment, and interventions in child abuse.
American College of Surgeons (ACOS)	{ST-32} Statement on Domestic Violence From web site (www.facs:80/fellows_info/statements/) October 1999 Meeting	N/A
American Dental Association (ADA)	American Dental Association Policies Excerpt from the Principles of Ethics and Code of Professional Conduct Policy Statement—Expansion of ADA Efforts to Educate Dental Professionals in Recognizing and Reporting Abuse and Neglect (1996:683)	**Resolved,** that the ADA expand existing efforts to educate dental professionals to recognize abuse and neglect beyond that of children alone, to include women, elders, people with developmental disabilities, the physically challenged, and any other person who might be the object of abuse or neglect and encourage training programs on how to report such abuse and neglect tot the proper authorities as required by state law, and be it further **Resolved,** that the ADA initiate a dialogue with other professional organizations, such as the American Medical Association

American Medical Association (AMA)	Update on the AMA's National Campaign Against Family Violence H-515.977 Policy Finders	to ensure that all health care professionals are working toward the same goals, and be it further **Resolved,** that these actions will not diminish any existing programs and that the ADA seek out existing programs in the dental community to try to coordinate them on a national level. The AMA should provide educational and training opportunities for physicians in diagnosing, treating, and referring cases of abuse constituting family violence.
American Medical Women's Association (AMWA)	AMWA Domestic Violence From web site (www.amwa-doc.org/Education/)	AMWA is developing an online continuing medical education course for health care providers, in an attempt to increase awareness of domestic violence, improve the diagnosis and treatment of victims of domestic violence, and provide physicians and other health care professionals with knowledge and understanding of key aspects of domestic violence.
American Nurses Association (ANA)	Position Statement: Physical Violence Against Women From web site (www.nursingworld.org/readroom/position/) Effective September 6, 1991. Originated by Council of Community Health Nurses, Congress of Nursing Practice. Adopted by ANA Board of Directors	The American Nurses Association supports: *Routine education of all nurses and health care providers in the skills necessary to prevent violence against women. *Inclusion of the topic of violence against women in all undergraduate nursing curricula.

continued on next page

Organization Name	Policy Name, Source And Date Established	Key Points Related to Education and Training
American Psychological Association (APA)	Public Interest Directorate • Front Matter for Including Information on Child Abuse and Neglect in the Undergraduate Curriculum • Front Matter for Including Information on Child Abuse and Neglect in the Graduate Curriculum From web site (http://www.apa.org/pi/ugradfront.html) Written April 1996	The APA working group on Implications for Education and Training of Child Abuse and Neglect Issues encouraged the development for this guide. This publication is designed to facilitate the inclusion of child abuse and neglect material in existing classes and the development of courses that focus on child abuse and neglect. It consists of an outline of the topics that could be included in a comprehensive semester-long course on child abuse and neglect and a series of references to the literature and other educational materials for each topic.
Emergency Nurses Association (ENA)	Position Statement From web site (www.ena.org/services/posistate/data/domvio.html)	ENA supports mandatory professional training, curriculum development, and continuing education for all health professionals on domestic violence.
Joint Commission on Accreditation of Healthcare Organizations (JCAHO)	Standards JCAHO: Comprehensive Accreditation Manual for Hospitals, Update 3, 1997	Standard PE.1.8 • The hospital has objective criteria for identifying and assessing possible victims of abuse and neglect, and they are used throughout the organization. Staff are to be trained in the use of these criteria. • The criteria focus on observable evidence and not on allegation alone. They address at least the following situations: physical assault, rape or other sexual molestation, domestic abuse, and abuse or neglect of elders and children.

| National Association of Orthopedic Nurses (NAON) | Comments to the Institute of Medicine's Committee on the Training Needs of Health Professionals to Respond to Family Violence Public Forum June 2000

Policy Recommendations by the National Association of Orthopedic Nurses Regarding Health Professionals' Screening, Detection, and Referral of Domestic Violence Victims | NAON recommendations on education:
Nurses must be educated to effectively deal with domestic violence victims including the elderly and disabled.
• NAON recommends education on domestic violence as a requirement for license renewal for professional associations, such as state medical and state nurses associations.
• NAON recommends health professional colleges develop curricula on domestic violence and elder abuse.
• NAON recommends that a minimum 10-hour curriculum on domestic violence be developed for nursing schools nationwide. |
| National Association of Social Workers (NASW) | Policy Statement for Family Violence

From "Social Work Speaks"

Policy Statement approved by the NASW Delegate Assembly, Nov. 1987, and reconfirmed by the Delegate Assembly, Aug. 1993. The 1999 Delegate Assembly voted to refer this policy statement to the 2002 Delegate Assembly for revision. | *NASW encourages schools of social work to develop and implement curricula to prepare students adequately to meet the demands of mandated witnesses and work in the field of family violence.
*NASW encourages the development of field experiences that reflect different approaches to assessment, treatment, and prevention in this field.
*NASW promotes the development of in-service training and continuing education on all forms of family violence to increase the awareness and intervention strategies of social work practitioners.
*NASW promotes the creation of interdisciplinary training, education, and comprehensive services to link and coordinate programs with health and protective services, the courts, schools, law enforcement agencies, the military, places of worship, workplace service providers, and social service systems for the effective treatment and prevention of family violence |

continued on next page

Organization Name	Policy Name, Source And Date Established	Key Points Related to Education and Training
The American College of Nurse-Midwives (ACNM)	Violence Against Women From "Violence Against Women" (Ad Hoc Committee) Approved by the ACNM BOD in Nov. 1995, revised Aug. 1997	N/A

Appendix C

Mandatory Reporting Laws for Family Violence

Child Abuse and Neglect

| | Who Must Report? | | | | | |
	Dentist	Doctor	Mental Health	Nurse	Social Worker	Standard for Reporting?
Alabama Ala. Code § 26-14-3 (2000)	Y	Y	Y	Y	Y	Knowledge *or* suspicion
Alaska Alaska Stat. § 47.17.020 (Michie 2000)	Y	Y	Y	Y	Y	Reasonable cause to suspect
Arizona Ariz. Rev. Stat. § 13-3620 (2000)	Y	Y	Y	Y	Y	Reasonable grounds to believe
Arkansas Ark. Code Ann. § 12-12-507 (Michie 1999)	Y	Y	Y	Y	Y	Reasonable cause to suspect
California Cal. [Penal] Code § 11166 (West 2000)	Y	Y	Y	Y	Y	Knowledge *or* reasonable suspicion
Colorado Colo. Rev. Stat. § 19-3-304 (1999)	Y	Y	Y	Y	Y	Reasonable cause to know *or* suspect
Connecticut Conn. Gen. Stat. §§ 17a-101 to -101b (1999)	Y	Y	Y	Y	Y	Reasonable cause to suspect *or* believe
Delaware Del. Code Ann. tit. 16, §§ 903-904 (1999)	Y	Y	Y	Y	Y	Knowledge *or* good faith suspicion
District of Columbia D.C. Code Ann. § 2-1352 (1999)	Y	Y	Y	Y	Y	Knowledge *or* reasonable cause to suspect
Florida Fla. Stat. ch. 39.201 (1999)	Y	Y	Y	Y	Y	Knowledge *or* reasonable cause to suspect
Georgia Ga. Code Ann. § 19-7-5 (1999)	Y	Y	Y	Y	Y	Reasonable cause to believe

Report What?	Report to Whom?	Report How?
Child abuse *or* neglect	Law enforcement *or* Department of Human Resources	Oral *and* written
Harm as a result of child abuse *or* neglect	Department of Health and Social Services	Not specified
Injury, commercial sexual exploitation of a minor, sexual exploitation of a minor, incest, child prostitution, death, abuse, *or* nonaccidental physical neglect	Law enforcement *or* Child Protective Services	Oral *and* written
Child maltreatment *or* conditions that will reasonably result in child maltreatment	Child abuse hotline	Oral
Child abuse	Child protective agency	Oral *and* written
Child abuse *or* neglect	County Department of Human Services *or* law enforcement	Not specified
Abuse, nonaccidental physical injury, *or* neglect	Commissioner of Children and Families *or* law enforcement agency	Oral
Child abuse *or* neglect	Division of Child Protective Services of Department of Services for Children, Youth, and Their Families	Oral *and* written (if requested)
Immediate danger of physical *or* mental abuse *or* neglect	Law enforcement *or* Child Protective Services	Not specified
Abuse, abandonment, *or* neglect	Department of Children and Family Services	Oral
Abuse	Child welfare agency designated by the Department of Human Resources *or* law enforcement	Oral *and* written (if requested)

continued on next page

Child Abuse and Neglect

| | Who Must Report? | | | | | |
	Dentist	Doctor	Mental Health	Nurse	Social Worker	Standard for Reporting?
Hawaii Haw. Rev. Stat. § 350-1.1 (1999)	Y	Y	Y	Y	Y	Reason to believe
Idaho Idaho Code § 16-1619 (1999)	Y	Y	Y	Y	Y	Reason to believe
Illinois 325 Ill. Comp. Stat. 5/4 (West 2000)	Y	Y	Y	Y	Y	Reasonable cause to believe
Indiana Ind. Code §§ 31-33-5-1 to -2, -4 (1999)	Y	Y	Y	Y	Y	Reason to believe
Iowa Iowa Code § 232.69 (1999)	Y	Y	Y	Y	Y	Reasonable belief
Kansas Kan. Stat. Ann. § 38-1522 (1999)	Y	Y	Y	Y	Y	Reason to suspect
Kentucky Ky. Rev. Stat. Ann. § 620.030 (Michie 1998)	Y	Y	Y	Y	Y	Knows *or* has reasonable cause to believe
Louisiana La. Civ. Stat. Ann. Art. 603, 609-610 (West 2000)	Y	Y	Y	Y	Y	Cause to believe
Maine Me. Rev. stat. Ann. Tit. 22 § 4011 (West 1999)	Y	Y	Y	Y	Y	Knowledge *or* reasonable cause to suspect
Maryland Md. Code Ann., [Fam. Law] § 5-704 (1999)	Y	Y	Y	Y	Y	Reason to believe

Report What?	Report to Whom?	Report How?
Child abuse *or* neglect *or* substantial risk of above in reasonably foreseeable future	Department of Human Services *and* law enforcement	Oral *and* written
Abuse, abandonment, *or* neglect *or* conditions that would reasonably result in any of above	Law enforcement *or* Department of Health and Welfare	Not specified
Abuse *or* neglect	Department of Children and Family Services	Not specified
Abuse *or* neglect	Child protective services *or* law enforcement	Oral
Child abuse	Department of Human Services	Oral *and* written
Injury resulting from physical, mental, *or* emotional abuse, neglect, *or* sexual abuse	Department of Social and Rehabilitation Services	Oral *and* written (if requested)
Dependency, neglect, *or* abuse	Law enforcement, Cabinet for Families and Children, *or* county attorney	Oral *or* written
Endangerment of child's physical *or* mental health *or* welfare due to neglect *or* abuse	Child Protection Unit of Department of Social Services	Written
Child likely to be *or* has been abused *or* neglected	Department of Human Services	Not specified
Abuse *or* neglect	Department of Social Services *or* law enforcement	Oral *and* written

continued on next page

Child Abuse and Neglect

| | Who Must Report? | | | | | |
	Dentist	Doctor	Mental Health	Nurse	Social Worker	Standard for Reporting?
Massachusetts Mass. Gen. Laws ch. 119, § 51A (2000)	Y	Y	Y	Y	Y	Reasonable cause to believe
Michigan Mich. Comp. Laws § 722.623 (1999)	Y	Y	Y	Y	Y	Reasonable cause to suspect
Minnesota Minn. Stat. § 626.556 (1999)	Y	Y	Y	Y	Y	Knows *or* has reason to believe
Mississippi Miss. Code Ann. § 43-21-353 (2000)	Y	Y	Y	Y	Y	Reasonable cause to suspect
Missouri Mo. Rev. Stat. § 210.115 (1999)	Y	Y	Y	Y	Y	Reasonable cause to suspect
Montana Mont. Code Ann. § 41-3-201 (1999)	Y	Y	Y	Y	Y	Knows *or* has reasonable cause to suspect
Nebraska Neb. Rev. Stat. § 28-711 (2000)	Y	Y	Y	Y	Y	Reasonable cause to believe
Nevada Nev. Rev. Stat. § 432B.220 (2000)	Y	Y	Y	Y	Y	Knowledge *or* reasonable cause to believe
New Hampshire N.H. Rev. Stat. Ann. §§ 169-C:29 to -C:30 (1999)	Y	Y	Y	Y	Y	Reason to suspect
New Jersey N.J. Stat. Ann. § 9:6-8.10 (West 2000)	Y	Y	Y	Y	Y	Reasonable cause to believe

Report What?	Report to Whom?	Report How?
Physical *or* emotional injury resulting from abuse which causes harm *or* substantial risk of harm to child's health *or* welfare;	Juvenile Court	Oral *and* written
Abuse *or* neglect	Department of Social Services	Oral *and* written
Neglect, *or* physical *or* sexual abuse, currently *or* within past three years	Welfare agency *or* law enforcement	Not specified
Neglect *or* abuse	Department of Human Services	Oral *and* written
Child has been *or* may be subjected to abuse *or* neglect *or* is being subjected to conditions that would reasonably result in abuse *or* neglect	Division of Family Services	Not specified
Abuse *or* neglect	Department of Public Health and Human Services	Not specified
Abuse *or* neglect *or* conditions that reasonably would result in abuse *or* neglect	Law enforcement *or* Department of Health and Human Services	Oral *and* written
Abuse *or* neglect	Law enforcement *or* protective services	Not specified
Abuse *or* neglect	Department of Health and Human Services	Oral *and* written (if requested)
Abuse	Division of Youth and Family Services	Oral *or* written

continued on next page

Child Abuse and Neglect

	Who Must Report?					
	Dentist	Doctor	Mental Health	Nurse	Social Worker	Standard for Reporting?
New Mexico N.M. Stat. Ann. § 32A-4-3 (Michie 2000)	Y	Y	Y	Y	Y	Knowledge *or* reasonable suspicion
New York N.Y. [Soc. Serv.] Law § 413 (McKinney1999)	Y	Y	Y	Y	Y	Reasonable cause to suspect
North Carolina N.C. Gen. Stat. § 7B-301 (1999)	Y	Y	Y	Y	Y	Cause to suspect
North Dakota N.D. Cent. Code § 50-25.1-03 (2000)	Y	Y	Y	Y	Y	Knowledge *or* reasonable cause to suspect
Ohio Ohio Rev. Code Ann. § 2151.421 (Anderson 1999)	Y	Y	Y	Y	Y	Knowledge *or* suspicion
Oklahoma Okla. Stat. tit. 10, § 7103 (1999)	Y	Y	Y	Y	Y	Reason to believe
Oregon *Or.* Rev. Stat. §§ 419B.005, .010-.015 (1997)	Y	Y	Y	Y	Y	Reasonable cause to believe
Pennsylvania 23 Pa. Cons. Stat. § 6311 (1999)	Y	Y	Y	Y	Y	Reasonable cause to suspect
Rhode Island R.I. Gen. Laws § 40-11-3 (2000)	Y	Y	Y	Y	Y	Reasonable cause to know *or* suspect

Report What?	Report to Whom?	Report How?
Abuse *or* neglect	Law enforcement *or* Department of Children, Youth, and Families *or* tribal law enforcement (if child resides in Indian country)	Not specified
Abuse *or* maltreatment	Central register of child abuse and maltreatment	Oral *and* written
Abuse, neglect, dependency, *or* death resulting from maltreatment	Department of Social Services	Oral *or* written
Abuse, neglect, *or* death resulting from abuse *or* neglect	Department of Human Services	Not specified
Suffers *or* faces threat of suffering abuse, neglect, physical *or* mental wound, injury *or* disability that reasonably indicates abuse *or* neglect	Public Children Services Agency *or* law enforcement	Oral *and* written (if requested)
Abuse *or* neglect	Department of Human Services	Oral *or* written
Abuse	Office for Services to Children and Families *or* law enforcement	Oral
Abuse	Department *or* appropriate county agency	Oral *and* written
Abuse, neglect, *or* sexual abuse perpetrated by another child	Department for Children and Their Families	Oral

continued on next page

Child Abuse and Neglect

	Who Must Report?					
	Dentist	Doctor	Mental Health	Nurse	Social Worker	Standard for Reporting?
South Carolina S.C. Code Ann. § 20-7-510 (Law. Co-op. 1999)	Y	Y	Y	Y	Y	Reason to believe
South Dakota S.D. Codified Laws §§ 26-8A-3, -6 (Michie 2000)	Y	Y	Y	Y	Y	Reasonable cause to suspect
Tennessee Tenn. Code Ann. § 37-1-403 (1999)	Y	Y	Y	Y	Y	Knowledge *or* reasonable indication *or* reasonable appearance
Texas Tex. [Fam.] Code Ann. §§ 261.101-.103 (West 2000)	Y	Y	Y	Y	Y	Cause to believe
Utah Utah Code Ann. § 62A-4a-403 (1999)	Y	Y	Y	Y	Y	Observes *or* has reason to believe
Vermont Vt. Stat. Ann. tit. 33, §§ 4913-4914 (2000)	Y	Y	Y	Y	Y	Reasonable cause to belive
Virginia Va. Code Ann. § 63.1-248.3 (Michie 1999)	Y	Y	Y	Y	Y	Reason to suspect
Washington Wash. Rev. Code § 26.44.030 (2000)	Y	Y	Y	Y	Y	Observation *or* reasonable cause to believe
West Virginia W. Va. Code § 49-6A-2 (2000)	Y	Y	Y	Y	Y	Reasonable cause to suspect

Report What?	Report to Whom?	Report How?
Physical *or* mental health *or* welfare has been *or* may be adversely affected by abuse *or* neglect	Department of Social Services *or* law enforcement	Oral
Abuse *or* neglect	State's attorney, Department of Social Services, *or* law enforcement	Oral
Wound, injury, disability, physical *or* mental condition caused by brutality, abuse, *or* neglect	Juvenile court judge, Department of Children's Services, *or* law enforcement	Oral *or* written
Physical *or* mental health *or* welfare adversely affected by abuse *or* neglect	Law enforcement *or* Department of Protective and Regulatory Services	Not specified
Incest, molestation, sexual exploitation, sexual abuse, physical abuse, neglect; *or* circumstances reasonably resulting in any of above	Law enforcement *or* Division of Child and Family Services	Not specified
Abuse *or* neglect	Commissioner of Social and Rehabilitation Services	Oral *and* written
Abuse *or* neglect	Department of Social Services	Oral
Abuse *or* neglect *or* conditions likely to result in abuse *or* neglect	Law enforcement *or* Department of Social and Health Services	Not specified
Neglect *or* abuse, *or* conditions likely to result in neglect *or* abuse	State Department of Human Services *and* Division of Public Safety *and* law enforcement (if serious)	Not specified

continued on next page

Child Abuse and Neglect

	Who Must Report?					
	Dentist	Doctor	Mental Health	Nurse	Social Worker	Standard for Reporting?
Wisconsin Wis. Stat. § 48.981 (1999)	Y	Y	Y	Y	Y	Reasonable cause to suspect *or* reason to believe
Wyoming Wyo. Stat. Ann. § 14-3-205 (Michie 2000)	Y	Y	Y	Y	Y	Knowledge *or* reasonable cause to believe *or* suspect

NOTE: Because the term "allied health professional" is defined variably among different states, this chart cannot accurately summarize the duties of all persons who might be included in this broad category.

Report What?	Report to Whom?	Report How?
Abuse *or* neglect, *or* threat of abuse *or* neglect	Department of Health and Family Services	Oral *and* written (if requested)
Abuse *or* neglect *or* subjection to conditions that would reasonably result in abuse *or* neglect	Child protective agency *or* law enforcement	Not specified

Elder Abuse and Neglect

	Who Must Report?					
	Dentist	Doctor	Mental Health	Nurse	Social Worker	Standard for Reporting?
Alabama Ala. Code § 38-9-8 (2000)	Y	Y	Y	Y	Y	Reasonable cause to believe
Alaska Alaska Stat. § 47.24.010 (Michie 2000)	N	Y	Y	Y	Y	Reasonable cause to believe
Arizona Ariz. Rev. Stat. § 46-454 (2000)	Y	Y	Y	Y	Y	Reasonable basis to believe
Arkansas Ark. Code Ann. § 5-28-203 (Michie 1999)	Y	Y	Y	Y	Y	Observation *or* reasonable cause to suspect
California Cal. [Welf. & Inst.] Code § 15630 (West 2000)	N	Y	Y	Y	Y	Observation *or* knowledge of *or* reasonably suspects
Connecticut Conn. Gen. Stat. § 17b-451 (1999)	Y	Y	Y	Y	Y	Reasonable cause to suspect *or* believe
Delaware Del. Code Ann. tit. 31, § 3910 (1999)	Y	Y	Y	Y	Y	Reasonable cause to believe
District of Columbia D.C. Code Ann. § 6-2503 (1999)	Y	Y	N	Y	Y	Substantial cause to believe
Florida Fla. Stat. ch. 415.1034 (1999)	Y	Y	Y	Y	Y	Knowledge of *or* reasonable cause to suspect
Georgia Ga. Code Ann. § 30-5-4 (1999)	Y	Y	Y	Y	Y	Reasonable cause to believe
Hawaii Haw. Rev. Stat. § 346-224 (1999)	Y	Y	Y	Y	Y	Knowledge *or* reason to believe

Report What?	Report to Whom?	Report How?
Physical abuse, neglect, exploitation, sexual abuse, *or* emotional abuse	County Department of Human Resources *or* law enforcement	Oral *and* written
Abandonment, exploitation, abuse, neglect, *or* self-neglect	Department of Health and Human Services' Central Information and Referral Service	Not specified
Abuse, neglect, *or* exploitation of property	Law enforcement *or* protective services worker	Oral *and* written
Abuse, sexual abuse, neglect, *or* exploitation	Central registry *or* law enforcement	Not specified
Abuse, abandonment, isolation *or* financial abuse *or* neglect	Adult protective services agency *or* law enforcement	Oral *and* written
Abuse, neglect, exploitation, *or* abandonment	Commissioner of Social Services	Not specified
In need of protective services	Department of Health and Social Services	Not specified
In need of protective services due to abuse *or* neglect	Department of Human Services	Oral *or* written
Abuse, neglect, *or* exploitation	Central abuse registry	Oral
Physical injury inflicted by nonaccidental means, neglect, *or* exploitation	Adult protection agency, law enforcement, *or* district attorney	Oral *or* written
Abuse *and* threat of imminent abuse	Department of Human Services	Oral *and* written

continued on next page

Elder Abuse and Neglect

| | Who Must Report? | | | | | |
	Dentist	Doctor	Mental Health	Nurse	Social Worker	Standard for Reporting?
Idaho Idaho Code § 39-5303 (1999)	Y	Y	Y	N	Y	Reasonable cause to believe
Illinois 320 Ill. Comp. Stat. 20/2, 20/4 (West 2000)	Y	Y	Y	Y	Y	Reason to believe
Indiana Ind. Code § 12-10-3-9 (1999)	Y	Y	Y	Y	Y	Belief *or* reason to believe
Iowa Iowa Code § 235B.3 (1999)	Y	Y	Y	Y	Y	Suspicion
Kansas Kan. Stat. Ann. § 39-1431 (1999)	N	Y	Y	Y	Y	Reasonable cause to believe
Kentucky Ky. Rev. Stat. Ann. § 209.030 (Michie 1998)	Y	Y	Y	Y	Y	Reasonable cause to suspect
Louisiana La. Rev. Stat. Ann. § 14/403/2 (West 2000)	Y	Y	Y	Y	Y	Cause to believe
Maine Me. Rev. Stat. Ann. tit. 22, § 3477 (West 1999)	Y	Y	Y	Y	Y	Reasonable cause to suspect
Maryland Md. Code Ann., [Fam. Law] § 14-302 (1999)	Y	Y	Y	Y	Y	Reason to believe
Massachusetts Mass. Gen. Laws ch. 19A, § 15 (1999)	Y	Y	Y	Y	Y	Reasonable cause to believe
Michigan Mich. Comp. Laws § 400.11a (1999)	Y	Y	Y	Y	Y	Suspicion *or* reasonable cause to believe

Report What?	Report to Whom?	Report How?
Abuse, neglect, *or* exploitation	Commission on Aging	Not specified
Abuse, neglect, *or* financial exploitation, within past 12 months	Department on Aging	Not specified
Endangered adult	Adult protective services *or* law enforcement *or* statewide telephone number	Not specified
Abuse	Department of Human Services	Not specified
Abuse, neglect, exploitation, *or* in need of protective services	Department of Social and Rehabilitation Services	Not specified
Abuse, neglect, *or* exploitation	Cabinet for Families and Children	Oral *or* written
Adverse effect on physical *or* mental health *or* welfare by abuse, neglect, *or* exploitation	Adult protection agency *or* law enforcement agency	Not specified
Abuse, neglect, *or* exploitation, accompanied by incapacitation	Department of Human Services	Oral *and* written
Abuse, neglect, self-neglect, *or* exploitation	Department of Social Services	Oral *or* written
Suffering from *or* death caused by abuse	Executive Office of Elder Affairs	Oral *and* written
Abuse, neglect, *or* exploitation	Department of Social Services	Oral

continued on next page

Elder Abuse and Neglect

	Who Must Report?					Standard for Reporting?
	Dentist	Doctor	Mental Health	Nurse	Social Worker	
Minnesota Minn. Stat. §§ 626.556, .557 (1999)	Y	Y	Y	Y	Y	Reason to believe
Mississippi Miss. Code Ann. § 43-47-7 (2000)	Y	Y	Y	Y	Y	Reasonable cause to believe
Missouri Mo. Rev. Stat. § 660.255 (1999)	Y	Y	Y	Y	Y	Reasonable cause to suspect
Montana Mont. Code Ann. § 52-3-811 (1999)	Y	Y	Y	Y	Y	Knowledge *or* reasonable cause to suspect
Nebraska Neb. Rev. Stat. § 28-372 (2000)	Y	N	Y	Y	Y	Reasonable cause to believe *or* observation
Nevada Nev. Rev. Stat. § 200.5093 (2000)	Y	Y	Y	Y	Y	Knowledge *or* reasonable cause to believe
New Hampshire N.H. Rev. Stat. Ann. § 161-F:46 (1999)	Y	Y	Y	Y	Y	Reason to believe
New Mexico Stat. Ann. § 27-7-30 (Michie 2000)	Y	Y	Y	Y	Y	Reasonable cause to believe
North Carolina N.C. Gen. Stat. § 108A-102 (1999)	Y	Y	Y	Y	Y	Reasonable cause to believe
Ohio Ohio Rev. Code Ann. § 5101.61 (Anderson 1999)	Y	Y	Y	Y	Y	Reasonable cause to believe
Oklahoma Okla. Stat. tit. 43A, § 10-104 (1999)	Y	Y	Y	Y	Y	Reasonable cause to believe

Report What?	Report to Whom?	Report How?
Maltreatment *or* physical injury not reasonably explained	Designated common entry point	Oral
Abuse, neglect, *or* exploitation	Department of Human Services *or* welfare department	Written *and/or* oral
Likelihood of suffering serious physical harm *and* in need of protective services	Department of Social Services	Oral *or* written
Abuse, sexual abuse, neglect, *or* exploitation	Department of Public Health and Human Services *or* county attorney	Not specified
Abuse *or* conditions reasonably resulting in abuse	Law enforcement *or* Department of Health and Human Services	Oral *and* written (if requested)
Abuse, neglect, exploitation, *or* isolation	Aging Services Division of Department of Human Resources *or* law enforcement	Not specified
Physical abuse, neglect, exploitation, *or* living in hazardous conditions	Commissioner of Health and Human Services	Oral *and* written (if requested)
Abuse, neglect, *or* exploitation	Children, Youth, and Families Department	Oral *or* written
Need of protective services	Director of Department of Social Services	Oral *or* written
Abuse, neglect, *or* exploitation	Department of Job and Family Services	Oral *and* written (if requested)
Abuse, neglect, *or* exploitation	Department of Human Services, district attorney, *or* law enforcement	Not specified

continued on next page

Elder Abuse and Neglect

	Who Must Report?					
	Dentist	Doctor	Mental Health	Nurse	Social Worker	Standard for Reporting?
Oregon Or. Rev. Stat. §§ 124.050, .060-.065 (1999)	Y	N	Y	Y	Y	Reasonable cause to believe
Rhode Island R.I. Gen. Laws § 42-66-8 (2000)	Y	Y	Y	Y	Y	Reasonable cause to believe
South Carolina S.C. Code Ann. § 43-35-25 (Law. Co-op. 1999)	Y	Y	Y	Y	Y	Reason to believe
Tennessee Tenn. Code Ann. § 71-6-103 (1999)	Y	Y	Y	Y	Y	Reasonable cause to suspect
Texas Tex. [Hum. Res.] Code Ann. § 48.051 (West 2000)	Y	Y	Y	Y	Y	Cause to believe
Utah Utah Code Ann. § 62A-3-302 (1999)	Y	Y	Y	Y	Y	Reason to believe
Vermont Vt. Stat. Ann. tit. 33, §§ 6903-6904 (2000)	Y	Y	Y	Y	Y	Knowledge, receipt of information, or reason to suspect
Virginia Va. Code Ann. § 63.1-55.3 (Michie 1999)	Y	Y	Y	Y	Y	Reason to suspect
Washington Wash. Rev. Code §§ 74.34.020, .035 (2000)	Y	Y	Y	Y	Y	Reasonable cause to believe
West Virginia W. Va. Code § 9-6-9 (2000)	Y	Y	Y	Y	Y	Reasonable cause to believe
Wyoming Wyo. Stat. Ann. § 35-20-103 (Michie 2000)	Y	Y	Y	Y	Y	Knowledge or reasonable cause to believe

NOTE: Because the term "allied health professional" is defined variably among different states, this chart cannot accurately summarize the duties of all persons who might be included in this broad category.

Report What?	Report to Whom?	Report How?
Abuse	Senior and Disabled Services Division *or* law enforcement	Oral
Abuse, neglect, exploitation, *or* abandonment	Director of Department of Elderly Affairs	Not specified
Occurrence *or* likelihood of abuse, neglect, *or* exploitation	Adult protective services program	Oral *or* written
Abuse, neglect, *or* exploitation	Department of Human Services	Oral *or* written
Abuse, neglect, *or* exploitation	Department of Protective and Regulatory Services	Oral *or* written
Abuse, emotional *or* psychological abuse, neglect, *or* exploitation	Law enforcement *or* adult protective services	Not specified
Abuse, neglect, *or* exploitation	Commissioner of the Department of Aging and Disabilities *or* law enforcement	Written
Abuse, neglect, *or* exploitation	Department of Public Welfare	Oral *or* written
Abandonment, abuse, financial exploitation, sexual *or* physical assault, *or* neglect	Law enforcement *and* Department of Social and Health Services	Oral *or* written
Neglect, abuse, *or* emergency situation	Protective services agency	Not specified
Abuse, neglect, exploitation, *or* abandonment	Law enforcement *or* Department of Family Services	Not specified

Intimate Partner Violence

	Who Must Report?					
	Dentist	Doctor	Mental Health	Nurse	Social Worker	Standard for Reporting?
California Cal. [Penal] Code § 11160 (Deering 2000)	Y	Y	N	Y	N	Knows *or* reasonably suspects
Colorado Colo. Rev. Stat. § 12-36-135 (1999)	N	Y	N	N	N	Believes *or* has reason to believe
Kentucky Ky. Rev. Stat. Ann. § 209.030 (Michie 1998)	Y	Y	Y	Y	Y	Reasonable cause to suspect
Rhode Island R.I. Gen. Laws § 12-29-9 (2000)	N	Y	N	Y	N	Reasonable cause to believe *or* victim statement

NOTE: Because the term "allied health professional" is defined variably among different states, this chart cannot accurately summarize the duties of all persons who might be included in this broad category.

Report What?	Report to Whom?	Report How?
Wound *or* other physical injury inflicted by firearm *or* wound *or* other physical injury resulting from assaultive *or* abusive conduct	Law enforcement agency	Oral *and* written
Injury caused by discharge of firearm *or* by sharp *or* pointed instrument *or* injury resulting from criminal act, including domestic violence	Law enforcement	Not specified
Abuse, neglect, *or* exploitation of adult	Cabinet for Families and Children	Oral *or* written
Domestic violence	Court's domestic violence training and monitoring unit	Written

Appendix D

Mandatory Education Laws for Family Violence

Child Abuse and Neglect

	Who Must Receive Continuing Education/Training?					What Information Must Be Conveyed?	Who Must Be Consulted and/or Must Approve?	When Is the Education/Training to Take Place?
	Dentist	Doctor	Mental Health	Nurse	Social Worker			
California Cal. [Bus. & Prof.] Code § 28 (Deering 2000)	N	N	Y	N	Y	Child abuse assessment *and* reporting	Board of Behavioral Science Examiners	Once (seven hours)
Iowa Iowa Code § 232.69 (2000)	Y	Y	Y	Y	Y	Child abuse identification *and* reporting	Department of Human Services	Two hours every five years
New York N.Y. [Soc. Serv.] Law § 421 (McKinney 2000)	Y	Y	Y	Y	N	Indicators of child abuse and maltreatment *and* reporting procedures	Department of Social Services	Two hours

Elder Abuse and Neglect

	Who Must Receive Continuing Education/Training?					What Information Must Be Conveyed?	Who Must Be Consulted and/or Must Approve?	When Is the Education/Training to Take Place?
	Dentist	Doctor	Mental Health	Nurse	Social Worker			
Iowa Iowa Code § 235B.16 (1999)	Y	Y	Y	Y	Y	Identification *and* reporting of dependent adult abuse	Department of Elder Affairs	Two hours within six months of initial employment *and* two hours every five years

Intimate Partner Violence

	Who Must Receive Continuing Education/Training?					What Information Must Be Conveyed?	Who Must Be Consulted and/or Must Approve?	When Is the Education/Training to Take Place?
	Dentist	Doctor	Mental Health	Nurse	Social Worker			
Alaska Alaska Stat. § 18.66.310 (Michie 1999)	Y	Y	Y	Y	Y	Nature, extent, and causes of intimate partner violence; procedures designed to promote victim safety; lethality issues; *and available resources*	Council on Domestic Violence and Sexual Assault	Not specified
Florida Fla. Stat. Ann. § 455.597 (West 1999)	Y	Y	Y	Y	Y	Number of patients likely to be victims and perpetrators; screening procedures, *and* resources in the local community	Division of Medical Quality Assurance	One hour every two years
Kentucky Ky. Rev. Stat. Ann. § 194A.540 (Michie 1998)	Y	Y	Y	Y	Y	Dynamics of intimate partner violence; effects on victims; legal remedies; lethality and risk issues; model protocols; available community resources; *and reporting requirements*	Legal, victim services victim advocacy, *and* mental health professionals with an expertise in intimate partner violence	Once (three hours)

Appendix E

Existing Curricula on Family Violence

Child Abuse and Neglect

Sponsoring Institution/ Developer	Title/Release Date	Audience	Training Approach	Description
	Focus on Child Abuse	Medical residents	Medium: slide format; self-assessment slides Method: educational brochures; fact sheets on a range of topics; articles; guide to current trends in child abuse and neglect; elective	Resident can diagnose possible child abuse cases; fact sheets cover shaken baby syndrome, managing stress, punishment versus discipline
	Curriculum for Pediatric Resident Education in Child Abuse and Neglect	Medical residents		Learn the basics of child abuse, child neglect, and abuse identification and management; identify and communicate with families at risk for abuse or neglect and provide appropriate intervention; attend lectures about physical abuse and sexual abuse; learn about forensic evaluations of child sexual abuse; evaluate children referred for PST consultation; conduct at least one psychosocial interview under supervision; review radiographic studies; evaluate children who may have been sexually abused
Alaska Family Violence Prevention Project (AFVPP)	Training Materials on Domestic Violence; developed 1999	Emergency medicine practitioners, psychologists, pediatricians, home visitors	Core curriculum (modules) with talking points for each slide Section 1: Core Curriculum on	Curriculum covers both domestic violence and child abuse: physical abuse ranking scale; examples of emotional abuse, sexual abuse; severity and frequency; prejudice and misunderstanding; clinical indicators; common diagnoses; nature and circumstance of injuries; related medical findings;

	Domestic Violence Section 2: Relationship Between Domestic Violence and Child Abuse Curriculum			mental health/psychological symptoms; relationship between domestic violence and child abuse; escalation of the violence; severe and fatal cases of child abuse; childhood history of abuse; child witnesses; screening for domestic violence and child abuse; goals when intervening in domestic violence and child abuse; child abuse reporting
American Academy of Pediatrics (AAP)	Visual Diagnosis of Child Sexual Abuse; developed 1998	AAP members, medical professionals	Medium: binder with 166 slides; 33-page study guide; Method: elective education program	Normal anatomy and variants; nonabusive pathology and trauma; examples in male and female children
American Academy of Pediatrics (AAP)	The Visual Diagnosis of Child Physical Abuse; developed 1994	AAP members, medical professionals	Medium: binder with 150 slides; 33-page study guide; Method: elective education program	Medical evidence of physical abuse: inflicted burns, bruises, abrasions, fractures; radiological diagnosis of head trauma; ocular findings
American Academy of Pediatrics (AAP)	Focus on Child Abuse: Resources for Prevention, Recognition, and Treatment, 2nd edition	Medical professionals	Medium: CD-ROM featuring 200 color slides; Method: presentation	200 color slides on CD-ROM; visual diagnosis of child physical abuse; visual self-assessment; parent and patient education/information; results of 50-state child abuse survey; AAP policies, manual excerpts; full-text articles from *Pediatrics*; AAP speaker's kit with slides, lecture notes, and handouts

continued on next page

Child Abuse and Neglect

Sponsoring Institution/ Developer	Title/Release Date	Audience	Training Approach	Description
American Psychological Association, Child Abuse and Neglect Working Group and Section on Child Maltreatment of the Division of Child, Youth, and Family Services	A Guide for Including Information on Child Abuse and Neglect in Professional Education and Training; A Guide for Including Information on Child Abuse and Neglect in the Undergraduate Curriculum; developed 1996	Graduate students of psychology	Medium: three-part guide with resources (graduate course on child abuse and neglect) Method: specialized training for clinical, counseling, and school psychologists (basic materials on child abuse and neglect)	Integrating child abuse and neglect into current course work; definitional issues; prevalence and consequences of child abuse and neglect; theories about the development of abusive and neglectful behaviors; recognition and referral of abused and neglected children and adults: child protection system, medical intervention, legal involvement, mental health interventions; prevention of child abuse and neglect; ethical issues; research methods; involvement with other professionals; assessment of child abuse and neglect victims and their families; interventions with abused and neglected children and families—issues for the psychologist; interventions with perpetrators of abuse and neglect
Boston Children's Hospital, AWAKE program (Advocacy for Women and Kids in Emergencies)	Health Care Services for Battered Women and Their Abused Children	Health care providers	Medium: 60-page manual; elective	Relationships between child abuse and woman abuse (also covers domestic violence); specific, practical information for a health system response
Brown University School of Medicine, Department of Pediatrics and Hasbro Children's Hospital, Providence, RI	Fellowship Program in Child Abuse and Neglect			

Center for Child Protection, Children's Hospital and Health Center, San Diego, CA	Gynecology and Obstetrics Preceptorship Clinical Training Program	Gynecology and obstetrics	Medium: clinical training program Method: lecture; vignettes; clinic	Manner in which sexual abuse medical evaluation can be effectively and atraumatically performed; team meetings for case review; 3-5 examples of cross-discipline cooperation; roles of law enforcement, child protective services, clinical forensic examiner/interviewer as they relate to investigation; anticipatory problems indicating need for referral for abuse counseling; filling out OCJP 925 medical reports; interpretation of examination findings; documentation; interpretation of photographs; literature review
Center for Child Protection, Children's Hospital and Health Center, San Diego, CA	Family Violence Rotation		Medium: student rotation Method: observation; educational videotapes; clinic; meetings; research project	Observe child protective services hotline for 1 hour as well as forensic videos, dv tro clinic, Oprah tape on incest dynamics and conference tape; article on child sexual abuse accommodation syndrome; observe/perform exams on children suspected of having been abused; participate in the failure-to-thrive clinic; standardized paper cases to demonstrate differences between medical and forensic history; law review; reporting forms; attendance at a navy family advocacy meeting; meeting with therapists; expert witness testimony
Center on Child Abuse and Neglect, University of Oklahoma Health Sciences Center	Interdisciplinary Training Program in Child Abuse and Neglect	Graduate-level students in law, psychology, social work, nursing, dentistry, public health, education, and related disciplines	Method: weekly seminars; two field practica; course projects; participation in a mock trial	Role of child protective services; interviewing children for suspected sexual abuse; substance abuse and child abuse and neglect; issues of child maltreatment in indian country; foster care; treatment of offenders and victims; mock trial; overview of prevention

continued on next page

Child Abuse and Neglect

Sponsoring Institution/ Developer	Title/Release Date	Audience	Training Approach	Description
Child Abuse and Neglect, American Academy of Pediatrics (AAP) 2000 Annual Meeting	Identifying Child Abuse: Can You Meet the Challenge?	AAP members	Medium: 3-hour lecture followed by "Award for Outstanding Service to Maltreated Children"; elective	Interactive case-based sessions with ARS; review common pitfalls in recognizing abuse; provide approaches for improving diagnostic acumen; and highlight disease mimickers of physical and sexual abuse
Children's Hospital of Philadelphia	The Child Abuse and Neglect Fellowship	Board-eligible or board-certified pediatricians	2 years	Court testimony; clinical care of children; education of medical personnel; multidisciplinary approach to caring for abused children; CARE clinic: work with social work coordinator of the clinic and attending physician to provide medical evaluations to children who are victims of physical and sexual abuse; in-patient evaluations: fellow provides consultation to the pediatric and surgery teams in the hospital when children are admitted as a result of abuse or neglect; research: develop research skills and learn proper research techniques under the guidance of pediatricians and epidemiologists with expertise in the medical research design; multidisciplinary work with the Child Advocacy Center, Philadelphia Child Fatality Review Team, Law Enforcement Child Abuse Project of Philadelphia, Medical Legal Advisory Board on Child Abuse
Children's Memorial Hospital, Chicago	Child Abuse Rotation Curriculum	PL_3 residents	Medium: 2-week rotation; required Method: clinic; consultations; review meetings; home visits	Hospital consults (mostly physical abuse and some neglect); outpatient sexual abuse clinic; death review meetings; juvenile court; home visits with Department of Children and Famly Services

Division of Emergency Medicine, Mayerson Center for Safe and Healthy Children, Children's Hospital Medical Center, University of Cincinnati	Fellowship in Child Forensics and Abuse; developed 1998	Pediatricians; completion of pediatric residency	Medium: 1-year fellowship Method: training; administrative; research	Training in the clinical areas of physical child abuse, sexual child abuse, medical neglect, Munchausen syndrome by proxy; administrative skills needed to direct a child abuse program; research skills required of medical investigators
Duke Medical Center	Pediatric residency rotation	Second-year residents	Medium: 1-month-long required course (however, 1 week of vacation time comes out of this month, and not every resident is able to rotate through the child abuse program/clinic because of limited space) Method: shadowing; clinic	Residents are with the physicians every day of the week but do not participate in child abuse coverage on evenings or weekends
Governor's Office, State of Pennsylvania	Governor's Proposal to Help Medical Professionals Identify and Prevent Child Abuse and Neglect; released April 1999	Physicians and other medical professionals	Medium: curriculum provided by 27 physicians and 32 county children and youth agencies in the state Method: lecture	How to identify child abuse and neglect and families at risk of child abuse and neglect; curriculum focuses on providing information on child protective services law and mandatory reporting provisions; hypothetical examples in which physicians and medical professionals may suspect child abuse and neglect; actual examples of child abuse compiled by the American Academy of Pediatrics; common themes that may indicate child abuse and neglect

continued on next page

Child Abuse and Neglect

Sponsoring Institution/ Developer	Title/Release Date	Audience	Training Approach	Description
Hawaii Dental Hygenists' Association	Dentistry's Role in Preventing Abuse and Neglect	Dentistry students	Medium: reading list; handout; worksheet Method: lectures	History and etiology of child abuse and neglect; risk factors for child abuse and neglect; warning signs; physical and behavioral indicators of child abuse and neglect; the relation of child abuse and neglect to other forms of family violence; statutory definitions; precipitating factors to family violence; recognition of physical abuse: clinical, general, head and neck, intraoral; sexual abuse; emotional abuse; conditions that mimic abuse; dental neglect; recognition of neglect; interventions; legal and liability issues; multipage resource/reading list; office protocol for identifying and reporting suspected child abuse and neglect
Louisiana County Department of Health Services	Family Violence for Health Professional Schools; 1981 (currently being updated)	Health professionals		Also covers elder abuse, domestic violence, and other special topics
Louisiana State University, School of Medicine, Department of Pediatrics	Child abuse rotation	All pediatrics interns, fourth-year elective, psychiatry fellows	Medium: 1-month rotation that consists of 40 hours per week outpatient clinic Method: clinic; consultations; review meetings; court attendance	One to three residents per month; outpatient clinic involves physical abuse, sexual abuse, failure to thrive and burns (inflicted); after hours; inpatient local death consultations; multidisciplinary staffing; attendance at review panels; elective attendance at pediatric autopsies; attendance in juvenile and criminal court; hired former prosecutor to plan/hold mock trial withthe resident being the expert once a month; planning to add a major/minor head injury

continued on next page

Organization	Title	Audience	Medium/Method	Content
Massachusetts Society for the Prevention of Cruelty to Children, Institute for Professional Education				clinic in conjunction with neurology and ophthalmology; psychiatry fellows concentrate on improving interview skills with children Medical evaluation of physical and sexual abuse; accidents and abuse: how to tell the difference; head trauma in child abuse; visceral injuries in child abuse; cutaneous manifestations of child abuse; skeletal injuries as a manifestation of child abuse; child neglect; unsafe manifestations of child abuse; Munchausen syndrome by proxy; conditions mistaken for child abuse; syndromes associated with child abuse, fatal child abuse, and sudden infant death syndrome, dental aspects of child abuse and neglect; critical injuries from falls
Nova Southeastern University Physician Assistant Program, College of Allied Health, Health Professions Division	Issues in Medicine: Domestic Violence; developed 1999	First-year physician assistant students, practicing physician assistants	Medium: on-line project or course during the "transition month" for physician assistant students; for CME [?] credits Method: 3-hour program	Presentation features epidemiology; diagnosis; treatment; patient education; counseling and prevention; state laws; reporting and case presentations; also covers spousal/mate abuse, elderly abuse, disabled abuse

Child Abuse and Neglect

Sponsoring Institution/ Developer	Title/Release Date	Audience	Training Approach	Description
Ohio State University College of Medicine, Columbus	The Child Abuse Program; developed 1998		1 year (July 1 through June 30)	Fellow attends five clinics in the Family Development Clinic each week; remaining time is spent in self-study, including pre- and posttesting, preparation of education materials, and community visits; attendance at weekly pediatric grand rounds and other appropriate educational programs at Children's Hospital; fellow and staff on all consultations, training programs, and court appearances; develop skills in research design, data collection, and data analysis; perform a forensic physical exam for abuse or neglect; complete an appropriate abuse form; participate in the interview of a child suspected of having been sexually abused; testify in court about findings as a fact witness; recognize sexual abuse; describe the roles of adjudication, identification, treatment, and prevention; date a bruise, subdural bleed, fracture; recognize 10 diseases that can be mistaken for child abuse; develop a community plan of action for child maltreatment; family development clinic
St. Joseph's Hospital, Phoenix	Children's Health Center, St. Joseph's Hospital Residents	Residents in their PL-2 year	Medium: 1-month-long required course Method: clinic; shadowing; rotation	Sexual abuse clinic; hospital consults; spend day with investigator; attend court with staff who are testifying; rotation initiated at the request of the students who wanted more training

State University of New York, Health Science Center at Syracuse University Health Center	Fellowship in Forensic and Child Abuse Pediatrics	Pediatricians	Medium: 2- to 3-year fellowship for one or two fellows. Method: teaching; research; patient care advocacy	Prepare pediatricians for teaching, research, patient care, legal and community responsibilities in the area of child maltreatment, including child abuse, forensics, foster care, sexual abuse, physical abuse, neglect and related issues; provide clinical treatment to maltreated children; plan, conduct, analyze, interpret, write studies related to maltreatment; advocate for children's issues, including courtroom time; teach medical students and residents, parent groups, and community professionals; program development for child abuse programs
Team for Children at Risk, Children's Mercy Hospital, Kansas City, MO	Child abuse curriculum			
University of California, Davis Medical Center, Sacramento	Child Abuse and Neglect Fellowship	Candidate either board certified or board eligible in pediatrics	Medium: 2-year fellowship training program. Method: teaching responsibilities; community involvement; research responsibilities; biomedical statistics course; writing workshop; computer workshop; literature searches; database management	Experimental design workshop, conferences, meetings; Child Protection Center Clinic responsibilities; on-call responsibilities; rotation/experiences; progress assessment; clinical and teaching assessment

continued on next page

Child Abuse and Neglect

Sponsoring Institution/ Developer	Title/Release Date	Audience	Training Approach	Description
University of Colorado Hospital and Kempe Children's Center, Denver	Child Abuse and Neglect Fellowship	Board-certified or board-eligible pediatricians, state medical license required	Medium: 1- to 2-year residency fellowship Method: first year is primarily clinical; second year can be designed around research with 60% clinical, 30% research, 10% outside involvement in advocacy center or consultation work; one or two positions yearly	Weekly child protection team; clinic sees primarily sexual abuse consultations for colposcopy and interviews; civil and criminal court involvement
University of Maryland Medical System's Child Protection Program	SEEK (Safe Environment for Every Kid): Provider Information Manual; developed March 2000	Community pediatricians, child health care providers	Manual with chapters on domestic violence, physical and sexual abuse, and child sexual abuse prevention	Assessment; initial management; referral information; questioning the child; questioning the parent; special considerations; documentation
University of Michigan	Practice Seminar in Child Maltreatment: Assessment and Treatment	Master's in social work students	Medium: class Method: lectures; discussion; demonstrations; video; role play; small-group exercises; duration 4 months (one semester)	Explores personal, professional, and societal responses to children at risk; discusses client issues and responses to child welfare interventions; discusses theories that explain child maltreatment

Institution	Course	Students	Medium/Method	Description
University of Michigan	Integrative Seminar in Child Maltreatment	Master's in social work students	Medium: class Method: lecture; discussion; small-group exercises; student presentation; guest speakers; elective	Examination of child welfare from perspective of community practice, direct practice and policy; integration of research findings related to child welfare; examines the relationship between child maltreatment and environmental factors
University of North Carolina at Chapel Hill, School of Medicine, Department of Social Medicine	Preventive Medicine Residency/Fellowship in Violence Prevention; developed 1998	Preventive medicine residents; must have completed a primary care training program in internal medicine, family practice, or pediatrics	Medium: 2-year fellowship Method: first year: learning research skills; acquiring master's in public health in epidemiology; outcomes research or maternal and child health; at end of program, fellows will be eligible for American Board of Preventive Medicine	Year 1: work in a multidisciplinary child abuse center; work on the consultation team for domestic violence Year 2: 30 working days at the state health department or a national health agency, completion of a major research project, and continued clinical work in one or more areas of violence specialization (also covers youth violence and domestic violence)
University of Pittsburgh	Child Sexual Abuse	Bachelor's in social work students	Medium: class Method: lecture; readings; written papers; duration is 4 months (one semester)	Overview of child sexual abuse; assessment of child abuse situations; examination of personal value/belief system; evaluation of effectiveness of treatment approaches
University of Pittsburgh	Child Maltreatment: Physical Abuse and Neglect	Bachelor's in social work students	Medium: class Method: discussion; role plays; readings; written assignments; duration 4 months (one semester)	Development of relevant treatment strategies for family members; identification of gender and racial issues in abuse/neglect situations; overview of how abuse and neglect are identified and integrated

continued on next page

Child Abuse and Neglect

Sponsoring Institution/ Developer	Title/Release Date	Audience	Training Approach	Description
University of Texas at Austin	Child Welfare	Bachelor's and master's in social work students	Medium: duration is 4 months (one semester); elective	
Vanderbilt University	Child Abuse Forensic Pediatric Rotation	First-year medical residents	Medium: 2 weeks, required as part of their ambulatory clinic months/ research month Method: slide review; history taking, visual diagnosis; management of acute and chronic sexual abuse presentations	Inpatient evaluation of suspected child abuse cases; two half-days per week at Our Kids, functioning as the primary medical provider, performing and documenting genital exams; take calls for both the CARE team and Our Kids during a month; interviewing techniques; attend review meetings with multidisciplinary review of cases; review and present a forensic pediatric case consult; attend x-ray rounds; attend court, depositions, or other legal matters with members of CARE and Our Kids; keep a log of patients and diagnoses; complete a pre- and posttest knowledge test on aspects of forensic pediatrics
Western Schools, Inc.	Child Abuse; developed 1993	Nurses	Medium: self-study book for nurses; continuing education credits	Characteristics of families at risk; underlying causes of violence against children; factors in a child's medical history that help professionals identify abuse; physical examination of the child; x-ray, ultrasound, and CAT scan studies; causes and detection of psychological abuse; legal aspects; failure to thrive; reporting; difference between juvenile and criminal courts; evidence; successful treatment approaches for families

Elder Abuse and Neglect

Sponsoring Institution/ Developer	Title/Release Date	Audience	Training Approach	Description
Benjamin Rose Institute, Alzheimer's Association of Cleveland, Department of Senior and Adult Protective Services	Model Intervention for Elder Abuse and Dementia; 19999	Cross-training service provider	Medium: comprehensive training manual on elder abuse and dementia Method: organized into three modules	Faculty guides; participant's workbooks; learning objectives; value statements; interactive exercises; case discussion guides Organized into three modules: (1) emphasizes the manifestations of various types of dementia; (2) provides background information on elder abuse, characteristics and theories of causation, how to screen for possible abuse, information on elder abuse laws, referral protocols; (3) integrative module promotes collaboration, discussion, ethical dilemmas, legal issues
Hawaii Dental Hygienists' Association	Dentistry's Role in Preventing Abuse and Neglect	Dentistry students	Method: reading list; handout; worksheet Method: lecture	Dentistry's role in preventing child abuse and neglect and domestic violence, also covers elder abuse: physical and behavioral indicators; history; relation to other forms of family violence; etiology; statutory definitions; precipitating factors to family violence; recognition of physical abuse; clinical, general, head and neck, intra-oral; sexual abuse; emotional abuse; conditions that mimic abuse; dental neglect; recognition of neglect; interventions; legal and liability issues; multipage resource/reading list; office protocol for identifying and reporting suspected abuse and neglect; warning signs; risk factors

continued on next page

Elder Abuse and Neglect

Sponsoring Institution/ Developer	Title/Release Date	Audience	Training Approach	Description
Integrated Health Services	Abuse Prohibition Program	Health care professionals	Medium: abuse prohibition program Method: PowerPoint presentation	Abuse, neglect, and misappropriation of property; prevention, identification, investigation of abuse; abuse protocol; definitions and examples of abuse; indicators that abuse may have occurred; guidelines for communication; suspected abuse reporting tools; abuse prohibition
New York State Office for the Aging	Shining Light on the Hidden Problem of Elder Abuse	Health care providers	Medium: elder abuse prevention training manual with overheads	Introduction to elder abuse, mistreatment, and neglect; high-risk factors and indicators; challenges in substantiating elder abuse; role of the financial community; role of the health care community; role of the law enforcement community; recommendations to reduce prevalence; resources
Nova Southeastern University Physician Assistant Program; College of Allied Health, Health Professions Division	Issues in Medicine: Domestic Violence; 1999	First-year physician assistant students, practicing physician assistants	Medium: On-line course or course during the "transition month" for physician assistant students; for continuing medical education credits, 3-hour program	Presentation features epidemiology, diagnosis, treatment, patient education, counseling and prevention, Florida laws, reporting, and case presentations; also features spousal/mate abuse, disabled abuse, child abuse
Terra Nova Films (ELDER)	Just to Have a Peaceful Life	Health professionals	Medium: 10-minute video; elective	Training video on older battered women's issues; complements materials produced by Wisconsin Coalition Against Domestic Violence Older Battered Women's Project

Wisconsin Bureau on Aging	Elder Abuse, Neglect, and Family Violence: A Guide for Health Care Professionals	Health care professionals	Medium: resource manual; elective	Descriptions of elder abuse, resources, key issues, addresses most commonly asked questions; also covers domestic violence
Wisconsin Coalition Against Domestic Violence (WCADV) Wisconsin Bureau on Aging and Long Term Care Resources (BALTCR)	Elder Abuse, Neglect, and Family Violence: A Guide for Health Care Professionals; 1999	Health care professionals	Medium: manual	Domestic abuse in later life; response to suspected elder abuse; answers to commonly asked questions; what can be done to help older victims of family violence; resources

Intimate Partner Violence

Sponsoring Institution/ Developer	Title/Release Date	Audience	Training Approach	Description
Alabama Coalition Against Domestic Violence	Domestic Violence: The Effective Medical Response	Health care providers	Lecture and discussion with accompanying 120-page resource manual 1-2 hours total	Training components: domestic violence 101; medical role in responding to domestic violence; domestic violence laws in Alabama; Alabama Coalition Against Domestic Violence resources; safety plan; medical resources; selected articles; resource material
Alaska Family Violence Prevention Project (AFVPP)	Developing a Domestic Violence Training Initiative: Technical Assistance Manual (Vol. 1)	Maternal and child health providers	Resource manual for background and planning (Vol. 1)	Vol. 1—Technical Assistance Manual Overview; domestic violence as a maternal and child health issue; building partnerships; local data sources; designing and conducting a needs assessment; locating resources; developing a training project; making the connection: family violence; funding sources
	Training Materials on Domestic Violence (Vol. 2); 1999		Didactic presentation; small-group discussion (variable duration) (Vol. 2)	Vol. 2—Training Materials on Domestic Violence Core curriculum on domestic violence; relationship between domestic violence and child abuse Training evaluation included
American College of Nurse Midwives	1995	Nurse midwifery students	50-page manual	Training manual for use by faculty of nurse midwifery education programs

| American College of Obstetricians and Gynecologists, Centers for Disease Control and Prevention, Work Group on the Prevention of Violence During Pregnancy | Intimate Partner Violence During Pregnancy: A Guide for Clinicians; 2000 | Reproductive health care providers: physicians—attending, fellows, residents, medical students, advanced-practice nurses, emergency department personnel, mental health providers, dentists | 30- to 60-minute slide lecture presentation with facilitator notes and talking points | 44 slides on CD with accompanying 73-page manual/facilitator guide; references; selected bibliography; resource listings |
| American College of Obstetricians and Gynecologists | Domestic Violence—The Role of the Physician in Identification, Intervention and Prevention; 1995 | Reproductive health care providers: physicians—attending, fellows, residents, medical students, advanced-practice nurses, other health care practitioners, general public | 30- to 60-minute slide lecture presentation with facilitator notes and talking points | 68 slides with accompanying 89-page manual/facilitator guide with lecture script; references; selected bibliography; resource listings

Targeted to obstetrics-gynecology residency training programs |

continued on next page

Intimate Partner Violence

Sponsoring Institution/ Developer	Title/Release Date	Audience	Training Approach	Description
American College of Physicians—American Society of Internal Medicine, Florida Chapter	Domestic Violence: How Do You Know and What Do You Do? A Guide For Physicians; 2000	Physicians	On-line self-instructional manual with accompanying self-test; continuing medical education (1-hour) for physicians	Instructional components: objectives; definition of domestic violence; signs of victimization; interviewing the victim; documentation; intervention; resources; RADAR; references; continuing medical education test
American Medical Women's Association	Domestic Violence; 1999	Health care providers (MDs and non-MDs)	On-line self-instruction	Text with interspersed audio and video clips of survivor interviews. On-line test for continuing medical education Modules: introduction; nature and dynamics; screening; assessment; documentation; presentations and assessment in clinic safety planning; referrals; legal aspects; children of domestic violence; the perpetrator; course evaluation
Arkansas: University of Arkansas for Medical Sciences	Student Syllabus: Domestic Violence	Medical students	Didactic presentation with accompanying independent study and small-group patient interview	Training components: lecture; small-group discussion with patient interview; journal entry
Association of Professors of Gynecology and Obstetrics (APGO) Medical Education Foundation	Women's Health: A Teaching Guide to Psychosocial Issues; 2000	Obstetricians and gynecologists	Chapter 17 in a textbook on teaching about psychosocial issues in women's health	Chapter 17: Violence Against Women: basic descriptive text; three case vignettes with discussion questions; appendix: sample safety plan; bibliography; web resources

Belson/Hanwright Video	Domestic Violence: Identification, Treatment, and Referral for the Health Professional; 1995	Health care providers	20-minute video	Three vignettes with discussion by a hospital-based domestic violence consult team
California: Health Education Alliance, San Jose	Why Does Daddy Hit Mommy?—A Course in Assessment and Intervention	Health professionals	Video presentation with accompanying written materials 12 continuing education hours for nurses	Training components: videos (2); course books; workbooks
California Medical Training Center	Improving the Healthcare Response to Violence; 1998	Health care providers, especially physicians, nurses, physician assistants, emergency department personnel, forensic examiners	Structured didactic presentations; panel presentations; role-play exercises; small-group discussions; skill labs (courses 2 and 3); photo review (course 2). (variable duration from 1 hour to 3 days, depending on course)	Four separate course offerings with course director and participant guides for each course: (1) Advanced training in domestic violence (1 day). Seven modules: prevalence; dynamics; screening; assessment; legal responsibilities; forensic exam; providing care; (2) pediatric sexual abuse evidentiary exam training; (3) sexual assault evidentiary exam (3 days); (4) elder and dependent adult abuse training (1-2 hours) Each course has complete facilitator notes; handouts; video illustrations; slides (35 mm or presentation on CD); full-text references; resource lists; bibliography
College of St. Catherine and University of St. Thomas	The Anatomy of Violence	Bachelor's in social work students	Medium: Class lecture Method: Attend a community antiviolence event; journal; written paper; written exams; meet once weekly for 4 months	Identifies issues related to cultural, racial, and interpersonal violence; explores the extent of violence and theoretical approaches to understanding violence; examines cultural/institutional sanctions for violence

continued on next page

Intimate Partner Violence

Sponsoring Institution/ Developer	Title/Release Date	Audience	Training Approach	Description
Colorado Department of Public Health and Environment, Injury Prevention and Control Program	Domestic Violence: Recognizing the Epidemic	Health care providers	30-minute training video	Designed for emergency health providers as an adjunct to other training about intimate partner violence; video consists of three clinical scenarios with discussion highlighting perspectives of physician, emergency department nurse, district attorney, police officer, perpetrator, treatment provider, shelter counselor, and victim-survivor
Connecticut Primary Care Association, University of Connecticut Health Center Domestic Violence Training Project	Domestic Violence Training Project: A Program for Health Professionals	Community health center staff	Lecture and small-group discussion	Clinic-wide curriculum; continuing medical education curriculum; train-the-trainer curriculum
Family Violence Prevention Fund	Improving the Health Care Response to Domestic Violence (2nd edition); 1998	Health care providers	Structured didactic presentations; role-play exercises; small-group protocol development exercises (2-day program)	1. Resource manual ("White Manual") 2. Trainer's manual ("Blue Manual") Discrete modules with background material, participant and facilitator notes; and handouts, understanding domestic violence; identification; assessment and intervention; health care responses to perpetrators; establishing an appropriate response; appendixes (forms, sample policies and protocols, etc.) Module on cultural competency included

Florida Department of Children and Families; Institute for Family Violence Studies, Florida State University, School of Social Family Practice Residency Program, Tallahassee Memorial Regional Medical Center	Domestic Violence: A Competency-Based Training Guide for Family Practice Residents; 1999	Family practice residents	106-page (plus appendixes) manual for self-instruction or classroom use	Ten-chapter manual for self-instruction or class/seminar use: overview of project; role of family practice residents in addressing domestic violence; encountering domestic violence in emergency room rotations; encountering domestic violence in obstetrics-gynecology rotations; encountering domestic violence in pediatric rotations; encountering domestic violence in orthopedic rotations; encountering domestic violence in medical rotations; working with special populations of domestic violence patients; legal issues present in domestic violence practice; utilizing community resources; references and bibliography; appendixes
Florida International University	Family Violence	Bachelor's in social work students	Medium: Elective course	
Group Health Cooperative of Puget Sound, Harborview Injury Prevention and Research Center, University of Washington	Managing Domestic Violence in Primary Care Settings; 1998	Adult health care providers	Two-hour training session with didactic components including overheads and video, accompanied by supporting materials for patient education and office support	Session 1: basic information; identification; assessment; documentation and referral skills Session 2: Skill building via role plays and survivor presentation; panel discussion on legal issues and community resources Multidisciplinary training team; evaluation of program published
Health Resources and Services Administration (HRSA), Office of Minority Health	Domestic Violence: Lessons, Community Partners; 2000	HRSA-funded community-based primary health care providers	Two-part satellite broadcast, each available as a 2-hour video	Broadcast series goal is to improve the capacity of community health centers to better recognize and treat abused women. Broadcast I: "Lessons" designed as "Domestic Violence 101." Covers awareness, assessment, and intervention Broadcast 2: "Community Partners." Covers strategies for developing a coordinated community response

continued on next page

Intimate Partner Violence

Sponsoring Institution/Developer	Title/Release Date	Audience	Training Approach	Description
Illinois: University of Chicago Pritzker School of Medicine, Abused Women Coalition, Cook County Hospital, Hospital Crisis Intervention Project	Improving the Health Care Response to Domestic Violence; 2000	Primary care internal medicine residents	Lectures; structured small-group discussions; site visit to an emergency shelter Integrated into residency training program	Intensive, interactive, 8-week elective course, 90 minutes per week; topics include overview of domestic violence; site visit to Greenhouse shelter; identifying, assessing, and intervening with domestic violence victims; working with diverse populations; the batterer; intervening with sexual assault patients; gun/community violence; child abuse; elder abuse and legal issues
Indiana University School of Medicine, National Centers of Excellence in Women's Health	Domestic Violence Curriculum—Medical Student Edition	Medical students	CD-ROM	CD-ROM with a combination of orally delivered didactic material, text material, and resources, plus four video demonstrations of clinical vignettes; includes a a knowledge-based posttest for student evaluation
Kentucky Board of Nursing	Domestic Violence, Recognition, Intervention, and Prevention—A Model Curriculum for Nursing Continuing Education; 1997	All nurses in Kentucky with active licensure	Lecture series (3 hours); 3-hour required continuing education	Four modules: dynamics of family violence (0.5 hours); victims of domestic/family violence (1 hour); prevention and intervention strategies: nursing protocols (1 hour); legal and social mandates (0.5 hours)
Kentucky Governor's Office of Child Abuse and Domestic Violence Services	Mental Health Intervention in Cases of Domestic Violence: Training Guide and Clinical Manual; 1996, revised 2001	Mental health clinicians	Lecture series (3 hours); 3-hour required continuing education	3-hour training program with 130-page companion manual for participants Five modules: scope and dynamics of domestic violence; domestic violence as an issue for mental health providers; correlation of domestic violence and chemical abuse; duties of mental health professionals in cases of domestic violence; application of criminal and civil law in cases of domestic violence

Kentucky Medical Association, Subcommittee on Domestic Violence, Committee on Community and Rural Health	Model Health Care Protocol on Abuse, Neglect, and Exploitation: Child, Spouse/Partner, Adult, and Elder; 1997	Physicians in primary care practice	Lecture series (3 hours)	Training modules: dynamics of domestic violence (45 minutes); effects of domestic violence and lethality and risk issues facing victims of domestic violence (75 minutes); societal issues and violence—laws and community resources for violence victims (45 minutes)
Louisiana State University	Family Violence	Master's in social work students	Medium: course Method: discussion; role play; small-group readings; written assignments; duration 4 months (one semester)	Examination of manifestations and dimensions of family violence; discussion of the dynamics of family violence as a social problem; applying social work skills to interventions
March of Dimes	Abuse During Pregnancy; 2001	Perinatal nurses, nurse midwives	Self-study or group study manual; self-administered exam for continuing education	60-page manual contains basic information, clinical protocols, vignettes of survivors, resource information, and pre- and postinstruction instruments and course evaluation
Maryland Alliance Against Family Violence, Medical and Surgical Faculty of Maryland (Maryland State Medical Society)	Maryland Physicians' Campaign Against Family Violence	Physicians	Didactic presentation and self-study manual with accompanying patient education and community outreach materials	Curriculum components: physicians' manual; curriculum guide; slides; posters; bus placards; clergy information packet; hospital information packet; patient information brochures

continued on next page

Intimate Partner Violence

Sponsoring Institution/ Developer	Title/Release Date	Audience	Training Approach	Description
Massachusetts: Boston Medical Center, Child Witness to Violence Project	Shelter from the Storm; 2000	Mental health clinicians	236-page trainer's manual; 12-hour curriculum of lectures; small-group discussion; case discussion	Training materials include training manual, 115 slides on disk, handout containing slide text, additional handouts
				Manual contains lecture/facilitator notes, case material, reproducible handouts; bibliography; list of resources, CD-ROM
			Designed to train mental health clinicians to provide services to children and families affected by intimate partner violence	Modules: domestic violence: principles of empowerment-based practice; impact of domestic violence on children; assessment of children affected by domestic violence; individual and group treatment of children affected by domestic violence; domestic violence; children; the courts; caring for the caregiver
Massachusetts: Children's Hospital of Boston, Family Violence Task Force AWAKE program (Advocacy for Women and Kids in Emergencies)	Health Care Services for Battered Women and Their Abused Children; 1997	Health care providers	2-hour lecture with accompanying 60-page training manual	Training focus: intimate partner violence; child abuse and neglect
				Training topics: definitions; prevalence; dynamics; myths; barriers; signs and symptoms; screening techniques; staff as victims or perpetrators; disclosure; children who witness violence; additional topics on request (personal safety, clinic security, confidentiality, human resources, role plays)

Massachusetts Medical Society	Seminar Series on Domestic Violence	Physicians, medical students, house officers, practicing physicians, other health care providers	Structured seminars, instructional video, interactive CD-ROM (6 hours total instructional time)	Four interactive structured seminars with comprehensive facilitator notes and handouts: background and dynamics of domestic violence; RADAR—a clinical model for screening, diagnosis, and intervention; skills development for clinical practice; a team approach to violence prevention and intervention 15-minute instructional video: "Diagnosis: Domestic Violence"; three-disc CD-ROM with three survivor interviews and four-visit primary care interactive "cases"; baseline and follow-up evaluation instruments; instructional "goal cards"; handouts; slides; guidelines for teaching section; designed for interested yet nonexpert faculty to teach effectively
Massachusetts: Office of the Attorney General	Diagnosis: Domestic Violence	Health care providers	24-minute video with accompanying monograph	Basic introduction to domestic violence featuring case histories; section on children as witnesses and characteristics of batterers
Massachusetts: University of Massachusetts Medical School	Interclerkship in Domestic Violence; 1995, updated yearly	Third-year medical students	Full-day multidisciplinary training	Lectures; workshops; small-group discussions; role plays; keynote address by a survivor Originally 3 days; now 1 day Required of all third-year medical students
MEDCEU	Domestic Violence Update; 2000 and 2001	Nurses, other medical professionals	On-line self-instructional monograph with posttest for nursing continuing education units	Instructional components: history, definitions and facts, health effects, dating violence, male batterers, references

continued on next page

Intimate Partner Violence

Sponsoring Institution/ Developer	Title/Release Date	Audience	Training Approach	Description
Medulogic	The Many Faces of Family Violence; 1999	Physicians, nurses dentists, social workers	Self-instructional CD-ROM, including printable text and video clips Physician, nursing and dental continuing education units (20 hours) Compatible with IBM-PC, not Macintosh computers	Instructional components: introduction and instructions; overview; survivor's story; dynamics; myths; domestic violence and health care system; recognizing and interviewing victims; documentation; advocacy; therapy and community action; same-sex intimate partner violence; understanding the batterer; elder abuse; child abuse; legal and reporting issues; resource kit for health care providers; resources; references
Minnesota: Allina Health System	Creating a Safe Place: Family Violence Screening in Health Care	Health care providers (primary care, social service, allied health, prehospital)	Modular teaching, including lecture, group discussion, video, clinical scenarios	Training components: Domestic Violence 101: definitions; statistics; dynamics; barriers to leaving; provider barriers; screening; assessment; documentation; community resources; self-care; 18-minute video and accompanying discussion guide; "Creating a Safe Place"; teaching scenarios
Minnesota: HealthPartners Family Violence Prevention Program	Screening and Intervening for Domestic Violence	Ambulatory health care providers and clinic staff	Brown-bag lunch discussions; 26-minute training video	Video: "Domestic Violence—How to Ask and What to Say" highlights three health care providers inquiring about abuse

Minnesota: University of Minnesota School of Dentistry, Program Against Sexual Violence	Family Violence: Intervention Model for Dental Professionals	Dental professionals	6-hour multicomponent training program, including didactic presentations, small-group discussion, role plays, case reviews, and two training videos Concurrent tracks for dentists and allied dental personnel	Training components: introduction; definition; myths; patterns; warning signs of abuse; clinical signs of abuse; role clarification; ethical and legal responsibilities; "healing voices: intervention model for dental professionals"; intervention techniques; development of office safety plans; team intervention techniques; community resources; Q&A Accompanying materials: training monograph; resource directory; selected articles; poster
Network for Continuing Medical Education	Domestic Violence: Intervention Strategies for the Physician; 2000	Physicians	60-minute video	Used as an independent or adjunctive training tool; can be used as a grand rounds presentation
Nova Southeastern University Physician Assistant Program; Ft. Lauderdale, FL	Issues in Medicine: Domestic Violence; 1999	First-year physician assistant students	3-hour course with reading assignments, lecture, case discussion, video scenarios and interviews	Course is part of a series of preclinical seminars offered during the "transition month" for physician assistant students entering clinical training
Ohio State Medical Association	Ohio Physicians' Domestic Violence Project: TRUST TALK; 1995	Physicians, nurses, other health care providers	58-page manual, 2-hour program; continuing medical education credit available	Designed for self-study or as a text for training classes; components: how to approach women who are battered; clinical guidelines for recognizing abuse, legal issues and reporting requirements, Ohio resources
Oregon Health Sciences University	Voices of Survivors: Domestic Violence Survivors Educate Physicians; 1999	Physicians	30-minute video consisting of a black-and-white photo montage with voiceover	Documentary video made from the perspectives of survivors of intimate partner violence; accompanying handbooks for learners and facilitators

continued on next page

Intimate Partner Violence

Sponsoring Institution/Developer	Title/Release Date	Audience	Training Approach	Description
Philadelphia Family Violence Working Group, Physicians for Social Responsibility	The RADAR Domestic Violence Training Project	Health center-based health care providers	3 to 6 hour didactic and video presentation delivered by a multidisciplinary team	Focus on trauma theory; instruction in RADAR approach to care; survivor presentation
Physicians for a Violence-Free Society (PVS)	PVS Documentation Course: Standardized Medical Documentation for Domestic Violence Injuries; 1999	Physicians	Four 40-minute structured didactic presentations on a standardized approach to medical documentation of injuries resulting from domestic violence; interactive session on how to use a camera designed for medical documentation	Curriculum contains slides and complete facilitator notes for each lecture, participant's syllabus (to be copied for each participant), chief instructor's guide, course coordinator's guide Participant syllabus contains narratives of each lecture, articles, course evaluation form, local resources Lecture summary: introduction and need for a medical response, medical response to domestic violence, living forensics: recognizing patterns of injury, medical-legal aspects of domestic violence Interactive session: learning to take pictures
Professional Resource Press	Domestic Violence and Spousal Abuse Program; 1994	Psychologists, psychiatrists, social workers, psychiatric nurses, other mental health providers	Home study continuing education course and self-exam based on book on spouse abuse; 3 hours of continuing education	Book sections: what kind of families are violent? how much do you know about partner abuse? assessment of spouse abuse; treatment of spouse abuse; final word on spouse abuse; references

Select Media	In Need of Special Attention	Emergency medical professionals	18-minute video	Emergency room training film demonstrates how emergency room personnel can identify and treat victims of spouse abuse
Society for Academic Emergency Medicine	Domestic Violence Presentation	Physicians	54-slide didactic presentation	Slide presentation for residency faculty to use as a teaching tool, for self-instruction, or for grand rounds presentations
Texas: Violence Intervention Prevention (VIP) Center Parkland Hospital, Dallas	Manual Strangulation in Victims of Domestic Violence	Physicians	PowerPoint presentation	Presentation components: rapid response intervention; in-depth assessment; case management, disposition, and placement; homicidal strangulation; literature on survivors of strangulation; information on walking and talking to the strangled patient
University of Iowa	Family Violence	Master's in social work students	Medium: course Methods: readings; lecture; written assignments; duration, 4 months (one semester)	Discussion of historical aspects of family violence; examination of family violence as a social issue; discussion of the role of "family" in society
University of Iowa	Selected Aspects of Social Work: Violence and Trauma	Social work students	Medium: lecture Method: readings; interview with trauma survivor or professional in field; written assignments; guest speakers; duration is 4 months (one semester)	Analyze violent content on television; overview of violence in community; effects of traumatic experiences

continued on next page

Intimate Partner Violence

Sponsoring Institution/Developer	Title/Release Date	Audience	Training Approach	Description
University of Kentucky	Family Violence: Social Work Interventions	Master's in social work students	Medium: course Method: readings; lecture; exams; duration, 4 weeks: meets twice a week for 3 hours	Evaluation of theories for understanding the etiology of child, spouse, elder, and sibling abuse; identify interventions to be used; identify implications of violence for social policy
University of Michigan	Family Violence Prevention and Intervention	Master's in social work students	Method: no information Medium: duration is 4 months (one semester); elective	Focus on methods of prevention; intervention and social change; provides overview of risk factors; emphasis is on needs of oppressed populations
University of Michigan	Special Issues in Interpersonal Violence	Master's in social work students	Method: no information Medium: duration is 4 months (one semester); required course	Integrates content on diversity, prevention, and social justice; use of social science theories and research is applied
University of Michigan	Integrative Seminar: Family Violence	Master's in social work students	Medium: models of interagency coordination; duration, 4 months (one semester)	Overview of risk factors; effects of trauma due to family violence are discussed; description of current models of prevention and intervention
University of Michigan	Practice Seminar in Child Maltreatment: Assessment and Treatment	Master's in social work students	Lectures; discussion; demonstrations; video role play; small-group exercises; duration, 4 months (one semester)	Explores personal, professional, and societal responses to children at risk; discusses client issues and responses to child welfare interventions; discusses theories that explain child maltreatment

Institution	Course	Students	Format/Method	Description
University of Michigan	Integrative Seminar in Child Maltreatment	Master's in social work students	Lecture; discussion; small-group exercises; student presentation; guest speaker	Examination of child welfare from perspective of community practice; direct practice and policy; integration of research findings related to child welfare; examines the relationship between child maltreatment and environmental factors
University of Minnesota Medical School	Domestic Abuse: The Role of the Physician; 1996	Medical students	Format includes lecture and video; class is 1 hour in length and is taught once every 2 months	Relationship of early intervention and prevention; prevalence of domestic abuse and violence; definitions; misconceptions and dynamics of domestic abuse; role and responsibilities of the health care provider; Joint Committee on Accreditation of Healthcare Organizatons hospital and ambulatory care standards; prevention in practice—a structure for change client services—advocacy and case management; where do we go from here?
University of Pittsburgh	Family Violence	Bachelor's in social work students	Medium: course Method: discussion; readings; written papers; written exam; presentation; duration is 4 months (one semester)	Exploration of aspects of family violence; treatment strategies presented; contains theoretical approach but with focus on practical social work experience
University of Pittsburgh	Child Sexual Abuse	Bachelor's in social work students	Lecture; readings; written papers; duration is 4 months (one semester)	Overview of child sexual abuse; assessment of child abuse situations; examination of personal value/belief system; evaluation of effectiveness of treatment approaches

continued on next page

Intimate Partner Violence

Sponsoring Institution/Developer	Title/Release Date	Audience	Training Approach	Description
University of Pittsburgh	Child Maltreatment: Physical Abuse and Neglect	Bachelor's in social work students	Discussion; role plays; readings; written assignments; duration is 4 months (one semester)	Development of relevant treatment strategies for family members; identification of gender and racial issues in abuse/neglect situations; overview of how abuse and neglect are identified and integrated
University of Texas at Austin	Contemporary Issues in Domestic Violence	Bachelor's and master's in social work students	Method: no information Duration is 4 months (one semester); elective	Dynamics of domestic violence and practice with individuals and families are discussed
University of Texas at Austin	Child Welfare	Bachelor's and master's in social work students	Duration is 4 months (one semester)	
U.S. Healthcare, Medical Education Collaborative	Current Concepts in Women's Health; Domestic Violence and Primary Care	Physicians and other women's health care providers	75-page self-study manual; 5 hours continuing medical education by the American Academy of Family Physicians, Administration on Aging	Components: overview and introduction; identification, diagnosis, and clinical findings; intervention and treatment; special considerations; appendix, including assessment documents; patient resources; bibliography

Provider	Title	Audience	Medium/Method	Description
Vantage Professional Education	Domestic Violence: Update for Healthcare Professionals; 2000	Nurses, dieticians	Self-study on-line or download and print; 4 contact hours—Georgia Nurses Associations; 4 continuing professional education credits—Commission on Dietetic Registration	Self-study document containing course objectives; what is domestic violence?; dynamics of violent relationships; effects of domestic violence on children; health care response to domestic violence case studies; sample forms and worksheets; bibliography and additional sources; continuing education test; answer sheet
Virtual Lecture Hall, Medical Directions, Inc.	The Current Management of Domestic Violence; 1999	Physicians	On-line self-study (no time duration indicated)	Case-based, interactive, downloadable forms; links to references and web sites; continuing medical education available
Washburn University	Clinical Practice with Survivors of Trauma	Master's in social work students	Medium: lectures Method: audio-visual aids; class exercises; readings; duration, 4 months (one semester)	Exploration of trauma on children and adults; impact of institutional and professional responses to traumas; strengths perspective
Washburn University	Clinical Practice with Survivors of Trauma: Adults	Master's in social work students	Medium: lectures Method: audiovisual aids; class exercises; readings; duration, 4 months (one semester)	Exploration of trauma on adults; impact of institutional and professional responses to traumas; strengths perspective
Washburn University	Clinical Practice with Survivors of Trauma: Professional Development	Master's in social work students	Medium: lecture Medium: discussions; readings; written assignments; duration, 4 months (one semester)	Focus on practitioner skills; transference and countertransference are discussed

continued on next page

Intimate Partner Violence

Sponsoring Institution/ Developer	Title/Release Date	Audience	Training Approach	Description
Washburn University	Clinical Practice with Survivors of Trauma: Adults	Master's in social work students	Medium: lectures Method: audiovisual aids; class exercises; readings; duration, 4 months (one semester)	Exploration of trauma on children; impact of institutional and professional responses to traumas; strengths perspective
Washington, DC: George Washington University	Sensitive Topics in Interviewing: Domestic Violence	Medical students	Videotape review; discussion; role play	Training components: videotape—the dynamics of domestic violence and the ethics of physician involvement; lecture/discussion; role plays followed by plenary discussion; selected articles as reference
Washington: Sacred Heart Medical Center, Spokane	A Time of Opportunity: Helping Battered Women in the Health Care Setting	Health professionals	22-minute video	Overview that includes basic information and interviews with survivors of physical, emotional, and sexual abuse and a number of professionals who work with battered women
Wisconsin: The Family Peace Project	Family Violence: A Self-Study Guide for Health Care Professionals in Primary Care; 1994	Health care providers	Self-study manual	Manual contains syllabus, required readings, background information, referral information, resource information

Training also includes survivor presentations; role plays; community resource assessment |

Appendix F

Summary of Evaluation Studies on Training of Health Care Professionals on Intimate Partner Violence

Knowledge, Attitudes, and Beliefs Outcome

Target Population (study citation)	Nature of Training Provided			Expected Outcomes and Measure	
	Intervention Group	Comparison Group (if applicable)	Study Design	Major Outcomes	Measure
Medical students (Ernst et al., 1998, 2000)	Type: Didactic Length: 3 hrs. Clinical aids: None		One group	Knowledge re IPV	Self-report (14 items)
Medical students (Haase et al., 1999)	Type: Mixed Length: 9 hrs. over 6 weeks Clinical aids: None	None	Two groups (one comparison group)	Perceived comfort, preparedness, questioning habits, and knowledge of resources re IPV	Self-report (five items, $\alpha = 0.70$)

	Timing		Sample Size and Attrition from Measurement		Results I = Intervention Group C = Comparison Group Pre = Baseline or Pretest Post = Posttest FU = Follow-up		
Base-line	Post-test (months)	Follow-ups (months)	Intervention	Comparison	Within-Group Change	Relative Group Difference	Comment
Yes	1	24	Eligible = 148 Pre = 144 Post = 141 (98%) FU = 104 (72%)		$I_{post} > I_{pre}$* (6 items) $I_{FU} > I_{pre}$* (5 items) $I_{FU} < I_{post}$* (2 items) and $I_{FU} = I_{post}$ (8 items)		Within-group comparisons were not based on matched groups (e.g., those with complete data on all measurement waves) due to the Institutional Review Board's requirement that participants be anonymous. Thus, the comparisons should be interpreted with caution.
No	24		Eligible = Not reported Post = 29	Eligible = Not reported Post = 86		$I_{post} > C_{post}$*	Although the training was a formal elective course, groups were created by self-report on the posttest rather than known course enrollment. The analysis controlled for gender. Analyses of individual items indicated that group differences were in knowledge and reported questioning habits rather than comfort and preparedness.

continued on next page

Knowledge, Attitudes, and Beliefs Outcome

| Target Population (study citation) | Nature of Training Provided | | | Expected Outcomes and Measure | |
	Intervention Group	Comparison Group (if applicable)	Study Design	Major Outcomes	Measure
Medical students (Jonassen et al., 1999)	Type: Mixed Length: 2-3.5 days		One group	Knowledge re IPV	Self-report (10 items)
	Clinical aids: Materials on local resources; screening algorithm			Attitudes re IPV	Self-report (26 items)
				Clinical skills and experience	Self-report (10 items)
Medical students (Short et al., 2000)	Type: Mixed Length: 4-week module Clinical aids: None	One lecture	Two groups (one comparison group)	Knowledge, attitudes, and behavioral intentions about IPV	Self-report (37 items, $\alpha = 0.80$, test-retest $= 0.87$)
				Appropriateness of intervening	Self-report (3-item subscale, $\alpha = 0.51$, test-retest $= 0.64$)
				Physician responsibility for IPV	Self-report (8-item subscale, $\alpha = 0.69$, test-retest $= 0.82$)
				Victim autonomy for decisions	Self-report (3-item subscale, $\alpha = 0.54$, test-retest $= 0.69$)

	Timing		Sample Size and Attrition from Measurement		Results I = Intervention Group C = Comparison Group Pre = Baseline or Pretest Post = Posttest FU = Follow-up		
Base-line	Post-test (months)	Follow-ups (months)	Intervention	Comparison	Within-Group Change	Relative Group Difference	Comment
Yes	Immedi-ately after training	6	Eligible = 205 Pre, Post, and FU = 144 (70%)		$I_{post} > I_{pre}$* $I_{FU} > I_{pre}$*		Test reliability was reported as adequate.
					$I_{post} > I_{pre}$* $I_{FU} > I_{pre}$* $I_{post} > I_{pre}$* $I_{FU} > I_{pre}$*		Results pertain to comparisons for two separate cohorts.
Yes	1		Eligible = 149 Pre = 124 Post = 87 (70%)	Eligible = 97 Pre = 88 Post = 66 (75%)	$I_{post} > I_{pre}$*	$I_{post} > C_{post}$*	
					$I_{post} < I_{pre}$	$I_{post} < C_{post}$	
					$I_{post} > I_{pre}$	$I_{post} > C_{post}$	
					$I_{post} > I_{pre}$	$I_{post} > C_{post}$	

continued on next page

Knowledge, Attitudes, and Beliefs Outcome

Target Population (study citation)	Nature of Training Provided		Study Design	Expected Outcomes and Measure	
	Intervention Group	Comparison Group (if applicable)		Major Outcomes	Measure
				Self-efficacy for detecting IPV	Self-report (6-item subscale, $\alpha = 0.72$, test-retest $= 0.72$)
				Behavioral intentions to screen	Self-report (6-item subscale, $\alpha = 0.66$, test-retest $= 0.83$)
Residents in all specialties (Coonrod et al., 2000)	Type: Mixed Length: 20 min. Clinical aids: Articles and pocket information cards	Didactic educational session on unrelated topic Length: 20 min. Clinical aids: Articles and pocket information cards on topic	Two groups (randomized)	Knowledge of IPV	Self-report (5-item subscale)

Timing			Sample Size and Attrition from Measurement		Results I = Intervention Group C = Comparison Group Pre = Baseline or Pretest Post = Posttest FU = Follow-up		
Base-line	Post-test (months)	Follow-ups (months)	Intervention	Comparison	Within-Group Change	Relative Group Difference	Comment
					$I_{post} > I_{pre}$*	$I_{post} > C_{post}$*	
					$I_{post} > I_{pre}$*	$I_{post} > C_{post}$*	
Yes	9-10		Eligible = 24 Pre = 24 Post = 12 (50%)	Eligible = 22 Pre = 22 Post = 11 (50%)		$I_{post} > C_{post}$*	Analysis controlled for pretest score.

continued on next page

Knowledge, Attitudes, and Beliefs Outcome

| Target Population (study citation) | Nature of Training Provided | | Study Design | Expected Outcomes and Measure | |
	Intervention Group	Comparison Group (if applicable)		Major Outcomes	Measure
Residents in internal medicine (Knight et al., 2000)	Type: Didactic Length: 105 min. Clinical aids: Local resource list; laminated card of screening questions and resource contacts		One group	Beliefs re IPV (including self-efficacy of victims)	Self-report (31 items)
Residents in internal medicine (Kripke et al., 1998)	Type: Mixed Length: 4 hrs. Clinical aids: None		One group	Knowledge re IPV	Self-report (10 items)
				Attitudes re IPV	Self-report (25 items)
				Perceptions re skills	Self-report (10 items)

Timing			Sample Size and Attrition from Measurement		Results I = Intervention Group C = Comparison Group Pre = Baseline or Pretest Post = Posttest FU = Follow-up		
Base-line	Post-test (months)	Follow-ups (months)	Intervention	Comparison	Within-Group Change	Relative Group Difference	Comment
Yes	Immedi-ately after training		Eligible = 45 Pre = 45 Post = 45 (100%)		$I_{post} = I_{pre}$		Measures used were those developed by Varvaro et al. (1997), who reported internal consistencies ranging from 0.62 to 0.90, depending on the subscale of interest. Results were affected by residents = complaints about the lengthiness of the survey and their careless responding.
Yes	Immedi-ately after training	6	Eligible = 55 Pre = 55 Post = 55 (100%) FU = 55 (100%)		$I_{post} > I_{pre}*$ $I_{FU} > I_{pre}*$ $I_{post} > I_{pre}*$ $I_{FU} > I_{pre}*$ $I_{post} > I_{pre}*$ $I_{FU} = I_{pre}$		The differences would have been statisti-cally signifi-cant if a one-tailed test had been used.

continued on next page

Knowledge, Attitudes, and Beliefs Outcome

Target Population (study citation)	Intervention Group	Comparison Group (if applicable)	Study Design	Major Outcomes	Measure
	Nature of Training Provided			**Expected Outcomes and Measure**	
ED staff and emergency medical technicians (Allert et al., 1997)	Type: Didactic Length: 90 min. Clinical aids: Copy of care guidelines; list of local resources		One group	Knowledge of written protocol, reporting requirements, and documentation	Self-report (4 items)
ED nurses (Bokunewicz & Copel, 1992)	Type: Didactic Length: 60 min. Clinical aids: None		One group	Beliefs re IPV	Self-report (questions on a scenario, $\alpha = 0.79$)
ED staff, including physicians, nurses, and social workers (Campbell et al., in press)	Type: Mixed Length: 2 days Clinical aids: Technical assistance if requested	Usual or available training	Two groups (group randomized)	Knowledge and attitudes about IPV	Self-report (23 items, $\alpha = 0.73$)

Timing			Sample Size and Attrition from Measurement		Results I = Intervention Group C = Comparison Group Pre = Baseline or Pretest Post = Posttest FU = Follow-up		
Base-line	Post-test (months)	Follow-ups (months)	Intervention	Comparison	Within-Group Change	Relative Group Difference	Comment
Yes	Immedi-ately after training	3	Eligible = 329 Pre = 266 Post = 266 (100%) FU = 213 (80%)		$I_{post} > I_{pre}$* (6 items) $I_{FU} > I_{pre}$* (6 items)		Total number of items in the instrument was not specified. The follow-up was done by telephone to a random sample, but the response rate was not reported. It is unclear whether the statistical tests took into account repeated measures.
Yes	Immedi-ately after training		Eligible = 42 Pre = 18 Post = 18 (100%)		$I_{post} > I_{pre}$*		
Yes	18-24		<u>3 EDs</u> Eligible = Not reported Pre = Not reported Post = 330	<u>3 EDs</u> Eligible = Not reported Pre = Not reported Post = 319	$I_{post} > I_{pre}$*	$I_{post} > C_{post}$*	An overall response rate for the posttest was 75%, but no information was provided regarding differential response rates for the two groups. The analyses controlled for gender, state, and pretest standing.

continued on next page

Knowledge, Attitudes, and Beliefs Outcome

Target Population (study citation)	Nature of Training Provided		Study Design	Expected Outcomes and Measure	
	Intervention Group	Comparison Group (if applicable)		Major Outcomes	Measure
Trauma center staff, including residents in surgery and emergency medicine, medical students, and surgeons (Davis et al., 2000)	Type: Didactic Length: Unclear Clinical aids: None		One group	Knowledge re IPV	Self-report (18 items)
ED staff, including physicians, interns, and nurses (Roberts et al., 1997b)	Type: Didactic Length: 1 hr. Clinical aids: Poster (protocol); pocket cards		One group	Knowledge of IPV	Self-report (43 items)

Timing			Sample Size and Attrition from Measurement		Results I = Intervention Group C = Comparison Group Pre = Baseline or Pretest Post = Posttest FU = Follow-up		
Base-line	Post-test (months)	Follow-ups (months)	Intervention	Comparison	Within-Group Change	Relative Group Difference	Comment
Yes	Immedi-ately after training		Eligible = Pre = 92 Post = 92 (100%)	Not reported	$I_{post} > I_{pre}$*		
Yes	Immedi-ately after training		Physicians Eligible = 72 Pre = 31 Post = 20 (65%) Nurses Eligible = 91 Pre = 69 Post = 48 (70%)		$I_{post} > I_{pre}$*		There were significant changes for the combined group of physicians and nurses, but nurses increased more than physicians. Overall, physicians incrased significantly but only in terms of knowl-edge of legal aspects of IPV.

continued on next page

Knowledge, Attitudes, and Beliefs Outcome

| Target Population (study citation) | Nature of Training Provided | | | Expected Outcomes and Measure | |
	Intervention Group	Comparison Group (if applicable)	Study Design	Major Outcomes	Measure
ED staff *(continued)*				Attitudes toward IPV	Self-report (10 items)
ED, critical care, and perinatal hospital staff (Short et al., in press)	Type: Length: Clinical aids: Protocol	Usual and available	Two groups (one comparison group)	Knowledge, attitudes, and behavioral intentions about IPV	Self-report (51 items)
				Understanding of abusive relationships	Self-report
				Beliefs about staff preparation and ability for addressing IPV	

	Timing		Sample Size and Attrition from Measurement		Results I = Intervention Group C = Comparison Group Pre = Baseline or Pretest Post = Posttest FU = Follow-up		
Base-line	Post-test (months)	Follow-ups (months)	Intervention	Comparison	Within-Group Change	Relative Group Difference	Comment
					$I_{post} > I_{pre}$		After training, 35% of physicians believed that there was little a doctor or nurse could do to stop IPV, 50% believed that victims did not want to discuss IPV with a health professional, and 45% did not know that emotional abuse is generally viewed as worse than physical abuse by victims.
Yes	12	12	Eligible = 417 Pre = 200 Post =	Eligible = 265 Pre = 127 Post =	$I_{FU2} > I_{pre}$	$I_{FU2} > C_{FU2}*$	Although exact results were not provided, the authors reported that psychometric
					$I_{FU2} > I_{pre}$	$I_{FU2} < C_{FU2}$	analyses found the scales were internally consistent.
					$I_{FU2} > I_{pre}$	$I_{FU2} > C_{FU2}*$	A total of 211 individuals had complete data for the outcome

continued on next page

Knowledge, Attitudes, and Beliefs Outcome

Target Population (study citation)	Nature of Training Provided			Expected Outcomes and Measure	
	Intervention Group	Comparison Group (if applicable)	Study Design	Major Outcomes	Measure
ED, critical care, and perinatal hospital staff *(continued)*				Victim autonomy for decisions	Self-report
				Staff responsibility to address domestic violence	Self-report
				Self-efficacy for detecting IPV and interacting with victims	Self-report
				Self-efficacy for referral and services	Self-report
				Own behaviors re screening and documentation	Self-report

Timing			Sample Size and Attrition from Measurement		Results I = Intervention Group C = Comparison Group Pre = Baseline or Pretest Post = Posttest FU = Follow-up		
Base-line	Post-test (months)	Follow-ups (months)	Intervention	Comparison	Within-Group Change	Relative Group Difference	Comment
					$I_{FU2} > I_{pre}$	$I_{FU2} > C_{FU2}*$	analyses, yielding an overall
					$I_{FU2} > I_{pre}$	$I_{FU2} > C_{FU2}$	response rate for the posttest of 65%. The extent to which
					$I_{FU2} > I_{pre}*$	$I_{FU2} > C_{FU2}$	differential attrition occurred between groups was not
					$I_{FU2} > I_{pre}*$	$I_{FU2} > C_{FU2}$	reported. Analyses controlled for
					$I_{FU2} > I_{pre}*$	$I_{FU2} > C_{FU2}*$	age, gender, position, department, exposure to training, and pretest score.

continued on next page

Knowledge, Attitudes, and Beliefs Outcome

| Target Population (study citation) | Nature of Training Provided | | Study Design | Expected Outcomes and Measure | |
	Intervention Group	Comparison Group (if applicable)		Major Outcomes	Measure
ED house staff (Varvaro et al., 1997)	Group 1 Type: Didactic Length: 1 hr. Clinical aids: None	Usual and available	Two groups (one comparison group)	Beliefs about IPV	Self-report (12 items, $\alpha = 0.89$)
	Group 2 Type: Didactic Length: 1 hr. Clinical aids: pocket IPV training manual			Attitudes re IPV (self-efficacy in IPV victims)	Self-report (31 items, as ranged from 0.62 to 0.90 for subscales)

Timing			Sample Size and Attrition from Measurement		Results I = Intervention Group C = Comparison Group Pre = Baseline or Pretest Post = Posttest FU = Follow-up		
Base-line	Post-test (months)	Follow-ups (months)	Intervention	Comparison	Within-Group Change	Relative Group Difference	Comment
Yes	0.5		<u>Group 1</u> Eligible = Not reported Pre = 13 Post = 13 (100%) <u>Group 2</u> Eligible = Not reported Pre = 13 Post = 13 (100%)	Eligible = Not reported Pre = 11 Post = 11 (100%) $I_{post} > I_{pres}$ (5 of 12 items)	$I_{post} = I_{pre}$	$I_{post} = C_{post}$	The lecture-only and the lecture plus manual groups differed on specific items regarding perceived self-efficacy at the posttest, but the differences did not consistently favor one group. No comparisons were made between these two groups and the control group. The ability to detect within-group changes and relative group differences was handicapped by the small sample sizes.

continued on next page

Knowledge, Attitudes, and Beliefs Outcome

	Nature of Training Provided			Expected Outcomes and Measure	
Target Population (study citation)	Intervention Group	Comparison Group (if applicable)	Study Design	Major Outcomes	Measure
Community health center staff, including physicians, mid-level practitioners, social workers, and psychologists (Harwell et al., 1998)	Type: Mixed Length: 3-6 hrs. Clinical aids: IPV screening pocket card; IPV assessment form; stamp to indicate screening and suspected or confirmed abuse; patient card of resources and safety tips; additional tailored follow-up training to some CHCs		One group	Knowledge of IPV Attitudes (comfort with IPV)	Self-report (13 items, $\alpha = 0.91$) Self-report (4 items, $\alpha = 0.82$)
Nurse-midwives (Paluzzi et al., 2000)	Type: Unclear Length: 8 hrs. Clinical aids: None		One group	Knowledge re IPV Attitudes re IPV Level of comfort in working with victims Perceived cultural competence	Self-report ($\alpha = 0.80$) Self-report ($\alpha = 0.61$) Self-report ($\alpha = 0.59$) Self-report ($\alpha = 0.96$)

					Results		
					I = Intervention Group		
			Sample Size and		C = Comparison Group		
			Attrition from		Pre = Baseline or Pretest		
Timing			Measurement		Post = Posttest FU = Follow-up		
Base-line	Post-test (months)	Follow-ups (months)	Intervention	Comparison	Within-Group Change	Relative Group Difference	Comment
Yes	Immedi-ately after training	3	Eligible = 108 Pre = 108 Post = 108 (100%) FU = 23 of 66 eligible (35%)		$I_{post} > I_{pre}$* $I_{FU} > I_{pre}$* $I_{FU} < I_{pre}$ $I_{post} > I_{pre}$* $I_{FU} > I_{pre}$ $I_{FU} < I_{post}$		Analyses were restricted to the direct care providers who received the training. Table 2 is not clear as to whether results at all waves were only for 23 in the follow-up.
Yes	6	12	Eligible = Not reported Pre = 165 Post = 80 (48%) FU = 23 (14%)		$I_{post} > I_{pre}$* $I_{FU} > I_{post}$ $I_{post} > I_{pre}$* $I_{FU} > I_{post}$ $I_{post} > I_{pre}$* $I_{FU} > I_{post}$ $I_{post} > I_{pre}$* $I_{FU} > I_{post}$		

continued on next page

Knowledge, Attitudes, and Beliefs Outcome

Target Population (study citation)	Nature of Training Provided			Expected Outcomes and Measure	
	Intervention Group	Comparison Group (if applicable)	Study Design	Major Outcomes	Measure
Primary care team members (Thompson et al., 2000)	Type: Mixed Length: two half-day sessions over 12 months Clinical aids: Posters; provider cue cards; routine exam forms; feedback	Usual and available training (e.g., manual)	Two groups (group randomized)	Self-efficacy re detecting IPV	Self-report (7-item subscale, $\alpha = 0.73$)
				System support	Self-report (4-item subscale, $\alpha = 0.73$)
				Blaming the victim	Self-report (7-item subscale, $\alpha = 0.80$)
				Fear of offending	Self-report (7-item subscale, $\alpha = 0.80$)
				Safety concerns	Self-report (8-item subscale, $\alpha = 0.91$)

Timing			Sample Size and Attrition from Measurement		Results I = Intervention Group C = Comparison Group Pre = Baseline or Pretest Post = Posttest FU = Follow-up		
Base-line	Post-test (months)	Follow-ups (months)	Intervention	Comparison	Within-Group Change	Relative Group Difference	Comment
Yes	9	21	Two clinics Eligible = Not reported Pre = 91 Post = Not reported FU = Not reported	Three clinics Eligible = Not reported Pre = 88 Post = Not reported FU = Not reported	$I_{post} > I_{pre}$* $I_{FU} > I_{pre}$*	$I_{post} > C_{post}$* $I_{FU} > C_{FU}$*	*Total number of eligible participants in all clinics was 208 of which 179 (86%) responded to the pretest. At
					$I_{post} > I_{pre}$ $I_{FU} = I_{pre}$	$I_{post} > C_{post}$ $I_{FU} > C_{FU}$	the posttest and follow-up, there were 190 eligible
					$I_{post} > I_{pre}$ $I_{FU} = I_{pre}$	$I_{post} > C_{post}$ $I_{FU} > C_{FU}$	providers of which 79% responded, and the correspond-
					$I_{post} > I_{pre}$* $I_{FU} > I_{pre}$*	$I_{post} > C_{post}$ $I_{FU} > C_{FU}$*	ing figures for the follow-up were 171 and 82%. The
					$I_{post} > I_{pre}$* $I_{FU} > I_{pre}$*	$I_{post} > C_{post}$ $I_{FU} > C_{FU}$*	extent to which the two groups differed with regard to attrition was not reported. Outcome analyses were adjusted for pretest and clustering.

Outcomes Related to Clinical Intervention Practices

Target Population (study citation)	Nature of Training Provided		Study Design	Expected Outcomes and Measure	
	Intervention Group	Comparison Group (if applicable)		Major Outcomes	Measure
Residents in internal medicine and family practice (Saunders et al., 1993)	Type: Mixed Length: Two 50-min. sessions or one 2-hr. session Clinical aids: None Number of participants: 17	Usual and available	Two groups, randomized	% covering psychosocial issues in patient interview	Standardized patient visit
				Extent to which history was taken during patient interview	Standardized patient visit
				Extent of planning conducted during patient interview	Standardized patient visit
ED staff, including physicians, nurses, and social workers (Campbell et al., in press)	Type: Mixed Length: 2 days Clinical aids: Technical assistance if requested	Usual or available training	Two groups (group randomized)	% of identified IPV cases with more appropriate interventions	Chart review
				Patient satisfaction with care received	Self-report of patients
				Commitment by EDs to detecting and treating IPV victims	Researcher ratings
ED staff (Fanslow et al., 1998, 1999)	Type: Didactic Length: 1 or 4 hrs. Clinical aids: Protocols; forms; body map; checklist; contact cards Number of participants: 33 nurses and 11 medical staff		Cohort	% of IPV cases where interventions were used (e.g., referrals)	Chart review

Timing			Sample Size and Attrition from Measurement		Results I = Intervention Group C = Comparison Group Pre = Baseline or Pretest Post = Posttest FU = Follow-up		
Base-line	Post-test (months)	Follow-ups (months)	Intervention	Comparison	Within-Group Change	Relative Group Difference	Comment
No	6		Post = 15	Post = 20		$I_{post} = C_{post}$	
						Unclear	
						Unclear	
Yes	12	18	3 hospitals: Pre = 600 Post = 600 FU = 600	3 hospitals: Pre = 600 Post = 600 FU = 600		$I_{post} = C_{post}$	
						$I_{post} > C_{post}*$	
					$I_{post} > I_{pre}*$ $I_{FU}t > I_{pre}*$	$I_{post} > C_{post}*$ $I_{FU}t > C_{FU}t*$	
Yes	12		Pre = 21 Post = 34	Pre = 26 Post = 13	$I_{post} > I_{pre}*$	$I_{post} > C_{post}*$ $I_{FU} = C_{FU}$	There was a difference in the number of interventions at the baseline.

continued on next page

Outcomes Related to Clinical Intervention Practices

Target Population (study citation)	Nature of Training Provided			Expected Outcomes and Measure	
	Intervention Group	Comparison Group (if applicable)	Study Design	Major Outcomes	Measure
Community health center staff, including physicians, mid-level practitioners, social workers, and psychologists (Harwell et al., 1998)	Type: Mixed Length: 3-6 hrs. Clinical aids: IPV screening pocket card; IPV assessment form; stamp to indicate screening and suspected or confirmed abuse; patient card of resources and safety tips; additional tailored follow-up training to some CHCs Number of participants: 108		Cohort	% of all cases with a completed safety assessment	Chart review
				% of all cases where a body map was completed	Chart review
				% of all cases with referral to CHC staff	Chart review
				% of all cases with referrals to outside agencies	Chart review
Public health nurses (Shepard et al., 1999)	Type: Mixed Length: 4 hrs. Clinical aids: Protocol and follow-ups Number of participants: Unclear		Cohort	% of identified IPV cases who were provided information	Chart review
				% of identified IPV cases who were directly referred to services	Chart review

	Timing		Sample Size and Attrition from Measurement		Results I = Intervention Group C = Comparison Group Pre = Baseline or Pretest Post = Posttest FU = Follow-up		
Base-line	Post-test (months)	Follow-ups (months)	Intervention	Comparison	Within-Group Change	Relative Group Difference	Comment
Yes	6		Pre = 251 Post = 255		$I_{post} > I_{pre}$*		
					$I_{post} = I_{pre}$		
					$I_{post} > I_{pre}$		
					$I_{post} > I_{pre}$*		
Yes	12	24	Pre = 31 Post = 23 FU = 18		$I_{post} > I_{pre}$* $I_{FU} > I_{pre}$*		Analyses controlled for age of patients.
					$I_{post} > I_{pre}$ $I_{FU} > I_{pre}$		

continued on next page

Outcomes Related to Clinical Intervention Practices

| Target Population (study citation) | Nature of Training Provided | | | Expected Outcomes and Measure | |
	Intervention Group	Comparison Group (if applicable)	Study Design	Major Outcomes	Measure
ED, critical care, and perinatal hospital staff (Short et al., in press)	Type: Length: Clinical aids: Protocol	Usual and available	Two groups (one comparison group)	% of cases with documentation of relevant social history	Chart review
				% of cases with documentation	Chart review
				% of documented referrals for IPV cases	Chart review
Primary care team members (Thompson et al., 2000)	Type: Mixed Length: 2 half-day sessions over 12 months Clinical aids: Posters; provider cue cards; routine exam forms; feedback Number of participants: Unclear	Usual and available training (e.g., manual)	Two groups (group randomized)	% of identified IPV cases whose quality of care was judged good or excellent	Chart review
Prenatal health clinic staff, including physicians, nurses, nutritionists, counselors, and clerical staff (Wist & McFarlane, 1999)	Type: Didactic Length: 90 min. Clinical aids: Protocol; follow-up Number of participants: Unclear	No protocol in one clinic	Two groups (one comparison group)	% of identified IPV cases who received referrals to outside agencies	Chart review

Timing			Sample Size and Attrition from Measurement		Results I = Intervention Group C = Comparison Group Pre = Baseline or Pretest Post = Posttest FU = Follow-up		
Base-line	Post-test (months)	Follow-ups (months)	Intervention	Comparison	Within-Group Change	Relative Group Difference	Comment
	15	18 21 24	Post, FU1, FU2, FU3 = Not reported	Post, FU1, FU2, FU3 = Not reported		$I_{FU}3 >$ $C_{FU}3^*$ $I_{FU}3 > C_{FU}3$ $I_{FU}3 > C_{FU}3^*$	A total of 2,531 charts were reviewed, but the numbers were not reported for each data collection wave.
Yes	9-10		2 clinics Pre = 27 Post = 37	3 clinics Pre = 32 Post = 35	$I_{post} = I_{pre}$ $C_{post} = C_{pre}$	$I_{post} = C_{post}$	
Yes	3	12	Pre = 3 Post = 9 FU = 17	Pre = 0 Post = 0 FU = 0	$I_{FU} > I_{pre}^*$		

Screening, Identification, and Detection of Intimate Partner Violence

Target Population (study citation)	Nature of Training Provided		Study Design	Expected Outcomes and Measure	
	Intervention Group	Comparison Group (if applicable)		Major Outcomes	Measure
Medical students (Jonassen et al., 1999)	Type: Mixed Length: 2-3.5 days Clinical aids: Materials on local resources; screening algorithm	Earlier cohort of third-year medical students who did not participate in the clerkship	Three groups (one comparison group)	Screening skills	Standardized patient
Medical students (Short et al., 2000)	Type: Mixed Length: 4-week module Clinical aids: None	One lecture	Two groups (one comparison group)	% correctly identifying IPV in patient % correctly identifying IPV in patient	Vignettes Standardized patient
Residents in family practice (Bolin & Elliott, 1996)	Type: Didactic Length: 2 hrs. Clinical aids: List of contacts; button	Type: Didactic Length: 2 hrs. Clinical aids: List of contacts	Two groups, randomized	No. of days that resident had conversations with patients about IPV	Self-report of residents (daily diary)
Residents in internal medicine (Knight et al., 2000)	Type: Didactic Length: 105 mins. Clinical aids: Local resource list; laminated card of screening questions and resource contacts Number of participants: 45		1 group	% of patients reporting that resident had asked about IPV	Patient exit interview (one item)

Timing			Sample Size and Attrition from Measurement		Results I = Intervention Group C = Comparison Group Pre = Baseline or Pretest Post = Posttest FU = Follow-up		
Base-line	Post-test (months)	Follow-ups (months)	Intervention	Comparison	Within-Group Change	Relative Group Difference	Comment
	9		Eligible = 205 Post = 205 (100%)	Eligible = 93 Post = 93 (100%)		$I_{post} > C_{pre}$*	Test reliability was reported as adequate. Results pertain to two separate cohorts who received the training.
Yes	1		Eligible = 149 Pre = 124 Post = 88 (71%)	Eligible (97) Pre = 88 Post = 66 (75%)	$I_{post} < I_{pre}$*	$I_{post} = C_{post}$	The standardized patient was designed as
No	1					$I_{post} = C_{post}$	test of interview techniques.
No	1		Eligible = Not reported Post = 6	Eligible = Not reported Post = 5		$I_{post} > C_{post}$*	
Yes	4 days		Pre = 122 Post = 116		$I_{post} > I_{pre}$*		Analyses were adjusted for patient age, income, and education, along with physician race.

continued on next page

Screening, Identification, and Detection of Intimate Partner Violence

	Nature of Training Provided			Expected Outcomes and Measure	
Target Population (study citation)	Intervention Group	Comparison Group (if applicable)	Study Design	Major Outcomes	Measure
Residents in internal medicine (Kripke et al., 1998)	Type: Mixed Length: 4 hrs. Clinical aids: None Number of participants: 55		One group	% of cases seen where patient was asked about IPV	Chart review
				% of cases where patient was identified as IPV victim	Chart review
Residents in family practice (Mandel & Marcotte, 1983)	Type: Mixed Length: Two sessions over 4 months Clinical aids: Checklist on appropriate practices Number of participants: 16	Usual and available	Two groups (one comparison group)	% identifying IPV	Standardized patient visit

					Results		
			Sample Size and		I = Intervention Group		
			Attrition from		C = Comparison Group		
	Timing		Measurement		Pre = Baseline or Pretest		
					Post = Posttest FU = Follow-up		
	Post-	Follow-			Within-	Relative	
Base-	test	ups			Group	Group	
line	(months)	(months)	Intervention	Comparison	Change	Difference	Comment
Yes	6		Pre = 693 Post = 277		$I_{post} > I_{pre}$		
					$I_{post} < I_{pre}$		
	4		Eligible = Not reported Post = 10	Eligible = Not reported Post = 6	$I_{post} = C_{post}$		Due to the small sample sizes, no statistical tests were performed.

continued on next page

Screening, Identification, and Detection of Intimate Partner Violence

Target Population (study citation)	Nature of Training Provided		Study Design	Expected Outcomes and Measure	
	Intervention Group	Comparison Group (if applicable)		Major Outcomes	Measure
Residents in internal medicine and family practice (Saunders et al., 1993)	Type: Mixed Length: Two 50-min. sessions or one 2-hr. session Clinical aids: None Number of participants: 17	Usual and available	Two groups, randomized	Time needed to detect IPV in interview	Standardized patient visit

Timing			Sample Size and Attrition from Measurement		Results I = Intervention Group C = Comparison Group Pre = Baseline or Pretest Post = Posttest FU = Follow-up		
Base-line	Post-test (months)	Follow-ups (months)	Intervention	Comparison	Within-Group Change	Relative Group Difference	Comment
No	6		Eligible = Not reported Post = 15	Eligible = Not reported Post = 20		$I_{post} = C_{post}$	Randomization was done by team in one site, and those who did not attend training were placed randomly in rotation sites. The outcome was in the expected direction but was not significant after physician gender, prior professional exposure, and number of IPV victims known were controlled for.

continued on next page

Screening, Identification, and Detection of Intimate Partner Violence

| Target Population (study citation) | Nature of Training Provided | | Study Design | Expected Outcomes and Measure | |
	Intervention Group	Comparison Group (if applicable)		Major Outcomes	Measure
ED staff, including physicians, nurses, and social workers (Campbell et al., in press)	Type: Mixed Length: 2 days Clinical aids: Technical assistance if requested	Usual or available training	Two groups (groups randomized)	% of women who asked about IPV % of self-identified IPV victims documented as such on medical record	Self-report of patients Chart review
ED psychiatric staff, including residents, medical students, and other staff (Currier & Briere, 2000)	Type: Didactic Length: 1 hr. Clinical aids: Protocol Number of participants: 10	Protocol only (8 staff)	Two groups, randomized	% of patients seen by staff where history of adult spouse abuse was identified in chart	Chart review

	Timing		Sample Size and Attrition from Measurement		Results I = Intervention Group C = Comparison Group Pre = Baseline or Pretest Post = Posttest FU = Follow-up		
Base- line	Post- test (months)	Follow- ups (months)	Intervention	Comparison	Within- Group Change	Relative Group Difference	Comment
Yes	9-12	18-24	Pre = Not reported Post = 330	Pre = Not reported FU2 = 319	$I_{FU} > I_{pre}$*	$I_{post} < C_{post}$ $I_{FU} > C_{FU}$ $I_{post} > C_{post}$ $I_{FU} > C_{FU}$	Analyses controlled for baseline differences. Although not statistically significant due to low statistical power, the ratio of self-reported IPV cases by patients to those documented in the medical record increased in the experimental hospitals but decreased in the comparison hospitals.
No	Unclear		Post = 84 patients	Post = 78 patients		$I_{post} > C_{post}$*	

continued on next page

Screening, Identification, and Detection of Intimate Partner Violence

	Nature of Training Provided			Expected Outcomes and Measure	
Target Population (study citation)	Intervention Group	Comparison Group (if applicable)	Study Design	Major Outcomes	Measure
ED staff (Fanslow et al., 1998, 1999)	Type: Didactic Length: 1 or 4 hrs. Clinical aids: Protocols; forms; body map; checklist; contact cards Number of participants: 33 nurses and 11 medical staff		Cohort	% of all cases identified as IPV victims	Chart review
				% of possible IPV cases that were confirmed	Chart review
				% of possible IPV cases with documentation	Chart review
ED staff (McLeer et al., 1989)	Type: Unclear Length: Unclear Clinical aids: Protocol Number of participants: Not clear		Cohort	% of all cases identified as IPV	Chart review
ED physicians (Olson et al., 1996)	Type: Didactic Length: 1 hr. Clinical aids: Stamped query on patient form Number of participants: Unclear		Cohort	% of all cases identified as IPV	Chart review

Timing			Sample Size and Attrition from Measurement		Results I = Intervention Group C = Comparison Group Pre = Baseline or Pretest Post = Posttest FU = Follow-up		
Base-line	Post-test (months)	Follow-ups (months)	Intervention	Comparison	Within-Group Change	Relative Group Difference	Comment
Yes	1-3	12-15	Pre = 2276 Post = 2287 FU = 1598	Pre = 1768 Post = 1720 FU = 1312	$I_{post} = I_{pre}$	$I_{post} = C_{post}$ $I_{FU} = C_{FU}$	The analyses did not incorporate additional
			Pre = 57 Post = 53 FU = 17	Pre = 54 Post = 45 FU = 30	$I_{post} > I_{pre}$ *	$I_{post} > C_{post}$ * $I_{FU} = C_{FU}$	variables (e.g., patient characteristics).
			Pre = 57 Post = 53 FU = 17	Pre = 54 Post = 45 FU = 17	$I_{post} > I_{pre}$ *	$I_{post} > C_{post}$ * $I_{FU} = C_{FU}$	Routine screening not adopted by ED staff.
Yes	12	96	Pre = 359 Post = 412 FU2 = 470		$I_{post} > I_{pre}$ * $I_{FU} > I_{pre}$ $I_{FU} < I_{post}$ *		At follow-up, the protocol was no longer in use nor any other formal assessment procedure.
	1 mo. prior	1	Pre = 1,272 Stamp-only = 1,444 Stamp & training = 1,356		$I_{post} > I_{pre}$ * $I_{FU} > I_{post}$		A significant increase in identification rates occurred after introduction of the stamp, but there was no change when education was added.

continued on next page

Screening, Identification, and Detection of Intimate Partner Violence

Target Population (study citation)	Nature of Training Provided		Study Design	Expected Outcomes and Measure	
	Intervention Group	Comparison Group (if applicable)		Major Outcomes	Measure
ED staff, including physicians, residents, interns, and nurses (Roberts et al., 1997a)	Type: Unclear (workshops and case presentations) Length: Unclear Clinical aids: None Number of participants: Unclear		Cohort	% of self-reported IPV victims who were noted as such on chart within 24 hours after presentation	Chart review
ED, critical care, and perinatal hospital staff (Short et al., in press)	Type: Length: Clinical aids: Protocol	Usual and available	Two groups (one comparison group)	% of cases with documentation of definite IPV	Chart review
				% of cases with documentation of suspected IPV	Chart review
ED nurses (Tilden & Shepherd, 1987)	Type: Didactic Length: 4 hrs. Clinical aids: Protocol and forms Number of participants: 22		Cohort	% of all cases identified as IPV	Chart review

Timing			Sample Size and Attrition from Measurement		Results I = Intervention Group C = Comparison Group Pre = Baseline or Pretest Post = Posttest FU = Follow-up		
Base-line	Post-test (months)	Follow-ups (months)	Intervention	Comparison	Within-Group Change	Relative Group Difference	Comment
Yes	12		Pre = 141 Post = 183			$I_{post} = C_{post}$	Low attendance at training and lack of social work referral services at times when victims showed in the emergency room may have contributed to the lack of differences.
	15	18 21 24	Post = FU1 = FU2 = FU3 =	Post = FU1 = FU2 = FU3 =		$I_{FU3} > C_{FU3}*$ $I_{FU3} > C_{FU3}*$	A total of 2,531 charts were reviewed, but the numbers were not reported for each data collection wave.
Yes	4		Pre = 447 Post = 445		$I_{post} > I_{pre}*$		

continued on next page

Screening, Identification, and Detection of Intimate Partner Violence

Target Population (study citation)	Nature of Training Provided			Expected Outcomes and Measure	
	Intervention Group	Comparison Group (if applicable)	Study Design	Major Outcomes	Measure
Maternity care coordinators in county health departments (Covington et al., 1997a)	Type: Didactic Length: Unclear Clinical aids: Protocol Number of participants:		Cohort	% of pregnant adolescents reporting IPV at first visit	Self-report of adolescent patients
				% of pregnant adolescents reporting IPV at any visit	Self-report of adolescent patients
Maternity care coordinators in county health departments (Covington et al., 1997b)	Type: Didactic Length: Unclear Clinical aids: Protocol Number of partcipants: Unclear		Cohort	% of pregnant adult clients reporting IPV at first visit	Self-report of pregnant patients
				% of pregnant adult clients reporting IPV at any visit	Self-report of pregnant patients

Timing			Sample Size and Attrition from Measurement		Results I = Intervention Group C = Comparison Group Pre = Baseline or Pretest Post = Posttest FU = Follow-up		
Base- line	Post- test (months)	Follow- ups (months)	Intervention	Comparison	Within- Group Change	Relative Group Difference	Comment
Yes	12		Pre = 129 Post = 117		$I_{post} > I_{pre}$		Analyses controlled for differences in race/ethnicity between the two patient cohorts. Although the rate of identification at the first visit doubled between baseline and the posttest, this was not a statistically reliable difference due to the small sample size.
					$I_{post} > I_{pre}$*		
Yes	12		Pre = 1,056 Post = 384		$I_{post} > I_{pre}$*		Analyses controlled for differences in race/ethnicity and age between the two patient cohorts. The baseline review of charts covered a 36-month time span, and no differences were found in identification rates among the three years.
					$I_{post} > I_{pre}$*		

continued on next page

Screening, Identification, and Detection of Intimate Partner Violence

Target Population (study citation)	Nature of Training Provided			Expected Outcomes and Measure	
	Intervention Group	Comparison Group (if applicable)	Study Design	Major Outcomes	Measure
Community health center staff, including physicians, mid-level practitioners, social workers, and psychologists (Harwell et al., 1998)	Type: Mixed Length: 3-6 hrs. Clinical aids: IPV screening pocket card; IPV assessment form; stamp to indicate screening and suspected or confirmed abuse; patient card of resources and safety tips; additional tailored follow-up training to some CHCs Number of participants: 108		Cohort	% of cases screened for IPV	Chart review
				% of cases where IPV was suspected	Chart review
				% of cases where IPV was confirmed	Chart review
Public health nurses (Shepard et al., 1999)	Type: Mixed Length: 4 hrs. Clinical aids: Protocol Follow-ups Number of participants: 12		Cohort	% of cases identified as IPV	Chart review

Timing			Sample Size and Attrition from Measurement		Results I = Intervention Group C = Comparison Group Pre = Baseline or Pretest Post = Posttest FU = Follow-up		
Base-line	Post-test (months)	Follow-ups (months)	Intervention	Comparison	Within-Group Change	Relative Group Difference	Comment
Yes	6		Pre = 251 Post = 255		$I_{post} > I_{pre}$* $I_{post} > I_{pre}$* $I_{post} > I_{pre}$		There was no significant change in positive identification of IPV victims in the chart.
Yes	12	24	Pre = 546 Post = 442 FU = 372		$I_{post} > I_{pre}$ $I_{FU1} > I_{pre}$		Differences in identification rates were not significant when age was controlled (although they were marginally significant).

continued on next page

Screening, Identification, and Detection of Intimate Partner Violence

Target Population (study citation)	Nature of Training Provided		Study Design	Expected Outcomes and Measure	
	Intervention Group	Comparison Group (if applicable)		Major Outcomes	Measure
Primary care team members (Thompson et al., 2000)	Type: Mixed Length: 2 half-day sessions over 12 months Clinical aids: Posters; provider cue cards; routine exam forms; feedback	Usual and available training (e.g., manual)	Two groups (group randomized)	% asking about IPV % of patients who were asked about IPV % of patients who were victims of IPV	Provider self-report (one item) Chart review Chart review
Prenatal health clinic staff, including physicians, nurses, nutritionists, counselors, and clerical staff (Wist & McFarlane, 1999)	Type: Didactic Length: 90 min. Clinical aids: Protocol; follow-up	No protocol in one clinic	Two groups (one comparison group)	% of patients identified as IPV	Chart review

Timing			Sample Size and Attrition from Measurement		Results: I = Intervention Group; C = Comparison Group; Pre = Baseline or Pretest; Post = Posttest; FU = Follow-up		
Base-line	Post-test (months)	Follow-ups (months)	Intervention	Comparison	Within-Group Change	Relative Group Difference	Comment
Yes	9		2 clinics Eligible = ? Pre = Post = 91	3 clinics Eligible = ? Pre = Post = 88	$I_{post} > I_{pre}$*	$I_{post} > C_{post}$* $I_{FU} > C_{FU}$	Differences in recorded asking occurred among those who had
Yes			Pre = 1,590 Post = 1,372 Same	Pre = 2,205 Post = 2,020 Same	$I_{post} > I_{pre}$*	$I_{post} > C_{post}$*	physical exams and screening questionnaire.
Yes					$I_{post} > I_{pre}$	$I_{post} > C_{post}$	
Yes	3	15	Pre = 360 Post = 110 FU2 = 250	Pre = 180 Post = 55 FU2 = 125	$I_{(post+FU)} >$	$I_{FU} > C_{FU}$* $I_{post} > C_{post}$*	The percent of charts at the intervention site that contained an abuse screen declined from 95% at the 3-month posttest to 85% at the 15-month follow-up.

Appendix G

Summary of Evaluation Studies on Training of Health Care Professionals on Child Abuse and Neglect

Child Abuse and Neglect

	Nature of Training Provided			Expected Outcomes and Measure	
Target Population (study citation)	Intervention Group	Comparison Group (if applicable)	Study Design	Major Outcomes	Measure
Medical students, residents, fellows, and attending physicians in pediatrics (Palusci & McHugh, 1995)	Type: Mixed Length: 9-15 hrs. in a clinical rotation Clinical aids: None	Other rotation comparison	Two-group, nonequivalent group	Knowledge of child sexual abuse	Self-report (30 items)
Residents in pediatrics (Dubowitz & Black, 1991)	Type: Mixed Length: Six 90-min. sessions Clinical aids: None	None	Two-group, comparison group	Knowledge, attitudes, and skills of child abuse	Self-report (31 items)
				Perceived competency to manage child abuse cases	Self-report (1 item)
Residents in pediatrics (Sugarman et al., 1997)	Type: Mixed Length: 8 hrs. Clinical aids: None Number of participants: 22		One group	Knowledge of child sexual abuse	Self-report (33 items)

Timing			Sample Size and Attrition from Measurement		Results — I = Intervention Group, C = Comparison Group, Pre = Baseline or Pretest, Post = Posttest, FU = Follow-up		
Base-line	Post-test (months)	Follow-ups (months)	Intervention	Comparison	Within-Group Change	Relative Group Difference	Comment
Yes	Immediately after training		Enrolled = 15 Post = 15 (100%)	Pre = 15 Pre = 15 (80%)	$I_{post} > I_{pre}$ * Post = 12	$I_{post} > C_{post}$ *	The study also included a reference group who received no training and was administered the pretest. It consisted of 127 students, residents, and physicians who attended report and continuity clinic conferences. All groups did not significantly differ at the pretest.
Yes	1	3-4	Eligible = 31 Pre = 31 Post = 31 (100%)	Eligible = 19 Pre = 19 Post = 19 (100%)	$I_{post}1 > I_{pre}$ *	$I_{post} > C_{post}$ * $I_{FU} > C_{FU}$ $I_{post} > C_{post}$ * $I_{FU} > C_{FU}$ *	The pretest scores of the two groups did not significantly differ.
Yes	Immediately after training		Eligible = Pre = 22 Post = 22 (100%)	Not reported	$I_{post}1 > I_{pre}$ *		

continued on next page

Child Abuse and Neglect

| Target Population (study citation) | Nature of Training Provided | | Study Design | Expected Outcomes and Measure | |
	Intervention Group	Comparison Group (if applicable)		Major Outcomes	Measure
Physicians, nurses, and caseworkers (Hibbard et al., 1987)	Type: Mixed Length: 1 day Clinical aids: Anatomically correct dolls; handbook of potential interventions		One group	Knowledge of child abuse	Self-report
Physicians, nurse-practitioners, family practice and public health nurses, social workers, and secondary health educators (Sullivan & Clancy, 1990)	Type: Mixed Length: 1 day Clinical aids: None		One group	Number of sexual abuse indicators recalled	Self-report
				Number of physical indicators of child abuse recalled	Self-report
				Number of psychological indicators of child abuse recalled	Self-report
				Number of behavioral indicators of child abuse recalled	Self-report
				Number of specific actions to take in interviews	Self-report

Timing			Sample Size and Attrition from Measurement		Results I = Intervention Group C = Comparison Group Pre = Baseline or Pretest Post = Posttest FU = Follow-up		
Base-line	Post-test (months)	Follow-ups (months)	Intervention	Comparison	Within-Group Change	Relative Group Difference	Comment
Yes	0.5	6	Eligible = 51 Pre = 38 (75%) Post = 35 (69%) FU = 21 (41%)		Medical staff: $I_{post}1 > I_{pre}$* $I_{FU} > I_{pre}$* Social workers: $I_{post}1 > I_{pre}$* $I_{FU} > I_{pre}$*		Increased use of anatomically dolls was noted at the 6-month follow-up, but no data were reported.
Yes	Immediately after training	3, 6	Eligible = 350 Posttest only: Assigned = 85 Post = 82 (97%) Pre- and posttest: Assigned = 96 Post = 65 (68%) Pre- and FU: Assigned = 88 Post = 65 (74%) Pre- and FU2: Assigned = 81 Post = 41 (81%)		$I_{post}1 > I_{pre}$* $I_{FU} > I_{pre}$* $I_{FU2} < I_{post}$ $I_{post}1 > I_{pre}$* $I_{post}1 > I_{pre}$* $I_{post}1 > I_{pre}$ $I_{post}1 > I_{pre}$*		Groups were randomized to one of the four testing conditions. Because the design (anonymity of subjects) did not permit pairing pretest, posttest, and follow-up scores, the results on within-group change should be interpreted with caution. Results indicated no pretest effect on the immediate posttest. Significant differences on all but sexual abuse indicators are for all posttests and follow-up combined.

continued on next page

Child Abuse and Neglect

	Nature of Training Provided			Expected Outcomes and Measure	
Target Population (study citation)	Intervention Group	Comparison Group (if applicable)	Study Design	Major Outcomes	Measure
Child protective service workers, including social workers (Cheung et al., 1991)	Type: Mixed Length: 6 hrs. Clinical aids: None		One group	Ability to complete initial case planning	Vignette (ratings)
				Ability to formulate goals	Vignette (ratings)
				Ability to set objectives for family	Vignette (ratings)
				Ability to develop a contract with family	Vignette (ratings)
Child protective service workers, including social workers (Leung & Cheung, 1998)	Type: Mixed Length: 3 mo. training program Clinical aids: None		One group	Perceived information and experience to:	
				Identify abuse	Self-report (1 item)
				Identify risk	Self-report (1 item)
				Recognize indicators	Self-report (1 item)
				Attitudes (e.g., value of family preservation and cultural differences)	Self-report (9-item subscale)

	Timing			Sample Size and Attrition from Measurement		Results I = Intervention Group C = Comparison Group Pre = Baseline or Pretest Post = Posttest FU = Follow-up		
Base-line	Post-test (months)	Follow-ups (months)		Intervention	Comparison	Within-Group Change	Relative Group Difference	Comment
Yes	Immedi-ately after training			Eligible = 18 Pre = 18 Post = 18		$I_{post}1 > I_{pre}$		
						$I_{post}1 > I_{pre}*$		
						$I_{post}1 > I_{pre}$		
						$I_{post}1 > I_{pre}*$		
Yes	Immedi-ately after training			Eligible = 413 Pre = 188 Post = 188 (100%)				The question-naire on perceived knowledge and experience included 16 items, all of which showed statistically significant improvement. Sample sizes for the performance evaluation varied, given that most of the workers were not yet eligible for their second-
						$I_{post}1 > I_{pre}*$		
						$I_{post}1 > I_{pre}*$		
						$I_{post}1 > I_{pre}*$		
Yes	Immedi-ately after training			Eligible = 23 Pre = 20 Post = 20 (100%)		$I_{post}1 > I_{pre}*$		

continued on next page

Child Abuse and Neglect

| Target Population (study citation) | Nature of Training Provided | | | Expected Outcomes and Measure | |
	Intervention Group	Comparison Group (if applicable)	Study Design	Major Outcomes	Measure
	Type: Mixed Length: 3 mo. training program Clinical aids: None	Not specified but some training as random sample of current caseworkers	Two-group, comparison group	Performance on job, including use of interviewing techniques, determining presence of child abuse or neglect, implementation of case management plans, and sufficient case documentation	Supervisor evaluation forms

Timing			Sample Size and Attrition from Measurement		Results I = Intervention Group C = Comparison Group Pre = Baseline or Pretest Post = Posttest FU = Follow-up		
Base-line	Post-test (months)	Follow-ups (months)	Intervention	Comparison	Within-Group Change	Relative Group Difference	Comment
No	6-9	12, 24	Eligible = 413 Post = 66 FU = 140 FU2 = 18	Eligible = ? Post = 39 FU = 50 FU2 = 46	$I_{FU} > I_{post}$* $I_{FU2} > I_{FU}$*	$I_{post} = C_{post}$	year evaluation.

Appendix H

Core Competencies for Family Violence

**COMPETENCIES NECESSARY FOR NURSES TO PROVIDE
HIGH-QUALITY CARE TO VICTIMS OF DOMESTIC VIOLENCE**

Competencies related to acknowledging the scope of the problem:

1. Recognize prevalence of domestic violence in all its forms.
2. Recognize risk factors for both victimization and perpetration of domestic violence.
3. Recognize the significant physical and mental health effects of both ongoing and prior domestic violence.
4. Recognize the effects of violence across the lifespan, including the long-term effects for children who are either victims or witnesses of domestic violence.
5. Recognize one's own attitudes about domestic violence, including possibility of own friends' or family members' victimization and the need to address ongoing issues arising from such experiences.

Competencies related to identification and documentation of abuse and its health effects:

1. Know developmentally appropriate questions to be used in screening in various settings (for example, McFarlane and Parker's (1994) "Abuse Assessment Screen").

2. If physical violence, assess particularly for forced sex, mental health status, old undiagnosed head injuries, risk of suicide and/or homicide (for example, Campbell's (1986) "Danger Assessment").
3. Assess for possibility of child abuse in the home and the effects of violence on children.
4. Assess for possibility of elder abuse in the home.
5. Document extent of current and prior injuries using body map and photographs if possible.

Competencies related to interventions to reduce vulnerability and increase safety, especially of women, children, and elders:

1. Know local, state, and national domestic violence referral resources, including abuse shelters and safe houses.
2. Communicate nonjudgmentally and compassionately with the victim.
3. Conduct safety planning with the victim.
4. Refer to social worker, shelter, and legal counsel as appropriate.

Competencies related to ethical, legal, and cultural issues of reporting and treatment:

1. Know state and national legal mandates regarding domestic violence, including mandatory reporting responsibilities.
2. Know appropriate methods for collection and documentation of data so that both the patient and the provider are protected.
3. Know the ethical principles that apply to patient confidentiality for victims.
4. Recognize that ethical dilemmas often arise from culture differences.
5. Recognize that cultural factors are important in influencing the occurrence and patterns of and responses to domestic violence in individuals, families, and communities.
6. Provide culturally competent assessment and intervention while maintaining human rights.

Competencies related to prevention activities:

1. Increase public awareness of domestic violence.
2. Promote activities to address prevention with populations at risk (e.g., child witnesses, pregnant women, and dependent-frail elderly).
3. Promote activities to assist with behavioral changes in battering and battered individuals.
4. Recognize the need to establish programs to support victims, their family members, and the abuser.

Source: American Association of Colleges of Nursing, "Appendix A: Competencies Necessary for Nurses to Provide High Quality Care to Victims of Domestic Violence," In "Position Statement: Violence as a Public Health Problem," http://www.aacn.nche.edu/Publications/positions/violence.htm [28 August 2000], Reprinted with permission.

Appendix I

Biographical Sketches of Committee Members and Staff

JOHN D. STOBO (*Chair*) is president of the University of Texas Medical Branch at Galveston. From 1976 to 1985, he served as head of the Section of Rheumatology and Clinical Immunology at the University of California, San Francisco, where he was an investigator of the Howard Hughes Medical Institute. In 1985, he was appointed the William Osler professor of medicine, director of the Department of Medicine, and physician-in-chief of the Johns Hopkins University Hospital. In 1994, he became the chairman and chief executive officer of Johns Hopkins Health Care, L.L.C., an organization created to address challenges in managed care on behalf of Johns Hopkins Medicine. He has served as president of the American Association of Professors of Medicine, president of the American College of Rheumatology, and chairman of the American Board of Internal Medicine. He is a member of the Institute of Medicine and chaired its Board on Health Sciences Policy. Stobo has an AB from Dartmouth College and an MD from S.U.N.Y. at Buffalo.

MARLA E. SALMON (*Vice Chair*) is dean and chief executive officer of the Nell Hodgson Woodruff School of Nursing at Emory University. Formerly an associate dean and director of graduate studies at the University of Pennsylvania School of Nursing, she also served as director of the Division of Nursing for the U.S. Department of Health and Human Services. Throughout her career, her research interests have included health policy, administration, and health workforce development, with particular emphasis on the importance of public health nursing. She has received numerous awards, including the Presidential Meritorious Executive Award and the U.S. Public Health Special Service Award.

She is a member of the Institute of Medicine and has been both nationally and internationally recognized for her contributions to health policies influencing health care delivery systems. She has a BS and a BSN from the University of Portland and an ScD from Johns Hopkins University.

ELAINE J. ALPERT has been on the faculty of the Boston University School of Public Health since 1984 and is currently an associate professor of public health and medicine and the assistant dean for student affairs. She has been active for several years in health professional education and community outreach in the area of family violence. She spearheaded the development of a model curriculum on family violence for the Boston University School of Medicine and has created a comprehensive postgraduate curriculum on domestic violence in collaboration with the Massachusetts Medical Society. She is also a faculty trainer for the Family Violence Prevention Fund. She serves on numerous state and national advisory panels concerned with the health professions' response to family violence and has spoken extensively to physicians, other health professions groups, and community organizations about the role of health care professionals in responding to and preventing family violence and abuse. Alpert has an MD from the University of Michigan School of Medicine and an MPH from the Boston University School of Public Health.

JACQUELYN C. CAMPBELL is the associate dean of doctoral education programs and research and is jointly appointed to the Johns Hopkins University School of Nursing and the School of Hygiene and Public Health Center for Injury Control. Her overall research focus is on women's physical, emotional, and behavioral responses to battering in intimate relationships, including marital rape, resultant homicide, abuse during pregnancy, and violence in adolescent relationships. She is also interested in cultural influences on intimate partner violence in Africa and Latin America as well as in local communities. She is a member of the Institute of Medicine and served on its Board of International Health; she also served on the National Research Council's Committee on Family Violence Intervention Evaluations. She is a member of the Department of Defense Task Force on Violence Against Women. She has provided consultation on intimate partner violence to the National Institute of Justice, the Ford and Robert Wood Johnson Foundations, the Milbank Fund, and the World Health Organization. Campbell has a BSN from the Duke University School of Nursing, an MSN from Wright State University, and a PhD from the University of Rochester School of Nursing.

MICHAEL I. COHEN has been chairman of the Department of Pediatrics at the Albert Einstein College of Medicine/Montefiore Medical Center since 1980 and a member of the faculty there since 1967. A graduate of Columbia College, he has an MD from Columbia University, did his pediatric training at Babies Hospital in New York City, and held a National Institutes of Health postdoctoral fellowship at Einstein before beginning his career in exploring the issues of adolescent development. He established one of the first programs in the nation in adolescent medicine at Montefiore in 1967, which has served as a prototype for similar programs throughout the United States. He is the former president and chief executive officer of the Montefiore Medical Center in New York and was elected a member of the Institute of Medicine in 1990. He served on the Council on Adolescent Development of the Carnegie Corporation of New York and was the vice chair of an advisory committee on adolescent health to the Office of Technology Assessment for the U.S. Congress. He is a trustee of the Foundation for Child Development.

FELICIA COHN (*Study Director*) is a program officer with the Board on Children, Youth, and Families of the Institute of Medicine and National Research Council. Previously, she was the director of the program in bioethics in the Department of Health Care Sciences and a senior scientist with the Center to Improve Care of the Dying of the George Washington University Medical Center. She teaches health professional students and serves on the Ethics Committee at George Washington Hospital. Cohn has written extensively on end-of-life care and ethics education and consults regularly on a number of ethical issues. She has an MA and a PhD in religious ethics (bioethics) from the University of Virginia.

DEBORAH EPSTEIN is an associate professor at the Georgetown University Law Center and has spent more than 15 years working as an advocate for victims of domestic violence. Since 1993, she has directed the Law Center's Domestic Violence Clinic, where she supervises students representing battered women in civil protection order cases. She is co-director of the D.C. Superior Court's Domestic Violence Intake Center and served as co-chair of the recent effort to create a specialized Domestic Violence Court in the District of Columbia. She has served on numerous local, national, and international advisory panels on the role of the justice system in responding to family violence. She has served as director and as a board member for various advocacy organizations in the domestic violence field. Epstein has a BA from Brown and a JD from New York University.

SHERYL HERON is an assistant residency director and an assistant professor in the Department of Emergency Medicine at the Emory University School of Medicine. She is a board-certified emergency medicine physician and was the 1996-97 injury control fellow for the Center for Injury Control at Emory. She was a member of the Georgia Commission on Family Violence Medical Protocols Committee that was charged with writing the medical protocol on domestic violence for the state of Georgia. Her primary research interest is the prevention of violence against women; other interests include resident education, international emergency medicine, and diversity. She has a BS from Tufts University, an MPH from Hunter College, and an MD from Howard University.

SUSAN R. JOHNSON is the associate dean for faculty affairs of the University of Iowa College of Medicine, professor of obstetrics and gynecology in that college, and professor of epidemiology in the College of Public Health. She is an examiner for the American Board of Obstetrics and Gynecology, a member of the National Board of Medical Examiners, and a member of the Iowa Board of Medical Examiners. Her clinical and research interests are in the areas of premenstrual syndrome (PMS) and menopausal health issues, particularly the use of hormones and other drugs in postmenopausal women. She directs both the PMS Clinic and the Menopause Clinic at the Women's Health Center of the University of Iowa Hospital and Clinics and serves as the medical director of the Family Planning Council of Iowa. She is an investigator with the Women's Health Initiative sponsored by the National Institutes of Health and is active at the national level in this trial. She also serves on the data, safety, and monitoring boards of several other multicenter clinical trials of various postmenopausal preventive drugs and has written numerous articles and chapters regarding these issues. Johnson has a BS, an MS, and an MD from the University of Iowa.

RICHARD D. KRUGMAN is professor of pediatrics and dean of the University of Colorado School of Medicine. His career has included a two-year appointment with the Public Health Service at the National Institutes of Health and the Food and Drug Administration, as well as a Robert Wood Johnson Health Policy Fellowship in the office of U.S. Senator Durenberger of Minnesota. He served as director of the C. Henry Kempe National Center for the Prevention and Treatment of Child Abuse and Neglect from 1981 to 1992. From 1988 to 1991, he headed the U.S. Advisory Board of Child Abuse and Neglect, which issued a landmark national report in 1990. He has chaired the American Academy of Pediatrics Child Abuse Committee and more recently worked with the Association of American Medical Colleges on family violence issues and the American Professional Society on the Abuse of Children Legislative Advisory Committee. He is editor-in-chief of *Child Abuse and Neglect: The International Journal* and is a past president of the International Society for the Prevention of Child Abuse and Neglect. Krugman has an MD from New York University School of Medicine and did a residency in pediatrics at the University of Colorado School of Medicine.

MARK S. LACHS is the director of geriatrics for the New York Presbyterian Health System and an associate professor of medicine and co-chief of the Division of Geriatric Medicine and Gerontology at the Weill Medical College of Cornell University. A graduate of the New York University School of Medicine, he completed his residency in internal medicine at the hospital of the University of Pennsylvania and is board certified in internal medicine with a certificate of added qualification in geriatric medicine. He was a Robert Wood Johnson clinical scholar at Yale University, where he also earned a master's degree in public health. He has published widely on issues in aging, including elder abuse and neglect, adult protective services, the measurement of functional status, ethics, and the financing of health care.

GARY B. MELTON is director of the Institute on Family and Neighborhood Life, professor of psychology, and an adjunct professor of family and youth development at Clemson University. A fellow of the American Psychological Association (APA) and eight of its divisions, he is a past president of the American Psychology-Law Society and the APA Division of Child, Youth, and Family Services. As director of the Consortium on Children, Families, and the Law, a national network of policy research centers, he organizes a regular congressional briefing series. His work has been cited by U.S. courts at all levels; he was the principal architect of the new national child protection strategy proposed by the U.S. Advisory Board on Child Abuse and Neglect. He also served as a member of the U.S. attorney general's Expert Panel on Youth Violence. The author of approximately 300 publications, he is active in research on services for children and families in diverse contexts. He has been principal investigator on projects funded by the National Institute of Mental Health, the National Center on Child Abuse and Neglect, the Office of Juvenile Justice and Delinquency Prevention, and various state agencies and private organizations. Melton has a BA from the University of Virginia and an MA and a PhD in clinical-community psychology from Boston University.

GREGORY J. PAVEZA is a professor in the School of Social Work at the University of South Florida. He has a BA in psychology from Lewis College in Illinois, an MSW from the School of Social Work at the University of Hawaii, and a PhD in public health sciences (psychiatric epidemiology) from the University of Illinois at Chicago. He has been a social work practitioner and an agency administrator. Since completing his doctorate in 1986, he has been a faculty member for the School of Public Health of the University of Illinois at Chicago; the director of the Center for Long Term Mental Health Evaluation, U.S. Department of Veterans Affairs; and an associate professor for the University of South Florida. His research interests include issues related to the social consequences of caregiving and Alzheimer's disease, including elder mistreatment in these families as well in the broader community.

GEORGINE M. PION is a research associate professor of psychology in the Department of Psychology and Human Development at Vanderbilt University and a senior fellow in the Vanderbilt Institute for Public Policy Studies. She has a PhD from Claremont Graduate School and did postdoctoral research training in the Division of Methodology and Evaluation Research at Northwestern University. She has served on committees involved in the evaluation of training programs for the National Research Council, the National Science Foundation, and the National Institute of Mental Health. Her interests include assessment of programs for at-risk populations, evaluation research and practitioner training, factors influencing career progression and outcomes in the biomedical and behavioral sciences, and evaluation and survey methodology.

MICHAEL A. RODRIGUEZ is an assistant professor in residence in the Department of Family and Community Medicine and the Department of Epidemiology and Biostatistics at the University of California, San Francisco (UCSF). He is also a faculty member at its Center for Aging in Diverse Communities. He is an undergraduate alumnus of the University of California, Berkeley, attended medical school at the University of California, Los Angeles, completed his residency training at UCSF, and has a public health degree from Johns Hopkins University School of Hygiene and Public Health. In addition, he was a Robert Wood Johnson clinical scholar and a Picker/Commonwealth scholar. He conducts research, collaborates with direct service and advocacy organizations, and is responsible for policy development on areas of concern to clinical practice, including violence prevention and minority health. His research includes a focus on improving the health care response to abused women from diverse backgrounds. He also teaches UCSF's residents and medical students while maintaining a family medicine practice at San Francisco General Hospital.

ROBERT S. THOMPSON is a clinical professor of pediatrics and health services research at the University of Washington and the director of the Department of Preventive Care at the Group Health Cooperative of Puget Sound. A member of the Centers for Disease Control and Prevention's National Task Force on Community Preventive Services since 1996, he has practiced pediatrics and worked as a clinical epidemiologist at the Group Health Cooperative since 1972. Since 1997, he has devoted professional time to the development, implementation, and evaluation of population-based clinical prevention services. His current funded research projects include adverse outcomes of immunizations, vaccine studies, domestic violence identification and management in primary care, HIV risk identification and management, "Healthy Steps"—a large-scale child development project—and translating knowledge on chlamydia screening into practice. He has a BA from Amherst College and an MD from Johns Hopkins University School of Medicine.

Index